Fodor's

FLORENCE & TUSCANY

Welcome to Florence and Tuscany

Florence and Tuscany enchant with remarkable works of art, memorable food and wine, and olive groves or cypress trees amid rolling landscapes. In Florence, you can visit ancient palaces and churches, see masterpieces by Michelangelo, and shop for artisanal wares. Tuscany's pleasures include sampling Chianti's wine and wandering through medieval towns. Note that this book was updated during the pandemic. When planning, please confirm that places are still open and let us know when we need to make updates at editors@fodors.com.

TOP REASONS TO GO

★ **Renaissance art:** Works by da Vinci and Michelangelo, the Uffizi's treasures, and more

★ **Authentic shops:** Leather goods, gold, and handmade paper delight discerning buyers

★ **Iconic churches:** Florence's Duomo and Arezzo's Basilica di San Francesco, to start

★ **Charming towns:** Lucca, Siena, Cortona, San Gimignano, and others are enthralling.

★ **Wineries:** At visitor-friendly vineyards, you can taste the wine and meet the makers.

★ **Traditional cuisine:** Tuscany's earthy, farm-fresh seasonal fare is heaven for foodies.

Contents

MAPS

Fodor's Features

Chapter 1

EXPERIENCE FLORENCE AND TUSCANY

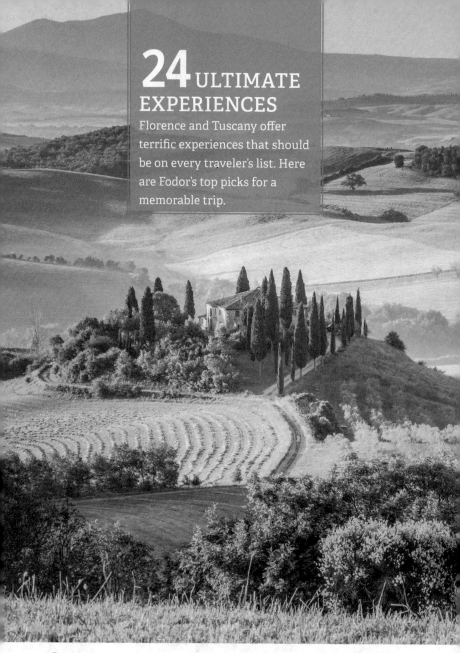

24 ULTIMATE EXPERIENCES

Florence and Tuscany offer terrific experiences that should be on every traveler's list. Here are Fodor's top picks for a memorable trip.

1 Relax in the Val d'Orcia

Spend a day exploring Montalcino and sipping wine from its Brunello vineyards, or taste distinctive pecorino cheeses in Pienza. For ultimate relaxation, try the Piscina Val di Sole public hot springs in Bagno Vignoni. *(Ch. 7)*

2 Visit Volterra

Visit Palazzo dei Priori, which is considered Tuscany's oldest town hall, with its central tower built in the 1200s. *(Ch. 5)*

3 Restore Your Soul in Assisi

Assisi, birthplace of St. Francis, has been a Christian pilgrimage site since he was buried there in the 1300s. *(Ch. 8)*

4 Explore Giardino di Boboli

If you are searching for green in Florence, head to the grounds of Palazzo Pitti and the Giardino di Boboli. Explore vine-covered pergolas, stone paths, and grand staircases. *(Ch. 3)*

5 See *Birth of Venus*

Anyone who has seen the famous painting of the golden-haired goddess of love as depicted in popular culture will be awed by Botticelli's original in the Uffizi Gallery. *(Ch. 3)*

6 Dip Cantucci in Vin Santo

At the end of *cena* (dinner) in Tuscany, order *cantucci* with *vin santo*. Cantucci are crunchy, twice-baked, oblong-shape almond biscuits with origins in the city of Prato. *(Ch. 4)*

7 People-Watch in Siena's Piazza del Campo

Siena's Piazza del Campo is an ideal spot for people-watching, whether seated on the cobblestone piazza or in one of the nearby restaurants and cafés. *(Ch. 5)*

8 Climb Florence's Duomo

Climb 463 steps through narrow passageways that were used during the dome's construction and out to the terrace for incredible Firenze views. *(Ch. 3)*

9 Soak in Terme di Saturnia

Legend says Saturn, irritated by the behavior he saw on Earth, threw a thunderbolt down, creating the bubbling mineral-rich waters of Saturnia. *(Ch. 7)*

10 Rub Il Porcellino for Good Luck

Il Porcellino ("the piglet"), a bronze statue in Florence's Mercato Nuevo, is said to bestow good luck on people who touch his snout. *(Ch. 3)*

11 Shop for Leather Goods

For gloves, try Madova in the Oltrano district. For bags and small leather goods, head to Scuola del Cuoio in the Santa Croce neighborhood. *(Ch. 3)*

12 Walk Along Lucca's Walls

This elevated walkway is the site of what for some is a daily ritual of *passeggiata delle mura* (walk along the walls). *(Ch. 4)*

13 Immerse Yourself in Renaissance Ideals

Through both architecture and art, Urbino's venerable Palazzo Ducale showcases the principles and values of the Renaissance. *(Ch. 8)*

14 Stare at the Leaning Tower of Pisa

The most popular site in Pisa is said to have begun its famous incline during construction in the 1100s and it has continued since. *(Ch. 4)*

15 Watch the Sunset Over Ponte Vecchio

It's best to stand on Ponte Santa Trinita, or anywhere along the Arno as the sun is setting, to see the sky changing hues. *(Ch. 3)*

16 Explore the Oltrarno

This has traditionally been home to Florence's working class, filled with leather makers, jewelers, artists, and other craftspeople. *(Ch. 3)*

17 Taste Wine in Chianti

With 17,000 acres of vineyards, sipping your way through Chianti is a fine way to spend a day. *(Ch. 5)*

18 Feel the Glow in Arezzo

If the main piazza of Arezzo looks familiar, it could be because scenes of Roberto Benigni's film *Life Is Beautiful* were shot here. *(Ch. 6)*

19 Climb San Gimignano's Towers

Today, 14 of this town's medieval high-rises remain, and you can climb them for sweeping Tuscan hillside views. *(Ch. 5)*

20 Eat Bistecca Alla Fiorentina

This 2½ pound T-bone steak is cooked rare on a wooden grill; side dishes are ordered separately.

21 Hike in Foreste Casentinesi

The forest's natural beauty is unmistakable, with waterfalls, sweeping vistas, and soaring eagles. Churches dot the hiking trails. *(Ch. 6)*

22 See Michelangelo's *David*

David, 17 feet of Carrara marble carved by Michelangelo in the 1500s and now in the Galleria dell'Accademia, could be the most famous man in the world. *(Ch. 3)*

23 See Views From San Miniato al Monte

Walk up the hill to San Miniato al Monte and you'll reach the Romanesque basilica's courtyard, where the views are spectacular and crowds are thin. *(Ch. 3)*

24 Find Views in Fiesole

Explore Roman baths, a Roman amphitheater, and Etruscan walls. The roads leading to Fiesole are lined with vine-covered walls and Tuscan villas. *(Ch. 3)*

WHAT'S WHERE

1 Florence. In the 15th century, Florence was at the center of the artistic revolution that would later be known as the Renaissance. Today, the Renaissance remains the main reason people visit—the abundance of art treasures is mind-boggling.

2 Northwest Tuscany. West of Florence the main attractions are Pisa, home of the Leaning Tower, and Lucca, a town with a charming historic center.

3 Central Tuscany. The hills spreading south from Florence to Siena make up Chianti, a region of sublime wine and marvelous views. Siena, once Florence's main rival, remains one of Italy's most appealing medieval towns. To its northwest, little San Gimignano is famous for its 13th- and 14th-century towers. Farther west still is Volterra, a town dating back to the Etruscans.

4 Eastern Tuscany. Arezzo, Tuscany's third-largest city (after Florence and Pisa), has a car-free historic center and a basilica containing beautiful frescoes. Cortona, perched on a steep hill

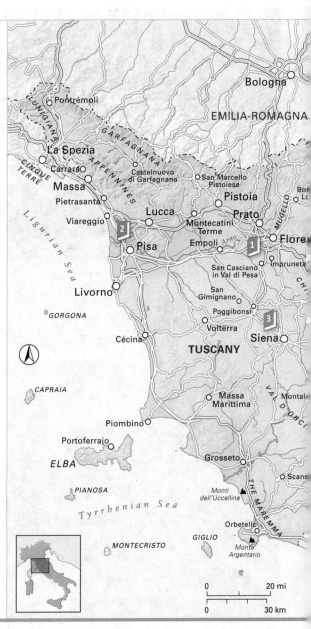

with sweeping views, exemplifies an alluringly old-fashioned way of life.

5 Southern Tuscany. In the Val d'Orcia, the towns of Montalcino and Montepulciano are surrounded by some of Italy's finest vineyards, and Pienza is a unique example of Renaissance urban planning. Farther south is the Maremma, Tuscany's cattle-ranching country. Off the coast, the lush island of Elba is a popular resort destination.

6 Umbria. Like Tuscany, Umbria has beautiful rolling hills topped by attractive old towns. Perugia is the region's largest city, but it's far from overwhelming, and it has a well-preserved medieval core. In Assisi, birthplace of St. Francis, the grand basilica draws millions of pilgrims annually. Spoleto is a quiet, elegant hill town, but, each summer, it brims with activity during the Festival dei Due Mondi. To the east, in the Marches region, Urbino is famed for its splendid Renaissance palace.

Best Hilltop Villages in Tuscany and Umbria

ORVIETO, UMBRIA

Although medieval architectural wonders adorn Orvieto, the labyrinth of subterranean tunnels beneath the town is even more fascinating. Orvieto is also recognized for its white and red wines, its olive oils, and its culinary classics—from boar and dove to pastas and pastries.

PITIGLIANO, TUSCANY

Although most Italian villages are overflowing with impressive churches, Pitigliano may be most famous for its synagogue, drawing attention to its rich history of Jewish settlement and giving the old town its nickname of Little Jerusalem. Of course, countless churches dot the rest of this Tuscan village. There's also a smattering of museums and other historic gems like the Palazzo Orsini, a Renaissance palace built on the ruins of medieval fortresses and containing both art and archaeological museums of its own.

SAN GIMIGNANO, TUSCANY

Most medieval towers have given way to war and erosion through the centuries, but San Gimignano retains so many that it has been dubbed the Town of Fine Towers and its historic center is a UNESCO World Heritage Site. Although it's packed with immaculate examples of medieval architecture, this village is among the more tourist-minded, with contemporary events like music festivals and art exhibitions and plenty of modern conveniences and services for travelers. San Gimignano even has its own app.

VOLTERRA, TUSCANY

Twelve miles from the better-known village of San Gimignano is the less visited (less crowded) Volterra. Although there are some serious medieval remnants in this village, especially its narrow streets in the town center, it's much more famous for the historical periods before and after. Some of its ancient Etruscan fortification walls still surround Roman ruins, including an impressive amphitheater worth exploring (there are also remains of ancient Roman baths and a forum). The Florentine influence of the Medici family left behind some dazzling Renaissance art and architecture throughout the once bustling mercantile village. The alabaster trade remains strong today and provides beautiful souvenirs of this Tuscan treasure.

SORANO, TUSCANY

Ham it up in Sorano, where the local ham is so revered that the town holds a festival for it every August. If you don't eat pork, don't worry; there are plenty of other local specialties highlighted during the event, particularly dairy products, including sheep's milk ricotta cheese, as well as oranges and other fruits and the ever-popular Italian liqueur, *limoncello*. Don't miss the Masso Leopoldina (sometimes called the Rocca Vecchia). It was once central to the defense of the town but is now a fabulous terrace that's a good place to enjoy panoramic views of Tuscany—and, perhaps, yet another limoncello.

San Gimignano

VINCI, TUSCANY

Yes, *that* Vinci. Established in the early Middle Ages among the rolling hills of Montalbano and with Arno Valley views, Vinci's claim to fame is Leonardo da Vinci (that, "Leonardo from Vinci"). The town is filled with tributes to him—like the imposing wooden sculpture, *Vitruvian Man,* by Mario Ceroli; the Biblioteca Leonardiana, an archive of his manuscripts and drawings; Santa Croce, the church where he was baptized; and the Museo Leonardiano Vinci, which houses his inventions and anatomical research, including drawings, studies, and replicas, in two buildings. You can also visit the birth home of this true Renaissance man in the nearby village of Anchiano. It's accessible via a 3-km (1.8-mile) walk up the *strade verde* (a dirt path with valley views) or by car or bus.

TODI, UMBRIA

Compact and ancient Todi is a hilltop citadel town with a beautiful patchwork of architecture that includes three sturdy walls, begun by the 3rd-century Etruscans followed by Roman and medieval dynasties. Starting at the café-community hub Piazza del Popolo, with an imposing 12th-century Romanesque-Gothic Duomo built upon a Roman temple, a maze of cobbled lanes and steep staircases fans out, inviting leisurely exploration. For grandstand views over roofs and the Umbrian hills beyond, climb the campanile of San Fortunato. Leafy walks abound in the Parco della Rocca, the city-wall park.

ASSISI, UMBRIA

Assisi claims history as ancient as 1000 BC and is probably best known for its most famous resident, St. Francis, whose 13th-century basilica is now a UNESCO World Heritage Site, as is the entire village itself. Plenty of other impressive churches, Roman ruins, and not one but two castles top the extensive list of the town's architectural offerings. From ceramics to medieval weaponry, Assisi's artisan history is also strong. Cured meats and chocolate are popular here, so grab a snack between sword fights, and refuel on the Assisi ribbon-type pasta *stringozzi,* often served with Norcia black truffles, asparagus, or *piccante* (spicy) tomato sauce.

Free Things to Do in Florence

GIARDINO DELLE ROSE

Florence has no shortage of gardens. One of the most beautiful is the Giardino delle Rose, whose terraces feature 400 varieties of roses as well as sculptures by Belgian artist Jean-Michel Folon. What's more, despite being free, it's less crowded than the Giardino di Boboli.

SANT'AMBROGIO MARKET

Even if you aren't interested in buying produce, walking through the local outdoor market is an entertaining (and free) activity all on its own. Every morning, an entire city block is filled with vendors selling fruits, vegetables, plants, and things like local honey.

IL DUOMO

As you walk around the center of Florence, Il Duomo (Santa Maria del Fiore, or Florence cathedral) is a monument that can't be missed. Standing before it and marveling at its intricate green and white marble facade might leave you in awe.

FESTA DELLA RIFICOLONA

If you are in Florence on September 7 and 8, don't miss one of the city's biggest street parties, celebrating the Virgin Mary's birthday. Festa della Rificolona is said to date from the 17th century when citizens across Florence and outside its city walls carried lanterns to guide their pilgrimage to the church of Santissima Annunziata, which is dedicated to the Virgin Mary, on the eve of her birth.

FIESOLE ANTIQUES MARKET

With only the price of a bus ticket, you can ride to Fiesole, in the northeast hills above Florence. The town is small, but, on the first Sunday of the month, its piazza is the site of a market selling vintage clothing, home wares, and other decades-old finds. You can spend an afternoon hunting for treasures.

LE MURATE

Florence may be known as an epicenter of Renaissance art, but if you want to see something different, and for free, head to Le Murate, a former convent and prison that is now a contemporary art gallery and event space. Artists from across the globe exhibit here with a particular emphasis on multimedia installations, which make use of former prison cells as showcasing rooms.

Piazzale Michelangelo

WANDER THE OLTRARNO DISTRICT

You're unlikely to visit Florence for its nightlife, but if you want a lively night out, the Oltrarno, whose streets are lined with bars and restaurants, is one option. La Cité, a popular Oltrarno bookstore, is a budget-friendly café for reading and studying by day and lingering with a cocktail at night.

LOGGIA DEI LANZI

The grand Piazza della Signoria (the square in front of Florence's city government building, Palazzo Vecchio) is made even grander by its open-air sculpture gallery—Loggia della Signoria, also called Loggia dei Lanzi. This 14th-century arched gallery, which is to your right as you walk toward the Galleria degli Uffizi, is free to enter at any time of night or day.

PIAZZALE MICHELANGELO

Whether you stand in Piazzale Michelangelo or sit on the steps leading up to it, be ready for crowds while enjoying the view of Florence's terra-cotta roofs—as well as Il Duomo, Ponte Vecchio, and Palazzo Vecchio—and the surrounding hills. The vistas are particularly striking at sunset.

SAN MINIATO AL MONTE

The Romanesque church San Miniato al Monte is a bit more challenging to reach than others in Florence, with its location high on a hill near Piazzale Michelangelo, but it's one of the most beautiful free attractions in the city. City views from its courtyard are spectacular.

What to Eat and Drink

FETTUNTA
Accompanying almost any meal at restaurants across Tuscany are bread, extra virgin olive oil, and salt.

RIBOLLITA
Ribollita is a thick stew of simmered vegetables like kale and carrots, white beans, and bread.

BRUNELLO DI MONTALCINO
Brunello di Montalcino reds are produced in the hill town Montalcino in the Val d'Orcia Valley.

CECINA
You can grab a slice of this savory mixture of olive oil, salt, and chickpea flour for a snack at bakeries throughout Florence and Tuscany.

TARTUFI
Tuscany's wild *tartufi*, or truffles, are a pungent, musky ingredient, whether shaved over pasta or added to sauces. White varieties are gathered by hunters from October to January, and black ones are more prevalent from June until fall.

CASTAGNACCIO
Gluten-free travelers can feast on this chestnut-flour dessert. It's often baked in fall, when chestnuts are most abundant, and combines the flour with pine nuts, sugar, and raisins for a dense consistency.

CINGHIALE RAGÙ
Wild boar, or *cinghiale*, roam Tuscany, making it a common meat dish. It's rich and a bit gamey and is frequently prepared as a *ragù* (meat sauce) to top *pappardelle*, a flat, wide, egg-based pasta with Tuscan origins.

PANZANELLA
Panzanella is the result of cooks combining leftovers with fresh ingredients to create a meal or a side dish. The aperitivo buffet staple is typically made from cubed bread, tomatoes, basil, and sometimes onions and cucumber.

Cecina

PICCIONE
Piccione (pigeon) is usually grilled or incorporated into a ragù. Sometimes it's served with spinach, pine nuts, and raisins.

PICI
These rounded, thick noodles resemble bulky spaghetti. Ask for *pici all'aglione,* served with a tomato sauce made with *aglione,* a variety of garlic that is cultivated in Tuscany and is known for its large bulbs and sweetness.

CROSTINI DI FEGATINI
Crostini—toasted pieces of bread with toppings—are an antipasti staple across Tuscany.

BUDINO DI RISO
Enjoy this tartlike pastry filled with vanilla-, orange-, or lemon-flavored rice pudding at many pasticcerie in Florence.

PAPPARDELLE ALLA LEPRE
A popular Tuscan meat is *lepre* (wild hare or rabbit), which is often served with pasta such as the broad, flat pappardelle.

PAPPA AL POMODORO
This Tuscan soup combines bread with tomatoes, basil, garlic, and olive oil.

10 Best Museums in Florence

PALAZZO PITTI

Florence's rich and powerful all walked down the halls of Palazzo Pitti. Today, its gallery rooms and royal apartments are lavishly decorated as a palace should be and contain more than 500 paintings (mostly Renaissance-era) including works by Raphael and Titian.

BARGELLO

The fortress-like Bargello has had many incarnations—family palace, government building, prison, and execution site (on its patio). As a nod to its conflicted past, it also houses a collection of weapons, armor, and medals from the powerful Medici family. The real draws, though, are Donatello's bronze *David*, standing victorious over the head of Goliath, and Michelangelo's marble *Bacchus*, as well as works by other major Renaissance sculptors.

GALLERIA DEGLI UFFIZI

It's one of the most visited museums in Florence, Italy, and the world for a reason. Head to the former offices of Florentine magistrates to see a wow-worthy collection of art. In one room, gaze at Sandro Botticelli's *Birth of Venus* and *Primavera*, and in another, Leonardo da Vinci's *Annunciation*. Works by Michelangelo, Raphael, Giotto, and Caravaggio are also here. Avoid the lines by booking tickets in advance on the Uffizi Gallery website.

GALLERIA DELL'ACCADEMIA

Come for *David*, stay to see everything else. There's no doubt that the line running down Via Ricasoli to enter a seemingly nondescript building is for Michelangelo's most famous man in the world—*Il Davide*. There is something marvelous about seeing his 17 feet of artfully carved Carrara marble "in the flesh," poised before his battle with Goliath. After you've caught your breath, check out the museum's early- to late-Renaissance works by Sandro Botticelli, and Andrea del Sarto; Florentine Gothic paintings; and collection of musical instruments.

MUSEO DELL'OPERA DEL DUOMO

When Santa Maria del Fiore—also known as Florence cathedral, or Il Duomo—and its baptistery and bell tower were completed in the 1400s, it was the largest church in Europe, and it was decorated by some of Italy's most celebrated artists. Today, however, some of its master works, like Lorenzo Ghiberti's famous bronze doors, or Gates of Paradise, which took him 27 years to finish, are fake. To save them from the elements, the doors and other decorative items and sculptures are now housed in the Museo dell'Opera del Duomo.

MUSEO SALVATORE FERRAGAMO

You may think that you've died and gone to shoe heaven at this museum in a palazzo featuring the work of southern Italian–born shoe designer, Salvatore Ferragamo (1898–1960). The permanent collection from the brand's archives includes a wedge sandal in gold and Technicolor rainbow colors that was designed for Judy Garland in 1938 and a cross-strap ballet flat that was created for Audrey Hepburn's slim feet in the 1950s and is still one of the label's signature styles. Because of Ferragamo's reputation as a "creator to the stars," the museum's temporary exhibits often merge film, art, and culture with fashion history.

PALAZZO STROZZI

Unlike Galleria degli Uffizi and other city-run museums, Palazzo Strozzi is an independent foundation. Hence, its exhibits are often eclectic, featuring, say, a retrospective of cinquecento Florentine art while at the same time showcasing avant-garde works such as a 65-foot spiral tunnel called *The Florence Experiment* or performance artist Marina Abramovic's *The Cleaner* (controversial for its use of nude actors). The permanent collection highlights the history of the palace, which was built for prominent Florentine banker, Filippo Strozzi, who died before it was completed.

PALAZZO VECCHIO

Also called Palazzo della Signoria, the monumental building surrounded by one of Italy's most famous piazzas has been home to Florence's city government since the Renaissance. Walk past a copy of Michelangelo's *David* at the entrance and up opulent marble staircases to see expansive gold-highlighted and frescoed ceilings and walls. The Salone dei Cinquecento is one of the grandest spaces, designed and painted by celebrated art historian (and artist in his own right), Giorgio Vasari.

SANTA CROCE

In Florence, churches are museums, too. At Santa Croce—considered the largest Franciscan church in the world (and said to be founded by St. Francis of Assisi)—you'll find 16 chapels that were once frequented by significant Florentine families who funded their decoration. There are frescoes by Renaissance master Giotto in the Bardi and Peruzzi chapels, and a terra-cotta altarpiece by another quattrocento heavy hitter, Andrea della Robbia. If the art isn't enough of a draw to visit, note that the basilica also contains the tombs of Michelangelo, Galileo, and Machiavelli.

Santa Croce

SANTA MARIA NOVELLA

Dominican monks founded the basilica of Santa Maria Novella in the 13th century, making it one of the most religiously significant churches in Florence—both then and now. The facade is a beauty, with green and white marble inlay work by Genoa-born Leon Battista Alberti. Inside are some of the world's finest examples of Renaissance art. On the main altar is Masaccio's *Trinita* fresco, which was painted in the 1400s, was covered and rediscovered in the 1800s, and is considered one of the earliest examples of perspective from the Renaissance period. Giotto's *Crucifix* is another master work that was likely painted in the late 1200s. In the basilica's largest chapel, Tornabuoni, Ghirlandaio painted frescoes about the life of the Virgin Mary, to whom the church is dedicated, in the late 1400s.

What to Read and Watch Before Your Trip

Gear up for your trip by learning about Italian culture with these books and films, from historical novels to contemporary movies.

THE AGONY AND THE ECSTASY BY IRVING STONE

Michelangelo, one of the most prolific Italian Renaissance artists, and his inspired life are the subjects of Irving Stone's 784-page *The Agony and the Ecstasy*. Read about the artist's most celebrated works in sculpture, painting, and architecture—*David*, the Sistine Chapel ceiling, and the dome of St. Peter's basilica—as well as his love affairs in this book that is long, but rightfully so.

A ROOM WITH A VIEW

Lucy Honeychurch and her cousin Charlotte Bartlett from Surrey, England, long for a "room with a view" for their holiday in Florence in 1987's Academy Award–winning (Best Adapted Screenplay, Best Art Direction, and Best Costume Design) film that's a very faithful adaptation of the E. M. Forster novel. Piazza della Signoria and Florence's skyline have key scenes as Lucy meets George Emerson at his family's pensione, which leads to a scandalous kiss between Lucy and George that's seen by Charlotte. Lucy returns to England and gets engaged to another man while her connection with George stays strong.

THE BIRTH OF VENUS BY SARAH DUNANT

Sarah Dunant's protagonist, Alessandra Cecchi, is the 14-year-old daughter of a Florentine cloth merchant who falls for a painter while he is decorating the family palazzo's chapel. A writer of successful thrillers, Dunant weaves a portrait of opulent 15th-century Florence in her 412-page novel as young Alessandra is married off to a wealthy older man while pursuing her love for her family's artist, his work, and the city where she lives.

THE CITY OF FLORENCE BY R. W. B. LEWIS

American literary scholar R. W. B. Lewis lived in Florence for several decades before writing this historical account of what is considered to be the birthplace of the Renaissance. The 320-page book examines the art, architecture, and history of the Tuscan city, beginning in the Middle Ages, through its artists; political leaders; and major sights like the Arno River, Ponte Vecchio, and Duomo.

THE ITALIANS BY JOHN HOOPER

In this 2015 book, longtime Rome correspondent John Hooper (who has written for the *Economist,* the *Guardian* and the *Observer*) addresses the complexities of contemporary Italy, attempting to reveal "what makes the Italian tick" with a generous *contorno* of humor. Here you'll learn the lexicon needed to negotiate and understand Italian culture. Of course, food, sex, and the weather—among other things—are heartily embraced in everyday life, but there's also an *amaro* (bitter) side. Hooper illustrates how the power of the *famiglia* (family) and the *chiesa* (church) has produced a society in which *furbizia* (cunning) is rewarded and meritocracy is replaced with *raccomandazioni* (favors) to get ahead in the world.

LIFE IS BEAUTIFUL

Roberto Benigni's Academy Award–winning film (for Best Actor and Best Foreign Language film in 1999), depicts the beauty and tragedy of life for Guido, Dora, and their young son Giosuè, in Italy during World War II. Guido (Benigni) is a fun-loving comic and the early parts of the film, much of which was shot in Cortona in Tuscany, follow the family's joy-filled lives. When the family is separated and sent to a concentration camp, Guido's humor shields his son by explaining the rules of the camp as a game to be won all the way to the end of film.

PBS *EMPIRES* SEASON 4: THE MEDICI

The fourth season of the American Public Broadcasting Service's historical miniseries, *Empires* (which also examines realms in Rome, Egypt, and Japan) focuses on Florence's Medici Dynasty. It begins with the establishment of the family's wealth in the 1400s and then continues with murder and intrigue. Michelangelo makes an appearance, and the story then follows a young Cosimo de'Medici taking over as Duke of Florence when his cousin is murdered.

INFERNO

The film adaptation of Dan Brown's novel sends Harvard University professor of religious iconology and symbology, Robert Langdon (Tom Hanks), on a dangerous mission across Florence and Venice. To track down a biological plague, Langdon follows a trail left by one of the film's villains, Betrand Zobrist, who was obsessed with Florentine poet Dante Alighieri. The mystery of the plague is tied to Dante's *Inferno,* and letters, phrases, objects and other clues that Langdon finds reveal not only the path to unraveling answers but bits of Dante's history and his significance during the Renaissance. With scenes shot in the bell tower of the Badia Fiorentina across the street from Dante's childhood home, Boboli Gardens, Vasari Corridor, and with views of Santa Maria del Fiore, you'll be transported to Florence, with your heart racing.

STEALING BEAUTY

In one of her first major film roles, Liv Tyler stars as Lucy Harmon in Italian director and screenwriter Bernardo Bertolucci's 1996 film, which is set in the Tuscan countryside. Lucy is a teenager who is sent to spend the summer at a family friend's Tuscan farmhouse after the death of her mother. Although she hopes to see a young man with whom she fell in love four years earlier, during the course of lively Italian dinners and parties, she is seduced by another guest at the house.

UNDER THE TUSCAN SUN BY FRANCES MAYES

When fortysomething writer Frances Mayes's marriage falls apart, she takes a vacation to Tuscany to change her perspective. That trip leads her to buy and remodel decrepit Villa Bramasole in Cortona, 65 miles northeast of Florence. The novel (which was made into a 2003 film starring Diane Lane) is Mayes's exploration of Tuscany through its local markets, people, and the discoveries she finds while unearthing decades' worth of history in her villa and the fertile land that surrounds it.

Florence and Tuscany Today

LA DOLCE VITA—TAKE IT SLOW

La dolce vita is perhaps the reason visitors flock to Tuscany and Umbria. The phrase literally translates as "the sweet life," meaning to take it easy and stop to smell the roses—perhaps with a glass of wine in hand while admiring the view.

Life here remains largely as it was centuries ago. Old-city skylines still look as good as they used to, as do views of the surrounding hills. In Tuscany, silver-gray olive trees dot the landscape, which is divided by rows of tall, noble cypresses.

The pace of life remains relatively unchanged, too. When they are not in their cars or on their Vespa scooters, Florentines still prefer to move to a more leisurely drumbeat. It's not just that the population is aging; it's that they don't like to appear rushed.

And so locals make a point of stopping to greet acquaintances, comment on the latest news, or catch up on gossip. Even waiters take their time, and you should be grateful to them for it. After all, why rush a meal with food that's this good and wine that's this divine?

SLOW FOOD

The Slow Food Movement, which was actually born in northern Italy, promotes seasonal cuisine that doesn't harm the environment and is mindful of animal welfare and consumer health. These principles starkly contrast with the notion of "fast food" and represent the joys of living a slow-paced lifestyle, beginning at the table. Although not all slow food is organic, the movement does promote the principles behind organic agriculture.

Throughout Tuscany and Umbria, keep an eye out for food purveyors and restaurants prominently displaying the Slow Food Movement emblem, which is a snail. These establishments are the standard-setters in terms of selling regional and seasonal specialties at reasonable prices.

That said, wherever food is sold, even in the larger supermarkets, you never go wrong by inquiring about local specialties or seasonal offerings. Most shopkeepers will appreciate your interest in what they are proudest to sell.

WINE-MAKING PROGRESSES

In 2013, a new category of Chianti Classico wine was created called the Gran Selezione. Grapes can come only from the same estate, with a lengthy release date of nearly three years. Vintners are equally divided about whether or not this is actually working.

Still, because of phenomenally high temperatures in July and August, many regional winemakers are fairly confident that future wines will be beyond-stellar quality—equal to, or possibly better than, those exquisite 1997, 2001, and 2003 vintages.

As across other wine-growing regions globally, Italy is part of the natural and biodynamic winemaking movement. With natural wines, organic or biodynamic grapes are processed from the vine and allowed to ferment naturally. Biodynamic generally refers to how the grapes are grown and harvested, and it follows more stringent requirements than wines labelled organic.

THE UFFIZI: STILL GROWING

The Uffizi Gallery, with arguably the world's greatest collections of Italian Renaissance art, is steadily expanding, striving to double its exhibition space. Although not all of its 99 rooms (and counting!) are always open, those containing the A-list works usually are.

In 2018, the rooms formerly known as Le Sale Blu (The Blue Rooms) became host to the Contini-Bonacossi collection, including the not-to-be-missed San Lorenzo sculpture by Bernini. That same year, the works of Leonardo da Vinci were finally given a glorious room of their own, and the works of Raphael were equally gifted.

The Terrace of Geographic Maps (Il Terrazzo delle Carte Geografiche), with its walls covered in late-16th century maps and frescoed ceilings, opened in 2021.

The Vasari Corridor—an enclosed, elevated passageway connecting Palazzo Vecchio with Palazzo Pitti via the Uffizi (its original intention in 1565)—has also received considerable attention, given its greatly anticipated reopening in 2022 after having been closed due to safety concerns since 2016.

OLD MEETS NEW IN THE WORLD OF ART

Echoing its past, modern-day Tuscany is a place for artists across genres to experiment and gain recognition, and regional museums are increasingly showcasing the works of both old masters and current artists. You'll find contemporary art installations throughout Florence, especially in Piazza della Signoria. Even the Uffizi now hosts temporary exhibits featuring modern-day works alongside museum masterpieces.

At Palazzo Strozzi, exhibitions focus on contemporary art installations, as well as works across genres and time periods, while highlighting the architectural details of the 15th century home of the Strozzi family.

Centro Pecci Prato's spaceship-like structure brings avant-garde to the region by showcasing research in the visual arts, music, cinema, and design.

Pietrasanta, 77 miles west of Florence on Tuscany's northern coast, was recognized during the Renaissance for its distinctive marble and is still a hub for artists. Public sculptures are on display in piazze and elsewhere throughout the town, as well as in its galleries and artists workshops.

MUSEUM DEALS

There's no doubt that, in a region with so many museums and so many masterpieces, deciding where to go first can be hard. The website of the Florentine State Museums (⊕ www.b-ticket.com/b-ticket/uffizi), which details and sells various tickets, is a good place to start.

As entrance fees can add up quickly, though, look into combo tickets that provide access to multiple sites at a discount. The PassePartOut ticket, for instance, can be used for five consecutive days at the Uffizi, Pitti Palace, and the Boboli Gardens and costs €18 (November–February) or €38 (March–October). A combined ticket for the Bargello, Medici Chapel, Palazzo Davanzati, Orsanmichele, and Casa Martelli museums costs €18.

Access to the various sites in the Piazza del Duomo (⊕ duomo.firenze.it/it/home) is via one of three passes that bundles admission and is valid for three days.

These include the €30 Brunelleschi Pass, the €20 Giotto Pass, and the €15 Ghiberti Pass. You can also purchase a ticket to visit Santa Croce, the Duomo Museum, and the Baptistery (⊕ *www.santacroce-opera.it/en/combo-ticket*) for €15.

Serious museumgoers might want to invest €85 in the Firenze Card (⊕ *www.firenzecard.it/en*), which grants entrance to most major museums, including the Uffizi and the Galleria dell'Accademia. Once it's activated, the card is good for 72 hours.

By adding the Firenze+ card for an additional €7, you'll have unlimited 72-hour access to the city's bus and tram system, too.

FASTER THAN A SPEEDING BULLET

High-speed train options—on the north–south Milan–Naples route as well as the east–west Venice–Bologna–Florence route—benefit from competition between the state-owned railway and privately owned Italo trains. Keep your eyes out for round-trip travel specials resulting from ongoing price wars: there are real deals to be had on ⊕ *www.italotreno.it/en* and ⊕ *www.trenitalia.com.*

Note, however, that local (*regionali*) commuter trains are still a state-controlled monopoly. Expect delays, crowds, cancellations, faulty air-conditioning in summer, and trains that need renovating. Patience is a virtue.

Remember that when there's a train strike, it is the commuter trains that are affected, not high-speed trains.

WHO'S WHO IN RENAISSANCE ART

Michelangelo. Leonardo da Vinci. Raphael. This heady triumvirate of the Italian Renaissance is synonymous with artistic genius. Yet they are only three of the remarkable cast of characters whose work defines the Renaissance, that extraordinary flourishing of art and culture in Italy, especially in Florence, as the Middle Ages drew to a close. The artists were visionaries, who redefined painting, sculpture, architecture, and even what it means to be an artist.

THE PIONEER. In the mid-14th century, a few artists began to move away the flat, two-dimensional painting of the Middle Ages. Giotto, who painted seemingly three-dimensional figures who show emotion, had a major impact on the artists of the next century.

THE GROUNDBREAKERS. The generations of Brunelleschi and Botticelli took center stage in the 15th century. Ghiberti, Masaccio, Donatello, Uccello, Fra Angelico, and Filippo Lippi were other major players. Part of the Renaissance (or "re-birth") was a renewed interest in classical sources—the texts, monuments, and sculpture of Ancient Greece and Rome. Perspective and the illusion of three-dimensional space in painting was another discovery of this era, known as the Early Renaissance. Suddenly the art appearing on the walls looked real, or more realistic than it used to.

Roman ruins were not the only thing to inspire these artists. There was an incredible exchange of ideas going on. In Santa Maria del Carmine, Filippo Lippi was inspired by the work of Masaccio, who in turn was a friend of Brunelleschi. Young artists also learned from the masters via the apprentice system. Ghiberti's workshop (bottega in Italian) included, at one time or another, Donatello, Masaccio, and Uccello. Botticelli was apprenticed to Filippo Lippi.

THE BIG THREE. The mathematical rationality and precision of 15th-century art gave way to what is known as the High Renaissance. Leonardo, Michelangelo, and Raphael were much more concerned with portraying the body in all its glory and with achieving harmony and grandeur in their work. Oil paint, used infrequently up until this time, became more widely employed: as a result, Leonardo's colors are deeper, more sensual, more alive. For one brief period, all three were in Florence at the same time. Michelangelo and Leonardo surely knew one another, as they were simultaneously working on frescoes (never completed) inside Palazzo Vecchio.

When Michelangelo left Florence for Rome in 1508, he began the slow drain of artistic exodus from Florence, which never really recovered her previous glory.

A RENAISSANCE TIMELINE

IN THE WORLD

Black Death in Europe kills one third of the population, 1347-50.

Joan of Arc burned at the stake, 1431.

IN FLORENCE

Dante, a native of Florence, writes The Divine Comedy, 1302-21.

Founding of the Medici bank, 1397.

Medici family made official papal bankers.

1434, Cosimo il Vecchio becomes de facto ruler of Florence. The Medici family will dominate the city until 1494.

1300

1400

IN ART

EARLY RENAISSANCE

Masaccio and Masolino fresco Santa Maria del Carmine, 1424-28.

GIOTTO (ca. 1267-1337)

Giotto fresoes in Santa Croce, 1320-25.

BRUNELLESCHI (1377-1446)

LORENZO GHIBERTI (ca. 1381-1455)

DONATELLO (ca. 1386-1466)

PAOLO UCCELLO (1397-1475)

FRA ANGELICO (ca. 1400-1455)

1334, 67-year-old Giotto is appointed chief architect of Santa Maria del Fiore, Florence's Duomo (below). He begins to work on the Campanile, which will be completed in 1359, after his death.

MASACCIO (1401-1428)

FILIPPO LIPPI (ca. 1406-1469)

Donatello sculpts his bronze David, ca. 1440.

Fra Angelico frescoes friars' cells in San Marco, ca. 1438-45.

Ghiberti wins the competition for the Baptistery doors (above) in Florence, 1401.

Uccello's Sir John Hawkwood, ca. 1436.

Brunelleschi wins the competition for the Duomo's cupola, 1418.

Gutenberg Bible is printed, 1455.

Columbus discovers America, 1492.

Martin Luther posts his 95 theses on the door at Wittenberg, kicking off the Protestant Reformation, 1517.

Constantinople falls to the Turks, 1453.

Machiavelli's Prince appears, 1513.

Copernicus proves that the earth is not the center of the universe, 1530-43.

Lorenzo "il Magnifico" (right), the Medici patron of the arts, rules in Florence, 1449-92.

Two Medici popes Leo X (1513-21) and Clement VII (1523-34) in Rome.

Catherine de'Medici becomes Queen of France, 1547.

1450   **1500**   **1550**

HIGH RENAISSANCE   MANNERISM

Fra Filippo Lippi's Madonna and Child, ca. 1452.

1508, Raphael begins work on the chambers in the Vatican, Rome.

Giorgio Vasari publishes his first edition of *Lives of the Artists*, 1550.

1504, Michelangelo's David is put on display in Piazza della Signoria, where it remains until 1873.

Botticelli paints the Birth of Venus, ca. 1482.

Michelangelo begins to fresco the Sistine Chapel ceiling, 1508.

BOTTICELLI (ca. 1444-1510)

LEONARDO DA VINCI (1452-1519)

RAPHAEL (1483-1520)

MICHELANGELO (1475-1564)

Leonardo paints The Last Supper (below) in Milan, 1495-98.

Giotto's Nativity

Donatello's St. John the Baptist

Ghiberti's Gates of Paradise

GIOTTO (CA. 1267-1337)

Painter/architect from a small town north of Florence.

He unequivocally set Italian painting on the course that led to the triumphs of the Renaissance masters. Unlike the rather flat, two-dimensional forms found in then prevailing Byzantine art, Giotto's figures have a fresh, life-like quality. The people in his paintings have bulk, and they show emotion, which you can see on their faces and in their gestures. This was something new in the late Middle Ages. Without Giotto, there wouldn't have been a Raphael.

In Florence: Santa Croce; Uffizi; Campanile; Santa Maria Novella

Elsewhere in Italy: Scrovegni Chapel, Padua; Vatican Museums, Rome

FILIPPO BRUNELLESCHI (1377-1446)

Architect/engineer from Florence.

If Brunelleschi had beaten Ghiberti in the Baptistery doors competition in Florence, the city's Duomo most likely would not have the striking appearance and authority that it has today. After his loss, he sulked off to Rome, where he studied the ancient Roman structures first-hand. Brunelleschi figured out how to vault the Duomo's dome, a structure unprecedented in its colossal size and great height. His Ospedale degli Innocenti employs classical elements in the creation of a stunning, new architectural statement; it is the first truly Renaissance structure.

In Florence: Duomo; Ospedale degli Innocenti; San Lorenzo; Santo Spirito; Baptistery Doors Competition Entry, Bargello; Santa Croce

LORENZO GHIBERTI (CA. 1381-1455)

Sculptor from Florence.

Ghiberti won a competition—besting his chief rival, Brunelleschi—to cast the gilded bronze North Doors of the Baptistery in Florence. These doors, and the East Doors that he subsequently executed, took up the next 50 years of his life. He created intricately worked figures that are more true-to-life than any since antiquity, and he was one of the first Renaissance sculptors to work in bronze. Ghiberti taught the next generation of artists; Donatello, Uccello, and Masaccio all passed through his studio.

In Florence: Door Copies, Baptistery; Original Doors, Museo dell'Opera del Duomo; Baptistry Door Competition Entry, Bargello; Orsanmichele

DONATELLO (CA. 1386-1466)

Sculptor from Florence.

Donatello was an innovator who, like his good friend Brunelleschi, spent most of his long life in Florence. Consumed with the science of optics, he used light and shadow to create the effects of nearness and distance. He made an essentially flat slab look like a three- dimensional scene. His bronze is probably the first free-standing male nude since antiquity. Not only technically brilliant, his work is also emotionally resonant; few sculptors are as expressive.

In Florence: David, Bargello; St. Mark, Orsanmichele; Palazzo Vecchio; Museo dell'Opera del Duomo; San Lorenzo; Santa Croce

Elsewhere in Italy: Padua; Prato; Venice

Fra Angelico's Déposition de Croix   Masaccio's Trinity   Filippo Lippi's Madonna and Child with Two Angels

PAOLO UCCELLO (1397-1475)
Painter from Florence.
Renaissance chronicler Vasari once observed that had Uccello not been so obsessed with the mathematical problems posed by perspective, he would have been a very good painter. The struggle to master single-point perspective and to render motion in two dimensions is nowhere more apparent than in his battle scenes. His first major commission in Florence was the gargantuan fresco of the English mercenary Sir John Hawkwood (the Italians called him Giovanni Acuto) in Florence's Duomo.
In Florence: **Sir John Hawkwood, Duomo; Battle of San Romano, Uffizi; Santa Maria Novella**
Elsewhere in Italy: **Urbino, Prato**

FRA ANGELICO (CA. 1400-1455)
Painter from a small town north of Florence.
A Dominican friar, who eventually made his way to the convent of San Marco, Fra Angelico and his assistants painted frescoes for aid in prayer and meditation. He was known for his piety; Vasari wrote that Fra Angelico could never paint a crucifix without a tear running down his face. Perhaps no other painter so successfully translated the mysteries of faith and the sacred into painting. And yet his figures emote, his command of perspective is superb, and his use of color startles even today.
In Florence: **Museo di San Marco; Uffizi**
Elsewhere in Italy: **Vatican Museums, Rome; Fiesole; Cortona; Perugia; Orvieto**

MASACCIO (1401-1428)
Painter from San Giovanni Valdarno, southeast of Florence.
Masaccio and Masolino, a frequent collaborator, worked most famously together at Santa Maria del Carmine. Their frescoes of the life of St. Peter use light to mold figures in the painting by imitating the way light falls on figures in real life. Masaccio also pioneered the use of single-point perspective, masterfully rendered in his His friend Brunelleschi probably introduced him to the technique, yet another step forward in rendering things the way the eye sees them. Masaccio died young and under mysterious circumstances.
In Florence: **Santa Maria del Carmine; Trinity, Santa Maria Novella**

FILIPPO LIPPI (CA. 1406-1469)
Painter from Prato.
At a young age, Filippo Lippi entered the friary of Santa Maria del Carmine, where he was highly influenced by Masaccio and Masolino's frescoes. His religious vows appear to have made less of an impact; his affair with a young nun produced a son, Filippino (Little Philip, who later apprenticed with Botticelli), and a daughter. His religious paintings often have a playful, humorous note; some of his angels are downright impish and look directly out at the viewer. Lippi links the earlier painters of the 15th century with those who follow; Botticelli apprenticed with him.
In Florence: **Uffizi; Palazzo Medici Riccardi; San Lorenzo; Palazzo Pitti**
Elsewhere in Italy: **Prato**

Botticelli's Primavera

Leonardo's Portrait of a Young Woman

Raphael's Madonna on the Meadow

BOTTICELLI (CA. 1444-1510)
Painter from Florence.
Botticelli's work is characterized by stunning, elongated blondes, cherubic angels (something he undoubtedly learned from his time with Filippo Lippi), and tender Christs. Though he did many religious paintings, he also painted monumental, nonreligious panels—his Birth of Venus and Primavera being the two most famous of these. A brief sojourn took him to Rome, where he and a number of other artists frescoed the Sistine Chapel walls.
In Florence:
Birth of Venus, Primavera, Uffizi; Palazzo Pitti
Elsewhere in Italy:
Vatican Museums, Rome

LEONARDO DA VINCI (1452-1519)
Painter/sculptor/engineer from Anchiano, a small town outside Vinci.
Leonardo never lingered long in any place; his restless nature and his international reputation led to commissions throughout Italy, and took him to Milan, Vigevano, Pavia, Rome, and, ultimately, France. Though he is most famous for his mysterious Mona Lisa (at the Louvre in Paris), he painted other penetrating, psychological portraits in addition to his scientific experiments: his design for a flying machine (never built) predates Kitty Hawk by nearly 500 years. The greatest collection of Leonardo's work in Italy can be seen on one wall in the Uffizi.
In Florence: **Adoration of the Magi, Uffizi**
Elsewhere in Italy: **Last Supper, Santa Maria delle Grazie, Milan**

RAPHAEL (1483-1520)
Painter/architect from Urbino.
Raphael spent only four highly productive years of his short life in Florence, where he turned out made-to-order panel paintings of the Madonna and Child for a hungry public; he also executed a number of portraits of Florentine aristocrats. Perhaps no other artist had such a fine command of line and color, and could render it, seemingly effortlessly, in paint. His painting acquired new authority after he came up against Michelangelo toiling away on the Sistine ceiling. Raphael worked nearly next door in the Vatican, where his figures take on an epic, Michelangelesque scale.
In Florence: **Uffizi; Palazzo Pitti**
Elsewhere in Italy: **Vatican Museums, Rome**

MICHELANGELO (1475-1564)
Painter/sculptor/architect from Caprese.
Although Florentine and proud of it (he famously signed his St. Peter's Pietà to avoid confusion about where he was from), he spent most of his 89 years outside his native city. He painted and sculpted the male body on an epic scale and glorified it while doing so. Though he complained throughout the proceedings that he was really a sculptor, Michelangelo's Sistine Chapel ceiling is arguably the greatest fresco cycle ever painted (and the massive figures owe no small debt to Giotto).
In Florence: **David, Galleria dell'Accademia; Uffizi; Casa Buonarroti; Bargello**
Elsewhere in Italy: **St. Peter's Basilica, Vatican Museums, and Piazza del Campidoglio in Rome**

Chapter 2

TRAVEL SMART

Updated by
Elizabeth Shemaria

★ **CAPITAL:**
Florence

♀♂ **POPULATION:**
3.7 million

🗨 **LANGUAGE:**
Italian

$ **CURRENCY:**
Euro

📠 **COUNTRY CODE:**
39

⚠ **EMERGENCIES:**
113

🚗 **DRIVING:**
On the right

⚡ **ELECTRICITY:**
200v/50 cycles; electrical
plugs have two round prongs

🕐 **TIME:**
Six hours ahead of New York

🌐 **WEB RESOURCES:**
www.italia.it
www.visittuscany.com
www.firenzeturismo.it

Know Before You Go

ITALIANS DON'T DRINK CAPPUCCINO AFTER BREAKFAST

Instead of cappuccino, you'll fit in if you drink espresso throughout the day, usually standing up and as a shot (it's not to be sipped). During a meal, order your espresso after dessert, not with it.

RESTROOM FACILITIES VARY GREATLY

The toilet might be small and low with no seat, or it might just be a porcelain hole in the floor. Restrooms in restaurants, hotel common areas, museums, and department stores tend to be the best equipped and cleanest; those in pubs, bars, and (some) gas stations far less so. Pay and attendant-supervised restrooms are options in large towns and cities. (Get a map of the pay toilets in Florence at city tourist-information offices.) Expect to pay or tip €1. Airports and train stations also have facilities; churches, post offices, and public beaches do not. Always carry tissues in case there's no toilet paper, as well as hand-sanitizing gel or wipes.

SAVE MONEY ON TRAIN FARE

If Italy is your only destination in Europe, consider purchasing a Eurail Italy Pass, which allows a limited number of travel days within one month. Prices for four days are about €153 (second class) or €204 (first class). Note that you must purchase your Eurail Italy Pass before arriving in in the country. Also, don't assume that having one guarantees a seat on the trains you wish to ride; you need to reserve seats ahead even if you use a rail pass. There's a nominal fee (usually €10) for the reservation.

FARMSTAYS ARE A POPULAR LODGING OPTION

Rural lodgings in the *agriturismo* (agricultural tourism) category—namely working farms or vineyards—are increasingly popular with both Italians and visitors.

Accommodations vary in size and range from luxury apartments, farmhouses, and villas to properties with very basic facilities. The Agriturist (⊕ *www.agriturist.it*) and Agriturismo (⊕ *www.agriturismo.it*) websites have hundreds of farm listings in Italy. Local tourist offices also have information.

DON'T GO HUNGRY

The crucial rule of restaurant dining is that you should order at least two courses. It's a common mistake for tourists to order only a *secondo* (second course), thinking they're getting a "main course" complete with a side dish (*contorno*). What they usually wind up with is one lonely piece of meat.

KEEP YOUR RECEIPT WITH YOU AFTER DINING

When you leave a dining establishment, take your meal bill or receipt with you; although not a common experience, the Italian finance (tax) police can approach you within 100 yards of the establishment at which you've eaten and ask for a receipt. If you don't have one, they can fine you and the business owner for not providing the receipt. The measure is intended to prevent tax evasion; it's not necessary to show receipts when leaving Italy.

THERE ARE DIFFERENT TYPES OF POLICE

Both Italy's national (*carabinieri*) and local (*polizia*) police are armed and can investigate crimes and make arrests. Traffic officers—colloquially known as *vigili* and officially known as *polizia municipale*—are responsible for handling minor traffic accidents, issuing parking tickets, and clamping cars. You can spot them in their white (in summer) or black uniforms. Many police stations have English-speaking staff to deal with travelers' problems. When reporting an incident, you'll need to fill out and sign a report form (*una denuncia*); keep a copy for your insurance company. Also, if you lose your passport, notify either the carabinieri or the police, as well as your embassy.

TRY TO LEARN SOME ITALIAN

Although in Florence and other cities most hotels have English speakers at their reception desks and you can always find someone who speaks at least a little English, you may run into a language barrier in the countryside. You need not strive for fluency: even just mastering a few basic words and terms is bound to make chatting with locals more rewarding and a phrasebook and the use of pantomime and expressive gestures will go a long way. Try to master a few phrases for daily use, and familiarize yourself with the terms you'll need for deciphering signs, menus, and museum labels. It helps, too, that the Italian language is often pronounced exactly as it is written.

COVER UP IN CHURCHES AND MONASTERIES

Many of Italy's churches contain significant works of art, but they are also places of worship, so be sure to dress appropriately when visiting them. Shorts, miniskirts, tank tops, spaghetti straps, and sleeveless garments are taboo; short shorts are inappropriate anywhere. When touring churches—especially in summer when it's hot and no sleeves are desirable—carry a sweater, large scarf, or a light shawl to wrap around your shoulders before entering. Also, remove your hat, and be sure your cell phone is turned off. While inside, don't drink from your water bottle. Do not enter a church if a service is in progress, and never enter with food.

MIND YOUR TABLE MANNERS

Table manners are formal; rarely do Italians share food from their plates. Spaghetti should be eaten with a fork only, although a little help from a spoon won't horrify locals the way cutting spaghetti into little pieces might. Flowers, dessert (in the form of a cake or torte from a pasticceria), or a bottle of wine are appropriate hostess gifts if you're invited to dinner.

DOGGY BAGS ARE REALLY ONLY FOR DOGS

Wiping your bowl clean with a small piece of bread is considered a sign of appreciation and not bad manners. Leftovers are left behind; don't ask for a doggy bag unless you really have a dog.

Getting Here and Around

Air

If you want to fly into Florence from the United States, you'll have to make connections in other major European cities like Paris, Frankfurt, or London.

AIRPORTS

The major gateways to Italy include Rome's Aeroporto Leonardo da Vinci (airport code FCO), better known as Fiumicino, and Milan's Aeroporto Malpensa (MIL). Flights to Florence make connections at Fiumicino, Malpensa, Paris, Amsterdam, Frankfurt, Munich, and London, among other airports.

Florence is served by Aeroporto A. Vespucci (FLR), also called Peretola, and by Aeroporto di Pisa (PSA), which is about a mile outside the center of Pisa and about one hour from Florence.

Italy's airports have restaurants, snack bars, and Wi-Fi access. Each airport has at least one nearby hotel, though the city centers of Florence and Pisa are only 15 minutes away by taxi, so if you encounter a long delay, spend it in town.

Airports in Italy have been ramping up security measures, which include random baggage inspections and the presence of bomb-sniffing dogs.

■ TIP→ **Ask the local tourist board about hotel and local transportation packages that include tickets to major museum exhibits or other special events.**

GROUND TRANSPORTATION

It takes about 20 minutes to get from Aeroporto A. Vespucci into Florence. Taxis are readily available, charging about €25, with a €1 surcharge for each bag and a €3 surcharge for nighttime trips. A tram line connects the airport to Santa Maria Novella train station from 5 am until midnight.

Taxis from Aeroporto di Pisa to central Pisa cost about €20. A train ride from Pisa to Florence takes just over an hour (€8.70), after connecting from the airport to Pisa train station using the People Mover (travel time about 5 minutes, €5 each way). You can also reach Florence from the Pisa airport by taxi (about €200) or by bus. The Sky Bus line service runs from the Pisa airport to the train station in Florence (60 minutes; one-way €13.90).

The train from Aeroporto Leonardo da Vinci stops at five stations in Rome and takes one hour (€14) to get to the city. A taxi from the airport to the central train station costs about €60.

Metered taxis are available outside both the arrival and departure areas of Aeroporto Malpensa. The journey time to central Milan is around 50 minutes; the fare is about €90. The Malpensa Express train departs every half hour from Milano Centrale and Milano Cadorna stations; it's €13 one-way and takes about an hour.

FLIGHTS
AIR TRAVEL TO FLORENCE AND TUSCANY

Air travel to Italy is frequent and virtually problem-free. Sometimes, however, airport- or airline-related union strikes cause delays, which are usually announced in advance. ITA, Italy's national flag carrier, has the most nonstop flights to Rome and Milan. Frequent flights are available from the United States aboard Lufthansa, Air France, American, United, and Delta; these stop once in Europe before they or their code-sharing partners continue on to Florence or Pisa.

WITHIN ITALY

ITA airways, major European airlines, and smaller, privately run companies such as Ryanair and EasyJet have an extensive network of flights within Italy.

🚌 Bus

Italy's bus network is extensive, but because of its low cost and convenience, train travel is usually a more attractive option. Bus schedules are often drawn up with commuters and students in mind, and service may be sporadic on Sunday. That said, if you don't have a car, regional buses are often the only options for reaching out-of-the-way places. Even when this isn't the case, buses can be faster and more direct than local trains, so it's a good idea to compare bus and train routes and schedules.

CLASSES

Both public and private buses offer only one class of service. Cleanliness and comfort levels are high on private buses, which have comfortable seats, but no toilets.

CUTTING COSTS

Public and private bus lines offer monthly passes and multiride cards. Children under three feet in height ride free if they're traveling with an adult and don't require their own seat. Infant car seats are permitted on private bus lines.

DISCOUNT PASSES

None of the cities in Tuscany or Umbria are big enough to make the various discount bus pass schemes that appear and disappear with regularity worth the trouble. Most weeklong tourists to Florence, the largest city, will ride the city buses no more than four times at a cost of €1.50 (or €2.50 if purchased on the bus) per ticket. A card with 10 rides is available for €14 and a month-long pass is available for €35 through the Autolinee Toscane system.

FARES AND SCHEDULES

You can buy public-transit tickets at newsstands or tobacco shops and at ticket machines at tram stops. The local public transportation service, Autolinee Toscane, allows customers to buy tickets in cash from the bus driver—exact fare is necessary, as no change is given, and the price is higher as there is a surcharge. Don't forget to validate your ticket in the machine on the bus.

Buy tickets for private buses at the bus station or at travel agencies bearing the bus line's logo. Again, be sure to validate the ticket either at the bus station or on the bus as soon as you board. Schedules for private line buses may be obtained online or at the bus station; city bus schedules for Florence (Autolinee Toscane) are available online at ⊕ www. at-bus.it.

PAYING

Credit cards may not be accepted for private-line bus tickets (some travel agencies may accept them), and public bus tickets purchased at newsstands and tobacco shops must often be paid for in cash.

RESERVATIONS

Public bus lines do not issue reservations. For some private bus line direct routes (i.e., during commute hours) reservations are required.

Car

Tuscany has an extensive network of *autostrade* (toll highways) that is complemented by (usually) well-maintained but free *superstrade* (expressways). The ticket you are issued upon entering an autostrada must be returned when you

Getting Here and Around

exit and pay the toll, though on some shorter autostrade, mainly connecting highways, the toll is paid upon entering. Telepass, debit payment cards on sale at many autostrada locations, make paying tolls easier and faster by avoiding the hunt for change to pay the toll.

A *raccordo* is a ring road surrounding a city. *Strade regionale* and *strade provinciale* (regional and provincial highways, denoted by *S, SS, SR,* or *SP* numbers) are usually two-lane roads, as are all secondary roads. Directions and turnoffs on toll roads and expressways are frequent and clear; secondary roads aren't always clearly marked. Regardless of the type of road, be prepared for fast and impatient fellow drivers.

GASOLINE

Gas stations are located at frequent intervals along the main highways and autostrade. In case you run out of gas along the toll roads or the main free superstrade, emergency telephones are provided. To find the phone, look on the pavement at the shoulder of the highway where painted arrows and the term "SOS" point in the direction of the nearest phone.

Gas stations on autostrade are usually open 24 hours. Those in towns and cities are usually on the periphery; they're rarely found in the city center. These stations are generally open Monday through Saturday 7–7 with a break at lunchtime.

Many stations have automatic self-service pumps that accept bills of €5, €10, €20, and €50 and don't give change (you can get a receipt to use the balance later); if you want a receipt (*ricevuta*), you might have to push a button before starting the process. Full-service stations or those with an attendant take both cash and credit cards. It's not customary to tip the attendant when full service is provided.

As of this writing, gas (*benzina*) costs about €1.80 a liter. It's available in unleaded (*verde*) and super unleaded (*super*). Many rental cars in Italy take only diesel (*gasolio*), which costs less per liter; ask about the fuel type before you leave the rental office.

PARKING

Parking is at a premium in most towns and cities, especially in their *centri storici* (historic centers), which are filled with narrow streets and restricted circulation zones. It's best to leave your car only in guarded parking areas. In Florence, such indoor parking costs about €23–€30 for 12–24 hours; outside attended parking costs about €10–€20.

Parking in an area signposted "Zona Disco" (Disk Zone), usually found only in small towns, is allowed for limited periods (from 30 minutes to two hours or more—the limit is posted. If you don't have the cardboard disk (located in the glove box of your rental car) to show what time you parked, you can use a piece of paper. The *parcometro,* the Italian version of metered parking in which you put coins into a machine for a stamped ticket that you leave on the dashboard, has been introduced in most large towns and cities.

Parking regulations are strictly enforced both in the cities and small towns. Fines run as high as €70 (more for taking a space designated for people with disabilities), and towing (or tire clamps) is a possible penalty in Florence. Car rental companies often use your credit card to be reimbursed for any fines you incur during your rental period.

In Tuscany vandalism and theft of cars are rare. Nevertheless, don't leave luggage or valuables in your car, especially in cities and large towns where thieves target rental cars. Be especially vigilant at Autogrills (rest stops).

ROAD CONDITIONS

Driving on the back roads of Tuscany isn't difficult as long as you're on the alert for bicycles, scooters, and passing cars. That said, street and road signs are often missing or placed in awkward spots, so a good map or GPS and patience are essential. Be aware that some maps may not use the newer *SR* or *SP* (strade regionale and strade provinciale) highway designations but rather the older *SS* designation—or no numbering at all.

Autostrade are well maintained, as are most interregional highways. The condition of provincial (county) roads varies, but maintenance at this level is generally good. In many small hill towns, the streets are winding and extremely narrow; consider parking at the edge of town and exploring on foot.

Most autostrade have two lanes in both directions; the left lane is used only for passing. Italians drive fast and are impatient with those who don't, so tailgating is the norm here. The only way to avoid it is to get out of the way.

ROAD MAPS

Michelin and Touring Club Italiano both produce good road maps. The Michelin website (⊕ *www.viamichelin.com*) is a good source of driving instructions and maps, though the travel times provided are highly optimistic. You can also get free street maps for most towns at local information offices.

RULES OF THE ROAD

Driving is on the right. Regulations largely resemble those in the United States, except that the police have the power to levy on-the-spot fines. In some Italian towns, the use of the horn is forbidden in certain, if not all, areas.

Speed limits are 130 kph (80 mph) on autostrade and 70 kph (43 mph) on state and provincial roads, unless otherwise marked. Enforcement of speed limits varies from region to region. If you are driving on superstrade, pay particular attention to the gray machines that appear periodically along the road. They snap photos if you're exceeding the speed limit, and the rental car company will eventually catch up with you to pay the fine.

The legal maximum blood-alcohol level is 0.05. Penalties for driving after drinking are heavy, including license suspension and the additional possibility of six months imprisonment.

Right turns on red lights are forbidden. Headlights are required to be on day and night while driving on all roads (large or small) outside of municipalities. Seat belts are required for adults, and infant and children's car seats are compulsory for babies and toddlers.

CAR RENTAL

When you reserve a car, ask about cancellation penalties, taxes, drop-off charges (if you're planning to pick up the car in one city and leave it in another), and surcharges (for being under or over a certain age, for additional drivers, or for driving across state or country borders or beyond a specific distance from your point of rental). All these things can add substantially to your costs. Request child car seats and other extras when you book, too.

Getting Here and Around

Rates are sometimes—but not always—better if you book in advance or reserve through a rental agency's website. There are other reasons to book ahead, though: for popular destinations, during busy times of the year, or to ensure that you get certain types of cars (vans, SUVs, exotic sports cars).

■ TIP➔ **Make sure that a confirmed reservation guarantees you a car. Agencies sometimes overbook, particularly for busy weekends and holiday periods.**

Tuscany has an intricate network of autostrade routes, good highways, and secondary roads, making renting a car a better but expensive alternative (because of high gas prices and freeway tolls) to public transportation. A rental car can be a particularly good investment for carefree countryside rambles, offering access to more remote towns. Having a car in major cities, however, often leads to parking and traffic headaches, plus the additional expense of garage and parking fees.

Florence, Siena, and other major cities have restricted, camera-monitored zones—"Zona Traffico Limitato" (or ZTL)—for cars. Although they're clearly marked, visitors often fail to see them. If you drive to your hotel in the centers of these cities, inquire at the front desk of your hotel as to whether your rental car's license tag number must be submitted by the hotel to the police or traffic authority. Failure to do this might result in a large fine being levied on your car-rental company and passed on to you.

Major car-rental companies offer Ford-type cars (such as the Ford Fusion) and Fiats in various sizes and in good condition, all with air-conditioning. Local companies provide good service and, depending on the time of year, may have greater availability than the well-known international companies. Because most Italian cars have standard transmissions, automatics are more expensive and must be reserved well in advance. Mileage is usually unlimited, although certain offers limit included mileage to 150 km (93 miles) a day, after which you must pay for additional miles.

Most major U.S. car-rental companies have offices or affiliates in Italy, but the rates are generally better if you make a reservation from abroad rather than from within Italy. Each company's rental prices are uniform throughout the country, so you won't save money by, for example, picking up a vehicle from a city rental office rather than from an airport location.

In Italy, a U.S. driver's license is acceptable to rent a car, but you should also get an International Driver's Permit (IDP). Italy, by law at least, requires non-Europeans to carry an IDP along with their domestic license because the IDP states in Italian (and a dozen other languages) that your license is valid. In practice, it depends on the police officer who pulls you over whether you will be penalized for not carrying the IDP.

In Italy you must be 18 years old to drive a car. Most rental companies will not rent to someone under age 21, refuse to rent any car larger than an economy or subcompact car to anyone under age 23, and further require customers under age 23 to pay by credit card. Additional drivers must be identified in the contract and must meet age requirements. There may be an additional daily fee for more than one driver.

Upon rental, all companies require credit cards as a warranty; to rent bigger cars (2,000 cc or more), you must often show two credit cards. There are no special restrictions on senior-citizen drivers. Book car seats, required for children under age three, in advance. The cost is generally about €36 for the duration of the rental.

Hiring a car with a driver can come in handy, particularly if you plan to do some wine tasting. Ask at your hotel for recommended drivers, or inquire at the local tourist-information office. Typically, drivers are paid by the day, and are usually rewarded with a tip of about 15% on completion of the journey.

CAR-RENTAL INSURANCE

Italy requires car-rental companies to include Collision Damage Waiver (CDW) coverage in quoted rates. Ask your rental company about other coverage when you reserve the car and/or pick it up.

Everyone who rents a car wonders whether the insurance that the rental companies offer is worth the expense. No one has a simple answer. It all depends on how much regular insurance you have, how comfortable you are with risk, and whether or not money is an issue.

Ferry

Ferries (*traghetti*) connect the mainland with the Tuscan islands, including Elba, Capraia, Pianosa, Giglio, and Giannutri. Hydrofoil (*aliscafo*) service is available to many destinations, too, and it is generally twice as fast as the ferries—and double the price. All ferries are considerably more frequent in summer.

Passenger and car ferries serve Elba. If you're traveling in July or August, try to make reservations at least a month in advance. Two ferry lines operate along the coast of Cinque Terre: Golfo Paradiso, which operates from June to September from Genoa and Camogli to the Cinque Terre villages of Monterosso al Mare

and Vernazza, and the smaller, but more frequent, Golfo dei Poeti, which stops at each village (from Portovenere to Riomaggiore, except for Corniglia) five times a day.

The easiest place to find schedules and fare information for Tuscany ferry service is on each company's website. If you are already in the area, local tourist offices, travel agencies, and port ticket offices have printed schedules. Most ferry operators accept credit cards or cash.

Train

Train service between Milan, Florence, Rome, and Naples is frequent throughout the day. The train from Rome to Florence takes 90 minutes; Milan to Florence takes about two hours. For the most part, trains stick to the schedule, although delays may occur during peak tourist season. Train strikes of various kinds are also frequent, so it's a good idea to make sure the train you want to take is in fact running: generally speaking, however, when train strikes happen high-speed trains are not affected.

The fastest trains on the Ferrovie dello Stato (FS), the Italian State Railways, are Le Frecce trains, operating on several main lines, including Rome–Milan via Florence and Bologna. There are four classes: Executive, Business, Premium, and Standard.

High-speed Le Frecce trains, called Frecciarossa, run at speeds of up to 300 km/h (190 mph) between Milan and Naples, stopping in Florence. On some journeys, you will find Frecciargento trains, which operate at speeds of up to 250 km/h (160 mph). Frecciabianca trains operate at up to 200 km/h (124 mph).

Getting Here and Around

All Le Frecce trains and the next-fastest trains, Intercity (IC) trains, require seat reservations. Italo, another line in direct competition with the Italian State Railways, runs high-speed trains to many major Italian cities. There is refreshment service on all long-distance trains, with mobile carts and a cafeteria or dining car. Tap water on trains is not drinkable.

Note that some Le Frecce trains have little aisle and luggage space, though there is a space near the door where you can put large bags. To avoid having to squeeze through narrow aisles, board only at your car (look for the number on the reservation ticket and match it to the number on the exterior of the car; it's usually on the door).

You'll find open seating on regionale and locale trains, which make more stops and are slower. Most cars are covered in graffiti and are dirty, crowded, and geared to commuters. When train workers go on strike (which is often), these are the trains that stop running.

Traveling overnight can be efficient but it's not inexpensive (compared to the cost of a hotel room). Just never leave your belongings unattended (even for a minute), and make sure the door of your compartment is locked.

BUYING TICKETS

You can buy train tickets for nearby destinations (within a 200-km [124-mile] range) at newsstands or tobacconists (usually only those inside the station), at ticket machines or windows in stations, and at travel agencies in town. You may also buy tickets online at ⊕ www.trenitalia.com or ⊕ www.italotreno.it and show tickets on your mobile phone or a printout on the train.

You must specify the day you want to travel, and, right before departure, you must validate paper tickets for regional and Intercity trains in the red, silver, and green bullet-shape machines that are usually found at the foot of many tracks. If you forget to stamp your ticket in the machine, or you didn't make it to the station in time to buy the ticket, you must immediately seek out a conductor. Don't wait for the conductor to find out that you're without a valid ticket (unless the train is overcrowded and walking becomes impossible), as they might charge you a hefty fine. However, you often can avoid getting fined if you immediately write the time, date, and name of the departure station on the back of the ticket and sign it—essentially "validating" it and making it unusable for another trip.

Kilometric tickets—tickets priced according to kilometer amounts instead of specific destinations—are sold at newsstands and can be a great time-saver if the line at the official ticket booth is too long (which it always is, especially during high season). Note, however, that you may have to round up amounts, and therefore pay more for your trip than if you purchased a destination-specific ticket. (For example, it's only 70 km [43 miles] from Florence to Pisa, but if the ticket amounts come only in 20-km [12-mile] denominations, you'd have to pay for an extra 10 km [6 miles].)

CLASSES

Many Italian trains have first and second classes, but regional trains don't. On interregional trains, the higher first-class fare gets you little more than a clean doily (metaphorically speaking) on the headrest of your seat, but on long-distance trains you get wider seats, more legroom, and better ventilation and lighting.

At peak travel times first-class train travel is worth the difference as the cars are almost always uncrowded—or, at the very least, less crowded than the second-class compartments. A first-class ticket, in Italian, is *prima classe*; second is *seconda classe*. Remember always to make seat reservations in advance, for either class and on either Le Frecce and Italo trains.

PAYING

You can pay for destination-specific train tickets in cash or with any major credit card such as American Express, Master-Card, and Visa. Newsstands accept only cash for kilometric tickets.

RESERVATIONS

Trains can be very crowded and reservations are a must on high-speed trains. In summer, it's fairly common to stand for a good part of the journey, especially if you are coming off a cruise ship and heading to Florence on a regional train. On the fast, direct Le Frecce and Italo trains, as well as some Intercity trains, reservations are mandatory. To avoid long lines at station windows, buy tickets and make seat reservations up to two months in advance online before you leave home at ⊕ *www.italotreno.it* and ⊕ *www. trenitalia.com* and print out your tickets in advance.

Tickets can also be purchased at the last minute, but seat reservations can be made only at agencies (or the train station) up until about three hours before the train departs from its city of origin. For trains that require a reservation, you may be able to get a seat assignment just before boarding; look for the conductor on the platform, but do this only as a last resort. If you plan on traveling in August, make sure to book your tickets well in advance. Italians make a mass exodus to the sea or mountains, and sardine-like conditions prevail in many cases.

Essentials

🌐 Customs and Duties

Travelers from the United States should experience little difficulty clearing customs at any airport in Italy.

Of goods obtained outside the EU, the allowances are (1) 200 cigarettes or 100 cigarillos (under 3 grams) or 50 cigars or 250 grams of tobacco; (2) 4 liters of still table wine or 1 liter of spirits over 22% volume; and (3) 50 milliliters of perfume and 250 milliliters of toilet water.

Of goods obtained (duty and tax paid) within another EU country, the allowances are (1) 800 cigarettes or 400 cigarillos (under 3 grams) or 200 cigars or 1 kilogram of tobacco; and (2) 90 liters of still table wine or 10 liters of spirits over 22% volume or 20 liters of spirits under 22% volume or 110 liters of beer.

There is no quarantine period in Italy, so it is possible to travel with Fido. Contact your nearest Italian consulate to find out what paperwork is needed for entry into Italy; generally, it is a certificate noting that the animal is healthy and up-to-date on its vaccinations. Keep in mind, however, that the United States has some stringent laws about reentry: pets must be free of all diseases, especially those communicable to humans, and they must be vaccinated against rabies at least 30 days before returning. This means that if you are in Italy for a short-term stay, you must find a veterinarian or have your pet vaccinated before departure. (This law does not apply to puppies less than three months old.) Pets should arrive at the point of entry with a statement, in English, attesting to this fact.

🍴 Dining

A meal in Tuscany and Umbria (and elsewhere in Italy) has traditionally consisted of five courses, and most menus are still organized accordingly. First up is the *antipasto* (appetizer), usually *affettati misto* consisting of cured meats, cheese, and crostini. Next to appear is the *primo*, usually pasta or soup, and after that the *secondo*, a meat or fish course with, perhaps, a *contorno* (a side dish, usually vegetables) on the side. A simple *dolce* (dessert) rounds out the meal. This, you've probably noticed, is a lot of food. Italians have noticed this as well—a full, five-course meal is an indulgence usually reserved for special occasions. Instead, restaurant meals are a mix-and-match affair: you might order a primo and a secondo, an antipasto and a primo, or a secondo and a contorno.

Not too long ago, *ristoranti* tended to be more elegant and expensive than *trattorie* and *osterie*, which serve traditional, home-style fare in an atmosphere to match. But the distinction has blurred considerably, and an osteria in the center of town might be far fancier (and pricier) than a ristorante across the street.

Although most restaurants in Tuscany and Umbria serve traditional local cuisine, you can find Asian and Middle Eastern alternatives in Florence, Perugia, and other cities (though they are often pale imitations of what you would get in other American and European cities). Menus are posted outside most restaurants (in English in tourist areas); if not, you might step inside and ask to take a look at the menu (but don't ask for a table unless you intend to stay).

Italians generally take their food as it is listed on the menu, without making special requests such as "dressing on the side" or "hold the olive oil." If you have special dietary needs, however, make them known; they can usually be accommodated. Although mineral water makes its way to almost every table, you can order a carafe of tap water (*acqua di rubinetto* or *acqua semplice*) instead, but keep in mind that such behavior is sneered at by just about everyone, who all deem it *brutta figura* (bad form).

The handiest and least expensive places for a quick snack between sights are bars, cafés, and pizza *al taglio* (by the slice) spots. Bars in Italy are primarily places to get a coffee and a bite to eat, rather than drinking establishments. Most have a selection of panini and *tramezzini* (sandwiches served on triangles of white bread). Some bars also serve prepared salads, fruit salads, and cold and hot pasta dishes. Most bars offer beer and a variety of alcohol, as well as wines by the glass.

A café (*caffè* in Italian) is like a bar but usually with more tables. If you place your order at the counter, ask whether you can sit down: some places charge extra for table service. In self-service bars and caffè, cleaning up your table before you leave is considered good manners. Note that in some places you have to pay before you place an order and then show your *scontrino* (receipt) when you move to the counter to order.

Pizza al taglio shops are easy to negotiate. They often sell pizza by weight: just point out which kind you want and how much. Very few pizza al taglio shops have seats.

MEALS AND MEALTIMES
The Italian breakfast (*la colazione*) is typically a cappuccino and a pastry (usually a brioche, which is similar to a croissant) served at the local bar. For lunch, Italians may eat a panino with a glass of wine while standing at a local bar. A more substantial lunch (*il pranzo*) consists of one or two courses at a trattoria. Dinner (*la cena*) is likely to be two or three courses at a restaurant or trattoria or pizza and a beer at a pizzeria.

At ristoranti, trattorie, and osterie, you're generally expected to order at least a two-course meal: a primo and a secondo; an antipasto followed by either primo or secondo; or, perhaps, a secondo and a dolce. Italian cuisine is still largely regional, so ask about the local specialties.

In an *enoteca* (wine bar) or pizzeria, it's not inappropriate to order one dish. An enoteca menu is often limited to a selection of cheeses, cured meats, salads, and desserts; if there's a kitchen, you may also find soups, pasta, meat, and fish. Most pizzerias don't offer just pizza, but also a variety of antipasti, salads, and simple pasta dishes, as well as dolce. Pizza at a caffè is to be avoided—it's usually frozen and reheated in a microwave oven.

Lunch is usually served from 12:30 to 2 and dinner from 7:30 to 9:30 or 10. Enoteche are open in the morning and late afternoon for a snack at the counter. Most pizzerias open at 7:30 pm and close around midnight or 1 am—sometimes later in summer and on weekends. Most bars and caffè are open 7 am to 8 or 9 pm; a few stay open until midnight or so. A happy development is that many spots are now opening at 11 in the morning, and the kitchen stays open until 11 pm.

Unless otherwise noted, the restaurants listed in this guide are open daily for lunch and dinner.

PAYING
Major credit cards are widely accepted in Italian eating establishments, though cash is usually the preferred, and sometimes the only, means of payment—especially in small towns and rural areas.

Essentials

(More restaurants take Visa and MasterCard rather than American Express; Discover is virtually unheard of here.)

Unless it's well past closing time, no waiter will put a bill on your table until you've requested it. When you've finished your meal and are ready to go, ask for the check (*il conto*) or head directly to the payment terminal.

Prices for goods and services in Italy include tax. The price of fish dishes is often given by weight (before cooking), so the price you see on the menu is for 100 grams of fish, not for the whole dish. (An average fish portion is about 350 grams.) Tuscan *bistecca alla fiorentina* (Florentine-style steak, seasoned with, perhaps, herbs, salt, pepper, and olive oil and traditionally served rare) is also often priced by weight, usually by the kilogram (2.2 pounds).

Most restaurants charge a separate "cover" per person, which, by law, is listed on the menu as *pane e coperto* (or just *coperto*); this charge is not for the service. A charge for service (*servizio*) may be included either as part of the menu prices or the total bill; if it is, tipping is unnecessary. It is customary to leave a small tip (no more than 5% unless you are at a high-falutin' restaurant) in appreciation of good service when the service charge is not included in the bill. Tips are always given in cash. At some places in Florence, if you pay by credit card the restaurant will automatically slap a 15% tip onto your bill, which means you should leave absolutely nothing on the table.

For guidelines on tipping, see the Tipping section of this chapter.

RESERVATIONS AND DRESS

Reservations are always a good idea in restaurants and trattorie, especially on weekends, holidays, and high season. Book as far ahead as you can, and reconfirm as soon as you arrive in town. (Large parties should always call ahead to check the reservations policy and should leave a 10% tip on the table if servizio is not included.)

Unless they're eating outdoors at a seaside resort and are perfectly tanned, Italian men never wear shorts or running shoes in a restaurant—no matter how humble—or in an enoteca. If you see people in shorts, you can be 100% sure that they are foreigners. The same "rules" apply to women's casual shorts, running shoes, plastic sandals, and clogs.

We mention dress only when men are required to wear a jacket and tie.

WINES, BEER, AND SPIRITS

The grape has been cultivated in Italy since the time of the Etruscans, and Italians justifiably take pride in their local vintages. Though almost every region produces good-quality wine, Tuscany is one of the most renowned areas. Wine in Italy is considerably less expensive than almost anywhere else, so it's often affordable to order a bottle of wine at a restaurant rather than to stick with the house wine (which, nevertheless, is probably quite good). Many bars have their own *aperitivo della casa* (house aperitif); Italians are imaginative with their mixed drinks, so you may want to try one.

You can purchase beer, wine, and spirits in any bar, grocery store, or enoteca any day of the week. Italian and German beers are readily available, but they can be more expensive than wine.

There's no minimum drinking age in Italy. Italian children begin drinking wine mixed with water at mealtimes when they are teens (or thereabouts). Italians are seldom seen drunk in public, and public drinking, except in a bar or eating establishment, isn't considered acceptable behavior. Bars usually close by 8 pm, though those in hotels and restaurants often stay open until midnight. Brewpubs and discos serve until about 2 am.

⊕ Health

Although COVID-19 brought travel to a virtual standstill from 2020 into early 2022, vaccinations have made travel possible and safe again. That said, flare ups are still a possibility, so requirements and restrictions may be implemented from time to time and place to place.

Check out the websites of the CDC and the U.S. Department of State, both of which have destination-specific, COVID-19 guidance. Also, in case travel is curtailed abruptly again, consider buying trip insurance. Just be sure to read the fine print: not all travel-insurance policies cover pandemic-related cancellations.

For travelers, the most common types of illnesses are caused by contaminated food and water, though in Italy, drinking tap water is safe as is eating out. As in any part of the world, as an extra precaution, avoid fresh vegetables and fruits that you haven't washed or peeled yourself. If you have problems, mild cases of traveler's diarrhea may respond to Imodium (known generically as loperamide) or Pepto-Bismol. Be sure to drink plenty of fluids; if you can't keep fluids down, seek medical help immediately.

🛏 Lodging

Hotels large and small, B&Bs, and rental properties—ranging from rustic agriturismi farmhouses to sophisticated villas—are plentiful across Tuscany and Umbria. Throughout the region, you'll also find historic buildings, including former palazzi and monasteries, that have been restored as luxurious hotels, either true to period or featuring chic, modern, Italian design. Increasingly, the region's famed wineries are offering rooms and apartments for longer stays.

Keep a few things in mind when choosing a place to stay. Although Italy has a star system for rating hotels, it is based on amenities provided and is not a definitive indication of an establishment's quality. Also, some hotels allow children under a certain age to stay in their parents' room at no extra charge, but others charge for them as extra adults; find out the cutoff age for discounts.

In addition, most hotels and other lodgings require credit-card details before they will confirm your reservation. However you book, get a confirmation in writing and have a copy of it handy when you check in.

Finally, be sure you understand the hotel's cancellation policy. Some places allow you to cancel without any penalty—even if you prepaid to secure a discounted rate—when you cancel at least 24 hours in advance. Others require you to cancel a week in advance or penalize you with the cost of one night. Small inns and B&Bs are most likely to require you to cancel far in advance.

APARTMENT AND HOUSE RENTALS

Italy gave birth to the Slow Food Movement, and it appears to be at the vanguard of a "slow travel" phenomenon as well. More and more, travelers are turning away from the three-countries-in-two-weeks style of touring and spending a week in one city or a month in the countryside. Renting an apartment, farmhouse, or villa can be an economical option for longer stays.

Essentials

Most properties are owned by individuals and managed by rental agents who advertise their offerings online. Note, though, that because many properties are represented by more than one agent, they're often given different names on various rental sites—so "Chianti Bella Vista," "Tuscan Sun Home," and "Casa Toscana Sole" could all be the same farmhouse. Also, the rental agent might meet you at the property for check-in, or the owner may be present, with the agent handling only the online reservation and financial arrangements.

Features to inquire about when renting an apartment in a city or town include: the type of neighborhood (ask about street noise, safety, and general ambience), the availability of an elevator or the number of stairs you'll have to climb, the available furnishings (including pots and pans and linens), where the nearest grocery store is, and the cost of utilities (included in the rate or not?). Inquiries about countryside properties should include all of that information plus an idea of how isolated the property is—do you have to drive for 45 minutes to reach the nearest town?

BED-AND-BREAKFASTS

You can find cozy B&Bs in towns and cities as well as in more rural areas. In towns and villages B&Bs tend to be personal, homey, simple, and clean. In the Tuscan countryside you can find private villas that offer B&B accommodations; many are very upscale.

CONVENTS AND MONASTERIES

For reasonably priced lodgings, look into staying at convents, monasteries, and religious houses. Religious orders usually charge €30–€60 per person per night for rooms that are clean, comfortable, and convenient. Most have private bathrooms; spacious lounge areas and secluded gardens or terraces are also common. A continental breakfast ordinarily comes with the room. Sometimes, for an extra fee, family-style lunches and dinners are available.

Be aware of three issues when considering a convent or monastery stay: most have a curfew of 11 pm or midnight; you need to book in advance, because they fill up quickly; and your best means of booking is usually email or fax—the person answering the phone may not speak English. For a list of stays visit ⊕ *ospitalitareligiosa.it*.

HOTELS

Italian hotels are awarded stars (one to five) based on their facilities and services. Keep in mind, however, that these are general indications, so a charming three-star might make for a better stay than a more expensive four-star. Note, too, that hotels with three or more stars always have bathrooms in all rooms.

In major cities, room rates are on a par with those in other European capitals, with four- and five-star rates that can be downright extravagant. In those categories, ask for a better room, because the less desirable rooms—and there usually are some—don't give you what you're paying for. Some may be very small by U.S. standards, with equally small bathrooms that have showers rather than bathtubs.

In all hotels, a rate card inside the door of your room or inside the closet door tells you the maximum rate that can be legally charged for that particular room (rates in the same hotel may vary according to the location and type of room). On this card, breakfast and any other options must be listed separately. Any discrepancy between the basic room rate and that charged on your bill is cause for complaint to the manager and to the police.

High season in Italy, when rooms are at a premium, generally runs from Easter through the middle of June, from early September to the middle of October, and then for two weeks at Christmas. During low season and whenever a hotel isn't full, it's often possible to negotiate a discounted rate. Major cities have no official off-season as far as hotel rates go, but some hotels do offer substantial discounts during the slower parts of the year and on weekends. Always inquire about special rates. Major cities have hotel-reservation service booths in train stations. It's always a good idea to confirm your reservation, dates, and rate in advance.

Although by law breakfast is supposed to be optional, many hotels quote room rates including breakfast. When you book a room, specifically ask whether the rate includes breakfast (*colazione*). The trick is to "offer" guests "complimentary" breakfast and have its cost built into the rate. However, it's encouraging to note that many of the hotels we recommend provide generous breakfasts instead of basic continental breakfasts. Remember, if the latter is the case, you can eat for less at the nearest coffee bar.

Hotels in the $ and $$ categories may charge extra for air-conditioning. In older hotels, the quality of the rooms may be very uneven; if you don't like the room you're given, request another. This applies to noise, too. Front rooms may be larger or have a view, but they also may have a lot of street noise. If you're a light sleeper, request a quiet room when making reservations.

Rooms in lodgings listed in this guide have a private bath unless otherwise noted. Remember to specify whether you prefer a bath or shower—not all rooms have both.

💲 Money

As in most countries, costs vary from region to region and are a bit lower in the countryside than in cities. Prices throughout this guide are given for adults, in euros. Substantially reduced fees are sometimes available for children, students, and senior citizens from the EU. Citizens of non-EU countries rarely get discounts, but be sure to inquire before you purchase tickets. Also, don't forget to look into combo tickets, which can offer substantial savings on admission to museums and other sights.

■ TIP → **Banks never have every foreign currency on hand, and it may take as long as a week to order. If you're planning to exchange funds before leaving home, don't wait until the last minute.**

ATMS AND BANKS

Fairly common in banks in large and small towns, as well as in airports and train stations, ATMs are the easiest way to get euros in Italy. All major banks are members of Cirrus and/or Plus. You usually won't find an ATM (*bancomat* in Italian) in hotels or grocery stores, however.

Your own bank may charge a fee for using ATMs abroad or charge for the cost of conversion from euros to dollars. Nevertheless, you'll usually get a better rate of exchange at an ATM than you will at a currency-exchange office or even when changing money inside a bank with a teller (and lately most banks are not offering this service). Extracting funds as you need them is also a safer option than carrying around a large amount of cash.

Check with your bank to confirm that you have an international PIN (*codice segreto*), to find out your maximum daily withdrawal allowance, and to learn what the bank fee is for withdrawing money. Before you leave home, memorize your

Essentials

PIN in numbers, not letters, because ATM keypads in Italy frequently don't show letters.

■TIP→ **PIN numbers with more than four digits are not recognized at ATMs in many countries. If yours has five or more, remember to change it before you leave. PIN numbers beginning with a 0 (zero) tend to be rejected in Italy.**

CREDIT CARDS

In Italy, Visa and MasterCard are preferred over American Express, but in tourist areas American Express is sometimes accepted. Although increasingly common, credit cards aren't accepted at all establishments, and some places require a minimum expenditure. If you want to pay with a card in a small hotel, store, or restaurant, it's a good idea to make your intentions known early on.

■TIP→ **Notify your credit-card companies of your travel plans before you leave home; the recent fraud-prevention programs frequently suspend a cardholder's credit when foreign activity is detected on the card.**

CURRENCY AND EXCHANGE

The euro is the main unit of currency in Italy, as well as in 19 other European countries. Under the euro system, there are eight coins: 1, 2, 5, 10, 20, and 50 *centesimi* (cents, at 100 centesimi to the euro), and 1 and 2 euros. There are seven notes: 5, 10, 20, 50, 100, 200, and 500 euros.

■TIP→ **Even if a currency-exchange booth has a sign promising no commission, rest assured that there's some kind of huge, hidden fee. As for rates, you're almost always better off getting foreign currency at an ATM.**

Packing

In summer, stick with light clothing—Florence is humid and steamy in June, July, and August—but throw in a sweater in case of cool evenings, especially if you're headed for the mountains and/or islands. Sunglasses, a hat, and sunblock are essential, as are comfortable walking shoes.

Winter weather used to be generally milder than in the northern and central United States, but things have changed. It often gets quite cold and sometimes snows in Florence. Bring a coat, gloves, a hat, a scarf, and sturdy but comfortable shoes or boots. Wool or flannel items are best.

As a rule, Italians are more particular about dress than Americans are. To their minds, shorts are for the beach or for hiking, not for urban settings. Men aren't required to wear ties or jackets in most places other than some of the grander hotel dining rooms and top-level restaurants, but they are expected to look reasonably sharp—and they do. Formal wear is the exception rather than the rule at the opera nowadays, though people in expensive seats usually do get dressed up.

Modesty of dress (no bare shoulders or knees) is expected of both men and women in all churches. For sightseeing, consider packing a pair of binoculars; they will help you get a good look at poorly lighted ceilings and domes.

⊕ Passports and Visas

You must have a valid passport for travel to Italy. U.S. citizens who plan to travel or live in Italy or the EU for longer than 90 days must acquire a valid visa from the Italian consulate serving their state before leaving the United States. Plan ahead, because the process of obtaining a visa will take at least 30 days, and the Italian government does not accept visa applications submitted by visa expediters.

■ TIP→ **Before your trip, make two copies of your passport's data page (one for someone at home and another for you to carry separately). Or scan or take a photo of the page and email it to someone at home and/ or yourself or store it on a secure drive.**

✚ Safety

Don't wear an exterior money belt or a waist pack, both of which peg you as a tourist. If you carry a bag or camera, be absolutely sure it has straps; you should sling it across your body bandolier-style and adjust the height to hip level or higher. Always be astutely aware of pickpockets, especially when on city buses, when making your way through train corridors, and in busy piazzas.

Women traveling alone in Tuscany and Umbria encounter few special problems. Younger women have to put up with male attention, but it's rarely dangerous. Ignoring whistling and questions is a good way to get rid of unwanted attention; a firm *no, vai via* ("no, go away") sometimes works, too.

■ TIP→ **Distribute your cash, credit cards, IDs, and other valuables between a deep front pocket, an inside jacket or vest pocket, and a hidden money pouch. Don't reach for the money pouch once you're in public.**

Tipping

If they tip at all, Italians do so in smaller amounts in smaller cities and towns. In restaurants in Tuscany and Umbria a service charge of 10% to 15% sometimes appears on your check. It's not necessary to tip in addition to this amount. If service is not included, leave a tip of €2. No one tips in bars in Florence.

Tip checkroom attendants 50 European cents per person and restroom attendants 50 European cents (more in expensive hotels and restaurants). Italians rarely tip taxi drivers, which is not to say that you shouldn't do it. A tip of 10%, depending on the length of the journey, is appreciated. Railway and airport porters charge a fixed rate per bag. Tip an additional 5% if the porter is especially helpful. Give a barber €1–€1.50 and a hairdresser's assistant €1.50–€4 for a shampoo or cut.

On sightseeing tours, tip guides about €2 per person for a half-day group tour, more if they are very good. In museums and other sights where admission is free, a contribution (€1) is expected. Service-station attendants are tipped only for special services, for example, 50 European cents for checking your tires.

In hotels, give the *portiere* (concierge) about 10% of his bill for services or €2.50–€5 if he has been generally helpful. For two people in a double room, leave the cleaning staff about €1 per day, or about €7 a week, in a moderately priced hotel; tip a minimum of €1 for valet or room service. Double amounts in expensive hotels. In very expensive hotels, tip porters €1 for calling a cab and €1 for carrying bags to the check-in desk, bellhops €2–€4 for carrying your bags to the room and €2–€3 for room service.

Helpful Italian Phrases

BASICS

Yes/no	Sí/No	see/no
Please	Per favore	pear fa-**vo**-ray
Thank you	Grazie	**grah**-tsee-ay
You're welcome	Prego	**pray**-go
I'm sorry (apology)	Mi dispiace	mee dis-pee-**atch**-ay
Excuse me, sorry	Scusi	**skoo**-zee
Good morning/ afternoon	Buongiorno	bwohn-**jor**-no
Good evening	Buona sera	**bwoh**-na **say**-ra
Good-bye	Arrivederci	a-ree-vah-**dare**-chee
Mr. (Sir)	Signore	see-**nyo**-ray
Mrs. (Ma'am)	Signora	see-**nyo**-ra
Miss	Signorina	see-nyo-**ree**-na
Pleased to meet you	Piacere	pee-ah-**chair**-ray
How are you?	Come sta?	ko-may-**stah**
Hello (phone)	Pronto?	**proan**-to

NUMBERS

one-half	mezzo	**mets**-zoh
one	uno	**oo**-no
two	due	**doo**-ay
three	tre	Tray
four	quattro	**kwah**-tro
five	cinque	**cheen**-kway
six	sei	Say
seven	sette	**set**-ay
eight	otto	**oh**-to
nine	nove	**no**-vay
ten	dieci	dee-**eh**-chee
eleven	undici	**oon**-dee-chee
twelve	dodici	**doh**-dee-chee
thirteen	tredici	**trey**-dee-chee
fourteen	quattordici	kwah-**tor**-dee-chee
fifteen	quindici	**kwin**-dee-chee
sixteen	sedici	**say**-dee-chee
seventeen	dicissette	dee-chee-**set**-ay
eighteen	diciotto	dee-chee-**oh**-to
nineteen	diciannove	dee-chee-ahn-**no**-vay
twenty	venti	**vain**-tee
twenty-one	ventuno	**vent**-oo-no
thirty	trenta	**train**-ta
forty	quaranta	kwa-**rahn**-ta
fifty	cinquanta	cheen-**kwahn**-ta
sixty	sessanta	seh-**sahn**-ta
seventy	settanta	seh-**tahn**-ta
eighty	ottanta	o-**tahn**-ta
ninety	novanta	no-**vahn**-ta
one hundred	cento	**chen**-to
one thousand	mille	**mee**-lay
one million	un milione	oon **mill**-oo-nay

COLORS

black	Nero	**nair**-ro
blue	Blu	bloo
brown	Marrone	ma-**rohn**-nay
green	Verde	**ver**-day
orange	Arancione	ah-rahn-**cho**-nay
red	Rosso	**rose**-so
white	Bianco	bee-**ahn**-koh
yellow	Giallo	**jaw**-low

DAYS OF THE WEEK

Sunday	Domenica	do-**meh**-nee-ka
Monday	Lunedi	loo-ne-**dee**
Tuesday	Martedi	mar-te-**dee**
Wednesday	Mercoledi	mer-ko-le-**dee**
Thursday	Giovedi	jo-ve-**dee**
Friday	Venerdì	ve-ner-**dee**
Saturday	Sabato	**sa**-ba-toh

MONTHS

January	Gennaio	jen-**ay**-o
February	Febbraio	feb-**rah**-yo
March	Marzo	**mart**-so
April	Aprile	a-**pril**-ay
May	Maggio	**mahd**-joe
June	Giugno	**joon**-yo
July	Luglio	**lool**-yo
August	Agosto	a-**gus**-to
September	Settembre	se-**tem**-bre
October	Ottobre	o-**toh**-bre
November	Novembre	no-**vem**-bre
December	Dicembre	di-**chem**-bre

USEFUL WORDS AND PHRASES

Do you speak English?	Parla Inglese?	par-la een-**glay**-zay
I don't speak Italian	Non parlo italiano	non **par**-lo ee-tal-**yah**-no
I don't understand	Non capisco	non ka-**peess**-ko
I don't know	Non lo so	non lo **so**
I understand	Capisco	ka-**peess**-ko
I'm American	Sono Americano(a)	**so**-no a-may-ree-**kah**-no(a)
I'm British	Sono inglese	so-no een-**glay**-zay
What's your name?	Come si chiama?	ko-may see kee-ah-ma
My name is …	Mi chiamo…	mee kee-ah-mo
What time is it?	Che ore sono?	kay **o**-ray so-no
How?	Come?	ko-may
When?	Quando?	**kwan**-doe
Yesterday/today/ tomorrow	Ieri/oggi/domani	yer-ee/ o-jee/ do-mah-nee

This morning	Stamattina/Oggi	sta-ma-**tee**-na/ **o**-jee
Afternoon	Pomeriggio	po-mer-**ee**-jo
Tonight	Stasera	sta-**ser**-a
What?	Che cosa?	kay **ko**-za
What is it?	Che cos'è?	kay ko-**zey**
Why?	Perchè?	pear-**kay**
Who?	Chi?	**Kee**
Where is ...	Dov'è...	doe-**veh**
the train station?	la stazione?	la sta-tsee-**oh**-nay
the subway?	la metropolitana?	la may-tro-po-lee-**tah**-na
the bus stop?	la fermata dell'autobus?	la **fer**-**mah**-ta del-ow-tor-**booss**
the airport	l'aeroporto	la-er-roh-**por**-toh
the post office?	l'ufficio postale	loo-**fee**-cho po-**stah**-lay
the bank?	la banca?	la **bahn**-ka
the hotel?	l'hotel...?	lo-**tel**
the museum?	Il museo	eel moo-**zay**-o
the hospital?	l'ospedale?	lo-spay-**dah**-lay
the elevator?	l'ascensore	la-shen-**so**-ray
the restrooms?	...il bagno	eel **bahn**-yo
Here/there	Qui/là	kwee/la
Left/right	A sinistra/a destra	a see-**neess**-tra/a **des**-tra
Is it near/far?	È vicino/lontano?	ay vee-**chee**-no/ lon-**tah**-no
I'd like ...	Vorrei...	vo-**ray**
a room	una camera	oo-na **kah**-may-ra
the key	la chiave	la kee-**ah**-vay
a newspaper	un giornale	oon jore-**nah**-vay
a stamp	un francobollo	oon frahn-ko-**bo**-lo
I'd like to buy ...	Vorrei comprare...	vo-**ray** kom-**prah**-ray
a city map	una mappa della città	oo-na **mah**-pa **day**-la chee-**tah**
a road map	una carta stradale	oo-na **car**-tah stra-**dahl**-lay
a magazine	una revista	oo-na ray-**vees**-tah
envelopes	buste	**boos**-tay
writing paper	carta de lettera	**car**-tah dah **leyt**-ter-rah
a postcard	una cartolina	oo-na car-tog-**leen**-ah
a ticket	un biglietto	oon bee-**yet**-toh
How much is it?	Quanto costa?	**kwahn**-toe **coast**-a
It's expensive/cheap	È caro/ economico	ay **car**-o/ ay-ko-**no**-mee-ko
A little/a lot	Poco/tanto	**po**-ko/**tahn**-to
More/less	Più/meno	pee-**oo**/**may**-no

Enough/too (much)	Abbastanza/ troppo	a-bas-**tahn**-sa/tro-po
I am sick	Sto male	sto **mah**-lay
Call a doctor	Chiama un dottore	kee-**ah**-mah-oondoe-**toe**-ray
Help!	Aiuto!	a-**yoo**-to
Stop!	Alt!	ahlt

DINING OUT

A bottle of ...	Una bottiglia di...	oo-na bo-**tee**-lee-ah dee
A cup of ...	Una tazza di...	oo-na **tah**-tsa dee
A glass of ...	Un bicchiere di...	oon bee-key-**air**-ay dee
Beer	La birra	la **beer**-rah
Bill/check	Il conto	eel **cone**-toe
Bread	Il pane	eel **pah**-nay
Breakfast	La prima colazione	la **pree**-ma ko-la-**tsee**-oh-nay
Butter	Il Burro	eel **boor**-roh
Cocktail/aperitif	L'aperitivo	la-pay-ree-**tee**-vo
Dinner	La cena	la **chen**-a
Fixed-price menu	Menù a prezzo fisso	may-**noo** a **pret**-so **fee**-so
Fork	La forchetta	la for-**ket**-a
I am vegetarian	Sono vegetariano(a)	**so**-no vay-jay-ta-ree-**ah**- -no/a
I cannot eat ...	Non posso mangiare	non **pose**-so mahn-gee-**are**-ay
I'd like to order	Vorrei ordinare	vo-**ray** or-dee-**nah**-ray
Is service included?	Il servizio è incluso?	eel ser-**vee**-tzee-o ay een-**kloo**-zo
I'm hungry/ thirsty	Ho fame/sede	oh **fah**-meh/**sehd**-ed
It's good/bad	È buono/cattivo	ay **bwo**-bo/ka-**tee**-vo
It's hot/cold	È caldo/freddo	ay **kahl**-doe/**fred**-o
Knife	Il coltello	eel kol-**tel**-o
Lunch	Il pranzo	eel **prahnt**-so
Menu	Il menu	eel may-**noo**
Napkin	Il tovagliolo	eel toe-va-lee-**oh**-lo
Pepper	Il pepe	eel **pep**-peh
Plate	Il piatto	eel pee-**aht**-toe
Please give me ...	Mi dia...	mee **dee**-a
Salt	Il sale	eel **sah**-lay
Spoon	Il cucchiaio	eel koo-kee-**ah**-yo
Tea	tè	tay
Water	acqua	**awk**-wah
Wine	vino	**vee**-noh

Great Itineraries

A Central Italy Itinerary

Visit central Italy for the great art, sumptuous countryside, and outstanding food and wine.

DAY 1: FLORENCE

If you're coming in on an international flight, you'll probably settle in Florence in time for an afternoon stroll or siesta (depending on your jet-lag strategy) before dinner.

Logistics: Begin anticipating the first dinner of your trip. Look for a place near your hotel, and when you arrive, reserve a table (or have your concierge do it for you). Making a meal the focus of your first day is a great way to ease into Italian life.

DAY 2: FLORENCE

Begin at the **Uffizi Gallery,** whose extensive collection will occupy much of your morning. Next, take in the neighboring **Piazza della Signoria,** then head a few blocks north to the **Duomo** to check out Ghiberti's famous bronze doors on the **Battistero** (actually high-quality copies; the originals are in the **Museo dell'Opera del Duomo**). Climb up Brunelleschi's cathedral dome to the cupola. Spend the afternoon wandering Florence's medieval streets; or head out to **Fiesole** to see the ancient amphitheater.

Logistics: It's a good idea to reserve Uffizi tickets online ahead of your visit; climbs up Brunelleschi's dome must be reserved in advance.

DAY 3: FLORENCE

Spend your morning seeing Michelangelo's *David* at the **Galleria dell'Accademia,** the **Medici Chapels,** the **Palazzo Pitti** and **Boboli Gardens,** and the churches of **Santa Maria Novella** and **Santa Croce.** If it's a clear day, spend the afternoon making your way up to **Piazzale Michelangelo** for sweeping views of the idyllic Florentine countryside. Recharge with a dinner featuring bistecca alla fiorentina.

Logistics: You can reach Piazzale Michelangelo by taxi or by taking Bus No. 12 or 13 from the Lungarno. Otherwise, do your best to get around on foot; Florence is a brilliant city for walking.

DAY 4: SAN GIMIGNANO

After breakfast, pick up your car and make the lazy drive from Florence to **San Gimignano.** Upon arriving in town, you'll no doubt be awed by its towers—medieval skyscrapers that provided security and served as symbols of wealth and power. After finding your way to a hotel in the old town, set out on foot to check out the city's turrets and alleyways, then enjoy a leisurely dinner.

Logistics: San Gimignano is only 57 km (35 miles) to the southwest. Consider taking a detour on the SS222 (Strada Chiantigiana) to a winery in one of the Chianti wine towns.

DAY 5: SIENA

In the morning, set out for nearby **Siena,** which is known worldwide for its Palio, a horse race involving the city's 17 *contrade* (medieval neighborhoods). You will be blown away by the precious medieval streets and memorable fan-shape **Piazza del Campo.** Don't miss the spectacular **Duomo,** the **Battistero,** and the **Spedale di Santa Maria della Scala,** an old hospital and hostel that now contains an underground archaeological museum.

Logistics: Parking can be a challenge. Look for the *stadio* (soccer stadium), where there's a parking lot that often has space.

DAY 6: AREZZO/CORTONA

From Siena you'll first head to **Arezzo,** home to the **Basilica di San Francesco,** which contains important frescoes by Piero della Francesca. Check out the **Piazza Grande** along with its beautiful Romanesque church of **Santa Maria della Pieve.** Try to do all of this before lunch, after which you'll head straight to **Cortona.** Cortona is a town for walking and relaxing, not sightseeing, so enjoy yourself as you wander through the **Piazza della Repubblica** and **Piazza Signorelli,** perhaps doing a bit of shopping.

Logistics: Siena to Arezzo is 70 km (43.5 miles) on the SS715 and A1 autostrada. From Arezzo to Cortona, it's just 30 km (18 miles)—take SR71.

DAY 7: ASSISI

Cross over into Umbria and see **Assisi,** the home of St. Francis that today hosts many religious pilgrims. After arrival and check-in, head straight for the **Basilica di San Francesco,** which displays the tomb of St. Francis and some unbelievable frescoes. From here, take Via San Francesco to **Piazza del Comune** and see the **Tempio di Minerva.** Break for lunch and then see **San Rufino,** the cathedral, before returning through the piazza to Corso Mazzini and **Santa Chiara.**

Logistics: From Cortona, take the SR71 to the A1 autostrada toward Perugia. After about 40 km (24 miles), take the Assisi exit (E45), and it's another 14 km (8 miles) to Assisi.

DAY 8: SPOLETO

This morning takes you to the walled city of **Spoleto,** renowned for its summer arts festival; its wonderful **Duomo;** its impressive **La Rocca** fortress; and its marvelous **Ponte delle Torri,** the 14th-century bridge that separates the town from Monteluco. Save your appetite for a serious last dinner in Italy. Try to sample black truffles, a proud product of the region, especially from mid-November to mid-March.

Logistics: The trip from Assisi to Spoleto is a pretty 47-km (29-mile) drive (SS75 to SS3) that should take less than an hour.

DAY 9: SPOLETO/DEPARTURE

It's a fair distance from Spoleto to the Florence airport, your point of departure. One alternative is to fly out of the tiny airport in Perugia. If you prefer to drive, get an early start and allow at least 2½ hours for the trip along the A1 autostrada.

Tours and Events

GUIDED TOURS

Tours aren't for everyone, but they can be just the thing for destinations where making travel arrangements is difficult or time-consuming. Plus, a knowledge-able guide can take you to places that you might never discover on your own. Although you generally travel along with a group, stay in prebooked hotels, eat with your fellow travelers, and follow a schedule, not all guided tours are an if-it's-Tuesday-this-must-be-Siena experiences. This is especially true of tours that focus on a special interest.

Whenever you book a guided tour, find out what's included and what isn't. A "land-only" tour includes all your travel in the destination, but not necessarily your flights to and from or even within it. Also, in most cases, prices in tour brochures don't include fees and taxes. And remember that you'll be expected to tip your guide (in cash) at the end of the tour.

SPECIAL-INTEREST TOURS

ART AND CULTURE

Abercrombie & Kent. ☎ 800/554–7016 ⊕ www.abercrombiekent.com.

Context Travel. ⊕ www.contexttravel.com.

BIKING

Backroads. ☎ 800/462–2848 ⊕ www.backroads.com.

Butterfield & Robinson. ☎ 866/551–9090 ⊕ www.butterfield.com.

Ciclismo Classico. ☎ 800/866–7314 ⊕ www.ciclismoclassico.com.

CULINARY

★ **Divina Cucina.** ⊕ www.divinacucina.com.

Joanne Weir. ☎ 415/262–0260 ⊕ www.joanneweir.com.

Taste Florence. ⊕ www.tasteflorence.com.

Toscana Saporita. ⊕ www.toscanasaporita.com.

Tuscan Women Cook. ⊕ www.tuscanwomencook.com.

HIKING

Backroads. ☎ 800/462–2848 ⊕ www.backroads.com.

Country Walkers. ☎ 800/234–6900 ⊕ www.countrywalkers.com.

WINE

Cellar Tours. ☎ 310/496–8061 ⊕ www.cellartours.com.

Food & Wine Trails. ☎ 800/367–5348 ⊕ www.foodandwinetrails.com.

FESTIVALS AND EVENTS

Celebrations can be serious business in Italy. From avant-garde musical performances to ribald street fairs, tremendous effort is expended to see that things are done right, with the pride of the community resting on the success of the event. The result is usually a great time for those who attend.

Carnevale, Viareggio, Northwest Tuscany. For the three weeks leading up to Lent, this coastal town does its own fanciful version of Mardi Gras.

Palio, Siena, Central Tuscany. Twice a year, on July 2 and August 16, Siena goes medieval with this bareback horse race around its main square.

Festa dei Ceri, Gubbio, Northern Umbria. Mid-May marks Gubbio's Festival of the Candles, highlighted by townsmen racing up a hill carrying three huge pillars—just as they've been doing every year since 1160.

Festival dei Due Mondi, Spoleto, Southern Umbria. Star performers from around the world flock to this Umbrian hill town every summer for two weeks to do their thing in piazzas and intimate theaters.

Contacts

✈ Air

**AIRLINE
INFORMATION American
Airlines.** ☎ *800/433–7300*
⊕ *www.americanair-
lines.it.* **Delta Airlines.**
☎ *800/221–1212 for U.S.
reservations* ⊕ *www.del-
ta.com.* **Ryanair.** ⊕ *www.
ryanair.com.* **United
Airlines.** ☎ *800/864–8331
for reservations while in
U.S.* ⊕ *www.united.com.*
ITA Airways. ⊕ *www.
itaspa.com.*

**AIRLINE SECURITY
ISSUES Transportation
Security Administration.**
⊕ *www.tsa.gov.*

**AIRPORT INFORMATION
Aeroporto A. Vespucci. (FLR,
usually called Peretola).**
☎ *055/30615* ⊕ *www.aero-
porto.firenze.it.* **Aeroporto di
Perugia San Francesco d'Assisi. (PEG).** ☎ *075/592141*
⊕ *www.airport.umbria.
it.* **Aeroporto Galileo Galilei.
(PSA).** ☎ *050/849111*
⊕ *www.pisa-airport.com.*
**Aeroporto Leonardo da
Vinci. (FCO, more common-
ly known as Fiumicino).**
☎ *06/65951* ⊕ *www.adr.it.*
Aeroporto Malpensa. (MIL).
☎ *02/232323* ⊕ *www.mila-
nomalpensa-airport.com.*

🚌 Bus

**INFORMATION Autolinee
Toscane.** ✉ *Florence*
☎ *800/142424* ⊕ *www.
at-bus.it/it.* **Bus Italia.**
⊕ *www.fsbusitalia.it.*
Firenze City SightSeeing.
⊕ *www.visitacity.com.*

🏳 Embassy/
Consulate

**INFORMATION
U.S. Consulate.** ✉ *Via
Lungarno Vespucci 38,
Florence* ☎ *055/266951*
⊕ *it.usembassy.gov/
embassy-consulates/
florence.* **U.S. Embassy.**
✉ *Via Vittorio Veneto
121, Rome* ☎ *06/46741*
⊕ *it.usembassy.gov/
embassy-consulates/rome.*

🛳 Ferry

**INFORMATION Golfo dei
Poeti.** ☎ *0187/732987*
⊕ *www.navigazionegolfo-
deipoeti.it.* **Golfo Paradiso.**
☎ *0185/772091* ⊕ *www.
golfoparadiso.it.* **Moby
Lines.** ☎ *02/7602–8132*
⊕ *www.moby.it.* **Toremar.**
☎ *800/304035* ⊕ *www.
toremar.it.*

🌐 Passport

**U.S. INFORMATION
U.S. Department of State.**
☎ *877/487–2778* ⊕ *travel.
state.gov/passport.*

**U.S. PASSPORT
EXPEDITERS Ameri-
can Passport Express.**
☎ *866/927–2106* ⊕ *www.
americanpassport.com.*
Travel Document Systems.
☎ *800/874–5104* ⊕ *www.
traveldocs.com.*

🚆 Train

**PASSES AND
INFORMATION Eurail Italy
Pass.** ⊕ *www.eurail.com.*
RailPass. ☎ *877/375–7245*
⊕ *www.railpass.com.*

RAIL INFORMATION Italo.
☎ *892020 in Italy; fee*
⊕ *www.italotreno.it.* **Trenitalia.** ☎ *800/892021 in Italy
(fee)* ⊕ *www.trenitalia.
com.*

Chapter 3

FLORENCE

3

Updated by
Patricia Rucidlo

⊙ Sights	🍴 Restaurants	🛏 Hotels	🛍 Shopping	🍸 Nightlife
★★★★★	★★★★★	★★★★★	★★★★★	★★★★☆

WELCOME TO FLORENCE

TOP REASONS TO GO

★ **Galleria degli Uffizi:** Italian Renaissance art doesn't get much better than this vast collection bequeathed in 1737 by the last Medici, Anna Maria Luisa.

★ **Brunelleschi's Dome:** His work of engineering genius is the city's undisputed centerpiece.

★ **Michelangelo's** *David:* One look, up close, and you'll know why this is one of the world's most famous sculptures.

★ **The view from Piazzale Michelangelo:** From this perch the city is laid out before you. The colors at sunset heighten the experience.

★ **Piazza Santa Croce:** After you've had your fill of Renaissance masterpieces, idle here and watch the world go by.

1 **Around the Duomo.** You're in the heart of Florence here. Among the numerous highlights are the city's greatest museum (the Uffizi) and arguably its most impressive square (Piazza della Signoria).

2 **San Lorenzo.** The complex of the basilica of San Lorenzo, the Palazzo Medici-Riccardi, and the Galleria dell'Accademia bears the imprints of the Medici and of Michelangelo, culminating in the latter's masterful statue *David.* Just to the north, the former convent of San Marco is an oasis of artistic treasures decorated with ethereal frescoes.

3 **Santa Maria Novella.** This part of town includes the train station, 16th-century palaces, and the city's swankest shopping street, Via Tornabuoni.

4 **Santa Croce.** The district centers on its namesake basilica, which is filled with the tombs of Renaissance (and other) luminaries. The area is also known for its leather shops.

5 **The Oltrarno.** Across the Arno you encounter the massive Palazzo Pitti and the narrow streets of the Santo Spirito neighborhood.

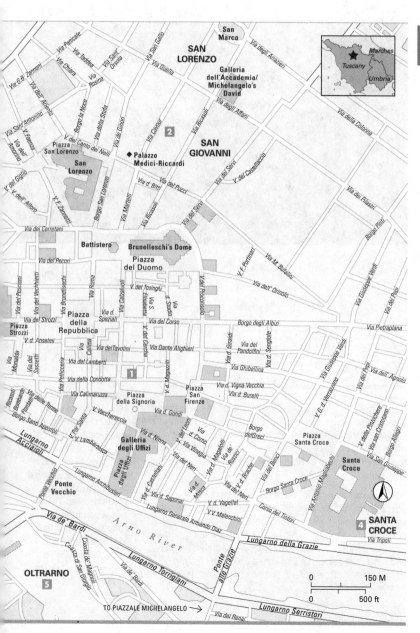

EATING AND DRINKING WELL IN FLORENCE

In Florence, simply prepared meats, grilled or roasted, are the culinary stars, usually paired with seasonal vegetables like artichokes or porcini. *Bistecca* (steak) is popular here, but there's plenty more that tastes great on the grill, too.

Traditionalists go for their gustatory pleasures in *trattorie* (casual restaurant) and *osterie* (down-home restaurant), places where decor is unimportant and place mats are mere paper. Culinary innovation comes slowly in this town, though some cutting-edge restaurants have been appearing.

By American standards, Florentines eat late: 1:30 or 2 pm is typical for lunch and 9 pm for dinner is considered early. Consuming a *primo* (first course), *secondo* (second course), and *dolce* (dessert) is largely a thing of the past. For lunch, many Florentines simply grab a panino and a glass of wine at a bar. Those opting for a simple trattoria lunch often order a plate of pasta and dessert.

STALE AND STELLAR

Stale bread is the basis for three classic Florentine primi: *pappa al pomodoro, ribollita,* and *panzanella.* Pappa is made with either fresh or canned tomatoes and that stale bread. Ribollita is a vegetable soup with *cavolo nero* (Tuscan kale) and cannellini beans, thickened with bread. Panzanella is reconstituted Tuscan bread combined with tomatoes, cucumber, and basil. They all are enhanced with a generous application of fragrant Tuscan olive oil.

A CLASSIC ANTIPASTO: CROSTINI DI FEGATINI

This beloved dish consists of a chicken-liver spread, presented warm or at room temperature, on toasted, garlic-rubbed bread. It can be served smooth, like a pâté, or in a chunkier, more rustic version. It's made by sautéing chicken livers with finely diced carrot and onion, enlivened with the addition of wine, broth, or Marsala reductions, and mashed anchovies and capers.

A CLASSIC SECONDO: BISTECCA FIORENTINA

The town's culinary pride and joy is a thick slab of beef, resembling a T-bone steak, from large white oxen called Chianina. The meat's slapped on the grill, seared on both sides, and served rare, sometimes with a pinch of salt.

A CLASSIC CONTORNO: CANNELLINI BEANS

Simply boiled, beans provide the perfect accompaniment to bistecca. The small white ones are best when they go straight from the garden into the pot. They should be anointed with a generous dose of Tuscan olive oil; the combination is oddly felicitous, and it goes a long way toward explaining why Tuscans are referred to as *mangiafagioli* (bean eaters) by other Italians.

A CLASSIC DOLCE: BISCOTTI DI PRATO

These are sometimes the only dessert on offer. *Biscotti* means twice-cooked (or, in this case, twice-baked). They are hard almond cookies that soften considerably when dipped languidly into *vin santo* ("holy wine"), a sweet dessert wine, or into a simple *caffè*.

A CLASSIC WINE: CHIANTI CLASSICO

This blend from the region just south of Florence relies mainly on the local, hardy sangiovese grape; it's aged for at least one year before hitting the market. (*Riserve*—reserve—is aged at least an additional six months.)

Chianti is usually the libation of choice for Florentines. Traditionalists opt for the younger, fruitier (and usually less expensive) versions often served in straw flasks. You can sample Chianti Classico all over town, and buy it in local supermarkets.

Florence, the city of the lily, gave birth to the Renaissance and changed the way we see the world. For centuries it has captured the imaginations of travelers, who have come seeking rooms with views and phenomenal art. Florence's is a subtle beauty—its staid, unprepossessing palaces built in local stone are not showy, even though they are very large.

They take on a certain magnificence when day breaks and when the sun sets. Their muted colors truly glow in the twilight.

Florence was "discovered" in the 1700s by upper-class visitors from everywhere making the grand tour. Today, millions of us follow in their footsteps. Navigating Piazza della Signoria, always packed with tourists, requires patience, but there's a reason why everyone flocks to it: the heart of the city is home to the Uffizi, the world's finest repository of Italian Renaissance art.

A walk along the Arno offers views that don't quit and haven't much changed in 700 years, and it's hard not to fall under the city's spell. As Mark Twain noted, when the sun sets over the Arno it, "overwhelms Florence with tides of color that make all the sharp lines dim and faint and turn the solid city to a city of dreams."

MAJOR REGIONS
Around the Duomo. You're in the heart of Florence here. Among the numerous highlights are the city's greatest museum (the Uffizi) and arguably its most impressive square (Piazza della Signoria).

San Lorenzo. The blocks from the basilica of San Lorenzo to the Galleria dell'Accademia bear the imprints of the Medici and of Michelangelo, culminating in the latter's masterful *David*. The former convent of San Marco is an oasis of artistic treasures.

Santa Maria Novella. This part of town includes the train station, 16th-century palaces, and the city's most swank shopping street, Via Tornabuoni.

Santa Croce. The district centers on its namesake basilica, which is filled with the tombs of Renaissance (and other) luminaries. The area is also known for its leather shops.

The Oltrarno. Across the Arno you encounter the massive Palazzo Pitti and the narrow streets of the Santo Spirito neighborhood, filled with artisans' workshops and antiques stores.

Planning

Getting Here and Around

AIR

To get into the city center from Aeroporto A. Vespucci (aka Peretola) by car, take the autostrada A11. The trip takes about 20 minutes. A tram travels between the airport and Stazione Santa Maria Novella in town.

BIKE AND MOPED

Cycling in Florence is difficult at best as you'll be up against hordes of tourists and those pesky *motorini* (mopeds). If you're a brave soul, though, you can rent bicycles at easy-to-spot locations at Fortezza da Basso, the Stazione Centrale di Santa Maria Novella, and Piazza Pitti. Otherwise, try **Alinari** (✉ *Via San Zanobi 38/r* ☎ *055/280500*).

The historic center can be circumnavigated via bike paths lining the *viali,* the ring road surrounding the area. For a safer ride, try Le Cascine, a former Medici hunting ground turned into a large public park with paved pathways.

If you want to go native, rent a noisy Vespa (Italian for "wasp") or other make of motorcycle or *motorino.* Try **Massimo** (✉ *Via Campo d'Arrigo 16/r* ☎ *055/573689*).

BUS

Florence's flat, compact city center is made for walking, but when your feet get weary you can use the efficient bus system, which includes small electric buses making the rounds in the center. Buses also climb to Piazzale Michelangelo and San Miniato south of the Arno.

Maps and timetables are available for a small fee at the ATAF (Azienda Trasporti Area Fiorentina) booth next to the train station or for free at visitor information offices. Tickets must be bought in advance from tobacco shops, newsstands, automatic ticket machines near main stops, or ATAF booths. The ticket must be validated in the machine immediately upon boarding.

You have several ticket options, all valid for one or more rides on all lines. A €1.20 ticket is good for one hour from the time it is first canceled. A multiple ticket—four tickets, each valid for 70 minutes—costs €4.50. A 24-hour tourist ticket costs €5. Two-, three-, and seven-day passes are also available.

Long-distance buses provide inexpensive service between Florence and other cities in Italy and Europe. **SITA** (✉ *Via Santa Caterina da Siena 17/r* ☎ *055/47821*) is the major line.

CAR

Florence is connected to the north and south of Italy by the Autostrada del Sole (A1). It takes about 1½ hours on scenic roads to reach Bologna (although heavy truck traffic over the Apennines often makes for slower going). It's about 3 hours to Rome and 3 to 3½ hours to Milan. The Tyrrhenian Coast is an hour west on the A11.

An automobile in Florence is a major liability. If your itinerary includes parts of Italy where you'll want a car, pick it up on your way out of town.

TAXI

Taxis usually wait at stands throughout the city (in front of the train station and in Piazza della Repubblica, for example). You can also call radio dispatch (☎ *055/4390* or *055/4242*) for one to pick you up wherever you are.

The meter starts at €3.30 if you get a taxi at a stand or €5.40 if you call for one. Extra charges apply at night, on Sunday, and for luggage. Women out on the town after midnight are entitled to a 10% discount on the fare; you must, however, request it.

TRAIN

Florence is on the principal Italian train route between most European capitals and Rome, and within Italy it is served frequently from Milan, Venice, and Rome by Intercity (IC) and nonstop Eurostar trains. ■TIP➔ **Avoid trains that stop only at the Campo di Marte or Rifredi stations, which are not convenient to the city center.**

Stazione Centrale di Santa Maria Novella. ✉ *Piazza della Stazione, Santa Maria Novella* ☎ *055/892–2021 Trenitalia in Italy (fee for call)* ⊕ *www.trenitalia.com.*

Making the Most of Your Time

With some planning, you can see Florence's most famous sights in a couple of days. Start off at the city's most awe-inspiring architectural wonder, the **Duomo,** climbing to the top of the dome if you have the stamina (and are not claustrophobic: it gets a little tight going up and coming back down). On the same piazza, check out Ghiberti's bronze doors at the **Battistero.** (They're actually high-quality copies; the Museo dell'Opera del Duomo has the originals.) Set aside the afternoon for the **Galleria degli Uffizi,** making sure to reserve tickets in advance.

On Day 2, visit Michelangelo's *David* in the **Galleria dell'Accademia**—reserve tickets here, too. Linger in **Piazza della Signoria,** Florence's central square, where a copy of *David* stands in the spot the original occupied for centuries, then head east a couple of blocks to **Santa Croce,** the city's most artistically rich church. Double back and walk across Florence's landmark bridge, the **Ponte Vecchio.**

But even after seeing those works, you'll have just scratched the surface. If you have more time, put the **Bargello,** the **Museo di San Marco,** and the **Cappelle Medicee** at the top of your list. When you're ready for an art break, stroll through the **Boboli Gardens** or explore Florence's lively shopping scene, from the food stalls of the **Mercato Centrale** to the chic boutiques of the **Via Tornabuoni.**

■TIP➔ **Even if you're the most dedicated of art enthusiasts, remember to pace yourself.** Allow time to wander, follow your whims, and watch the world go by while relaxing—without any guilt—in a café. Florence isn't a city that can be "done." Rather, it's a place you can return to again and again, confident there will always be more treasures to discover.

Uffizi Reservations

At most times of day a line of people snakes around the Uffizi. They're waiting to buy tickets, and you don't want to be one of them. Instead, call ahead for a reservation (☎ *055/294883*).

You'll be given a reservation number and an admission time—the sooner you call, the more time slots you'll have to choose from. Go to the museum's reservation door 10 minutes before the appointed hour (at least 30 minutes before in high season), give the clerk your number, pick up your ticket, and go inside. You'll pay €4 for this privilege, but it's money well spent.

You can also book through the ticketing website (⊕ *www.b-ticket.com/b-ticket/ uffizi*). The process takes some patience, but it works, and money-saving combo tickets are available as well. Use the same reservation service to book tickets for the Galleria dell'Accademia, where lines rival those of the Uffizi.

Reservations can also be made for the Palazzo Pitti, the Bargello, and several other sights, but they usually aren't needed—although, lately, in summer, lines can be long at Palazzo Pitti. An alternative strategy is to check with your hotel—many will handle reservations.

Florentine Hours

Florence's sights keep tricky hours. Some are closed Wednesday, some Monday, some every other Monday. Quite a few shut their doors each day (or on most days) by 2 pm.

Here's a rundown of things to keep in mind when timing visits to major sights. Check listings throughout this chapter for more details, and be aware that hours are subject to change: always confirm them in advance.

The **Accademia** and the **Uffizi** are both closed Monday. Note, too, that on the first Sunday of the month, all state museums, including these two, are free and do not accept reservations.

The **Bargello** is closed on Tuesday and the first, third, and last Sunday of the month. Otherwise, it's open from 8:45 am until 7 pm.

The **Battistero** is open daily 9 am to 7:30 pm.

The **Cappelle Medicee** are closed alternating Sundays and Mondays (those Sundays and Mondays when the Bargello is open).

The **Duomo** is closed on Sunday and is open from 10:15 am to 4:30 pm the rest of the week.

Museo di San Marco closes at 1:50 weekdays but stays open until 7 weekends—except for alternating Sundays and Mondays, when it's closed entirely.

Palazzo Medici-Riccardi is closed Wednesday.

Hotels

Florence has so many famous landmarks that it's not hard to find lodging with a panoramic view. In addition, the city's importance as a tourist destination and convention hub (it's also the site of the Pitti fashion collections) guarantees a variety of accommodations. You'll find both budget and luxury hotels in the *centro storico* (historic center), along the Arno, and elsewhere.

You can even still find the equivalent of the genteel *pensioni* of yesteryear, though they are now officially classified as hotels. Generally small and intimate, these often have a quaint appeal that usually doesn't preclude modern plumbing.

High demand for accommodations means that, except in winter, reservations are a must. If, however, you find yourself in Florence with no reservations, reach out to **Consorzio ITA** (✉ *Stazione Centrale, Santa Maria Novella* ☎ *055/282893*). Note that you must appear in person to make a booking.

Hotel reviews have been shortened. For full information, visit Fodors.com. Hotel prices are the lowest cost of a standard double room in high season.

WHAT IT COSTS in Euros			
$	$$	$$$	$$$$
HOTELS			
under €125	€125–€200	€201–€300	over €300

Nightlife

Florentines are rather proud of their nightlife options. Most bars now have some sort of happy hour, which usually lasts for many hours and often has snacks that can substitute for a light dinner. (Check whether the buffet is free or comes with the price of a drink.) Clubs typically don't open until very late in the evening, so they don't get crowded until 1 or 2 in the morning.

Performing Arts

Florence has a lively classical music scene. The internationally famous annual Maggio Musicale lights up the musical calendar in early spring and continues throughout most of the year. Fans of rock, pop, and hip-hop might be somewhat surprised by the absence of live acts that make it to town (for such offerings, traveling to Rome or Milan is often a necessity). What it lacks in contemporary music, however, it makes up for with its many theatrical offerings.

FESTIVALS AND SPECIAL EVENTS

Festa di San Giovanni (*Feast of St. John the Baptist*)

FESTIVALS | On June 24, Florence mostly grinds to a halt to for celebrations honoring the city's patron saint. Many shops and bars close, and, at night, a fireworks display lights up the Arno and attracts thousands. ⊠ *Florence.*

Scoppio del Carro (*Explosion of the Cart*)

FESTIVALS | On Easter Sunday, Florentines and foreigners alike flock to the Piazza del Duomo to watch as the Scoppio del Carro, a monstrosity of a carriage pulled by two huge oxen decorated for the occasion, arrives in the piazza after making its way through the city center. Using an elaborate wiring system, an object representing a dove is sent from inside the cathedral to the Baptistery across the way. The dove sets off an explosion of fireworks that come streaming from the carriage. You have to see it to believe it. ⊠ *Piazza del Duomo, Florence.*

Restaurants

Florence's popularity with tourists means that, unfortunately, there's a higher percentage of mediocre restaurants here than elsewhere in Italy. Some owners cut corners and let standards slip, knowing that a customer today is unlikely to return tomorrow. So, if you're looking to eat well, it pays to do some research, starting with the recommendations here.

Cafés in Italy serve not only coffee concoctions and pastries but also sweets, drinks, and panini; some also offer hot pasta and lunch dishes. They're usually open from early in the morning until late at night, except on Sunday, when many are closed entirely.

At other restaurants, service starts at around 1 pm for lunch and 8 pm for dinner. (Just remember that many of Florence's restaurants are small, so reservations are a must.) You can sample such specialties as creamy *fegatini* (a chicken-liver spread) and *ribollita* (minestrone thickened with bread and beans and swirled with extra-virgin olive oil) in a bustling, convivial trattoria, where you share long wooden tables set with paper place mats, or in an upscale ristorante with linen tablecloths and napkins.

Consider following the Florentine lead by taking a daytime break at an *enoteca* (wine bar), where you'll discover some excellent Chiantis and Super Tuscans from small producers who rarely export. Also, if you have a sense of culinary adventure, try a tripe sandwich. Served from stands throughout town, this Florentine favorite comes with a fragrant *salsa verde* (green sauce) or a piquant red sauce—or both.

Although Florentine pizza can't compete with that in Rome or Naples, you can find tasty approximations. Note, too, that international cuisine is a hit-or-miss affair here. Despite the fact that the city has numerous Asian restaurants, only a select few are worth a visit.

Restaurant reviews have been shortened. For full information, visit Fodors. com. Restaurant prices are the average cost of a main course at dinner or, if dinner is not served, at lunch.

WHAT IT COSTS in Euros			
$	$$	$$$	$$$$
RESTAURANTS			
under €15	€15–€24	€25–€35	over €35

Shopping

Window-shopping in Florence is like visiting an enormous contemporary art gallery. Many of today's greatest Italian artists are fashion designers, and most keep shops in Florence. The usual suspects—Prada, Gucci, Versace, to name but a few—all have shops here. But if you want to buy Florentine in Florence, stick to Gucci, Pucci, and Ferragamo.

Discerning shoppers will find bargains on Italian clothing outside the city. There are also deals to be had at street markets. ■TIP➔ **Do not buy Prada or other high-end "designer" goods from street hawkers. It's illegal to purchase knockoffs. If the police catch you, the fines that you—not the vendor—will pay are astronomical.**

Shops are generally open 9 to 1 and 3:30 to 7:30; they're closed all day Sunday and on Monday mornings most of the year. Summer (June to September) hours are usually 9 to 1 and 4 to 8, with some shops closing on Saturday afternoon instead of Monday morning.

When looking for addresses, you'll see two color-coded numbering systems on each street. The red numbers are commercial addresses and are indicated, for example, as 31/r. The blue or black numbers are residential addresses. Most shops take major credit cards and ship purchases, but because of possible delays, it's wise to take your purchases with you.

SHOPPING DISTRICTS
Florence's most fashionable shops are concentrated in the center of town, with the fanciest designers situated mainly on Via Tornabuoni and Via della Vigna Nuova. The city's largest concentrations of antiques shops are along Borgo Ognissanti and the Oltrarno's Via Maggio.

The Ponte Vecchio houses reputable but expensive jewelry shops, as it has since the 16th century. The area near Santa Croce is the heart of the leather merchants' district.

Visitor Information

The Florence tourist office (☎ 039/055000 ⊕ www.feelflorence. it), also known as the APT, has branches at the airport, next to the Palazzo Medici-Riccardi, across the street from Stazione di Santa Maria Novella (the main train station), and at the Bigallo in Piazza del Duomo. The offices are generally open from 9 am until 7 pm. The multilingual staff will answer questions, give you directions, and provide information on the latest performing-arts happenings and other events. The website also provides information in English.

Around the Duomo

The heart of Florence, stretching from the Piazza del Duomo south to the Arno, is as dense with artistic treasures as any place in the world. Its churches, medieval towers, Renaissance palaces, and world-class museums and galleries contain some of the most outstanding achievements of Western art.

Much of the centro storico is closed to automobile traffic, but you still must dodge mopeds, cyclists, and masses of fellow tourists as you walk the narrow streets, especially in the area bounded by the Duomo, Piazza della Signoria, Galleria degli Uffizi, and the Ponte Vecchio. Via dei Calzaiuoli, between Piazza del Duomo and Piazza della Signoria, is the city's favorite *passeggiata* (leisurely stroll).

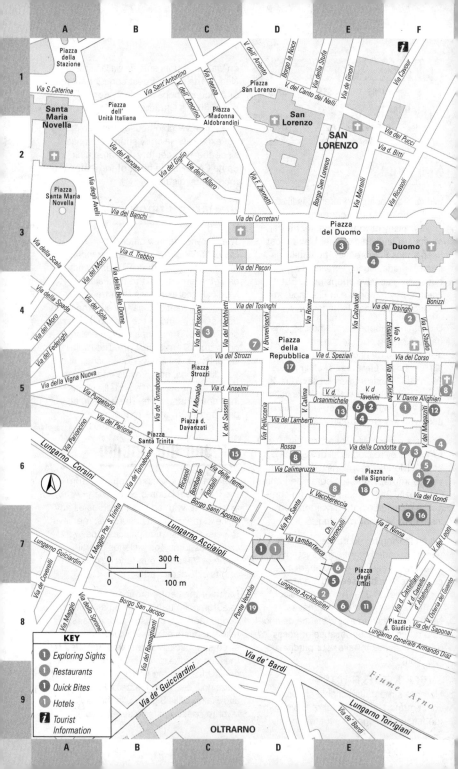

Around the Duomo

3

Florence AROUND THE DUOMO

Sights ▼

1 Badia Fiorentina G6
2 Bargello............................. G6
3 Battistero E3
4 Campanile E3
5 Duomo E3
6 Galleria degli Uffizi E8
7 Gucci Garden F6
8 Mercato Nuovo D6
9 Museo dei Ragazzi F6
10 Museo dell'Opera del Duomo.... G3
11 Museo Galileo...................... E8
12 Oratorio dei Buonomini
    di San Martino F5
13 Orsanmichele E5
14 Ospedale Santa Maria Nuova..... I3
15 Palazzo Davanzati C6
16 Palazzo Vecchio F6
17 Piazza della Repubblica........... D5
18 Piazza della Signoria E6
19 Ponte Vecchio D8
20 San Michele Visdomini G2

Restaurants ▼

1 Birreria Centrale F5
2 Coquinarius......................... F4
3 Gucci Giardino 25................... F6
4 Gucci Osteria........................ F6
5 Le Mossacce........................ G4
6 Ora d'Aria........................... E7
7 Ristorante Frescobaldi Firenze.... F6
8 Rivoire.............................. E6

Quick Bites ▼

1 Caffè delle Carrozze.............. D7
2 Cantinetta dei Verrazzano E5
3 Gelateria Carabe.................. G1
4 I Fratellini E5
5 'ino................................. E7
6 Perché No! E5

Hotels ▼

1 Hermitage D7
2 Hotel degli Orafi................... E8
3 Hotel Helvetia and Bristol......... C4
4 Hotel Renaissance F6
5 In Piazza della Signoria F6
6 Palazzo Niccolini al Duomo G3
7 Palazzo Vecchietti D4
8 Sani Tourist House................. F5

Sights

Badia Fiorentina

CHURCH | Originally endowed by Willa, Marquess of Tuscany, in 978, this ancient church is an interesting mélange of 13th-century, Renaissance, baroque, and 18th-century architectural refurbishing. Its graceful bell tower, best seen from the interior courtyard, is beautiful for its unusual construction—a hexagonal tower built on a quadrangular base.

The interior of the church was halfheartedly remodeled in the baroque style during the 17th century. Three tombs by Mino da Fiesole (circa 1430–84) line the walls, including the *monumento funebre di Conte Ugo* (tomb sculpture of Count Ugo), widely regarded as Mino's masterpiece. Executed in 1469–81, it shows Mino at his most lyrical: the faces seem to be lit from within—no small feat in marble.

The best-known work of art here is the delicate *Vision of St. Bernard,* by Filippino Lippi (circa 1457–1504), on the left as you enter. The painting—one of Filippino's finest—is in superb condition; note the Virgin Mary's hands, perhaps the most beautifully rendered in the city. On the right side of the church, above the cappella di San Mauro, is a monumental organ dating from 1558. Constructed by Onofrio Zeffirini da Cortona (1510–86), it's largely intact but is missing its 16th-century keyboard. ⊠ *Via Dante Alighieri 1, Bargello* ☎ *055/264402* ⊕ *www.badiafiorentina. org* ⊠ *Free* ⊙ *Closed Sun.*

Bargello

ART MUSEUM | This building started out in the Middle Ages as the headquarters for the Capitano del Popolo (Captain of the People) and was later a prison. Today, it houses the Museo Nazionale, home to what is probably the finest collection of Renaissance sculpture in Italy. The remarkable masterpieces by Michelangelo (1475–1564), Donatello (circa 1386–1466), and Benvenuto Cellini (1500–71) are distributed amid an eclectic collection of arms, ceramics, and miniature bronzes, among other things.

In 1401, Filippo Brunelleschi (1377–1446) and Lorenzo Ghiberti (circa 1378–1455) competed to earn the most prestigious commission of the day: the decoration of the north doors of the Baptistery in Piazza del Duomo. For the contest, each designed a bronze bas-relief panel depicting the sacrifice of Isaac; the panels are displayed together in the room devoted to the sculpture of Donatello, on the upper floor. According to Ghiberti, the judges chose him, though Brunelleschi maintained that they were both hired for the commission. See who you believe after visiting. ⊠ *Via del Proconsolo 4, Bargello* ☎ *055/294883* ⊕ *www.museodelbargello.it* ⊠ *€12* ⊙ *Closed 2nd and 4th Mon. of the month.*

Battistero (*Baptistery*)

RELIGIOUS BUILDING | The octagonal Baptistery is one of the supreme monuments of the Italian Romanesque style and one of Florence's oldest structures. Local legend has it that it was once a Roman temple dedicated to Mars (it wasn't), and modern excavations suggest that its foundations date from the 1st century AD. The round Romanesque arches on the exterior date from the 11th century, and the interior dome mosaics from the beginning of the mid-13th century are justly renowned, but—glittering beauties though they are—they could never outshine the building's famed bronze Renaissance doors decorated with panels crafted by Lorenzo Ghiberti. Copies of the doors on which Ghiberti worked (1403–52) most of his adult life are on the north and east sides of the Baptistery (to protect them from pollution and acid rain, the original doors were moved to the Museo dell'Opera del Duomo, where they're now on display). The Gothic panels on the south door were designed by Andrea Pisano (circa 1290–1348) in 1330.

Florence through the Ages

Guelph vs. Ghibelline. Although Florence can lay claim to a modest importance in the ancient world, it didn't come into its own until the Middle Ages. In the early 1200s the city, like most of the rest of Italy, was rent by civic unrest. Two factions, the Guelphs and the Ghibellines, competed for power. The Guelphs supported the papacy, and the Ghibellines supported the Holy Roman Empire. Bloody battles—most notably one at Montaperti in 1260—tore Florence and other Italian cities apart. By the end of the 13th century the Guelphs ruled securely, and the Ghibellines had been vanquished. This didn't end civic strife, however: the Guelphs split into the Whites and the Blacks for reasons still debated by historians. Dante, author of *The Divine Comedy*, was banished from Florence in 1301 because he was a White.

The Guilded Age. Local merchants had organized themselves into guilds by some time beginning in the 12th century. In 1250, they proclaimed themselves the *primo popolo* (literally, "first people"), making a landmark attempt at elective, republican rule. Though the episode lasted only 10 years, it constituted a breakthrough in Western history. Such a daring stance by the merchant class was a by-product of Florence's emergence as an economic powerhouse. Florentines were papal bankers; they instituted the system of international letters of credit; the gold florin became the international standard of currency. With this economic strength came a building boom. Sculptors such as Ghiberti and Donatello decorated the new churches; painters such as Giotto and Masaccio frescoed their walls.

Mighty Medici. Though ostensibly a republic, Florence was blessed (or cursed) with one very powerful family, the Medici, who came to prominence in 1434 and were initially the de facto rulers and then the absolute rulers of Florence for several hundred years. It was under patriarch Cosimo il Vecchio (1389–1464) that the Medici's position in Florence was securely established. Florence's golden age occurred during the reign of his grandson Lorenzo de' Medici (1449–92). Lorenzo was not only an astute politician but also a highly educated man and a great patron of the arts. Called "Il Magnifico" (the Magnificent), he gathered around him poets, artists, philosophers, architects, and musicians.

Lorenzo's son Piero (1471–1503) proved inept at handling the city's affairs. He was run out of town in 1494, and Florence briefly enjoyed its status as a republic while dominated by the Dominican friar Girolamo Savonarola (1452–98). After a decade of internal unrest, the republic fell and the Medici returned to power, but Florence never regained its former prestige. By the 1530s most of the major artistic talent had left the city—Michelangelo, for one, had settled in Rome. The now-ineffectual Medici, eventually attaining the title of grand dukes, remained nominally in power until the line died out in 1737, after which time Florence passed from the Austrians to the French and back again until the unification of Italy (1865–70), when it briefly became the capital under King Vittorio Emanuele II.

3

Florence AROUND THE DUOMO

Ghiberti's north doors depict scenes from the life of Christ; his later east doors (1425–52), facing the Duomo facade, render scenes from the Old Testament. Both merit close examination, for they are very different in style and illustrate the artistic changes that marked the beginning of the Renaissance. Look at the far right panel of the middle row on the earlier (1403–24) north doors (*Jesus Calming the Waters*). Here, Ghiberti captured the chaos of a storm at sea with great skill and economy. The artistic conventions he used, however, are basically pre-Renaissance: Jesus is the most important figure, so he is the largest; the disciples are next in size, being next in importance; the ship on which they founder looks like a mere toy.

The exquisitely rendered panels on the east doors are larger, more expansive, more sweeping—and more convincing. The middle panel on the left-hand door tells the story of Jacob and Esau, and the various episodes of the story—the selling of the birthright, Isaac ordering Esau to go hunting, the blessing of Jacob, and so forth—have been merged into a single beautifully realized street scene. Ghiberti's use of perspective suggests depth: the background architecture looks credible, the figures in the foreground are grouped realistically, and the naturalism and grace of the poses (look at Esau's left leg and the dog next to him) have nothing to do with the sacred message being conveyed. Although the religious content remains, the figures and their place in the natural world are given new prominence and are portrayed with a realism not seen in art since the fall of the Roman Empire nearly a thousand years before.

As a footnote to Ghiberti's panels, one small detail of the east doors is worth a special look. To the lower left of the Jacob and Esau panel, Ghiberti placed a tiny self-portrait bust. From either side, the portrait is extremely appealing—Ghiberti looks like everyone's favorite uncle—but the bust is carefully placed so that you can make direct eye contact with the tiny head from a single spot. When that contact is made, the impression of intelligent life—of *modern* intelligent life—is astonishing. It's no wonder that these doors received one of the most famous compliments in the history of art from an artist known to be notoriously stingy with praise: Michelangelo declared them so beautiful that they could serve as the Gates of Paradise. ⌧ *Piazza del Duomo, Duomo* ☎ *055/230–2885* ⊕ *duomo. firenze.it/it/home* ✉ *Admission is via one of 3 combo tickets, each valid for 3 days: €30 Brunelleschi Pass (with Campanile, Cupola of the Duomo, Museo dell'Opera del Duomo, and Santa Reparata Basilica Cripta); €20 Giotto Pass (with Campanile, Museo dell'Opera, and Cripta); €15 Ghiberti Pass (with Museo dell'Opera and Cripta).*

Campanile

NOTABLE BUILDING | FAMILY | The Gothic bell tower designed by Giotto (circa 1266–1337) is a soaring structure of multicolor marble originally decorated with sculptures by Donatello and reliefs by Giotto, Andrea Pisano, and others (which are now in the Museo dell'Opera del Duomo). A climb of 414 steps rewards you with a close-up of Brunelleschi's cupola on the Duomo next door and a sweeping view of the city. ⌧ *Piazza del Duomo, Duomo* ☎ *055/230–2885* ⊕ *duomo.firenze.it/it/home* ✉ *Admission is via one of 2 combo tickets, each valid for 3 days: €30 Brunelleschi Pass (with Battistero, Cupola of the Duomo, Museo dell'Opera del Duomo, and Santa Reparata Basilica Cripta); €20 for Giotto Pass (with Battistero, Museo dell'Opera, and Cripta).* ☉ *Closed Sun. morning.*

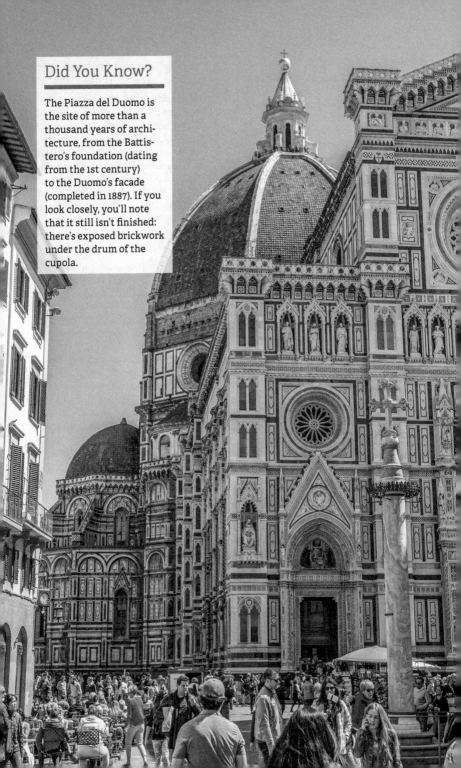

★ Duomo

(*Cattedrale di Santa Maria del Fiore*)
CHURCH | In 1296, Arnolfo di Cambio (circa 1245–1310) was commissioned to build "the loftiest, most sumptuous edifice human invention could devise" in the Romanesque style on the site of the old church of Santa Reparata. The immense Duomo was consecrated in 1436, but work continued over the centuries. The imposing facade dates only from the 19th century; its neo-Gothic style somewhat complements Giotto's genuine Gothic 14th-century campanile. The real glory of the Duomo, however, is Filippo Brunelleschi's dome, presiding over the cathedral with a dignity and grace that few domes to this day can match.

Brunelleschi's cupola was an ingenious engineering feat. The space to be enclosed by the dome was so large and so high above the ground that traditional methods of dome construction—wooden centering and scaffolding—were of no use whatsoever. So Brunelleschi developed entirely new building methods, including a novel scaffolding system, that he implemented with equipment of his own design. Beginning work in 1420, he built not one dome but two, one inside the other, and connected them with ribbing that stretched across the intervening empty space, thereby considerably lessening the crushing weight of the structure. He also employed a new method of bricklaying, based on an ancient herringbone pattern, interlocking each course of bricks with the course below in a way that made the growing structure self-supporting.

The result was one of the great engineering breakthroughs of all time: most of Europe's later domes, including that of St. Peter's in Rome, were built employing Brunelleschi's methods, and today the Duomo has come to symbolize Florence in the same way that the Eiffel Tower symbolizes Paris. The Florentines are justly proud of it, and to this day the Florentine phrase for "homesick" is *nostalgia del cupolone* (homesick for the dome).

The interior is a fine example of Florentine Gothic. Although of the cathedral's best-known art has been moved to the nearby Museo dell'Opera del Duomo, notable among the works that remain are two massive equestrian frescoes, both on the left nave, that honor famous soldiers: Niccolò da Tolentino, painted in 1456 by Andrea del Castagno (circa 1419–57), and Sir John Hawkwood, painted 20 years earlier by Paolo Uccello (1397–1475).

A 1995 restoration repaired the dome and cleaned the vastly crowded fresco of the Last Judgment, executed by Giorgio Vasari (1511–74) and Zuccari, on its interior. Originally Brunelleschi wanted mosaics to cover the interior of the great ribbed cupola, but by the time the Florentines got around to commissioning the decoration, 150 years later, tastes had changed. The climb to the top of the dome (463 steps) is not for the faint of heart, but the view is superb. ■TIP→ **Admission to the Duomo is free; there is, however, an entrance fee for the cupola (included in some combo tickets), and timed-entry reservations to visit it are required.** ✉ *Piazza del Duomo, Duomo* ☎ *055/230–2885* ⊕ *duomo.firenze.it/it/home* 🎫 *Church is free. Admission to the cupola is via the €30 Brunelleschi Pass, a 3-day combo ticket that also includes the Battistero, Campanile, Museo dell'Opera del Duomo, and Santa Reparata Basilica Cripta.* ☉ *Closed Sun.* ♿ *Timed-entry reservations required for the cupola.*

★ Galleria degli Uffizi

ART MUSEUM | The venerable Uffizi Gallery occupies two floors of the U-shape Palazzo degli Uffizi, designed by Giorgio Vasari (1511–74) in 1560 to hold the *uffici* (administrative offices) of the Medici Grand Duke Cosimo I (1519–74).

Among the highlights is the *Battle of San Romano* by Paolo Uccello (1397–1475). Gloriously restored in 2012, its brutal chaos of lances is one of the finest visual metaphors for warfare ever captured in paint. Equally noteworthy is the *Madonna and Child with Two Angels* in which Fra Filippo Lippi (1406–69) depicts eye contact established by the angel that would have been unthinkable prior to the Renaissance. In Sandro Botticelli's (1445–1510) *Birth of Venus*, the goddess seems to float in the air, and in his *Primavera*, a fairy-tale charm demonstrates the painter's idiosyncratic genius at its zenith.

Other significant works include the portraits of the Renaissance duke Federico da Montefeltro and his wife, Battista Sforza, by Piero della Francesca (circa 1420–92); Raphael's (1483–1520) *Madonna of the Goldfinch*, which is distinguished by the brilliant blues of the sky and the eye contact between mother and child, both clearly anticipating the painful future; Michelangelo's *Doni Tondo*; the *Venus of Urbino* by Titian (circa 1488/90–1576); and the splendid *Bacchus* by Caravaggio (circa 1571/72–1610). In the last two works, the approaches to myth and sexuality are diametrically opposed (to put it mildly).

Late in the afternoon is the least crowded time to visit. For a €4 fee, advance tickets can be reserved by phone, online, or, once in Florence, at the Uffizi reservation booth (✉ *Consorzio ITA, Piazza Pitti* ☎ *055/294883*), at least one day in advance of your visit. Keep the confirmation number, and take it with you to the door at the museum marked "reservations." In the past, you were ushered in almost immediately. But overbooking (especially in high season) has led to long lines and long waits even with a reservation. Taking photographs in the Uffizi has been legal since 2014, and this has contributed to making what

ought to be a sublime museum-going experience more like a day at the zoo. ✉ *Piazzale degli Uffizi 6, Piazza della Signoria* ☎ *055/294883* ⊕ *www.uffizi.it* 🎟 *From €20* ⊗ *Closed Mon.*

Gucci Garden

OTHER MUSEUM | This museum has all the class and elegance associated with the Gucci name. Tasteful displays of the design house's famous luggage, shoes, and sporting goods (including snorkels and flippers) fill the 14th-century Palazzo del Tribunale di Mercatanzia. Centuries ago, this building heard and tried cases by disgruntled guildsmen. Today, it offers some interesting juxtapositions, including an early 15th-century fresco of Christ crucified located in a room that's now filled with displays of 20th-century jewelry. ✉ *Piazza della Signoria 10, Duomo* ☎ *055/7592–7010* ⊕ *guccigarden.gucci. com, www.gucci.com* 🎟 *€8.*

Mercato Nuovo (*New Market*)

MARKET | FAMILY | The open-air loggia, built in 1551, teems with souvenir stands, but the real attraction is a copy of Pietro Tacca's bronze *Porcellino* (which translates as "little pig" despite the fact the animal is, in fact, a wild boar). The sculpture is Florence's equivalent of the Trevi Fountain: put a coin in his mouth, and if it falls through the grate below (according to one interpretation), it means you'll return to Florence someday. What you're seeing is a copy of a copy: Tacca's original version, in the Museo Bardini, is actually a copy of an ancient Greek work. ✉ *Via Por Santa Maria at Via Porta Rossa, Piazza della Repubblica* ⊗ *Closed Sun.*

Museo dei Ragazzi

CHILDREN'S MUSEUM | FAMILY | Florence's Children's Museum may be the best-kept public-access secret in Florence. A series of interactive tours includes "Encounters with History," during which participants meet and talk with Giorgio Vasari or Galileo Galilei and explore secret

3

Florence AROUND THE DUOMO

Continued on page 89

THE DUOMO

FLORENCE'S BIGGEST MASTERPIECE

For all its monumental art and architecture, Florence has one undisputed centerpiece: the Cathedral of Santa Maria del Fiore, better known as the Duomo. Its cupola dominates the skyline, presiding over the city's rooftops like a red hen over her brood. Little wonder that when Florentines feel homesick, they say they have "*nostalgia del cupolone.*"

The Duomo's construction began in 1296, following the design of Arnolfo di Cambio, Florence's greatest architect of the time. By modern standards, construction was slow and haphazard—it continued through the 14th and into the 15th century, with some dozen architects having a hand in the project.

In 1366, Neri di Fioravante created a model for the hugely ambitious cupola: it was to be the largest dome in the world, surpassing Rome's Pantheon. But when the time finally came to build the dome in 1418, no one was sure how—or even if—it could be done. Florence was faced with a 143 foot hole in the roof of its cathedral, and one of the greatest challenges in the history of architecture.

Fortunately, local genius Filippo Brunelleschi was just the man for the job. Brunelleschi won the 1418 competition to design the dome, and for the next 18 years he oversaw its construction. The enormity of his achievement can hardly be overstated. Working on such a large scale (the dome weighs 37,000 tons and uses 4 million bricks) required him to invent hoists and cranes that were engineering marvels. A "dome within a dome" design and a novel herringbone bricklaying pattern were just two of the innovations used to establish structural integrity. Perhaps most remarkably, he executed the construction without a supporting wooden framework, which had previously been thought indispensable.

Brunelleschi designed the lantern atop the dome, but he died soon after its first stone was laid in 1446; it wouldn't be completed until 1461. Another 400 years passed before the Duomo received its facade, a 19th-century neo-Gothic creation.

DUOMO TIMELINE

1296 Work begins, following design by Arnolfo di Cambio.

1302 Arnolfo dies; work continues, with sporadic interruptions.

1331 Management of construction taken over by the Wool Merchants guild.

1334 Giotto appointed project overseer, designs campanile.

1337 Giotto dies; Andrea Pisano takes leadership role.

1348 The Black Plague; all work ceases.

1366 Vaulting on nave completed; Neri di Fioravante makes model for dome.

1417 Drum for dome completed.

1418 Competition is held to design the dome.

1420 Brunelleschi begins work on the dome.

1436 Dome completed.

1446 Construction of lantern begins; Brunelleschi dies.

1461 Antonio Manetti, a student of Brunelleschi, completes lantern.

1469 Gilt copper ball and cross added by Verrocchio.

1587 Original facade is torn down by Medici court.

1871 Emilio de Fabris wins competition to design new facade.

1887 Facade completed.

WHAT TO LOOK FOR INSIDE THE DUOMO

The interior of the Duomo is a fine example of Florentine Gothic with a beautiful marble floor, but the space feels strangely barren—a result of its great size and the fact that some of the best art has been moved to the nearby **Museo dell'Opera del Duomo**.

Notable among the works that remain are two towering equestrian frescoes of famous mercenaries: Niccolò da Tolentino (1456) by Andrea del Castagno, and Sir John Hawkwood (1436) by Paolo Uccello. There's also fine terra-cotta work by Luca della Robbia. Ghiberti, Brunelleschi's great rival, is responsible for much of the stained glass, as well as a reliquary urn with gorgeous reliefs. A vast fresco of the Last Judgment, painted by Vasari and Zuccari, covers the dome's interior. Brunelleschi had wanted mosaics to go there; it's a pity he didn't get his wish.

In the crypt beneath the cathedral, you can explore excavations of a Roman wall and mosaic fragments from the late 6th century; entry is near the first pier on the right. On the way down you pass Brunelleschi's modest tomb.

1. Entrance; stained glass by Ghiberti
2. Fresco of Niccolò da Tolentino by Andrea del Castagno
3. Fresco of John Hawkwood by Paolo Uccello
4. Dante and the Divine Comedy by Domenico di Michelino
5. Lunette: Ascension by Luca della Robbia
6. Above altar: two angels by Luca della Robbia. Below the altar: reliquary of St. Zenobius by Ghiberti
7. Lunette: Resurrection by Luca della Robbia
8. Entrance to dome
9. Bust of Brunelleschi by Buggiano
10. Stairs to crypt
11. Campanile

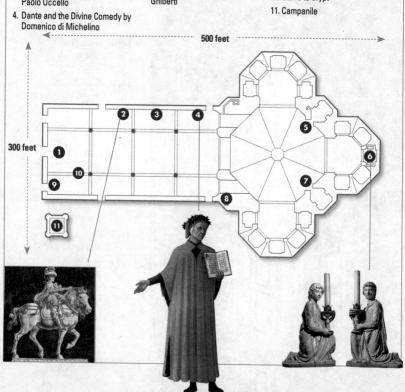

MAKING THE CLIMB

Climbing the 463 steps to the top of the dome is not for the faint of heart—or for the claustrophobic—but those who do it will be rewarded a smashing view of Florence (left). Keep in mind that the way up is also the way down, which means that while you're huffing and puffing in the ascent, people very close to you in a narrow staircase (below) are making their way down.

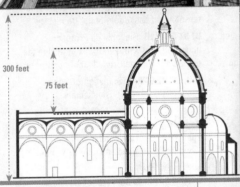

300 feet

75 feet

DUOMO BASICS

- Admission to the church is free, but there's a fee to visit the cupola, and timed-entry reservations are required.

- For an alternative to the dome, consider climbing the less trafficked campanile, which gives you a view from on high of the dome itself.

- Dress code essentials: covered shoulders, no short shorts, and hats off upon entering.

THE CRYPT

The crypt is worth a visit: computer modeling allows visitors to see its ancient Roman fabric and subsequent rebuilding. A transparent plastic model shows exactly what the earlier church looked like.

BRUNELLESCHI vs. GHIBERTI
The Rivalry of Two Renaissance Geniuses

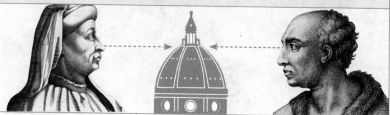

In Renaissance Florence, painters, sculptors, and architects competed for major commissions, with the winner earning the right to undertake a project that might occupy him (and keep him paid) for a decade or more. Stakes were high, and the resulting rivalries fierce—none more so than that between Filippo Brunelleschi and Lorenzo Ghiberti.

The two first clashed in 1401, for the commission to create the bronze doors of the Baptistery. When Ghiberti won, Brunelleschi took it hard, fleeing to Rome, where he would remain for 15 years. Their rematch came in 1418, over the design of the Duomo's cupola, with Brunelleschi triumphant. For the remainder of their lives, the two would miss no opportunity to belittle each other's work.

FILIPPO BRUNELLESCHI (1377–1446)

MASTERPIECE: The dome of Santa Maria del Fiore.

BEST FRIENDS: Donatello, whom he stayed with in Rome after losing the Baptistery doors competition; the Medici family, who rescued him from bankruptcy.

SIGNATURE TRAITS: Paranoid, secretive, bad tempered, practical joker, inept businessman.

SAVVIEST POLITICAL MOVE: Feigned sickness and left for Rome after his dome plans were publicly criticized by Ghiberti, who was second-in-command. The project proved too much for Ghiberti to manage on his own, and Brunelleschi returned triumphant.

MOST EMBARRASSING MOMENT: In 1434, he was imprisoned for two weeks for failure to pay a small guild fee. The humiliation might have been orchestrated by Ghiberti.

OTHER CAREER: Shipbuilder. He built a huge vessel, *Il Badalone*, to transport marble for the dome up the Arno. It sank on its first voyage.

INSPIRED: The dome of St. Peter's in Rome.

LORENZO GHIBERTI (1378–1455)

MASTERPIECE: The Gates of Paradise, the ten-paneled east doors of the Baptistery.

BEST FRIEND: Giovanni da Prato, an underling who wrote diatribes attacking the dome's design and Brunelleschi's character.

SIGNATURE TRAITS: Instigator, egoist, know-it-all, shrewd businessman.

SAVVIEST POLITICAL MOVE: During the Baptistery doors competition, he had an open studio and welcomed opinions on his work, while Brunelleschi labored behind closed doors.

OTHER CAREER: Collector of classical artifacts, historian.

INSPIRED: The Gates of Hell by Auguste Rodin.

The Gates of Paradise detail

passageways. Events occur at different venues (Palazzo Vecchio, Museo Stibbert, Cappella Brancacci, and the Museo Galileo). Tours are in English and must be booked in advance. Though most of the tours are geared for the three- to eight-year-old crowd, adults will find them lots of fun, too. ⊠ *Piazza della Signoria 1, Piazza della Signoria* ☎ *055/276–8224* ⊕ *musefirenze.it/musei/museo-di-palaz-zo-vecchio* ⊠ *€10.*

★ Museo dell'Opera del Duomo
(*Cathedral Museum*)
ART MUSEUM | A seven-year restoration, completed in 2015, gave Florence one of its most modern, up-to-date museums. The exhibition space was doubled, and the old facade of the cathedral, torn down in the 1580s, was re-created with a 1:1 relationship to the real thing. Both sets of Ghiberti's doors adorn the same room. Michelangelo's *Pietà* finally has the space it deserves, as does Donatello's *Mary Magdalene.* ⊠ *Piazza del Duomo 9, Duomo* ☎ *055/230–2885* ⊕ *duomo.firen-ze.it/it/home* ⊠ *Admission is via one of 3 combo tickets, each valid for 3 days: €30 Brunelleschi Pass (with Battistero, Cam-panile, Cupola of the Duomo, and Santa Reparata Basilica Cripta); €20 Giotto Pass (with Battistero, Campanile, and Cripta); €15 Ghiberti Pass (with Battistero and Cripta)* ☉ *Closed 1st Tues. of month.*

Museo Galileo
SCIENCE MUSEUM | FAMILY | Although it tends to be obscured by the glamour of the neighboring Uffizi, this science museum has much to brag about: Galileo's own instruments, antique armillary spheres, and other reminders of the artistic and scientific feats of the Renaissance. ⊠ *Piazza dei Giudici 1, Piaz-za della Signoria* ☎ *055/265311* ⊕ *www. museogalileo.it* ⊠ *€11* ⚅ *Reservations are recommended.*

Oratorio dei Buonomini di San Martino
RELIGIOUS BUILDING | Founded in 1441 by Antoninus, Bishop of Florence, to offer alms to the *poveri vergognosi* (the ashamed poor), this one-room oratory is decorated with 15th-century frescoes by the school of Ghirlandaio that vividly depict the confraternity's activities. More than 500 years later, the Compagnia dei Buonomini, or Confraternity of the Good Men, continues to perform charitable works, linking Renaissance notions of charity to the 21st century. ⊠ *Piazza San Martino, Bargello* ⊕ *www.buonominidis-anmartino.it* ⊠ *Free* ☉ *Closed Sun. and Mon. afternoon.*

Orsanmichele
CHURCH | This structure has served mul-tiple purposes. Built in the 8th century as an oratory, in 1290, it was turned into an open-air loggia for selling grain. Destroyed by fire in 1304, it was rebuilt as a loggia-market. Between 1367 and 1380 its arcades were closed and two stories were added above. Finally, at cen-tury's end, it was turned into a church.

Although the interior contains a beautifully detailed 14th-century Gothic tabernacle by Andrea Orcagna (1308–68), its the exterior that is most interesting. Niches contain sculptures (all copies) dating from the early 1400s to the early 1600s by Donatello and Verrocchio (1435–88), among others, which were paid for by the guilds. Although it is a copy, Verroc-chio's *Doubting Thomas* (circa 1470) is particularly deserving of attention. Here you see Christ, like the building's other figures, entirely framed within the niche, and St. Thomas standing on its bottom ledge, with his right foot outside the niche frame. This one detail, the positioning of a single foot, brings the whole composition to life. It's possible to see the original sculptures at the Museo di Orsanmichele, which is open on Tuesday afternoon and Saturday morning only. ⊠ *Via dei*

Calzaiuoli, Piazza della Repubblica ☎ *055/284944* ⊕ *www.polomuseale.firenze.it* ⊠ *€2* ⊘ *Closed Sun. and Mon. and Wed.–Fri.* ⊸ *Reservations recommended.*

Ospedale Santa Maria Nuova

HOSPITAL | Folco Portinari, the father of Dante's Beatrice, founded this sprawling complex in 1288. It was originally a hostel for pilgrims and other travelers. During the Black Death of 1348, it served as a hospice. At another point, it served as an office where money could be exchanged and deposited and letters could be received; Michelangelo did his banking here. It had been lavishly decorated by the top Florentine artists of the day, but most of the works, such as the frescoes by Domenico Veneziano and Piero della Francesca, have disappeared or been moved to the Uffizi for safekeeping.

Today, it functions as a hospital in the modern sense of the word, but you can visit the single-nave church of Sant'Egidio, in the middle of the complex, where the frescoes would have stood. Imagine, too, Hugo van der Goes's (1435–82) magnificent *Portinari Altarpiece,* which once crowned the high altar; it's now in the Uffizi. Commissioned by Tommaso Portinari, a descendent of Folco's, it arrived from Bruges in 1483 and created quite a stir. Bernardo Rossellino's immense marble tabernacle (1450), still in the church, is worth a look. ⊠ *Via Sant'Egidio and Piazza di Santa Maria Nuova, San Lorenzo* ⊕ *www.fondazionesantamarianuova.com.*

Palazzo Davanzati

CASTLE/PALACE | The prestigious Davizzi family owned this 14th-century palace in one of Florence's swankiest medieval neighborhoods (it was sold to the Davanzati in the 15th century). The place is a delight, as you can wander through the surprisingly light-filled courtyard and climb the steep stairs to the piano nobile (there's also an elevator), where the family did most of its living. The beautiful Sala dei Pappagalli (Parrot Room) is adorned with trompe-l'oeil tapestries and gaily painted birds. ⊠ *Piazza Davanzati 13, Piazza della Repubblica* ☎ *055/064–9460* ⊕ *www.polomuseale.firenze.it* ⊠ *€6* ⊘ *Closed Mon. and 1st, 3rd, 5th Sun. of month.*

Palazzo Vecchio (*Old Palace*)

CASTLE/PALACE | FAMILY | Florence's forbidding, fortress-like city hall was begun in 1299, presumably designed by Arnolfo di Cambio, and its massive bulk and towering campanile dominate Piazza della Signoria. It was built as a meeting place for the guildsmen governing the city at the time; today, it is still City Hall. The interior courtyard is a good deal less severe, having been remodeled by Michelozzo (1396–1472) in 1453; a copy of Verrocchio's bronze *puttino* (cherub), topping the central fountain, softens the space. (The original is upstairs.)

The main attraction is on the second floor: two adjoining rooms that supply one of the most startling contrasts in Florence. The first is the opulently vast Sala dei Cinquecento (Room of the Five Hundred), named for the 500-member Great Council, the people's assembly established after the death of Lorenzo the Magnificent, that met here. Giorgio Vasari and others decorated the room, around 1563–65, with gargantuan frescoes celebrating Florentine history; depictions of battles with nearby cities predominate. Continuing the martial theme, is Michelangelo's *Victory,* intended for the tomb of Pope Julius II (1443–1513), plus other sculptures of decidedly lesser quality.

In comparison, the little Studiolo, just off the Sala dei Cinquecento's entrance, was a private room meant for the duke and those whom he invited in. Here's where the melancholy Francesco I (1541–87), son of Cosimo I, stored his priceless treasures and conducted scientific experiments. Designed by Vasari, it was decorated by him, Giambologna, and many others. Note, too, that spectacular

360-degree views may be had from the battlements (only 77 steps) and the tower (223 more). ☒ *Piazza della Signoria, Piazza della Signoria* ☎ *055/276–8325* ⊕ *museicivicifiorentini.comune.fi.it* ☒ *From €13.*

Piazza della Repubblica

PLAZA/SQUARE | The square marks the site of an ancient forum, which was the core of the original Roman settlement and which was replaced in the Middle Ages by the Mercato Vecchio (Old Market). The current piazza, constructed between 1885 and 1895 as a neoclassical showpiece, is lined with outdoor cafés, affording an excellent opportunity for people-watching. ☒ *Florence.*

Piazza della Signoria

PLAZA/SQUARE | Here, in 1497 and in 1498, the famous "bonfire of the vanities" took place, when the fanatical Dominican friar Savonarola induced his followers to hurl their worldly goods into the flames. It was also here, a year later, that he was hanged as a heretic and, ironically, burned. A plaque in the piazza pavement marks the spot of his execution.

Cellini's famous bronze *Perseus*, shown holding the severed head of Medusa, is among the most important sculptures in the Loggia dei Lanzi. Also noteworthy are *The Rape of the Sabine Women* and *Hercules and the Centaur*, both late-16th-century works by Giambologna (1529–1608). But it's the Neptune Fountain, created between 1550 and 1575 by Bartolomeo Ammannati, that dominates the square. The Florentines call it "il Biancone," which may be translated as "the big white man" or "the big white lump." Giambologna's equestrian statue, to the left of the fountain, portrays Grand Duke Cosimo I. Occupying the steps of the Palazzo Vecchio is a copy of Michelangelo's *David*, as well as Baccio Bandinelli's *Hercules*. ☒ *Florence.*

Ponte Vecchio (*Old Bridge*)

BRIDGE | This charmingly simple bridge was built in 1345 to replace an earlier one that was swept away by a flood. Its shops first housed butchers, then grocers, blacksmiths, and other merchants. But, in 1593, the Medici grand duke Ferdinando I (1549–1609), whose private corridor linking the Medici palace (Palazzo Pitti) with the Medici offices (the Uffizi) crossed the bridge atop the shops, decided that all this plebeian commerce under his feet was unseemly. So he threw out the butchers and blacksmiths and installed 41 goldsmiths and eight jewelers. The bridge has been devoted solely to these two trades ever since.

The Corridoio Vasariano (☒ *Piazzale degli Uffizi 6, Piazza della Signoria* ☎ *055/294883*), the private Medici elevated passageway, was built by Vasari in 1565. Though the ostensible reason for its construction was one of security, it was more likely designed so that the Medici family wouldn't have to walk amid the commoners. Take a moment to study the Ponte Santa Trinita, the next bridge downriver, from either the bridge or the corridor. It was designed by Bartolomeo Ammannati in 1567 (probably from sketches by Michelangelo), blown up by the retreating Germans during World War II, and painstakingly reconstructed after the war. The view *from* the Ponte Santa Trinita is also beautiful, which might explain why so many young lovers hang out there. ☒ *Florence.*

San Michele Visdomini

CHURCH | Aficionados of 16th-century mannerism should stop in this church, which has a *Sacra Conversazione* by Jacopo Pontormo (1494–1556). The early work, said by Vasari to have been executed on paper, is in dire need of a cleaning. Its palette is somewhat bereft of the lively colors typically associated with Pontormo. ☒ *Via dei Servi at Via Bufalini, Duomo* ☒ *Free.*

🍴 Restaurants

Birreria Centrale

$$ | ECLECTIC | The feel here is more Munich beer hall than Florentine trattoria; indeed, although the menu lists plenty of Italian dishes, it also emphasizes sausages and sauerkraut. Heavy wooden tables are set closely together, and copies of 19th-century paintings adorn the intensely yellow walls, along with two frescoed Michelangelesque nudes that cavort over a brick arch. **Known for:** copious portions; cheerful staff; outdoor seating. $ *Average main: €16* ✉ *Piazza Cimatori 1/r, Duomo* ☎ *055/211915* ⊕ *www.birreria-centrale.it* ⊘ *Closed Sun.*

Coquinarius

$$ | ITALIAN | This rustically elegant space, which has served many purposes over the past 600 years, offers some of the tastiest food in town at great prices. It's the perfect place to come if you aren't sure what you're hungry for, as they offer a little bit of everything: salad lovers will have a hard time choosing from among the lengthy list (the Scozzese, with poached chicken, avocado, and bacon, is a winner); those with a yen for pasta will face agonizing choices (the ravioli with pecorino and pears is particularly good). **Known for:** inconsistent service; reasonably priced wine list; marvelous salads. $ *Average main: €18* ✉ *Via delle Oche 15/r, Duomo* ☎ *055/230–2153* ⊕ *www.coquinarius.it* ⊘ *Closed Sun.*

Gucci Giardino 25

$$ | ITALIAN | Piazza Signoria has a new-as-of-February 2022 hotspot. Breakfast, light lunches (where the dishes have fanciful name), dessert, and afternoon tea are all possibilities. **Known for:** closes after midnight; chic setting in a trendy space; opens early. $ *Average main: €16* ✉ *Piazza della Signoria 37/r, Piazza della Signoria* ⊕ *guccigarden.gucci.com.*

★ Gucci Osteria

$$$ | FUSION | Chef, artist, and visionary Massimo Bottura has joined forces with the creative folk at Gucci to develop a marvelous menu that is both classic and innovative. Though he trained with Ducasse and Adrià, his major influence was his grandmother's cooking. **Known for:** outdoor seating in one of Florence's most beautiful squares; an ever-changing menu; tortellini in crema di Parmigiano Reggiano. $ *Average main: €35* ✉ *Piazza della Signoria 10, Piazza della Signoria* ☎ *055/7592–7038* ⊕ *guccigarden.gucci.com.*

Le Mossacce

$ | TUSCAN | Come to this tiny, cramped, and boisterous place for hearty, stick-to-your-ribs Florentine dishes such as *ribollita* (Tuscan bread soup). Seating is communal, with diners sharing big, straw-covered flasks of wine; service is prompt and efficient; and two nimble cooks with impeccable timing staff the small kitchen. **Known for:** frequented by locals; generous portions; authentic home cooking. $ *Average main: €10* ✉ *Via del Proconsolo 55/r, Duomo* ☎ *055/294361* ⊕ *www.trattorialemossacce.it* ⊘ *Closed Sat.*

Ora d'Aria

$$$$ | MODERN ITALIAN | The name means "Hour of Air" and refers to the time of day when prisoners were let outside for fresh air—alluding to the fact that this gem began life across the street from an old prison. In the kitchen, gifted chef Marco Stabile turns out exquisite Tuscan classics as well as more fanciful dishes, which are as beautiful as they are delicious. **Known for:** lunchtime tapas menu; graceful staff; unusual food combinations. $ *Average main: €40* ✉ *Via Georgofili 11/r, Piazza della Signoria* ☎ *055/200–1699* ⊕ *www.oradariaristorante.com* ⊘ *Closed Sun. No lunch.*

Ristorante Frescobaldi Firenze

$$$ | TUSCAN | The Frescobaldi family has run a vineyard for more than 700 years, and this swanky establishment offers tasty and sumptuous fare to accompany some seriously fine wines. The menu is typically Tuscan, but turned up a notch or two: the *faraona in umido con l'uva* (stewed guinea fowl with grapes) comes with a side of feather-light mashed potatoes. **Known for:** fine fish options; vegans will not go hungry; seasonal ingredients used in creative ways. $ *Average main: €28* ⊠ *Piazza della Signoria 31, Piazza della Signoria* ☎ *055/284724* ⊕ *www. frescobaldifirenze.it* ⊗ *Closed Mon. No lunch Sun.*

★ Rivoire

$$ | ITALIAN | One of the best spots in Florence for people-watching offers stellar service, light snacks, and terrific aperitivi. It's been around since the 1860s, and has been famous for its hot and cold chocolate (with or without cream) for more than a century. **Known for:** the view on the piazza; friendly bartenders; hot chocolate. $ *Average main: €15* ⊠ *Via Vacchereccia 4/r, Piazza della Signoria* ☎ *055/214412* ⊕ *rivoire.it/ en* ⊗ *Closed Mon.*

🍽 Coffee and Quick Bites

Caffè delle Carrozze

$ | ITALIAN | FAMILY | Around the corner from the Uffizi and practically at the foot of the Ponte Vecchio, this café is a great spot to take a break and enjoy a sandwich or a gelato. Of its many terrific offerings, the chocolate-chip laced coffee flavor is especially good. **Known for:** outdoor seating looking onto the Ponte Vecchio; sandwiches; flavorful ice cream. $ *Average main: €3* ⊠ *Piazza del Pesce 3–5/r, Piazza della Signoria* ☎ *055/239–6810* ▭ *No credit cards.*

Cantinetta dei Verrazzano

$ | WINE BAR | Although there are some serious wine offerings at this spot in the heart of the centro storico, it's also a good place for tasty breakfast baked treats and light lunches. **Known for:** outdoor seating; good coffee; delicious breads and cakes. $ *Average main: €13* ⊠ *Via dei Tavolini 18/20/r, Piazza della Signoria* ☎ *055/268590* ⊕ *www.verrazzano.com/la-cantinetta-in-firenze.*

Gelateria Carabe

$ | ICE CREAM | FAMILY | Specializing in things Sicilian, this shop is known for its tart and flavorful *granitàs* (flavored ices), which are great thirst-quenchers. It's also a great place to grab a gelato after seeing Michelangelo's *David*. **Known for:** some of the best gelato around; close to the Accademia; no-frills shop. $ *Average main: €3* ⊠ *Via Ricasoli 60/r, San Marco* ☎ *055/289476* ⊕ *www.ilparcocarabe.it* ▭ *No credit cards.*

★ I Fratellini

$ | WINE BAR | A hop, skip, and a jump from Orsanmichele in the centro storico and in existence since 1875, I Fratellini sells wines by the glass and has a lengthy list of panini, including pecorino with sundried tomatoes and spicy wild-boar salami with goat cheese. There are no tables: this is strictly a sandwich counter. **Known for:** great prices; charming sandwich-makers; creative sandwich combinations. $ *Average main: €4* ⊠ *Via dei Cimatori 38/r, Piazza della Signoria* ☎ *055/239–6096.*

★ 'ino

$ | ITALIAN | This is the perfect place to grab a bite and/or a glass of wine after a visit to the nearby Uffizi. Only the very best ingredients go into owner Alessandro Frassica's delectable panini. **Known for:** delicious bread; top-notch ingredients; interesting panini combinations. $ *Average main: €8* ⊠ *Via dei Georgofili 3/r–7/r, Piazza della Signoria* ☎ *055/214154* ⊕ *www.inofirenze.com* ⊗ *Closed Mon.*

★ Perché No!

$ | **ICE CREAM** | **FAMILY** | What many consider the best gelateria in the centro storico embodies the "practice makes perfect" adage. It's been making ice cream since 1939. **Known for:** unusual flavors and vegan options; one of the oldest gelaterias in the city; gelati made daily. [$] *Average main: €3* ✉ *Via dei Tavolini 19r, Duomo* ☎ *055/239–8969* 🌐 *www.facebook.com/GelateriaPercheNo.*

Hotels

Hermitage

$$ | **HOTEL** | Some rooms here have views of the Palazzo Vecchio, and others of the Arno; the rooftop terrace, where you can have breakfast or an aperitivo, is decked with flowers. **Pros:** views; enviable position a stone's throw from the Ponte Vecchio; friendly staff. **Cons:** street noise sometimes a problem; might be time for a refurbishing; short flight of stairs to reach elevator. [$] *Rooms from: €151* ✉ *Vicolo Marzio 1, Piazza della Signoria* ☎ *055/287216* 🌐 *www.hermitagehotel.com* 🛏 *28 rooms* 🍴 *No Meals.*

Hotel degli Orafi

$$$$ | **HOTEL** | A key scene in *A Room with a View* was shot in this pensione, which is today a luxury hotel adorned with chintz and marble. **Pros:** stellar Arno views; quiet location during the evenings; rooftop bar. **Cons:** somewhat pricey; on the path of many tour groups during the day; some street noise in river-facing rooms. [$] *Rooms from: €310* ✉ *Lungarno Archibusieri 4, Piazza della Signoria* ☎ *055/26622* 🌐 *www.hoteldegliorafi.it* 🛏 *50 rooms* 🍴 *Free Breakfast.*

Hotel Helvetia and Bristol

$$$$ | **HOTEL** | From the cozy yet sophisticated lobby with its stone columns to the guest rooms decorated with prints, you might feel as if you're a guest in a sophisticated manor house. **Pros:** central location; old-world charm; excellent restaurant. **Cons:** books up quickly; breakfast is not always included in the price of a room; rooms facing the street get some noise. [$] *Rooms from: €700* ✉ *Via dei Pescioni 2, Piazza della Repubblica* ☎ *055/26651* 🌐 *www.starhotelscollezione.com* 🛏 *89 rooms* 🍴 *Free Breakfast.*

Hotel Renaissance

$$ | **HOTEL** | Nestled in an old building just a stone's throw from the main civic square (Piazza Signoria), this charming little boutique hotel offers peace in quiet elegance. **Pros:** the staff; the location; the sumptuous breakfast. **Cons:** books up quickly; some street noise in some rooms; steps up to the elevator. [$] *Rooms from: €150* ✉ *Via della Condotta 4, Piazza della Signoria* ☎ *055/213996* 🌐 *www.hotelrenaissancefirenze.com* 🛏 *9 rooms* 🍴 *Free Breakfast.*

★ In Piazza della Signoria

$$$ | **B&B/INN** | In this home that is part of a 15th-century palazzo, a cozy feeling permeates the charming rooms, all of which are uniquely decorated and lovingly furnished; some have damask curtains, others fanciful frescoes in the bathroom. **Pros:** marvelous staff; some rooms easily accommodate three; tasty breakfast with a view of Piazza della Signoria. **Cons:** books up quickly during high season; some of the rooms have steps up into showers and bathtubs; short flight of stairs to reach elevator. [$] *Rooms from: €300* ✉ *Via dei Magazzini 2, Piazza della Signoria* ☎ *055/239–9546* 🌐 *www.boutiquehotelinpiazza.com* 🛏 *13 rooms* 🍴 *Free Breakfast.*

★ Palazzo Niccolini al Duomo

$$$$ | **HOTEL** | The graceful Marchesa Ginevra Niccolini di Camugliano has taken the palazzo of her husband's family (acquired by an ancestor in 1532) and turned it into a luxurious place that still manages to evoke a cozy, yet highly sophisticated, home. **Pros:** steps away from the Duomo; the well-appointed honor bar; the hardwood floors. **Cons:** some hallway noise a possibility; in high season, books up quickly; street

noise sometimes a problem. **$** *Rooms from: €310* ✉ *Via dei Servi 2, Florence* ☎ *055/282412* ⊕ *www.niccolinidomepalace.com* 🛏 *14 rooms* ❍❙ *No Meals.*

Palazzo Vecchietti

$$$$ | **HOTEL** | If you're looking for a swank setting, and the possibility of staying in for a meal (each room has a tiny kitchenette), look no further than this hotel which, while thoroughly modern, dates to the 15th century. **Pros:** great service; public room has a Renaissance fireplace and high ceilings; central location. **Cons:** it's expensive; some street noise a possibility; no restaurant. **$** *Rooms from: €399* ✉ *Via degli Strozzi 4, Duomo* ☎ *055/230–2802* ⊕ *www.palazzovecchietti.com* 🛏 *14 rooms* ❍❙ *Free Breakfast.*

Sani Tourist House

$ | **B&B/INN** | Hosts Elizabeth and Remi have taken their former no-frills accommodation and spruced it up, adding such amenities as air-conditioning and the occasional private bath. **Pros:** good deals for single travelers, even lower rates off-season; central location in a quiet cul-de-sac; kind hosts. **Cons:** books up quickly; not all rooms have en suite bathrooms; no reception. **$** *Rooms from: €60* ✉ *Piazza dei Giuochi 1, Duomo* ☎ *335/822–4133* ⊕ *www.sanibnb.it* 🛏 *6 rooms* ❍❙ *No Meals.*

🎭 Performing Arts

British Institute of Florence

FILM | The British Institute of Florence runs several English-language film series; the programmer has a penchant for classic movies. Also on offer here are weekly lectures, courses, and a stunning library. ✉ *Palazzo Lanfredini, Lungarno Guicciardini 9, Lungarno South* ☎ *055/2677–8270* ⊕ *www.britishinstitute.it.*

Odeon Firenze

FILM | This magnificent art deco theater shows first-run English-language films throughout the week. ✉ *Piazza Strozzi 2, Piazza della Repubblica* ☎ *055/295051* ⊕ *www.odeonfirenze.com.*

Orchestra da Camera Fiorentina

MUSIC | This orchestra performs various concerts of classical music throughout the year at Orsanmichele, the grain-market–turned–church. ✉ *Via Monferrato 2, Piazza della Signoria* ☎ *055/783374* ⊕ *orchestradacamerafiorentina.it.*

Shopping

★ Bernardo

MEN'S CLOTHING | Come here for men's trousers, cashmere sweaters, and shirts with details like mother-of-pearl buttons. ✉ *Via Porta Rossa 87/r, Piazza della Repubblica* ☎ *055/283333* ⊕ *www.bernardofirenze.it.*

Cabó

MIXED CLOTHING | Missoni knitwear is the main draw at Cabó. ✉ *Via Porta Rossa 77–79/r, Piazza della Repubblica* ☎ *055/215774.*

Carlo Piccini

JEWELRY & WATCHES | Still in operation after four generations, this Florentine institution sells antique jewelry and makes pieces to order; you can also get old jewelry reset here. ✉ *Ponte Vecchio 31/r, Piazza della Signoria* ☎ *055/294768* ⊕ *www.fratellipiccini.com* ❍ *Closed Sun. and Mon.*

Diesel

MIXED CLOTHING | Trendy Diesel started in Vicenza; its gear is on the "must have" list of many Italian teens. ✉ *Via degli Speziali 16/r, Piazza della Signoria* ☎ *055/239–9963* ⊕ *www.diesel.com.*

Gherardi

JEWELRY & WATCHES | Florence's king of coral, Gherardi has the city's largest selection of finely crafted pieces, as well as cultured pearls, jade, and turquoise. ✉ *Ponte Vecchio 36/r, Piazza della Signoria* ☎ *055/211809* ⊕ *www.gherardigioielli.it.*

★ il Papiro

STATIONERY | One of several locations in the historic center, this place has been making that classic Florentine peacock paper for decades. ⊠ *Via de' Tavolini 13/r, Duomo* ☎ *055/213823* ⊕ *ilpapirofirenze. eu/en.*

Liu-Jo

WOMEN'S CLOTHING | For something to wear for a night out, check out Liu-Jo. ⊠ *Via Calimala 14/r, Piazza della Repubblica* ☎ *055/264–5881* ⊕ *www.liujo.com.*

Luisa Via Roma

MIXED CLOTHING | The surreal window displays hint at the trendy yet tasteful clothing inside this fascinating *alta moda* (high-style) boutique, which stocks the world's top designers as well as Luisa's own line. ⊠ *Via Roma 19–21/r, Duomo* ☎ *055/906–4116* ⊕ *www.luisaviaroma. com.*

Mandragora Art Store

MUSEUM SHOP | This is one of the first attempts in Florence to cash in on the museum-store craze. Look for reproductions of valued works of art and jewelry. ⊠ *Piazza del Duomo 50/r, Duomo* ☎ *055/265–4384* ⊕ *www.mandragora.it.*

Mercato dei Fiori (*Flower Markete*)

MARKET | Every Thursday morning from September through June the covered loggia in Piazza della Repubblica hosts this lively market—a riot of plants, flowers, and difficult-to-find herbs. ⊠ *Piazza della Repubblica, Florence.*

Mercato del Porcellino

MARKET | FAMILY | If you're looking for cheery, inexpensive trinkets to take home, roam through the stalls under the loggia of the Mercato del Porcellino. ⊠ *Via Por Santa Maria at Via Porta Rossa, Piazza della Repubblica.*

Oro Due

JEWELRY & WATCHES | Gold jewelry and other beauteous objects are priced according to the level of craftsmanship and the value of gold bullion that day. ⊠ *Via Lambertesca 12/r, Piazza della Signoria* ☎ *055/292143.*

Patrizia Pepe

WOMEN'S CLOTHING | The Florentine designer has clothes for mostly really thin young people, especially for women with a tiny streak of rebelliousness. Sizes run extremely small. ⊠ *Piazza San Giovanni 12/r, Duomo* ☎ *055/264–5056* ⊕ *www.patriziapepe.com.*

★ Pegna

FOOD | This shop has been selling both Italian and non-Italian food since 1860. If you're tired of mozzarella and feel the need for some cheddar, this is the place to find it. ⊠ *Via dello Studio 8, Duomo* ☎ *055/282701* ⊕ *pegna.sangiustosrl.com.*

★ Penko

JEWELRY & WATCHES | Renaissance goldsmiths provide the inspiration for this dazzling jewelry with a contemporary feel. ⊠ *Via Ferdinando Zannetti 14–16/r, Duomo* ☎ *055/211661* ⊕ *www.paolopenko.com* ☉ *Closed Sun. and Mon.*

Quercioli & Lucherini

LINGERIE | This shop has been vending high-quality clothing—the kind that goes next to bare skin—since 1895. Remember that luxury comes at a price. ⊠ *Via Porta Rossa 45/r, Piazza della Repubblica.*

San Lorenzo

A sculptor, painter, architect, and poet, Florentine native son Michelangelo was a consummate genius, and some of his finest creations remain in his hometown. The Biblioteca Medicea Laurenziana is perhaps his most fanciful work of architecture. A key to understanding Michelangelo's genius can be found in the magnificent Cappelle Medicee, where both his sculptural and architectural prowess can be clearly seen.

Planned frescoes were never completed, sadly, for they would have shown in one space the artistic triple threat that he certainly was. The towering yet graceful *David,* perhaps his most famous work, resides in the Galleria dell'Accademia.

■TIP➜ **After seeing the Basilica di San Lorenzo, visit the other area churches and museums, which tend to close early (the Museo di San Marco, for instance, closes at 1:30 on weekdays), before exploring the market, which stays open until 7 pm.**

Sights

Basilica di San Lorenzo
CHURCH | Filippo Brunelleschi designed this basilica, as well as that of Santo Spirito in the Oltrarno, in the 15th century. He never lived to see either finished. The two interiors are similar in design and effect. San Lorenzo, however, has a grid of dark, inlaid marble lines on the floor, which considerably heightens the dramatic effect. The grid makes the rigorous geometry of the interior immediately visible, and is an illuminating lesson on the laws of perspective. If you stand in the middle of the nave at the church entrance, on the line that stretches to the high altar, every element in the church—the grid, the nave columns, the side aisles, the coffered nave ceiling—seems to march inexorably toward a hypothetical vanishing point beyond the high altar, exactly as in a single-point-perspective painting. Brunelleschi's Sagrestia Vecchia (Old Sacristy) has stucco decorations by Donatello; it's at the end of the left transept. ⊠ *Piazza San Lorenzo, San Lorenzo* ⊕ *sanlorenzo-firenze.it* ✉ *€7* ⊗ *Closed Sun.*

Biblioteca Medicea Laurenziana
(*Laurentian Library*)
LIBRARY | Michelangelo the architect was every bit as original as Michelangelo the sculptor. Unlike Brunelleschi (the architect of the Spedale degli Innocenti), however, he wasn't obsessed with proportion and perfect geometry. He was interested in experimentation, invention, and the expression of a personal vision that was at times highly idiosyncratic.

It was never more idiosyncratic than in the Laurentian Library, begun in 1524 and finished in 1568 by Bartolomeo Ammannati. Its famous *vestibolo,* a strangely shaped anteroom, has had scholars scratching their heads for centuries. In a space more than two stories high, why did Michelangelo limit his use of columns and pilasters to the upper two-thirds of the wall? Why didn't he rest them on strong pedestals instead of on huge, decorative curlicue scrolls, which rob them of all visual support? Why did he recess them into the wall, which makes them look weaker still? The architectural elements here do not stand firm and strong and tall as inside San Lorenzo next door; instead, they seem to be pressed into the wall as if into putty, giving the room a soft, rubbery look that is one of the strangest effects ever achieved by 16th-century architecture. It's almost as if Michelangelo intentionally flouted the conventions of the High Renaissance to see what kind of bizarre, mannered effect might result.

His innovations were tremendously influential, and produced a period of architectural experimentation. As his contemporary Giorgio Vasari put it, "Artisans have been infinitely and perpetually indebted to him because he broke the bonds and chains of a way of working that had become habitual by common usage."

The anteroom's staircase (best viewed straight on), which emerges from the library with the visual force of an unstoppable lava flow, has been exempted from the criticism, however. In its highly sculptural conception and execution, it is quite simply one of the most original and fluid staircases in the world. Note that this site has seen temporary closures. Check on its status before visiting. ⊠ *Piazza San Lorenzo 9, entrance to left of San Lorenzo, San Lorenzo* ⊕ *www.bmlonline. it* ✉ *Special exhibitions €3* ⊗ *Check ahead on opening days and times as this site has seen temporary closures.*

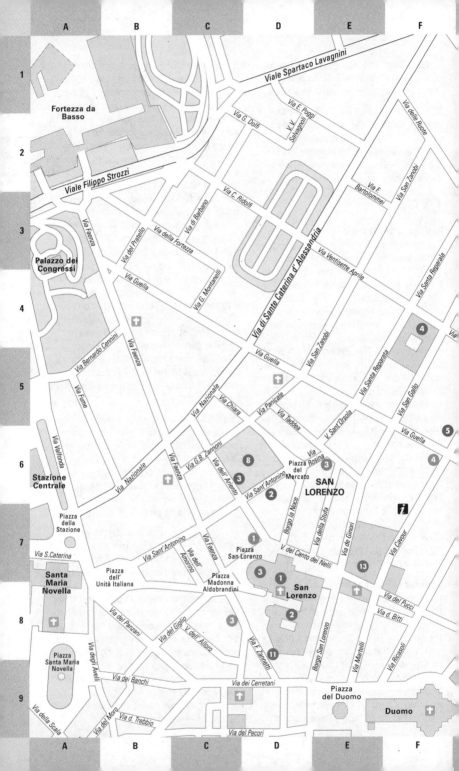

San Lorenzo

Sights ▼

1 Basilica di San Lorenzo **D7**
2 Biblioteca Medicea
   Laurenziana **D8**
3 Cappelle Medicee **D7**
4 Cenacolo di Sant'Apollonia **F4**
5 Chiostro dello Scalzo **H3**
6 Galleria dell'Accademia **H6**
7 Giardino dei Semplici **I4**
8 Mercato Centrale **D6**
9 Museo Archeologico **I6**
10 Museo dell'Opificio delle
   Pietre Dure **H6**
11 Museo di Casa Martelli **D8**
12 Museo di San Marco **H4**
13 Palazzo Medici-Riccardi **E7**
14 Santa Maria Maddalena
   dei Pazzi **J7**
15 Santissima Annunziata **I6**
16 Spedale degli Innocenti **I6**

Restaurants ▼

1 da Sergio **D7**
2 La Mescita **H7**
3 Mario **E6**

Quick Bites ▼

1 Alfio e Beppe **G5**
2 Casa del Vino **D6**
3 da Nerbone **C6**
4 Pugi **G5**
5 Shake **F6**

Hotels ▼

1 Antica Dimora Firenze **H3**
2 Antica Dimora Johlea **H2**
3 Firenze Number Nine **C8**
4 Il Guelfo Bianco **F6**

KEY

1 *Exploring Sights*
1 *Restaurants*
1 *Quick Bites*
1 *Hotels*
🛈 *Tourist Information*

Cappelle Medicee (*Medici Chapels*)
CHURCH | This magnificent complex includes the Cappella dei Principi, the Medici chapel and mausoleum that was begun in 1605 and kept marble workers busy for several hundred years, and the Sagrestia Nuova (New Sacristy), designed by Michelangelo and so called to distinguish it from Brunelleschi's Sagrestia Vecchia (Old Sacristy) in San Lorenzo.

Michelangelo received the commission for the New Sacristy in 1520 from Cardinal Giulio de' Medici (1478–1534), who later became Pope Clement VII. The cardinal wanted a new burial chapel for his cousins Giuliano, Duke of Nemours (1478–1534), and Lorenzo, Duke of Urbino (1492–1519). He also wanted to honor his father, also named Giuliano, and his uncle, Lorenzo il Magnifico. The result was a tour de force of architecture and sculpture.

Architecturally, Michelangelo was as original and inventive here as ever, but it is, quite properly, the powerfully sculpted tombs that dominate the room. The scheme is allegorical: on the tomb on the right are figures representing Day and Night, and on the tomb to the left are figures representing Dawn and Dusk. Above them are idealized sculptures of the two men, usually interpreted to represent the active life and the contemplative life. But the allegorical meanings are secondary; what is most important is the intense presence of the sculptural figures and the force with which they hit the viewer. ⊠ *Piazza di Madonna degli Aldobrandini, San Lorenzo* ☎ *055/294883 reservations* ⊕ *www.cappellemedicee. it* ⊠ *€9* ☉ *Closed Tues., and 1st, 3rd, and 5th Sun. of month.*

Cenacolo di Sant'Apollonia
CHURCH | The frescoes in the refectory of a former Benedictine nunnery were painted in sinewy style by Andrea del Castagno, a follower of Masaccio (1401–28). The *Last Supper* is a powerful version of this typical refectory theme. From the entrance, walk around the corner to Via San Gallo 25 and take a peek at the lovely 15th-century cloister that belonged to the same monastery but is now part of the University of Florence. ⊠ *Via XXVII Aprile 1, San Marco* ☎ *055/294883* ⊕ *www.polomuseale. firenze.it* ⊠ *Free* ☉ *Closed 1st, 3rd, and 5th Sat. and Sun. of month.*

Chiostro dello Scalzo
RELIGIOUS BUILDING | Often overlooked, this small, peaceful 16th-century cloister was frescoed in grisaille by Andrea del Sarto (1486–1530) and Franciabigio with scenes from the life of St. John the Baptist, Florence's patron saint. Note that temporary closures are a possibility at this site, so check on accessibility before visiting. ⊠ *Via Cavour 69, San Marco* ☎ *055/294883* ⊕ *www.polomuseale. firenze.it* ⊠ *Free* ☉ *Check ahead on temporary closures and possible opening days and times.*

Galleria dell'Accademia
(*Accademia Gallery*)
ART MUSEUM | FAMILY | The collection of Florentine paintings, dating from the 13th to 18th century, is largely unremarkable, but the sculptures by Michelangelo are worth the price of admission. The unfinished *Slaves,* fighting their way out of their marble prisons, were meant for the tomb of Michelangelo's overly demanding patron, Pope Julius II (1443–1513). But the focal point is the original *David,* moved here from Piazza della Signoria in 1873. It was commissioned in 1501 by the Opera del Duomo (Cathedral Works Committee), which gave the 26-year-old sculptor a leftover block of marble that had been ruined 40 years earlier by two other sculptors. Michelangelo's success with the block was so dramatic that the city showered him with honors, and the Opera del Duomo voted to build him a house and a studio in which to live and work.

The bounty at Florence's Mercato Centrale

Today, *David* is beset not by Goliath but by tourists, and seeing the statue at all—much less really studying it—can be a trial. Save yourself a long wait in line by reserving tickets in advance. A plexiglass barrier surrounds the sculpture, following a 1991 attack on it by a self-proclaimed hammer-wielding art anarchist who, luckily, inflicted only a few minor nicks on the toes. The statue is not quite what it seems. It is so poised and graceful and alert—so miraculously alive—that it is often considered the definitive sculptural embodiment of High Renaissance perfection. But its true place in the history of art is a bit more complicated.

As Michelangelo well knew, the Renaissance painting and sculpture that preceded his work were deeply concerned with ideal form. Perfection of proportion was the ever-sought Holy Grail; during the Renaissance, ideal proportion was equated with ideal beauty, and ideal beauty was equated with spiritual perfection. But *David*, despite its supremely calm and dignified pose, departs from these ideals. Michelangelo didn't give the statue perfect proportions. The head is slightly too large for the body, the arms are too large for the torso, and the hands are dramatically large for the arms.

The work was originally commissioned to adorn the exterior of the Duomo and was intended to be seen from below and at a distance. Michelangelo knew exactly what he was doing, calculating that the perspective of the viewer would be such that, in order for the statue to appear proportioned, the upper body, head, and arms would have to be bigger, as they would be farther away. But he also sculpted it to express and embody, as powerfully as possible in a single figure, an entire biblical story. David's hands *are* big, but so was Goliath, and these are the hands that slew him.

■TIP➜ **Music lovers might want to check out the Museo delgli Instrumenti Musicali, also within the Accademia; its Stradivarius is the main attraction.** ✉ *Via Ricasoli 60, San Marco* ☎ *055/294883 reservations, 055/238-8609 gallery* ⊕ *www.polomuseale.firenze.it* ☎ *€12* ⊙ *Closed Mon.*

Giardino dei Semplici

GARDEN | Created by Cosimo I in 1550, this delightful garden was designed by favorite Medici architect Niccolò Tribolo. Many of the plants here have been grown since the 16th century. Springtime, especially May, is a particularly beautiful time to visit, as multitudes of azaleas create a riot of color. ⊠ *Via Pier Micheli 3, San Marco* ☎ *055/275–6799* ⊕ *www.ortobotanicoitalia.it* 🎫 *€3* ⊘ *Closed Mon.*

★ Mercato Centrale

MARKET | FAMILY | Some of the food at this huge, two-story market hall is remarkably exotic. The ground floor contains meat and cheese stalls, as well as some very good bars that have panini. The upstairs food hall is eerily reminiscent of food halls everywhere, but the quality of the food served more than makes up for this. The downstairs market is closed on Sunday; the upstairs food hall is always open. ⊠ *Piazza del Mercato Centrale, San Lorenzo* ☎ *239–9798* ⊕ *www.mercatocentrale.it.*

Museo Archeologico

(*Archaeological Museum*)
HISTORY MUSEUM | FAMILY | Of the Etruscan, Egyptian, and Greco-Roman antiquities here, the Etruscan collection is particularly notable—one of the most important in Italy (the other being in Turin). The famous bronze *Chimera* was discovered without its tail, which is a 16th-century reconstruction by Cellini. If you're traveling with kids, they might particularly enjoy the small mummy collection. Those with a fondness for gardens should visit on Saturday morning, when the tiny but eminently pleasurable garden is open for tours. If you're going to the Uffizi, hang on to your ticket, as admission to this museum is free. ⊠ *Piazza Santissima Annunziata 9/b, Santissima Annunziata* ☎ *055/23575* ⊕ *www.polomusealetoscana.beniculturali.it* 🎫 *€8* ⊘ *Closed 2nd, 3rd, 4th, and 5th Sun. of month.*

Museo dell'Opificio delle Pietre Dure

ART MUSEUM | Adjacent to this fascinating small museum is an *opificio*, or workshop, that Ferdinando I established in 1588 to train craftsmen in the art of working with precious and semiprecious stones and marble (*pietre dure* means hard stones). Four hundred–plus years later, the workshop is renowned as a center for the restoration of mosaics and inlays in semiprecious stones. The museum is highly informative and includes some magnificent late-Renaissance examples of this highly specialized and beautiful craft. If you're going to the Uffizi, do keep your ticket, as entrance to this museum is free. ⊠ *Via degli Alfani 78, San Marco* ☎ *055/26511* ⊕ *www.opificiodellepietredure.it* 🎫 *€4* ⊘ *Closed Sun.*

Museo di Casa Martelli

HISTORIC HOME | The wealthy Martelli family, long associated with the all-powerful Medici, lived, from the 16th century, in this palace on a quiet street near the Basilica of San Lorenzo. The last Martelli died in 1986, and, in October 2009, the *casa-museo* (house-museum) opened to the public. It's the only nonreconstructed example of such a house in all of Florence, and for that reason alone it's worth a visit. The family collected art, and while most of the stuff is B-list, a few gems by Beccafumi, Salvatore Rosa, and Piero di Cosimo adorn the walls. Reservations are essential, and you will be shown the glories of this place by well-informed, English-speaking guides. Tours are available Saturday mornings on the hour. An €18 ticket, good for 72 hours, allows entrance to the Bargello, Cappelle Medicee, Palazzo Davanzati, and Orsanmichele. ⊠ *Via Zanetti 8, San Lorenzo* ☎ *055/294883* ⊕ *www.polomuseale.firenze.it* 🎫 *€18* ⊘ *Closed Sun.–Fri.* ♿ *Reservations essential.*

Museo di San Marco

ART MUSEUM | A former Dominican convent adjacent to the church of San Marco houses this museum, which contains many stunning works by Fra Angelico (circa 1400–55), the Dominican friar famous for his piety as well as for his painting. When the friars' cells were restructured between 1439 and 1444, he decorated many of them with frescoes meant to spur religious contemplation. His unostentatious and direct paintings exalt the simple beauties of the contemplative life. Don't miss the famous *Annunciation*, on the upper floor, and the works in the gallery off the cloister as you enter. Here you can see his beautiful *Last Judgment*; as usual, the tortures of the damned are far more inventive and interesting than the pleasures of the redeemed. ⊠ *Piazza San Marco 1, San Lorenzo* ☎ *055/294883* ⊕ *www.polomusealetoscana.beniculturali.it* 🎟 *€8* 🕓 *Closed 1st, 3rd, and 5th Sun. and 2nd and 4th Mon. of month.*

Palazzo Medici-Riccardi

CASTLE/PALACE | The main attraction of this palace, begun in 1444 by Michelozzo for Cosimo de' Medici, is the interior chapel, the Cappella dei Magi, on the *piano nobile* (main floor). Painted on its walls is Benozzo Gozzoli's famous *Procession of the Magi*, finished in 1460 and celebrating both the birth of Christ and the greatness of the Medici family. Gozzoli wasn't a revolutionary painter and today is considered by some not quite first-rate because of his technique, which was old-fashioned even for his day. Gozzoli's gift, however, was for entrancing the eye, not challenging the mind, and in this regard his success here is beyond question. Entering the chapel is like walking into the middle of a magnificently illustrated children's storybook, and this beauty makes it one of the most enjoyable rooms in the city. Keep in mind that the admission fee is a bit pricey when you consider that visits are limited to 15 minutes and the chapel is the only interesting thing to see in the building. ⊠ *Via Cavour 1, San Lorenzo* ☎ *055/276–8224* ⊕ *www.palazzomediciriccardi.it* 🎟 *€10* 🕓 *Closed Wed.*

Santa Maria Maddalena dei Pazzi

CHURCH | One of Florence's hidden treasures, a cool and composed *Crucifixion* by Perugino (circa 1445/50–1523), is in the chapter house of the monastery below this church. Here you can see the Virgin Mary and St. John the Evangelist with Mary Magdalene and saints Benedict and Bernard of Clairvaux posed against a simple but haunting landscape. The figure of Christ crucified occupies the center of this brilliantly hued fresco. Perugino's colors radiate—note the juxtaposition of the yellow-green cuff against the orange tones of Magdalene's robe. Entrance to this beauteous fresco is through the Liceo Michelangelo (a high school). Check on temporary closures, a possibility at this site, before visiting. ⊠ *Via della Colonna 9, Santa Croce* 🎟 *Suggested donation €1* 🕓 *Check on opening days and times as this site has experienced temporary closures.*

Santissima Annunziata

CHURCH | Dating from the mid-13th century, this church was restructured in 1447 by Michelozzo, who gave it an uncommon (and lovely) entrance cloister with frescoes by Andrea del Sarto (1486–1530), Pontormo (1494–1556), and Rosso Fiorentino (1494–1540). The interior is a rarity for Florence: an overwhelming example of baroque. But it's not really a fair example, because it's merely 17th-century baroque decoration applied willy-nilly to an earlier structure—exactly the sort of violent remodeling exercise that has given baroque a bad name.

The Cappella dell'Annunziata, immediately inside the entrance to the left, illustrates the point. The lower half, with its stately Corinthian columns and carved frieze bearing the Medici arms, was commissioned by Piero de' Medici in 1447; the upper half, with its erupting curves and impish sculpted cherubs, was added 200 years later. Fifteenth-century-fresco enthusiasts should also note the very fine *Holy Trinity with St. Jerome* in the second chapel on the left. Done by Andrea del Castagno (circa 1421–57), it shows a wiry and emaciated St. Jerome with Paula and Eustochium, two of his closest followers. This church, unlike many others in Florence, is highly active: please do not enter if Mass is in progress. ⊠ *Piazza di Santissima Annunziata, San Lorenzo* 🖃 *Free.*

Spedale degli Innocenti

ART MUSEUM | FAMILY | The building built by Brunelleschi in 1419 to serve as an orphanage takes the historical prize as the very first Renaissance building. Brunelleschi designed its portico with his usual rigor, constructing it from the two shapes he considered mathematically (and therefore philosophically and aesthetically) perfect: the square and the circle. Below the level of the arches, the portico encloses a row of perfect cubes; above the level of the arches, the portico encloses a row of intersecting hemispheres. The entire geometric scheme is articulated with Corinthian columns, capitals, and arches borrowed directly from antiquity.

At the time he designed the portico, Brunelleschi was also designing the interior of San Lorenzo, using the same basic ideas. But because the portico was finished before San Lorenzo, the Spedale degli Innocenti can claim the honor of ushering in Renaissance architecture. The 10 ceramic medallions depicting swaddled infants that decorate the portico are by Andrea della Robbia (1435–1525/28), done in about 1487.

Within the building is the small Museo degli Innocenti. Although most of the objects are minor works by major artists, they're still worth a look. Of note is Domenico Ghirlandaio's (1449–94) *Adorazione dei Magi* (*Adoration of the Magi*), executed in 1488. His use of color, and his eye for flora and fauna, shows

that art from north of the Alps made a great impression on him. ⊠ *Piazza di Santissima Annunziata 12, San Lorenzo* ☎ *055/20371* ⊕ *www.museodeglinnocenti.it* 🖃 *€13* ⊙ *Closed Tues.*

Restaurants

★ da Sergio

$ | TUSCAN | This restaurant just across the way from the Basilica of San Lorenzo and run by the Gozzi family since 1915 serves food that's as delicious as it is affordable. The menu short menu changes daily, though the *lombatina alla griglia* (grilled veal T-bone steak) is almost always available, and meat eaters should not miss it. **Known for:** terrific pastas; ever-changing menu; local favorite. 💲 *Average main: €10* ⊠ *Piazza San Lorenzo 8/r, San Lorenzo* ☎ *055/281941* ⊙ *Closed Sun. No dinner Mon.–Thurs.*

La Mescita

$ | TUSCAN | Come early (or late) to grab a seat at this tiny spot frequented by Florentine university students and businesspeople, who come to enjoy the day's primi (the lasagna is terrific), perhaps followed by the *polpettone* (meat loaf) and tomato sauce. Though seats are cramped, and the wine is no great shakes, the service is friendly, and the food hits the spot. **Known for:** delicious pastas at rock-bottom prices; jovial staff; its longevity (it's been around since the 1920s). 💲 *Average main: €9* ⊠ *Via degli Alfani 70/r, Florence* ☎ *347/795–1604* 🖃 *No credit cards* ⊙ *Closed Wed. No dinner.*

★ Mario

$ | TUSCAN | Florentines flock to this narrow, family-run trattoria near San Lorenzo to feast on Tuscan favorites served at simple tables under a wooden ceiling dating from 1536. A distinct cafeteria feel and genuine Florentine hospitality prevail: you'll be seated wherever there's room, which often means with strangers. **Known for:** festive atmosphere; roasted potatoes; grilled meats. $ *Average main: €13* ⊠ *Via Rosina 2/r, corner of Piazza del Mercato Centrale, San Lorenzo* ☎ *055/218550* ⊕ *www.trattoriamario.com* ⊗ *Closed Sun. and Aug. No dinner.*

Coffee and Quick Bites

Alfio e Beppe

$ | **ITALIAN** | Watch chickens roast over high flames while you decide which of the delightful side dishes you'd like to enjoy as well. Although this place is strictly takeout (there are no tables), it's open on Sunday when most places are not. **Known for:** delicious roasted potatoes; roast chicken to go; good ribs. $ *Average main: €9* ⊠ *Via Cavour 118–120/r, San Marco* ☎ *055/214108* ⊗ *Closed Sat.*

★ Casa del Vino

$ | **WINE BAR** | Come here for creative panini, such as *sgrombri e carciofini sott'olio* (mackerel and marinated baby artichokes), and an ever-changing list of significant wines by the glass. It also has a good selection of bottles to go. **Known for:** divine porchetta; lively local clientele; tasty crostini. $ *Average main: €5* ⊠ *Via dell'Ariento 16/r, San Lorenzo* ☎ *055/215609* ⊕ *www.casadelvino.it* ⊗ *Closed Sun.*

★ da Nerbone

$ | **TUSCAN** | This *tavola calda* (cafeteria) in the middle of the covered Mercato Centrale has been serving Florentines since 1872. Tasty primi and secondi are always available, as are *bollitos* (boiled beef sandwiches), but the cognoscenti come for the *panino con il lampredotto* (tripe sandwich)—best when it's prepared *bagnato* (with the bread quickly dipped in the tripe cooking liquid) and served slathered with the green and/or spicier red sauce. **Known for:** favorite dishes sell out fast; frequented by locals (and everyone else); tripe sandwich. $ *Average main: €10* ⊠ *Mercato San Lorenzo, Florence* ⊗ *Closed Sun. No dinner.*

Pugi

$ | **PIZZA** | **FAMILY** | Conveniently across the piazza from San Marco, Pugi sells the popular pizza *a taglio* (by the slice) as well as delicious focaccie. It's a great place to grab a quick lunch or snack. **Known for:** pizza by the slice; convenient location; great bread. $ *Average main: €3* ⊠ *Piazza San Marco 9/b, San Marco* ☎ *055/280981* ⊕ *www.fornopugi.it* ⊟ *No credit cards* ⊗ *Closed Sun.*

Shake

$ | **ITALIAN** | Handily located between Piazza San Marco and Piazza San Lorenzo, Shake serves up creative juices, tasty baked goods, wonderful salads, and great bowls. It's committed to sustainability and to keeping its carbon footprint small. **Known for:** remarkable way with juices (the De-Tox is especially good); courtyard seating; nice, cheerful staff. $ *Average main: €7* ⊠ *Via Camillo Cavour 67/69r, San Lorenzo* ☎ *055/051–5418* ⊕ *www.shakecafe.bio* ⊗ *Closed Wed.*

Hotels

Antica Dimora Firenze

$$ | **B&B/INN** | Each simply furnished room in this *residenza* (guesthouse) is painted a different pastel color—peach, rose, powder-blue—and double-glazed windows ensure a peaceful night's sleep. **Pros:** ample DVD library; honor bar with Antinori wines; complimentary coffee, tea, and fresh fruit available all day in the sitting room. **Cons:** some might consider it too small; might be too removed for some; books up quickly. $ *Rooms from: €160* ⊠ *Via San Gallo 72, San Marco* ☎ *055/462–7296* ⊕ *www.antichedimore-fiorentine.it* ⊟ *No credit cards* ⇄ *6 rooms* ⊚❙ *Free Breakfast.*

★ Antica Dimora Johlea

$$$ | **B&B/INN** | In addition to guest rooms with four-poster beds and sweeping drapes, this 19th-century palazzo has a charming, flower-filled terrace where you can sip a glass of wine while taking in a

view of Brunelleschi's cupola. **Pros:** great staff; honor bar; cheerful rooms. **Cons:** steps to breakfast room; staircase to roof terrace is narrow; staff goes home at 7:30. $ *Rooms from: €220 ⊠ Via San Gallo 80, San Marco* ☎ *055/463–3292* ⊕ *www.antichedimorefiorentine.it* ⇆ *6 rooms* ❘○❘ *Free Breakfast.*

Firenze Number Nine

$$$ | **HOTEL** | At this elegant hotel, swank reception rooms have comfortable couches and contemporary artwork, and guest rooms feature parquet floors, high ceilings, and furnishings that combine Scandinavian sleekness with the Italian love for fine fabric (think: damask draperies). **Pros:** historic center location; sumptuous breakfast; walk-in gym and spa. **Cons:** books up quickly; might be too trendy for some; some street noise. $ *Rooms from: €300 ⊠ Via del Conti 9, San Lorenzo* ☎ *055/293777* ⊕ *firenzenumbernine.com* ⇆ *45 rooms* ❘○❘ *Free Breakfast.*

Il Guelfo Bianco

$$ | **HOTEL** | The 15th-century building has all modern conveniences, but Renaissance charm still shines in the high-ceiling rooms. **Pros:** great staff; sumptuous breakfast; beautiful floors made of either parquet or marble. **Cons:** not all rooms are well lit; might be too removed for some; rooms facing the street can be noisy. $ *Rooms from: €150 ⊠ Via Cavour 29, San Marco* ☎ *055/288330* ⊕ *ilguelfobianco.it* ⇆ *40 rooms* ❘○❘ *Free Breakfast.*

🛍 Shopping

★ Baroni

FOOD | The cheese selection at Baroni may be the most comprehensive in Florence. It also sells high-quality truffle products, vinegars, and other delicacies, many of which are, or can be, packed for shipping. ⊠ *Mercato Central, enter at Via Signa, San Lorenzo* ☎ *055/289576* ⊕ *www.baronialimentari.it* ⊗ *Closed Sun.*

furò e punteruolo

LEATHER GOODS | Paolo Fattori and his wife, Luisa, handcraft exquisite, one-of-a-kind bags and other leather accessories at this one-room store and workshop. ⊠ *Via del Giglio 29/r, Florence* ☎ *055/013–0427* ⊕ *www.furoepunteruolo.com* ⊗ *Closed Sun.*

Mercato Centrale

MARKET | FAMILY | This huge indoor food market offers a staggering selection of all things edible. Downstairs is full of vendors hawking their wares—meat, fish, fruit, vegetables—upstairs (daily 8 am–midnight) is full of food stalls serving up the best of what Italy has to offer. ⊠ *Piazza del Mercato Centrale, San Lorenzo* ☎ *239–9798* ⊕ *www.mercato-centrale.it* ⊗ *Downstairs closed Sun. and after 2 pm Mon.–Sat.*

Mercato di San Lorenzo

MARKET | FAMILY | The clothing and leather-goods stalls of the Mercato di San Lorenzo in the streets next to the church of San Lorenzo have bargains for shoppers on a budget. ⊠ *Florence.*

★ Penko

JEWELRY & WATCHES | Renaissance goldsmiths provide the inspiration for this dazzling jewelry with a contemporary feel. ⊠ *Via Ferdinando Zannetti 14–16/r, Duomo* ☎ *055/211661* ⊕ *www.paolopenko.com* ⊗ *Closed Sun. and Mon.*

★ Perini

FOOD | It's possible to break the bank at what might be the best salumeria in Florence. Perini sells prosciutto, mixed meats, sauces for pasta, and a wide assortment of *antipasti* (starters). ⊠ *Mercato Centrale, enter at Via dell'Aretino, San Lorenzo* ☎ *055/239–8306* ⊗ *Closed Sun.*

via de'Ginori 23/r

LEATHER GOODS | Family-run and operated, this shop sells beautifully handcrafted leather items just down the street from the Basilica of San Lorenzo. ⊠ *Via de'Ginori 23/r, Florence* ☎ *055/239–8031* ⊕ *www.viadeginori23r.com* ⊗ *Closed Sun.*

Meet the Medici

The Medici were the dominant family of Renaissance Florence, wielding political power and financing some of the world's greatest art. You'll see their names at every turn around the city. These are some of the more notable family members.

Cosimo il Vecchio (1389–1464): incredibly wealthy banker to the popes and the first in the family line to act as de facto ruler of Florence. He was a great patron of the arts and architecture; he was the moving force behind the family palace and the Dominican complex of San Marco.

Lorenzo il Magnifico (1449–92): grandson of Cosimo il Vecchio who presided over a Florence largely at peace with its neighbors. A collector of cameos, a writer of sonnets, and a lover of ancient texts, he was the preeminent Renaissance man and, like his grandfather, the de facto ruler of Florence.

Leo X (1475–1521): also known as Giovanni de' Medici, he became the first Medici pope, helping extend the family power base to include Rome and the Papal States. His reign was characterized by a host of problems, the biggest one being a former friar named Martin Luther.

Catherine de' Medici (1519–89): was married by her great uncle Pope Clement VII to Henry of Valois, who later became Henry II of France. Wife of one king and mother of three, she was the first Medici to marry into European royalty. Lorenzo il Magnifico, her great-grandfather, would have been thrilled.

Cosimo I (1537–74): the first grand duke of Tuscany, not to be confused with his ancestor, Cosimo il Vecchio.

Santa Maria Novella

Piazza Santa Maria Novella is a gorgeous, pedestrian-only square, with grass (laced with roses) and plenty of places to sit and rest your feet. The streets in and around it have their share of architectural treasures, including some of Florence's most tasteful palaces. Between Santa Maria Novella and the Arno is Via Tornabuoni, Florence's swankiest shopping street.

 Sights

Colonna della Giustizia
PUBLIC ART | In the center of Piazza Santa Trinita is this column from Rome's Terme di Caracalla, given to the Medici grand duke Cosimo I by Pope Pius IV in 1560. Typical of Medici self-assurance, the name translates as the Column of Justice. ⊠ *Piazza Santa Trinita, Santa Maria Novella.*

Croce al Trebbio
MONUMENT | In 1338, the Dominican friars (the Dominican church of Santa Maria Novella is down the street) erected this little granite column near Piazza Santa Maria Novella to commemorate a famous local victory: it was here in 1244 that they defeated their avowed enemies, the Patarene heretics, in a bloody street brawl. ⊠ *Via del Trebbio, Santa Maria Novella.*

Le Cascine
CITY PARK | **FAMILY** | In the 16th century, this vast park belonged to the Medici, who used it for hunting, one of their favorite pastimes. It was opened to the public in the 19th century. The park runs for nearly 3 km (2 miles) along the Arno

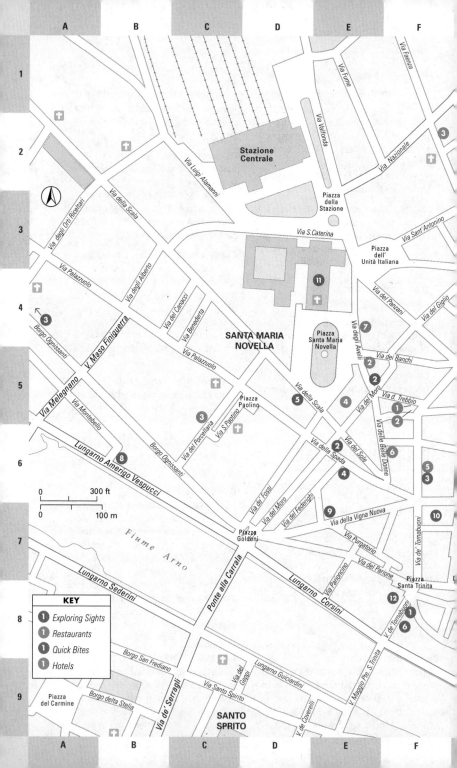

KEY

- **1** Exploring Sights
- **1** Restaurants
- **1** Quick Bites
- **1** Hotels

Stazione Centrale

Piazza della Stazione

Via S.Caterina

Piazza dell' Unità Italiana

SANTA MARIA NOVELLA

Piazza Santa Maria Novella

Piazza Paolino

Piazza Goldoni

Fiume Arno

0 — 300 ft
0 — 100 m

SANTO SPRITO

Piazza del Carmine

Piazza Santa Trinita

Santa Maria Novella

Sights ▼

1 Colonna della Giustizia **F8**
2 Croce al Trebbio **E5**
3 Le Cascine.......................... **A4**
4 Museo Marino Marini and
  Cappella Rucellai.................. **E6**
5 Museo Novecento.................. **D5**
6 Museo Salvatore Ferragamo...... **F8**
7 Museo Stibbart **G1**
8 Ognissanti **B6**
9 Palazzo Rucellai **E7**
10 Palazzo Strozzi **F7**
11 Santa Maria Novella **E4**
12 Santa Trinita........................ **F8**

Restaurants ▼

1 Buca Lapi............................ **F5**
2 Cantinetta Antinori **F5**
3 La Sostanza **C5**
4 Mangiafoco **G8**
5 Obicà................................ **F6**
6 Osteria delle Belle Donne **F6**
7 Ristorante Vincanto **E4**

Quick Bites ▼

1 Amblé **G9**
2 La Spada............................ **E6**
3 Procacci............................ **F6**

Hotels ▼

1 Gallery Hotel Art **G9**
2 Hotel L'Orologio **E5**
3 Nuova Italia **F2**
4 The Place Firenze.................. **E5**

and has roughly 291 acres. It's ideal for strolling on sunny days, and there are paths for jogging, allées perfect for biking, grassy fields for picnicking, and lots of space for rollerblading (as well as a place to rent skates). At the northern tip of the park is the Piazzaletto dell'Indiano, an oddly moving monument dedicated to Rajaram Cuttraputti, Marajah of Kolepoor, who died in Florence in 1870. The park hosts sports enthusiasts, a weekly open-air market, and discotheques. But be warned: at night there's a booming sex-for-sale trade. ⊠ *Main entrance: Piazza Vittorio Veneto, Viale Fratelli Roselli (at Ponte della Vittoria), Florence.*

Museo Marino Marini and Cappella Rucellai

ART MUSEUM | A 21-foot-tall bronze horse and rider, one of the major works by artist Marino Marini (1901–80), dominates the space of the main gallery here. The museum itself is an eruption of contemporary space in a deconsecrated 9th-century church, designed with a series of open stairways, walkways, and balconies that allow you to peer at Marini's work from all angles. In addition to his Etruscanesque sculpture, the museum houses Marini's paintings, drawings, and engravings. The Cappella Rucellai, commissioned by one of Florence's most powerful families, shows Renaissance man Leon Battista Alberti (1404–72) at the height of his architectural powers. ⊠ *Piazza San Pancrazio, Santa Maria Novella* ☎ *055/219432* ⊕ *www.museomarinomarini.it* 🖅 *€6* ⊗ *Closed Tues.–Fri.*

Museo Novecento

ART MUSEUM | It began life as a 13th-century Franciscan hostel offering shelter to tired pilgrims. It later became a convalescent home, and, in the late 18th century, it was a school for poor girls. Now the former Ospedale di San Paolo houses a museum devoted to Italian art of the 20th century. Most of these artists are not exactly household names, but the museum is so beautifully done that it's worth a visit. The second floor contains works by artists from the second half of the century; start on the third floor, and go directly to the collection of Alberto della Ragione, a naval engineer determined to be on the cutting edge of art collecting. The museum frequently hosts temporary exhibitions of very contemporary art. ⊠ *Piazza Santa Maria Novella 10, Santa Maria Novella* ☎ *055/286132* ⊕ *www.museonovecento.it* 🖅 *€9.*

Museo Salvatore Ferragamo

ART MUSEUM | A shrine to footwear, the shoes in this dramatically displayed collection were designed by Salvatore Ferragamo (1898–1960) beginning in the early 20th century. Born in southern Italy, Ferragamo jump-started his career in Hollywood by creating shoes for the likes of Mary Pickford and Rudolph Valentino. He then returned to Florence and set up shop in the 13th-century Palazzo Spini Ferroni. The collection includes about 16,000 shoes, and those on display are frequently rotated. Special exhibitions are also mounted here and are well worth visiting—past shows have been devoted to Audrey Hepburn, Greta Garbo, and Marilyn Monroe. ⊠ *Via dei Tornabuoni 2, Santa Maria Novella* ☎ *055/356–2846* ⊕ *www.ferragamo.com* 🖅 *€15.*

Museo Stibbert

ART MUSEUM | Frederick Stibbert (1838–1906), born in Florence to an Italian mother and an English father, liked to collect things. Over a lifetime of doing so, he amassed some 50,000 objects. This museum, which was also his home, displays many of them. He had a fascination with medieval armor, as well as costumes, particularly Uzbek costumes, which are exhibited in a room called the Moresque Hall. These are mingled with an extensive collection of swords, guns, and other devices whose sole function was to kill people. The paintings, most of which date from the 15th century, are largely second-rate. The house itself is an interesting amalgam of neo-Gothic,

Renaissance, and English eccentric. To get here, take Bus 4 (across from the station at Santa Maria Novella) and get off at the stop marked "Fabbroni 4," then follow signs to the museum. ⊠ *Via Federico Stibbert 26, Florence* ☎ *055/486049* ⊕ *www.museostibbert.it* ⊠ *€8* ⊗ *Closed Thurs.*

Ognissanti

CHURCH | The Umiliati owned this architectural hodgepodge of a church before the Franciscans took it over in the mid-16th century. Beyond the fanciful baroque facade by Matteo Nigetti (1560–1649) are a couple of wonderful 15th-century gems. On the right in the nave is the *Madonna della Misericordia* by Ghirlandaio; a little farther down is Botticelli's *St. Augustine in His Study*. A companion piece, directly across the way, is Ghirlandaio's *St. Jerome*. Also worth seeing is the wooden crucifix by Giotto: the colors dazzle. Pass through the rather dreadfully frescoed cloister to view Ghirlandaio's superb *Last Supper.* ⊠ *Piazza Ognissanti, Santa Maria Novella* ☎ *055/239–8700* ⊕ *chiesaognissanti.it* ⊠ *Church free; donation requested for the Last Supper* ↻ *Check ahead on access to the Last Supper.*

Palazzo Rucellai

CASTLE/PALACE | Architect Leon Battista Alberti (1404–72) designed perhaps the very first private residence inspired by antique models—which goes a step further than the Palazzo Strozzi. A comparison between the two is illuminating. Evident on the facade of the Palazzo Rucellai, dating between 1455 and 1470, is the ordered arrangement of windows and rusticated stonework seen on the Palazzo Strozzi, but Alberti's facade is far less forbidding. He devoted a far larger proportion of his wall space to windows, which lighten the facade's appearance, and filled in the remainder with rigorously ordered classical elements borrowed from antiquity. The result, though still severe, is less fortresslike, and Alberti

strove for this effect purposely (he is on record as saying that only tyrants need fortresses).

Ironically, the Palazzo Rucellai was built some 30 years *before* the Palazzo Strozzi. Alberti's civilizing ideas here, it turned out, had little influence on the Florentine palazzi that followed. To Renaissance Florentines, power—in architecture, as in life—was equally as impressive as beauty. While you are admiring the facade (the palazzo isn't open to the public), turn around and look at the Loggia dei Rucellai across the street. Built in 1463–66, it was the private "terrace" of the Rucellai family, in-laws to the Medici. Its soaring heights and grand arches are a firm testament to the family's status and wealth. ⊠ *Via della Vigna Nuova, Santa Maria Novella.*

Palazzo Strozzi

CASTLE/PALACE | The Strozzi family built this imposing palazzo in an attempt to outshine the nearby Palazzo Medici. Based on a model by Giuliano da Sangallo (circa 1452–1516) dating from around 1489 and executed between 1489 and 1504 under il Cronaca (1457–1508) and Benedetto da Maiano (1442–97), it was inspired by Michelozzo's earlier Palazzo Medici-Riccardi. The exterior is simple, severe, and massive: it's a testament to the wealth of a patrician, 15th-century Florentine family. The interior courtyard is another matter altogether. It is here that the classical vocabulary—columns, capitals, pilasters, arches, and cornices—is given uninhibited and powerful expression. The palazzo frequently hosts blockbuster art shows. ⊠ *Via Tornabuoni, Piazza della Repubblica* ☎ *055/264-5155* ⊕ *www.palazzostrozzi.org* ⊠ *Free.*

Santa Maria Novella

CHURCH | The facade of this church looks distinctly clumsy by later Renaissance standards, and with good reason: it is an architectural hybrid. The lower half was completed mostly in the 14th century, and its pointed-arch niches and decorative marble patterns reflect the Gothic style of the day. About 100 years later (around 1456), architect Leon Battista Alberti was called in to complete the job. The marble decoration of his upper story clearly defers to the already existing work below, but the architectural motifs he added evince an entirely different style. The central doorway, the four ground-floor half-columns with Corinthian capitals, the triangular pediment atop the second story, the inscribed frieze immediately below the pediment—these are borrowings from antiquity, and they reflect the new Renaissance style in architecture, born some 35 years earlier at the Spedale degli Innocenti.

Alberti's most important addition—the S-curve scrolls (called volutes) surmounting the decorative circles on either side of the upper story—had no precedent whatsoever in antiquity. The problem was to soften the abrupt transition between wide ground floor and narrow upper story. Alberti's solution turned out to be definitive. Once you start to look for them, you will find scrolls such as these (or sculptural variations of them) on churches all over Italy, and every one of them derives from Alberti's example here.

The architecture of the interior is, like that of the Duomo, a dignified but somber example of Florentine Gothic. Exploration is essential, however, because the church's store of art treasures is remarkable. Highlights include the 14th-century, stained-glass-rose window depicting the *Coronation of the Virgin* (above the central entrance); the Cappella Filippo Strozzi (to the right of the altar), containing late-15th-century frescoes and stained glass by Filippino Lippi; the *cappella maggiore* (the area around the high altar), displaying frescoes by Ghirlandaio; and the Cappella Gondi (to the left of the altar), containing Filippo Brunelleschi's famous wood crucifix, carved around 1410 and said to have so stunned the

great Donatello when he first saw it that he dropped a basket of eggs.

Of special interest for its great historical importance and beauty is Masaccio's *Trinity*, on the left-hand wall, almost halfway down the nave. Painted around 1426–27 (at the same time he was working on his frescoes in Santa Maria del Carmine), it unequivocally announced the arrival of the Renaissance. The realism of the figure of Christ was revolutionary in itself, but what was probably even more startling to contemporary Florentines was the barrel vault in the background. The mathematical rules for employing single-point perspective in painting had just been discovered (probably by Brunelleschi), and this was one of the first works of art to employ them with utterly convincing success.

In the first cloister is a faded and damaged fresco cycle by Paolo Uccello depicting tales from Genesis, with a dramatic vision of the Deluge (at this writing, in restoration). Earlier and better-preserved frescoes painted in 1348–55 by Andrea da Firenze are in the chapter house, or the Cappellone degli Spagnoli (Spanish Chapel), off the cloister. ✉ *Piazza Santa Maria Novella 19, Florence* ☎ *055/219257 museo* ⊕ *www. smn.it/en* ⬛ *€8* ⊙ *Closed Sun. morning.*

Santa Trinita

CHURCH | Started in the 11th century by Vallombrosian monks and originally Romanesque in style, this church underwent a Gothic remodeling during the 14th century. (Remains of the Romanesque construction are visible on the interior front wall.) The major works are the fresco cycle and altarpiece in the Cappella Sassetti, the second to the high altar's right, painted by Ghirlandaio between 1480 and 1485. His work here possesses graceful decorative appeal and proudly depicts his native city, as most of the cityscapes show 15th-century Florence in all its glory. The wall frescoes illustrate scenes from the life of

St. Francis, and the altarpiece, depicting the *Adoration of the Shepherds,* veritably glows. ✉ *Piazza Santa Trinita, Santa Maria Novella* ⏲ *Closed Sun. 10:45–4.*

🍴 Restaurants

Buca Lapi
$$$$ | **ITALIAN** | The Antinori family started selling wine from their palace's basement in the 15th century, and, 600 years later, this *buca* (hole) is a lively, subterranean spot filled with Florentine aristocrats chowing down on what might be the best—and the most expensive—*bistecca fiorentina* (flavorful, lightly seasoned beef) in town. The classic Tuscan menu has the usual suspects: *crostino di cavolo nero* (black cabbage on toasted garlic bread), along with *ribollita* (vegetable, bean, and bread soup) and *pappa al pomodoro* (tomato and bread soup). **Known for:** gargantuan bistecca fiorentina; pet-friendly; adherence to Tuscan classics. [$] *Average main: €40* ✉ *Via del Trebbio 1* ☎ *055/213768* 🌐 *www.bucalapi.com/en* ⏲ *Closed Sun. No lunch.*

Cantinetta Antinori
$$$ | **TUSCAN** | After a morning of shopping on Via Tornabuoni, stop for lunch in this 15th-century palazzo, a place to see and be seen as well as to dine. The panache of the clientele is matched by that of the food, with dishes such as *tramezzino con pane di campagna al tartufo* (bread served with country pâté and truffles) and *insalata di gamberoni e gamberetti con carciofi freschi* (crayfish and prawn salad with shaved raw artichokes). **Known for:** outdoor seating in a 15th-century courtyard; most ingredients come from the family farm; chic clientele. [$] *Average main: €31* ✉ *Piazza Antinori 3, Santa Maria Novella* ☎ *055/292234* 🌐 *cantinetta-antinori.com/en* ⏲ *Closed Sun., 20 days in Aug., and Dec. 25–Jan. 6.*

★ **La Sostanza**
$$ | **TUSCAN** | Since opening its doors in 1869, this trattoria has been serving top-notch, unpretentious food to Florentines who like their bistecca very large and, of course, very rare, as that's the only way to eat it. The *tartino di carciofi* (artichoke tart) and the *pollo al burro* (chicken with butter) are signature dishes. **Known for:** Tuscan classics; no frills, 19th-century decor; delicious desserts (especially the semifreddo). [$] *Average main: €16* ✉ *Via del Porcellana 25/r, Lungarno North* ☎ *055/212691* 💳 *No credit cards* ⏲ *Closed Sun.*

★ **Mangiafoco**
$$ | **TUSCAN** | On a romantic medieval side street in the heart of the centro storico, this small restaurant serves Tuscan classics that reflect both the whims of the chef and what's in season. The menu features creative salads and pasta, meat, and truffle dishes, as well as *taglieri* (mixed meat and cheese plates) that are often served with jams made from Chianti, vin santo, or balsamic vinegar. **Known for:** great service; house-made breads and desserts; phenomenal wines by the glass or the bottle. [$] *Average main: €20* ✉ *Borgo Santi Apostoli 26/r, Santa Maria Novella* ☎ *055/265–8170* 🌐 *www.mangiafoco.com* ⏲ *Closed Wed.*

Obicà
$$ | **ITALIAN** | Mozzarella takes center stage at this sleek eatery on Florence's swankiest street. The cheese, along with its culinary cousin *burrata* (a fresh cheese filled with cream), arrives daily from southern Italy to become the centerpiece for various salads and pastas. **Known for:** outdoor seating in nice weather; outstanding pizza and desserts; mozzarella-laden menu. [$] *Average main: €18* ✉ *Via Tornabuoni 16, Santa Maria Novella* ☎ *055/277–3526* 🌐 *www.obica.com.*

Osteria delle Belle Donne

$$ | TUSCAN | Down the street from the church of Santa Maria Novella, this gaily decorated spot, always festooned with some sort of creative decoration (ropes of garlic and other vegetables have figured in the past) has an ever-changing menu and stellar service. The list of Tuscan standards is shaken up with alternatives such as *sedani con bacon, verza, e uova* (thick noodles sauced with bacon, cabbage, and egg); when avocados are ripe, they're on the menu, too, either with cold boiled shrimp or expertly grilled chicken breast. **Known for:** dessert; many dishes not typical of Tuscany; seasonal ingredients. $ *Average main: €19* ⊠ *Via delle Belle Donne 16/r, Santa Maria Novella* ☎ *055/238–2609* ⊕ *www. belledonneosteria.it.*

Ristorante Vincanto

$$ | ITALIAN | It opens at 11 am and closes at midnight—rare for Florentine restaurants—and it offers a bit of everything, including fine pastas (don't miss the *gnudi*), salads, and pizza. And all of this can be enjoyed with a splendid view of Piazza Santa Maria Novella. **Known for:** open early to late; something for everyone; view of Piazza Santa Maria Novella. $ *Average main: €18* ⊠ *Piazza Santa Maria Novella 23/r, Santa Maria Novella* ☎ *055/274–1555* ⊕ *www.ristorantevincanto.com.*

☕ Coffee and Quick Bites

Amblé

$ | ITALIAN | Hidden in a little cul-de-sac just down the street from the Ponte Vecchio, this colorful eatery has a variety of sandwiches (both hot and cold, most of which are served on five-grain bread), crostini, salads, and various tartares. Vegetarian and vegan options abound, but the kitchen also has a way with Italian cured meats. **Known for:** delicious sandwiches; outdoor seating in a lovely little piazza; young, lively staff. $ *Average main: €10* ⊠ *Piazzetta dei Del Bene 7/A,*

Florence ☎ *055/568528* ⊕ *www.amble.it* ◷ *Closed Mon.*

La Spada

$ | ITALIAN | FAMILY | Near Santa Maria Novella is La Spada. Walk in and inhale the fragrant aromas of meats cooking in the wood-burning oven. **Known for:** eat in or order takeout; adherence to Tuscan cuisine; grilled meats and aromatic pastas. $ *Average main: €11* ⊠ *Via della Spada 62/r, Santa Maria Novella* ☎ *055/218757* ⊕ *ristorantelaspada.it.*

★ Procacci

$$ | ITALIAN | At this classy Florentine institution dating from 1885, try one of the truffle panini and swish it down with a glass of prosecco. **Known for:** serene (but tiny) space; excellent wines by the glass; pane tartufato. $ *Average main: €15* ⊠ *Via Tornabuoni 64/r, Santa Maria Novella* ☎ *055/211656* ⊕ *www.procacci1885.it.*

Hotels

Gallery Hotel Art

$$$$ | HOTEL | High design resides at this art showcase near the Ponte Vecchio, where sleek, uncluttered rooms are dressed mostly in neutrals but have luxe touches such as leather headboards and kimono robes. **Pros:** trendy atmosphere; the in-house Fusion Bar serves delightful cocktails; artistic touches. **Cons:** might be too trendy for some; books up quickly; some street noise. $ *Rooms from: €680* ⊠ *Vicolo dell'Oro 5, Santa Maria Novella* ☎ *055/27263* ⊕ *www.lungarnocollection. com/gallery-hotel-art* ➡ *63 rooms* ⧉ *Free Breakfast.*

Hotel L'Orologio

$$$ | HOTEL | The owner of this quietly understated, elegant hotel has a real passion for watches, which is why he chose to name his hotel after them (and why you will see them throughout the property). **Pros:** location; stunning breakfast room; great staff. **Cons:** holds conferences from time to time; gets the occasional

tour group; some folks think it's too close to the train station. $ *Rooms from: €250* ✉ *Piazza Santa Maria Novella 24, Santa Maria Novella* ☎ *055/277380* ⊕ *www. hotelorologioflorence.com* ⇘ *60 rooms* ¶○¶ *Free Breakfast.*

Nuova Italia
$$ | HOTEL | FAMILY | The genial Viti family oversees this property with clean and simple rooms near the train station and well within walking distance of the sights. **Pros:** reasonable rates; great for those on a budget; close to everything. **Cons:** some street noise; the neighborhood is highly trafficked; no elevator. $ *Rooms from: €119* ✉ *Via Faenza 26, Santa Maria Novella* ☎ *055/287508* ⊕ *www.hotel-nuovaitalia.com* ⊘ *Closed Dec. 20–Dec. 27* ⇘ *20 rooms* ¶○¶ *Free Breakfast.*

★ The Place Firenze
$$$$ | HOTEL | Hard to spot from the street, this sumptuous place provides all the comforts of a luxe home away from home—expect soothing earth tones in the guest rooms, free minibars, crisp linens, and room service offering organic dishes. **Pros:** private, intimate feel; small dogs allowed; stellar staff. **Cons:** might be too trendy for some; books up quickly; breakfast at a shared table. $ *Rooms from: €660* ✉ *Piazza Santa Maria Novella 7, Florence* ☎ *055/264–5181* ⊕ *www.theplacefirenze. com* ⇘ *20 rooms* ¶○¶ *Free Breakfast.*

◉ Performing Arts

Maggio Musicale Fiorentino
MUSIC | In 2014, a new music hall opened in the area now called the Parco della Musica (Music Park), which was designed by Paolo Desideri and associates. Maggio Musicale Fiorentino has taken up residence there, and continues to hold forth at the Teatro Comunale (✉ *Corso Italia 16, Lungarno North* ☎ *055/287222*). Within Italy you can purchase tickets from late April through July directly at the box office or by phone

(☎ *055/277–9309*). You can also buy them online. ✉ *Via Alamanni 39, Florence* ☎ *055/200–1278* ⊕ *www.maggiofioren-tino.it.*

Tuscany Hall
FESTIVALS | This large exhibition space, formerly Teatro Saschall, hosts many events throughout the year, including a big and boisterous Christmas bazaar run by the Red Cross, visiting rock stars, and trendy bands from all over Europe. ✉ *Lungarno Aldo Moro 3, Santa Maria Novella* ☎ *055/650–4112* ⊕ *www.tuscanyhall.it.*

◖ Shopping

Alberto Cozzi
STATIONERY | You'll find an extensive line of Florentine papers and paper products in this shop, where artisans also rebind and restore books and works on paper. Opening hours are tricky, so it's best to call before stopping by. ✉ *Via del Parione 35/r, Santa Maria Novella* ☎ *055/294968.*

★ Angela Caputi
JEWELRY & WATCHES | Angela Caputi wows Florentine cognoscenti with her highly creative, often outsize, acrylic jewelry. A small but equally creative collection of women's clothing made of fine fabrics is also on offer. ✉ *Borgo Santi Apostoli 44/46, Florence* ☎ *055/292993* ⊕ *www. angelacaputi.com.*

Antica Officina del Farmacista Dr. Vranjes
PERFUME | Dr. Vranjes elevates aromatherapy to an art form with scents for the body and home. ✉ *Via della Vigna Nuova 30/r, Santa Maria Novella* ☎ *055/094–5851* ⊕ *www.drvranjes.it.*

Brandimarte
HOUSEWARES | Most people want to buy gold when they come to Florence (for which it is justly famous). That said, Brandimarte, which has specialized in exquisitely crafted silver objects since 1955, is well worth a visit. ✉ *Via del Moro 92/r, Santa Maria Novella* ☎ *349/422–0269* ⊕ *www.brandimarte.com.*

Cellerini

LEATHER GOODS | In a city where it seems just about everybody carries an expensive leather bag, Cellerini is an institution. ⊠ *Via del Sole 9/r, Santa Maria Novella* ☎ *055/282533* ⊕ *www.cellerini.it.*

Emilio Pucci

WOMEN'S CLOTHING | The aristocratic Marchese di Barsento, Emilio Pucci, became an international name in the late 1950s when the stretch ski clothes he designed for himself caught on with the *dolce vita* ("sweet life") crowd—his pseudopsychedelic prints and "palazzo pajamas" became all the rage. ⊠ *Via Tornabuoni 20–22/r, Santa Maria Novella* ☎ *055/265–8082* ⊕ *www.emiliopucci.com.*

Emporio Armani

MIXED CLOTHING | The sister store of the Giorgio Armani boutique has slightly more affordable nightclub- and office-friendly garb. ⊠ *Via Roma 14/r, Santa Maria Novella* ☎ *055/284315* ⊕ *www.armani.com.*

Ferragamo

SHOES | This classy institution, in a 13th-century palazzo, displays designer clothing and accessories, though elegant footwear still underlies the Ferragamo success. ⊠ *Via Tornabuoni 14/r, Santa Maria Novella* ☎ *055/292123* ⊕ *store. ferragamo.com.*

Gatto Bianco

JEWELRY & WATCHES | This contemporary jeweler has breathtakingly beautiful pieces featuring semiprecious and precious stones. ⊠ *Borgo Santi Apostoli 12/r, Santa Maria Novella* ☎ *055/282989* ⊕ *www. gattobiancogioielli.com.*

G.B. Frugone 1885

MIXED CLOTHING | If you're shopping for elegant cashmere, look no further. This Genoese-based company has been making scarves, dresses, and sweaters (among other things) for men and women since 1885. ⊠ *Via delle Belle Donne 35/r, Santa Maria Novella* ☎ *055/287820* ⊕ *www.frugonecashmere.com.*

Giorgio Armani

MIXED CLOTHING | The sleek, classic boutique Giorgio Armani is a centerpiece of the dazzling high-end shops clustered in this part of town. ⊠ *Via Tornabuoni 83/r, Santa Maria Novella* ☎ *055/219041* ⊕ *www.armani.com.*

Giotti

LEATHER GOODS | You'll find multiple lines of leather bags, wallets, and other accessories here. ⊠ *Piazza Ognissanti 3–4/r, Lungarno North* ☎ *055/294265* ⊕ *www. bottegagiotti.com/collection.*

Gucci

MIXED CLOTHING | Florentine perennial Gucci puts its famous initials on just about everything it sells. ⊠ *Via Tornabuoni 73/r, Santa Maria Novella* ☎ *055/264011* ⊕ *www.gucci.com.*

Libreria Sacchi

BOOKS | Genial proprietor and bibliophile Franco Cioncolini presides at this small shop specializing in old books, old prints, and the occasional contemporary painting. ⊠ *Via Lambertesca 18/r, Santa Maria Novella* ☎ *055/290805* ⊕ *www.libreria-sacchi.com.*

★ Loretta Caponi

MIXED CLOTHING | Synonymous with Florentine embroidery, this shop sells luxury lace, linens, and lingerie that have earned the eponymous signora worldwide renown. There's also beautiful (and expensive) clothing for children. ⊠ *Via delle Belle Donne 28/r, Santa Maria Novella* ☎ *055/213668* ⊕ *www.lorettacaponi.it/en.*

★ Officina Profumo Farmaceutica di Santa Maria Novella

PERFUME | The essence of a Florentine holiday is captured in the sachets of this art nouveau emporium of herbal cosmetics and soaps that are made following centuries-old recipes created by friars. ⊠ *Via della Scala 16, Santa Maria Novella* ☎ *055/216276* ⊕ *www.smnovella.it.*

★ Pineider

STATIONERY | Although it has shops throughout the world, Pineider started out in Florence in 1774 and still does all its printing here. Stationery and business cards are the mainstay, but the stores also sell fine-leather desk accessories as well as a less stuffy, more lighthearted line of products. ☒ *Piazza Rucellai 4/7/r, Santa Maria Novella* ☎ *055/284655* ⊕ *www.pineider.com.*

Prada

MIXED CLOTHING | Known to mix school-marmish sensibility with sexy cuts and funky fabrics, Prada appeals to an exclusive clientele. ☒ *Via Tornabuoni 67/r, Santa Maria Novella* ☎ *055/267471* ⊕ *www.prada.com.*

Principe

DEPARTMENT STORE | This Florentine institution sells casual clothes for men, women, and children at far-from-casual prices. It also has a great housewares department. ☒ *Via del Sole 2, Santa Maria Novella* ☎ *055/292843* ⊕ *www.principedifirenze.com.*

Valli

FABRICS | Gifted seamstresses (and seamsters) should look no further than this place, which sells sumptuous silks, beaded fabrics, lace, wool, and tweeds by the meter. ☒ *Via della Vigna Nuova 81/r, Santa Maria Novella* ☎ *055/282485* ⊕ *www.vallitessuti.com.*

Santa Croce

The Santa Croce quarter, on the southeast fringe of the historic center, was built up in the Middle Ages outside the second set of medieval city walls. The centerpiece of the neighborhood was (and is) the basilica of Santa Croce, which could hold great numbers of worshippers. The vast piazza could accommodate any overflow and also served as a fairground and, allegedly since the middle of the 16th century, as a playing field for no-holds-barred soccer games. A center of leather-working since the Middle Ages, the neighborhood is still packed with artisans and leather shops.

Sights

Casa Buonarroti

ART MUSEUM | If you really enjoy walking in the footsteps of the great genius, you may want to complete the picture by visiting the Buonarroti family home. Michelangelo lived here from 1516 to 1525, and later gave it to his nephew, whose son, Michelangelo il Giovane (Michelangelo the Younger), turned it into a gallery dedicated to his great-uncle. The artist's descendants filled it with art treasures, some by Michelangelo himself. Two early marble works—the *Madonna of the Stairs* and *Battle of the Centaurs*—demonstrate his genius. ☒ *Via Ghibellina 70, Santa Croce* ☎ *055/241752* ⊕ *www.casabuonarroti.it* ☑ *€8* ☉ *Closed Tues.*

Cimitero degli Inglesi (*English Cemetery*)

CEMETERY | The final resting place for some 1,400 souls was designed in 1828 by Carlo Reishammer and originally intended for the Swiss community in Florence. Just outside the city's 14th-century walls (no longer visible), the cemetery grew to accommodate other foreigners living here, and thus earned another of its names, the Protestant Cemetery. It's also referred to as the "Island of the Dead." Indeed, Swiss painter Arnold Böcklin (1827–1901) used the cemetery as inspiration for his haunting painting of that name.

Perhaps its most famous resident is Elizabeth Barrett Browning (1809–61), who spent the last 15 years of her life in the city. Other noteworthy expats buried here include the English poets Arthur Clough and Walter Savage Landor, Frances Trollope (mother of Anthony), and the American preacher Theodore Parker. ☒ *Piazzale Donatello 38, Santa*

3

Sights ▼

1 Casa Buonarroti **F7**
2 Cimitero degli Inglesi.............. **J1**
3 Florence American Cemetery ... **D9**
4 Museo del Cenacolo **J5**
5 Museo Horne...................... **D9**
6 Piazza dei Ciompi **G6**
7 Piazza Santa Croce................ **E8**
8 Santa Croce **F8**
9 Sant'Ambrogio **H6**
10 Sinagoga............................ **H5**

Restaurants ▼

1 Antico Noè **E6**
2 Ciblèo **H6**
3 Cibrèo Ristorante **H6**
4 Cibrèo Trattoria **H6**
5 Dim Sum **C9**
6 Enoteca Pinchiorri................. **F7**
7 La Giostra.......................... **E5**
8 Pizzeria Caffè Italiano............. **D7**
9 Ruth's.............................. **H5**

Quick Bites ▼

1 da Rocco............................ **I7**
2 Finisterrae Firenze
  Pasticceria **E8**
3 I Dolci di Patrizio Cosi **E6**
4 La Ghiotta.......................... **H6**

Hotels ▼

1 Borgo Pinti.......................... **E5**
2 The Four Seasons **H1**
3 Hotel Regency **J2**
4 Monna Lisa **F4**
5 Morandi alla Crocetta.............. **F1**

Croce ☎ 055/582608 ✉ Free; suggested €3 per person for large groups ⊘ Closed weekends, Mon. afternoon, and Tues.– Fri. morning.

Florence American Cemetery

CEMETERY | About 8 km (5 miles) south of Florence on the road to Siena is one of two American cemeteries in Italy (the other is in Nettuno). It contains 4,392 bodies of Americans who died in Italy during World War II. Spread across a gently rolling hill, the simple crosses and Stars of David bearing only name, date of death, and state seem to stretch endlessly. Atop the hill is a place for reflection and large mosaic maps depicting the Allied assault in 1943. The two fronts—called the Gothic Line and the Gustav Line—are vividly rendered. So, too, is the list containing 1,409 names of those missing in action. ✉ Via Cassia, Florence ⊹ From Florence, take Via Cassia south to Località Scopeti ☎ 055/202–0020 ⊕ www.abmc.gov/Florence ✉ Free.

Museo del Cenacolo (Museum of the Last Supper)

ART MUSEUM | This way-off-the-beaten-path museum has a stunning fresco by Andrea del Sarto. Begun sometime around 1511 and finished in 1526–27, the fresco depicts the moment when Christ announced that one of his apostles would betray him. Andrea has rendered the scene in subtle yet still brilliant colors. Also on display are a couple of lesser-known works by Pontormo and copies of other 16th-century works.

Down the street is the church of San Salvi, founded by John Gualbert and begun in 1048. Though it suffered damage during the siege of 1529–30, the interior has a modest but lovely Madonna and Child by Lorenzo di Bicci as well as a 16th-century wooden cross on the altar. To get here, take Bus 6 from Piazza San Marco and get off at the Lungo L'Affrico stop—it's the first stop after crossing

the railroad tracks. ✉ Via San Salvi 16, Florence ☎ 055/064–9489 ⊕ www.polo-musealetoscana.beniculturali.it ✉ Free ⊘ Closed Mon.

Museo Horne

CASTLE/PALACE | Englishman Herbert P. Horne (1864–1916), architect, art historian, and collector, spent much of his life in his 15th-century palazzo surrounded by carefully culled paintings, sculptures, and other decorative arts mostly from the 14th to 16th century. His home has since been turned into a museum, and the jewel of the collection is Giotto's St. Stephen. The rest of the collection is decidedly B-list (he owned plenty of minor works by major artists such as Masaccio and Bernini), but it's still worth a visit to see how a gentleman lived in the 19th century. Many of the furnishings, such as the 15th-century lettuccio (divan), are exemplary. Note that this museum has been undergoing development and may be closed; check ahead on its status before visiting. ✉ Via dei Benci 6, Santa Croce ☎ 055/244661 ⊕ www.museohorne.it ✉ €7 ☞ Check ahead on opening days and hrs.

Piazza dei Ciompi

PLAZA/SQUARE | In the 14th century, this piazza (once the site of a daily flea market) was part of a working-class neighborhood of primarily wool- and silk-trade workers. The disenfranchised wool workers, forbidden entry to the Arte della Lana (the Wool Guild, whose members included those who traded in wool), briefly seized control of the government. It was a short-lived exercise in rule by the nonrepresented and was eventually overpowered by the ruling upper class. The loggia, executed in 1567, is by Giorgio Vasari. ✉ Piazza dei Ciompi, Santa Croce.

Piazza Santa Croce

PLAZA/SQUARE | Originally outside the city's 12th-century walls, this piazza grew with the Franciscans, who used it for

Continued on page 126

SANTA CROCE

The Duomo may catch your eye first, but to discover Florence's most impressive tombs and finest church art, cross town to this Gothic masterpiece.

Construction of Santa Croce was initiated in 1294 by Florence's Franciscan friars, who were aiming to outdo Santa Maria Novella, the church of their Dominican rivals. In the centuries that followed, Santa Croce would fulfill this goal in ways the Franciscans never could have imagined: it became the resting place of Italian geniuses—a sort of Florentine Westminister Abbey—and the site of revolutionary frescoes that helped change the course of Western art.

Clockwise from left: Sacristy inside Santa Croce; detail from Michelangelo's tomb; exterior of Sante Croce; Dante Alighieri monument.

WHAT TO LOOK FOR INSIDE SANTA CROCE

THE ART WITHIN SANTA CROCE is the most impressive of any church in Florence. Historically, the most significant works are the Giotto frescoes. Time hasn't been kind to them; over the centuries, they've been whitewashed, plastered over, and clumsily restored. But you can still sense the realism and drama of Giotto's work—it may look primitive, but in the 14th century it sparked a revolution. Before Giotto, the role of painting was to symbolize the attributes of God; after him, it was to imitate life.

Donatello's *Crucifixion*

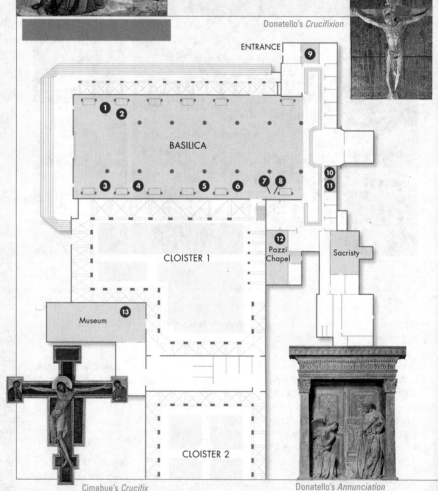

ENTRANCE

BASILICA

CLOISTER 1

Pazzi Chapel

Sacristy

Museum

CLOISTER 2

Cimabue's *Crucifix*

Donatello's *Annunciation*

6 Donatello's *Annunciation* (c. 1435) exquisitely renders the surprise of the Virgin as Gabriel announces that the Lord is with her.

9 Donatello's *Crucifixion* (1425) is located in the Cappella Bardi di Vernio, the chapel at the end of the left transept.

10 Giotto's **Cappella Bardi frescoes** (1320–25), in the first chapel to the right of the main altar, show scenes from the life of St. Francis.

11 Giotto's **Cappella Peruzzi frescoes** (1320–25), in the second chapel to the right of the main altar, depict scenes from the lives of John the Evangelist and Baptist.

12 Brunelleschi's **Cappella Pazzi** (begun 1429) shows the master architect in an intimate light; Brunelleschi did not live to see it completed.

13 Cimabue's *Crucifix* (1287–88), in the attached Museo dell'Opera di Santa Croce, heartbreakingly shows what damage the flood of 1966 did to some very important works of art.

TOMBS & MONUMENTS OF GREAT MEN

1 Galileo Galilei (1564–1642). Galileo's tomb wasn't given prominence until 100 years after his death, as his evidence that the Earth was not the center of the universe was highly displeasing to the Church.

2 Lorenzo Ghiberti (1378–1455). The tomb slab of sculptor Lorenzo Ghiberti, who created the Baptistery doors, is on the floor near Galileo's tomb.

3 Michelangelo (1475–1564; tomb shown above). The great master supposedly picked this spot so he'd see Brunelleschi's dome on Judgment Day.

4 Dante Alighieri (1265–1321). A memorial to Dante was built in 1829 to honor the poet, who was banished from Florence and buried in Ravenna.

5 Niccolò Machiavelli (1469–1527). The Renaissance political theoretician has the quote "*Tanto nomini nullum par elogium*" ("For so great a name, no praise is adequate") on his tomb, built in 1787.

7 Leonardo Bruni (1370–1444). Bernardo Rossellino's Tomb of Leonardo Bruni (1444–45), one of Santa Croce's finest works, depicts the humanist chancellor of Florence, the first *uomo illustre* (illlustrious man) to be buried in the church.

8 Gioacchino Rossini (1792–1868). The great Italian composer wrote more than 30 operas; his most famous was *Il barbiere di Siviglia* (*The Barber of Seville*).

Santa Croce Basics

Like the Duomo, Santa Croce is Gothic in design, and in all likelihood the two churches had the same initial architect, Arnolfo di Cambio. In the typical fashion of the Middle Ages, construction continued for decades—the church was finally consecrated by Pope Eugene IV in 1442. And, also like the Duomo, Santa Croce's neo-Gothic facade is a 19th-century addition.

✉ Piazza Santa Croce 16
☎ 055/246–6105
🎟 €8 Basilica and museum (combined ticket)
🕓 Closed Tues.

public preaching. During the Renaissance, it hosted *giostre* (jousts), including one sponsored by Lorenzo de' Medici. Lined with many palazzi dating from the 15th and 16th centuries, the square remains one of Florence's loveliest and is a great place to people-watch. ⊠ *Piazza Santa Croce, Santa Croce.*

★ Santa Croce

CHURCH | As a burial place, this Gothic church (whose facade dates from the 19th century) contains the skeletons of many Renaissance celebrities. The tomb of Michelangelo is on the right at the front of the basilica, a location he is said to have chosen so that the first thing he would see on Judgment Day, when the graves of the dead fly open, would be Brunelleschi's dome through Santa Croce's open doors. The tomb of Galileo Galilei (1564–1642) is on the left wall. He was not granted a Christian burial until 100 years after his death because of his controversial contention that Earth was not the center of the universe. The tomb of Niccolò Machiavelli (1469–1527), the political theoretician whose brutally pragmatic philosophy so influenced the Medici, is halfway down the nave on the right. The grave of Lorenzo Ghiberti, creator of the Baptistery doors, is halfway down the nave on the left. Composer Gioachino Rossini (1792–1868) is buried at the end of the nave on the right. The monument to Dante Alighieri (1265–1321), the greatest Italian poet, is a memorial rather than a tomb (he is buried in Ravenna); it's on the right wall near the tomb of Michelangelo.

The complex's collection of art is by far the most important of any church in Florence. The most famous works are the Giotto frescoes in the two chapels immediately to the right of the high altar. They illustrate scenes from the lives of St. John the Evangelist and St. John the Baptist (in the right-hand chapel), as well as those from the life of St. Francis (in the left-hand chapel). Time has not been kind to these frescoes; through the centuries, wall tombs were placed in the middle of them, they were whitewashed and plastered over, and they suffered a clumsy 19th-century restoration. But the reality that Giotto introduced into painting can still be seen. He did not paint beautifully stylized religious icons, as the Byzantine style that preceded him prescribed. Instead, he painted drama—St. Francis surrounded by grieving friars at the very moment of his death. This was a radical shift in emphasis: before Giotto, painting's role was to symbolize the attributes of God; after him, it was to imitate life. His work is indeed primitive compared with later painting, but in the early 14th century it caused a sensation that was not equaled for another 100 years. He was, for his time, the equal of both Masaccio and Michelangelo.

Other highlights are Donatello's *Annunciation,* a moving expression of surprise (on the right wall two-thirds of the way down the nave); 14th-century frescoes by Taddeo Gaddi (circa 1300–66) illustrating scenes from the life of the Virgin Mary, clearly showing the influence of Giotto (in the chapel at the end of the right transept); and Donatello's *Crucifix,* criticized by Brunelleschi for making Christ look like a peasant (in the chapel at the end of the left transept). Outside the church proper, in the Museo dell'Opera di Santa Croce off the cloister, is the 13th-century *Crucifix* by Cimabue (circa 1240–1302), badly damaged by the flood of 1966. A model of architectural geometry, the Cappella Pazzi, at the end of the cloister, is the work of Brunelleschi. ⊠ *Piazza Santa Croce 16, Santa Croce* ☎ *055/246–6105 reservations* ⊕ *www.santacroceopera. it* ⊡ *Church and museum €8* ⊗ *Closed Tues.*

Sant'Ambrogio

CHURCH | Named for the Bishop of Milan, this 10th-century church once belonged to an order of Benedictine nuns. Just this side of austere, the church is one of the oldest in Florence. Though its facade is 19th century, inside are 15th-century panel paintings and a lovely but rather damaged 1486 fresco by Cosimo Roselli, in the chapel to the left of the high altar. The tabernacle of the Blessed Sacrament was carved by Mino da Fiesole, who, like Verrocchio, il Cronaca, and Francesco Granacci (1469/77–1543), is buried here. ⊠ *Piazza Sant'Ambrogio, Santa Croce* 🎟 *Free.*

Sinagoga

SYNAGOGUE | Jews were well settled in Florence by the end of the 14th century. By 1574, however, they were required to live within the large "ghetto" at the north side of today's Piazza della Repubblica, by decree of Cosimo I. Construction of the modern Moorish-style synagogue began in 1874 as a bequest of David Levi, who wished to endow a synagogue "worthy of the city." Falcini, Micheli, and Treves designed the building on a domed Greek cross plan with galleries in the transept and a roofline bearing three distinctive copper cupolas visible from all over Florence. The exterior has alternating bands of tan travertine and pink granite, reflecting an Islamic style repeated in Giovanni Panti's ornate interior. Note the cast-iron gates by Pasquale Franci, the eternal light by Francesco Morini, and the Murano glass mosaics by Giacomo dal Medico.

The gilded doors of the Moorish ark, which fronts the pulpit and is flanked by extravagant candelabra, are decorated with symbols of the ancient Temple of Jerusalem and bear bayonet marks from vandals. The synagogue was used as a garage by the Nazis, who failed to inflict much damage in spite attempting to blow it up with dynamite. Only the left-side columns were destroyed, and, even then, the Women's Balcony above did not collapse. Note the Star of David in black and yellow marble inlay on the floor. The original capitals can be seen in the garden. ⊠ *Via Farini 4, Santa Croce* 🕿 *055/245252* ⊕ *www.firenzebraica.it/sinagoga* 🎟 *Synagogue and museum €7* ⏱ *Closed weekends and Jewish holidays.*

Restaurants

Antico Noè

$$ | **TUSCAN** | **FAMILY** | The short menu at the one-room eatery relies heavily on seasonal ingredients picked up daily at the market. Although the secondi are good, the antipasti and primi really shine, and the menu really comes alive during truffle and artichoke seasons (don't miss the grilled artichokes if they're available). **Known for:** porcini dishes; artichoke dishes; attention to seasonal vegetables. 💲 *Average main: €18* ⊠ *Volta di San Piero 6/r, Santa Croce* 🕿 *055/234–0838* ⊕ *www.anticonoe.com* ⏱ *Closed 2 wks in Aug. No dinner Sun.*

★ Ciblèo

$$$$ | **FUSION** | This tiny eatery brilliantly blends the cuisine of Tuscany with that of Korea and Japan. Here you'll find wacky and marvelous combinations in the dumplings, ravioli, and more on a seasonally changing menu. **Known for:** a collection of sakes; one seating per evening at 7 pm; startling flavor combinations. 💲 *Average main: €50* ⊠ *Via del Verrocchio 2/r, Florence* 🕿 *055/477881* ⊕ *www.cibreo.com/en/cibleo-en* ⏱ *Closed Sun. and Mon.*

★ Cibrèo Ristorante

$$$$ | **TUSCAN** | This upscale trattoria serves sumptuous options like the creamy crostini *di fegatini* (with a savory chicken-liver spread) and melt-in-your-mouth desserts. Many Florentines hail this as the city's best restaurant, and justifiably so—chef-owner Fabio Picchi knows Tuscan food better than anyone, and it shows. **Known for:** multilingual staff; no written menu; authentic Tuscan food. 💲 *Average main: €40* ⊠ *Via A. del Verrocchio 8/r, Santa Croce* 🕿 *055/234–1100* ⊕ *www.cibreo.com/en/cibreo-restaurant* ⏱ *Closed Sun. and Mon.*

Cibrèo Trattoria

$ | TUSCAN | This intimate trattoria, known to locals as Cibreino, shares its name and its kitchen with the famed Florentine restaurant but has a shorter, less-expensive menu. Save room for dessert, as the pastry chef has a deft hand with chocolate tarts. **Known for:** need to come early or late to avoid a wait; clever riffs on classic dishes; excellent meal at a moderate price. $ *Average main: €13 ⊠ Via dei Macci 122/r, Santa Croce ☎ 055/234–1100 ⊕ www.cibreo.com/en/cibreo-trattoria ۞ Closed Sun., Mon., and July 25–Sept. 5.*

Dim Sum

$ | ASIAN FUSION | Florence has long been in dire need of a top-notch Asian restaurant, and now it finally has one. You can watch as classic dumplings and Tuscan variations (beef with *lardo di colonnata* or truffled beef) are made. **Known for:** classic and fusion dishes; rolls and noodle dishes; open kitchen lets you see the food being prepared. $ *Average main: €11 ⊠ Via Magliabecchi 9/r, Santa Croce ☎ 055/284331 ⊕ www.dimsumrestaurant.it ۞ No lunch Mon.*

Enoteca Pinchiorri

$$$$ | ITALIAN | A sumptuous Renaissance palace with high, frescoed ceilings and bouquets in silver vases provides the backdrop for this restaurant, one of the most expensive in Italy. Some consider it one of the best, and others consider it inauthentic, as the cuisine extends far beyond Italian. **Known for:** exorbitantly high prices; wine cellar; creative food. $ *Average main: €90 ⊠ Via Ghibellina 87, Santa Croce ☎ 055/242777 ⊕ www.enotecapinchiorri.it ۞ Closed Sun., Mon., and Aug. No lunch ⌂ Jacket required.*

★ La Giostra

$$$ | ITALIAN | This clubby spot, whose name means "carousel," was created by the late Prince Dimitri Kunz d'Asburgo Lorena and is now expertly run by Soldano, one of his twin sons. The ever-changing menu generally has vegetarian and vegan options. **Known for:** vegetarian and vegan options; carefully curated wine list; sublime tiramisù and a wonderfully gooey Sacher torte. $ *Average main: €30 ⊠ Borgo Pinti 12/r, Santa Croce ☎ 055/241341 ⊕ ristorantelagiostra.com ۞ No lunch weekends.*

Pizzeria Caffè Italiano

$ | PIZZA | This small pizzeria is favored by locals. Come early to grab one of the few tables in front or round the back, and don't mind the fact that service here is intentionally rushed: turning tables is paramount. **Known for:** limited seating; local favorite; its limited (but very tasty) pizza offerings. $ *Average main: €10 ⊠ Via Isole delle Stinche 11/r, Santa Croce ☎ 055/289080 ⊕ caffeitaliano.it ▭ No credit cards.*

Ruth's

$$ | TUSCAN | The only kosher–vegetarian restaurant in Tuscany is Ruth's, adjacent to Florence's synagogue. On the menu: inexpensive vegetarian and Mediterranean dishes and a large selection of kosher wines. **Known for:** nice wine list; friendly staff; harissa. $ *Average main: €15 ⊠ Via Farini 2/a, Santa Croce ☎ 055/248–0888 ⊕ www.kosheruth.com ۞ No dinner Fri. No lunch Sat.*

☕ Coffee and Quick Bites

da Rocco

$ | TUSCAN | At one of Florence's biggest markets, you can grab lunch to go, or you can cram into one of the booths and pour from the straw-cloaked flask (wine here is *da consumo,* which means they charge you for how much you drink). Food is abundant, Tuscan, and fast; locals pack in. **Known for:** takeout; ever-changing menu; tasty food at rock-bottom prices. $ *Average main: €8 ⊠ Mercato Sant'Ambrogio, Piazza Ghiberti, Santa Croce ☎ 339/838–4555 ⊕ trattoria-da-rocco-lunch-restaurant.business.site ۞ Closed Sun. No dinner.*

Finisterrae Firenze Pasticceria

$ | **ITALIAN** | Conveniently placed very near the ticket office of the Basilica of Santa Croce, this bar does it all: great coffee, terrific pastries, fine wines by the glass, and tasty sandwiches. **Known for:** counter for pastries and sandwiches; prices that won't break the bank; convenient location. $ *Average main: €5* ⊠ *Piazza Santa Croce 12, Florence* ☎ *055/263–8675* ⊕ *www.finisterraefirenze.com.*

I Dolci di Patrizio Cosi

$ | **DESSERTS** | Florentines in the know come here for the deliciously bewildering selection of chocolate- and cream-filled pastries. **Known for:** cream-stuffed pastries; excellent coffee; walnut-stuffed pastries. $ *Average main: €10* ⊠ *Borgo Albizi 15/r, Santa Croce* ☎ *055/248–0367* ⊕ *www.pasticceriacosifirenze.it* ⊗ *Closed Sun. afternoon.*

La Ghiotta

$ | **FAST FOOD** | You can assemble a perfect dinner, from soup to nuts, at this Florentine favorite, which specializes in whole and half chickens, grilled or roasted. Order takeout or eat in, which is what many locals do. **Known for:** local favorite; chicken prepared various ways; great vegetable dishes. $ *Average main: €13* ⊠ *Via Pietrapiana 7/r, Santa Croce* ☎ *055/241237* ⊕ *www.laghiottafirenze.it* ▭ *No credit cards* ⊗ *No dinner Mon.*

 ## Hotels

Borgo Pinti

$ | **B&B/INN** | Nuns of the Oblates of the Assumption run this convent holiday house, where some of the simple but spotlessly clean rooms have views of the Duomo's cupola, and others look out onto a garden where you are welcome to relax. **Pros:** great location and (mostly) quiet rooms; a soothing, somewhat untended garden; Mass held daily. **Cons:** rooms are frugal; rooms facing the street can be noisy; some have observed that there's hall noise. $ *Rooms from:*

€88 ⊠ *Borgo Pinti 15, Santa Croce* ☎ *055/234–6291* ⊕ *www.oblate.it* ⇨ *40 rooms* ◎ *Free Breakfast.*

The Four Seasons

$$$$ | **HOTEL** | This 15th-century palazzo is perhaps the city's most luxurious hotel, where many guest rooms have original 17th-century frescoes, and an 11-acre garden is dotted with centuries-old trees. **Pros:** pool; Michelin-starred Il Palagio restaurant; state-of-the-art spa. **Cons:** small rooms; splashing children in the pool can be a nuisance for some; ultra-pricey. $ *Rooms from: €1220* ⊠ *Borgo Pinti 99e, Santa Croce* ☎ *055/26261* ⊕ *www.fourseasons.com/florence* ⇨ *117 rooms* ◎ *No Meals.*

Hotel Regency

$$$$ | **HOTEL** | Though it's just 10 minutes from the Accademia and Michelangelo's *David,* this hotel—in a 19th-century mansion adorned with rich fabrics and period-appropriate furnishings—is a true retreat from the city's noise and crowds. **Pros:** faces one of the few green spaces in central Florence; lovely, on-site Relais le Jardin restaurant; quiet residential setting. **Cons:** books up quickly; rooms facing the park can be noisy; somewhat removed from the city center. $ *Rooms from: €350* ⊠ *Piazza d'Azeglio 3, Santa Croce* ☎ *055/245247* ⊕ *www.regency-hotel.com* ⇨ *31 rooms* ◎ *Free Breakfast.*

★ Monna Lisa

$$ | **HOTEL** | Although some rooms are small, all are tastefully decorated and housed in a 15th-century palazzo that retains its original staircase and some of its wood-coffered ceilings. **Pros:** lavish buffet breakfast; pretty garden; cheerful, multilingual staff. **Cons:** thin walls have been noted; street noise in some rooms; rooms in annex are less charming than those in palazzo. $ *Rooms from: €195* ⊠ *Borgo Pinti 27, Santa Croce* ☎ *055/247–9751* ⊕ *www.monnalisa.it* ⇨ *48 rooms* ◎ *Free Breakfast.*

★ Morandi alla Crocetta

$ | **B&B/INN** | You're made to feel like friends of the family at this charming and distinguished residence, furnished comfortably in the classic style of a gracious Florentine home and former convent. **Pros:** interesting, offbeat location near the sights; historic touches like fragments of a 17th-century fresco; affable staff. **Cons:** some say breakfast could be better; far from the "true" historical center; books up quickly. [$] *Rooms from: €115* ✉ *Via Laura 50, Santissima Annunziata* ☎ *055/234–4747* 🌐 *www.hotelmorandi.it* 🛏 *10 rooms* 🍴 *Free Breakfast.*

Nightlife

Caffè Sant'Ambrogio

BARS | Come here when it's summer for outdoor seating with a view of an 11th-century church (Sant'Ambrogio) directly across the street. Come here at any time of the year for perfectly mixed drinks and a lively atmosphere filled with (mostly) locals. ✉ *Piazza Sant'Ambrogio 7–8/r, Santa Croce* ☎ *055/247–7277.*

Jazz Club

LIVE MUSIC | Enjoy live music in this small basement club. ✉ *Via Nuova de' Caccini 3, at Borgo Pinti, Santa Croce.*

Rex

BARS | A trendy, artsy clientele frequents this bar at aperitivo time. By 10 pm, the place is packed with mostly young folks sipping artful cocktails. ✉ *Via Fiesolana 23–25/r, Santa Croce* ☎ *055/248–0331* 🌐 *www.rexfirenze.com.*

Performing Arts

Amici della Musica

MUSIC | This organization sponsors classical and contemporary concerts at the Teatro della Pergola (✉ *Box office, Via delle Carceri 1* ☎ *055/210804*). ✉ *Via Pier Capponi 41, Florence* 🌐 *amicimusicafirenze.it.*

Festival dei Popoli

FILM | This weeklong documentary film festival happens in November or December with screenings at various venues around town. ✉ *Via della Robbia 66, Santa Croce* ☎ *055/244778* 🌐 *www.festivaldeipopoli.org.*

Orchestra della Toscana

MUSIC | The concert season of the Orchestra della Toscana runs from November to June. ✉ *Via Verdi 5, Santa Croce* ☎ *055/234–0710* 🌐 *www.orchestradellatoscana.it.*

Teatro della Pergola

THEATER | From mid-October to mid-April, see Italian plays at this 1656 theater, which was once the private venue of the grand dukes and which has undergone several metamorphoses. Its present incarnation dates from the early 19th century. ✉ *Via della Pergola 12/r, Santissima Annunziata* ☎ *055/076–3333 ticket office* 🌐 *www.teatrodellapergola.com.*

Shopping

Antico Salumificio Anzuini

FOOD | This salumeria shrink-wraps its own high-quality pork products, making it a snap to take home some *salame di cinghiale* (wild boar salami). It's also known for its exceptional prosciutto. ✉ *Via de' Neri 84/r, Santa Croce* ☎ *055/294901* 🌐 *www.salumificioanzuini.it.*

★ AquaFlor Firenze

PERFUME | Candles, soaps, and other heavenly products for the body and house may be found in this shop, which is set in a Renaissance palace. ✉ *Borgo Santa Croce 6, Santa Croce* ☎ *055/234–3471* 🌐 *www.aquaflor.it.*

Libreria Salimbeni

BOOKS | One of Florence's best art-book shops has an outstanding selection. ✉ *Via Matteo Palmieri 14–16/r, Santa Croce* ☎ *055/234–0905* 🌐 *www.libreriasalimbeni.com.*

Mercato di Sant'Ambrogio

MARKET | FAMILY | It's possible to strike gold at this lively market, where clothing stalls abut those with fruits and vegetables. ⊠ *Piazza Ghiberti, off Via dei Macci, Santa Croce.*

Oreria

JEWELRY & WATCHES | The two women who run Oreria create divine designs using silver and semiprecious stones. Send suitors to purchase significant gifts here. ⊠ *Borgo Pinti 87/a, Santa Croce* ☎ *055/244708* ⊕ *www.oreria.net.*

Paolo Carandini

HOUSEWARES | Stop in here for exquisite leather picture frames, jewelry boxes, and desk accessories. ⊠ *Borgo Allegri 7/r, Santa Croce* ☎ *334/735–5954* ⊕ *www. paolocarandini.net.*

Sbigoli Terrecotte

CERAMICS | Traditional Tuscan terra-cotta and ceramic vases, pots, and cups and saucers are on offer at this shop. ⊠ *Via Sant'Egidio 4/r, Santa Croce* ☎ *055/247– 9713* ⊕ *www.sbigoliterrecotte.it.*

★ Scuola del Cuoio

LEATHER GOODS | Leatherworkers ply their trade at Scuola del Cuoio (Leather School), a consortium in the former dormitory of the convent of Santa Croce. High-quality, fairly priced jackets, belts, and purses are sold here. ⊠ *Piazza Santa Croce 16, Florence* ☎ *055/244533* ⊕ *www.scuoladelcuoio.com.*

The Oltrarno

A walk through the Oltrarno (literally "the other side of the Arno") takes in two very different aspects of Florence: the splendor of the Medici, manifest in the riches of the mammoth Palazzo Pitti and the gracious Giardino di Boboli, and the charm of a slightly gentrified but still fiercely proud working-class neighborhood with artisans' and antiques shops.

Farther east across the Arno, a series of ramps and stairs climb to Piazzale Michelangelo, where the city lies before you in all its glory (save this trip for a clear day). More stairs (behind La Loggia restaurant) lead to the church of San Miniato al Monte.

You can avoid the long walk by taking Bus 12 or 13 at the west end of Ponte alle Grazie and getting off at Piazzale Michelangelo. You still have to climb the monumental stairs to and from San Miniato, but you can then take the bus from Piazzale Michelangelo back to the center of town. Just remember to buy your bus ticket before you board.

Sights

Certosa

CHURCH | This incredible Carthusian complex was largely funded in 1342 by the wealthy Florentine banker Niccolò Acciaiuoli, whose guilt at having amassed so much money must have been at least temporarily assuaged with the creation of such a structure to honor God. In the grand cloister are stunning (but faded) frescoes of *Christ's Passion* by Pontormo. Though much of the paint is missing, their power is still unmistakable.

Also of great interest are the monks' cells; the monks could spend most of their lives tending their own private gardens without dealing with any other monks. To get here, you must either take Bus 37 to the stop marked "Certosa" or have a car. Tours, which are mandatory, are given only in Italian, but even if you can't understand what's being said, you can still take in the sights. ⊠ *Via della Certosa 1, Galluzzo, Florence* ✛ *From Florence, take Viale Petrarca to Via Senese and follow it for about 10 mins; Certosa is on right* ☎ *055/204–9226* ⊕ *www. certosadifirenze.it* 🎟 *€5* ⊗ *Closed Mon.*

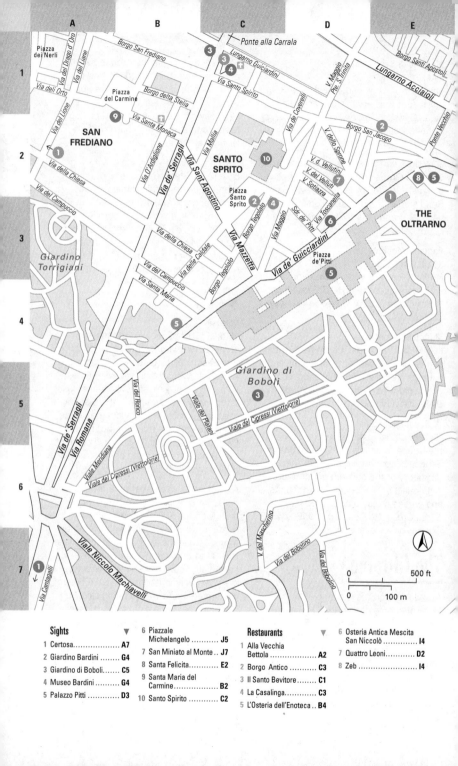

Sights ▼

1 Certosa.................. **A7**
2 Giardino Bardini **G4**
3 Giardino di Boboli..... **C5**
4 Museo Bardini **G4**
5 Palazzo Pitti **D3**
6 Piazzale
  Michelangelo **J5**
7 San Miniato al Monte .. **J7**
8 Santa Felicita........... **E2**
9 Santa Maria del
  Carmine................ **B2**
10 Santo Spirito **C2**

Restaurants ▼

1 Alla Vecchia
  Bettola **A2**
2 Borgo Antico **C3**
3 Il Santo Bevitore **C1**
4 La Casalinga............ **C3**
5 L'Osteria dell'Enoteca .. **B4**
6 Osteria Antica Mescita
  San Niccolò **I4**
7 Quattro Leoni........... **D2**
8 Zeb **I4**

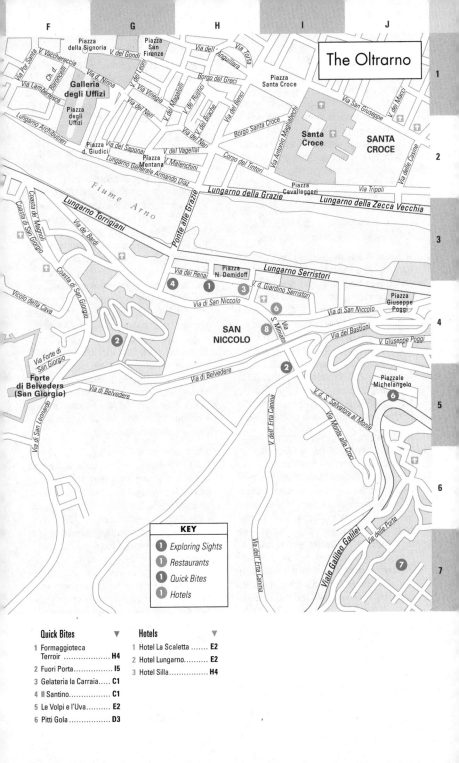

The Oltrarno

KEY
1 Exploring Sights
1 Restaurants
1 Quick Bites
1 Hotels

Giardino Bardini

GARDEN | Garden lovers, those who crave a view, and those who enjoy a nice hike should visit this lovely villa, whose history spans centuries. It had a walled garden as early as the 14th century; its "Grand Stairs"—a zigzag ascent well worth scaling—have been around since the 16th. The garden is filled with irises, roses, and heirloom flowers. It also has a Japanese garden and statuary. ⊠ *Via de'Bardini, San Niccolò* ☎ *055/263–8599* ⊕ *www.villabardini.it* 🎟 *€10* ⊘ *Closed Mon. (with occasional exceptions).*

Giardino di Boboli (*Boboli Gardens*)

GARDEN | The main entrance to these gardens is from the right side of the courtyard of Palazzo Pitti. The landscaping began to take shape in 1549, when the Pitti family sold the palazzo to Eleanor of Toledo, wife of the Medici grand duke Cosimo I. Niccolò Tribolo (1500–50) laid out the first plans, and, after his death, Ammannati, Giambologna, Bernardo Buontalenti (circa 1536–1608), Giulio (1571–1635), and Alfonso Parigi (1606–56), among others, continued his work.

Italian landscaping is less formal than French, but it's still full of sweeping drama. A copy of the famous *Morgante,* Cosimo I's favorite dwarf astride a particularly unhappy tortoise, is near the exit. Sculpted by Valerio Cioli (circa 1529–99), the work seems to illustrate the perils of culinary overindulgence. A visit here can be disappointing because the gardens are somewhat sparse, but the pleasant walk offers excellent views. ⊠ *Piazza de' Pitti, Palazzo Pitti* ☎ *055/294883* ⊕ *www. uffizi.it/giardino-boboli* 🎟 *€10* ⊘ *Closed 1st and last Mon. of month Nov.–May.*

Museo Bardini

ART MUSEUM | The 19th-century collector and antiquarian Stefano Bardini turned his palace into his own private museum. Upon his death, the collection was turned over to the state and includes an interesting assortment of Etruscan pieces, sculpture, paintings, and furniture that dates mostly from the Renaissance and the baroque. ⊠ *Via dei Renai 1, Oltrarno* ☎ *055/234-2427* ⊕ *musefirenze. it/en/musei/museo-stefano-bardini* 🎟 *€7* ⊘ *Closed Tues.–Thurs.*

Palazzo Pitti

ART MUSEUM | This enormous palace is one of Florence's largest architectural set pieces. The original palazzo, built for the Pitti family around 1460, consisted of the main entrance and the sections extending as far as three windows on either side. In 1549, the property was sold to the Medici, and Bartolomeo Ammannati was called in to make substantial additions. Although he apparently operated on the principle that more is better, he succeeded only in producing proof that more is just that: more. Today, the palace houses several museums. The Museo degli Argenti displays a vast collection of Medici treasures, including exquisite antique vases belonging to Lorenzo the Magnificent. The Galleria del Costume showcases fashions from the past 300 years. The Galleria d'Arte Moderna holds a collection of 19th- and 20th-century paintings, mostly Tuscan.

Most famous of the Pitti galleries is the Galleria Palatina, which contains a broad collection of paintings from the 15th to the 17th century. Its rooms remain much as the Lorena, the rulers who took over after the last Medici died in 1737, left them. Their floor-to-ceiling paintings are considered by some to be Italy's most egregious exercise in conspicuous consumption, aesthetic overkill, and trumpery. Still, the collection possesses high points, including a number of paintings by Titian and an unparalleled collection of paintings by Raphael. The price of admission to the Galleria Palatina also allows you to explore the former Appartamenti Reali, containing furnishings from a remodeling done in the 19th century. ⊠ *Piazza Pitti, Palazzo Pitti* ☎ *055/294883* ⊕ *www.uffizi.it/palazzo-pitti* 🎟 *From €16* ⊘ *Closed Mon.*

Piazzale Michelangelo

PLAZA/SQUARE | FAMILY | From this lookout you have a marvelous view of Florence and the hills around it, rivaling the vista from the Forte di Belvedere. A copy of Michelangelo's *David* overlooks outdoor cafés packed with tourists during the day and with Florentines in the evening. In May, the Giardino dell'Iris (Iris Garden) off the piazza is abloom with more than 2,500 varieties of the flower. The Giardino delle Rose (Rose Garden) on the terraces below the piazza is also in full bloom in May and June. ⊠ *Piazzale Michelangelo, San Niccolò*.

San Miniato al Monte

CHURCH | This abbey, like the Baptistery a fine example of Romanesque architecture, is one of the oldest churches in Florence, dating from the 11th century. A 12th-century mosaic topped by a gilt bronze eagle, emblem of San Miniato's sponsors, the Calimala (cloth merchants' guild), crowns the green-and-white marble facade. Inside are a 13th-century inlaid-marble floor and apse mosaic. Artist Spinello Aretino (1350–1410) covered the walls of the Sagrestia with frescoes of scenes from the life of St. Benedict.

The Cappella del Cardinale del Portogallo (Chapel of the Portuguese Cardinal) is one of the richest 15th-century Renaissance works in Florence. It contains the tomb of a young Portuguese cardinal, Prince James of Lusitania, who died in Florence in 1459. Its glorious ceiling is by Luca della Robbia, and the sculpted tomb by Antonio Rossellino (1427–79). Everyday at 6:30 pm, the monks fill the church with the sounds of Gregorian chanting and celebrate vespers in Latin. ⊠ *Viale Galileo Galilei, San Niccolò* ☎ *055/234–2731* ⊕ *www.sanminiatoalmonte.it*.

Santa Felicita

CHURCH | This late baroque church (its facade was remodeled between 1736 and 1739) contains the mannerist Jacopo Pontormo's *Deposition*, the centerpiece of the Cappella Capponi (executed 1525–28) and a masterpiece of 16th-century Florentine art. The remote figures, which transcend the realm of Renaissance classical form, are portrayed in tangled shapes and intense pastel colors (well preserved because of the low lights in the church) in a space and depth that defy reality. Note, too, the exquisitely frescoed *Annunciation*, also by Pontormo, at a right angle to the *Deposition*. The granite column in the piazza was erected in 1381 and marks a Christian cemetery. ⊠ *Via Guicciardini, Piazza Santa Felicita, Palazzo Pitti* ⊗ *Closed Sun.*

Santa Maria del Carmine

CHURCH | Fire destroyed most of this church in the 18th century, but, miraculously, the Cappella Brancacci—at the end of the right transept and containing a masterpiece of Renaissance painting—survived almost intact. The fresco cycle here changed the course of Western art and is the work of three artists: Masaccio and Masolino (1383–circa 1447), who began it around 1424, and Filippino Lippi, who finished it some 50 years later, after a long interruption when the sponsoring Brancacci family was exiled. It was, however, Masaccio's work that opened a new frontier for painting, as he was among the first artists to employ single-point perspective; tragically, he died in 1428 at the age of 27, so he didn't live to experience the revolution his innovations caused.

Masaccio collaborated with Masolino on several of the frescoes, but his style predominates in the *Tribute Money*, on the upper-left wall; *St. Peter Baptizing*, on the upper altar wall; the *Distribution of Goods*, on the lower altar wall; and the *Expulsion of Adam and Eve*, on the chapel's upper-left entrance pier. If you compare the last painting with some of the chapel's other works, you'll see a pronounced difference.

The figures of Adam and Eve possess a startling presence thanks to the dramatic way in which their bodies seem to reflect

A Good Walk: Florentine Piazzas

You may come to Florence for the art, but once here, you'll likely be won over by the pedestrian-friendly street life of its wonderfully varied piazzas. This walk takes you through many of them, though it bypasses some of the most prominent ones, which you'll inevitably encounter while sightseeing.

Start off in **Piazza Santa Maria Novella**, by the train station. Note the glorious facade by Leon Battista Alberti decorating the square's church. Take Via delle Belle Donne, a narrow street running southeast from the piazza, and go left heading toward Via del Trebbio. Here you'll see a cross marking the site of a 13th-century street scuffle between Dominican friars and Patarene heretics. (The Dominicans won.) A right on Via Tornabuoni takes you to tiny **Piazza Antinori**. The 15th-century Antinori palace has been in the hands of its wine-producing namesake family for generations.

Continue south on Via Tornabuoni, stopping in **Piazza Strozzi** to admire the gargantuan Palazzo Strozzi, a 16th-century family palace designed specifically to dwarf the Palazzo Medici, and step into the delicate courtyard. Next stop on Via Tornabuoni is the lovely little **Piazza Santa Trinita**. Pop into the church of Santa Trinita; in its Sassetti Chapel in the right transept, Ghirlandaio's 15th-century frescoes depict the square in which you were just standing.

Continue south to the Arno, and cross it via the Ponte Trinita. Go south on Via Maggio, then make a right on Via Michelozzi, which leads to **Piazza Santo Spirito**, one of the liveliest squares in Florence. Walking away from the piazza's church (heading south), make a left on Via Sant'Agostino, which turns into Via Mazzetta. Stop in **Piazza San Felice** and note Number 8, home of English poets Elizabeth Barrett Browning and Robert Browning from 1849 to 1861.

Via Guicciardini takes you to **Piazza dei Pitti**, which was intended to outsize Palazzo Strozzi, and it succeeds. Behind the palazzo is the Giardino di Boboli. Walking to its top, you'll pass man-made lakes, waterfalls, and grottoes. Head for the 18th-century Giardino dei Cavalieri, where you should pause and admire the view. It's hard to believe the scene in front of you, complete with olive groves, is in the city center.

Head back toward the Arno along Via Guicciardini. Just before the Ponte Vecchio, turn right onto Via de' Bardi. Stop in **Piazza Maria Sopr'Arno**, and check out the eerie 20th-century sculpture of John the Baptist, patron saint of Florence. Continue along Via de' Bardi until it becomes Via San Niccolò. Make a right on Via San Miniato, passing through the city walls at Porta San Niccolò. Head up, steeply, on Via Monte alle Croci, and veer left, taking the steps of Via di San Salvatore al Monte. At the top is **Piazzale Michelangelo**, where your effort is rewarded with a breathtaking view of Florence below.

light. Masaccio shaded his figures consistently, so as to suggest a single, strong source of light within the world of the painting but outside its frame. In so doing, he imitated with paint the real-world effect of light on mass, giving his figures a sculptural reality unprecedented in his day. But his skill went beyond mere technical innovation. In the faces of Adam and Eve, you see more than finely modeled figures; you see terrible shame and suffering depicted with a humanity rarely achieved in art. ✉ *Piazza del Carmine, Santo Spirito* ☎ *055/276–8224 reservations* 🌐 *cultura.comune.fi.it/musei* 🎟 *€10* 🕒 *Closed Tues. and Thurs.* ✍ *Reservations to visit the Cappella Brancacci are essential.*

Santo Spirito

CHURCH | The plain, unfinished facade belies and interior that is one of the most important examples of Renaissance architecture in Italy. It's one of a pair designed in Florence by Filippo Brunelleschi in the early decades of the 15th century (the other is San Lorenzo). It was here that Brunelleschi supplied definitive solutions to the two major problems of interior Renaissance church design: how to build a cross-shape interior using classical architectural elements borrowed from antiquity and how to reflect in that interior the order and regularity that Renaissance scientists (among them Brunelleschi himself) were at the time discovering in the natural world around them.

Brunelleschi's solution to the first problem was brilliantly simple: turn a Greek temple inside out. While ancient Greek temples were walled buildings surrounded by classical colonnades, Brunelleschi's churches were classical arcades surrounded by walled buildings. This brilliant architectural idea overthrew the previous era's religious taboo against pagan architecture once and for all, triumphantly claiming that architecture for Christian use.

Brunelleschi's solution to the second problem—making the entire interior orderly and regular—was mathematically precise: he designed the ground plan of the church so that all its parts were proportionally related. The transepts and nave have exactly the same width; the side aisles are precisely half as wide as the nave; the little chapels off the side aisles are exactly half as deep as the side aisles; the chancel and transepts are exactly one-eighth the depth of the nave; and so on, with dizzying exactitude. For Brunelleschi, such a design technique was a matter of passionate conviction. Like most theoreticians of his day, he believed that mathematical regularity and aesthetic beauty were flip sides of the same coin, that one was not possible without the other. In the refectory, adjacent to the church, you can see Andrea Orcagna's highly damaged fresco of the Crucifixion. ✉ *Piazza Santo Spirito 30, Oltrarno* ☎ *055/210030* 🌐 *www.basilicasantospirito.it* 🎟 *Church: free. Tour: €2* 🕒 *Closed Wed.*

🍴 Restaurants

Alla Vecchia Bettola

$ | TUSCAN | The name doesn't exactly mean "old dive," but it comes pretty close. The recipes here come from "wise grandmothers" and celebrate Tuscan food in its glorious simplicity—prosciutto is sliced with a knife, grilled meats are tender, service is friendly, and the wine list is well priced and good. **Known for:** just outside the centro storico but worth the taxi ride; firmly Tuscan menu; grilled meats. [$] *Average main: €14* ✉ *Viale Vasco Pratolini, Oltrarno* ☎ *055/224158* 🕒 *Closed Sun. and Mon.*

Borgo Antico

$ | PIZZA | While you wait for your pizza or other trattoria fare, enjoy a glass of wine or a cocktail. **Known for:** outdoor seating on a beautiful piazza; lively, mostly young, clientele; tasty pizzas. [$] *Average main: €14* ✉ *Piazza Santo Spirito 6/r, Santo Spirito* ☎ *055/210437* 🌐 *www.borgoanticofirenze.com.*

★ Il Santo Bevitore

$ | **TUSCAN** | Florentines and other lovers of good food flock to "The Holy Drinker" for tasty, well-priced dishes. Unpretentious white walls, dark wood furniture, and paper place mats provide the simple decor; start with the exceptional *verdure sott'olio* (vegetables in oil) or the *terrina di fegatini* (a creamy chicken-liver spread) before sampling any of the divine pastas. **Known for:** friendly waitstaff; delicious potato gratin; pasta. [$] *Average main: €11* ✉ *Via Santo Spirito 64/66r, Santo Spirito* ☎ *055/211264* 🌐 *www.ilsantobevitore.com* 🕒 *No lunch Sun.*

★ La Casalinga

$ | **TUSCAN** | *Casalinga* means "housewife," and this place, which has been around since 1963, has the nostalgic charm of a mid-century kitchen with Tuscan comfort food to match. If you eat ribollita anywhere in Florence, eat it here—it couldn't be more authentic. **Known for:** often packed; liver, Venetian style; ribollita. [$] *Average main: €14* ✉ *Via Michelozzi 9/r, Santo Spirito* ☎ *055/218624* 🌐 *www.trattorialacasalinga.it* 🕒 *Closed Sun., 1 wk at Christmas, and 3 wks in Aug.*

L'Osteria dell'Enoteca

$$ | **TUSCAN** | This innovative, charming place serves up remarkable food. Anyone looking for sublime bistecca fiorentina should stop here: it serves the cut from different places on the planet, so you can sample and decide. **Known for:** secondi with dash and fantasy; beyond gracious service; fantastic primi. [$] *Average main: €15* ✉ *Via Romana 70/r, Santo Spirito* ☎ *055/228–6018* 🌐 *www.osteriadellenoteca.com* 🕒 *Closed Tues. No lunch Mon., Wed., and Thurs.*

Osteria Antica Mescita San Niccolò

$ | **TUSCAN** | Always crowded—but always good and inexpensive—this osteria is next to the church of San Niccolò, and, if you sit in the lower part, you'll be in what was once a chapel dating from the 11th century. The subtle but dramatic background nicely complements the food, which is simple Tuscan at its best. **Known for:** outdoor seating in a small, lovely square; great, simple salads; delicious soup. [$] *Average main: €11* ✉ *Via San Niccolò 60/r, San Niccolò* ☎ *055/234–2836* 🌐 *www.osteriasanniccolo.it.*

Quattro Leoni

$$ | **ITALIAN** | The eclectic staff at this trattoria in a small piazza is an appropriate match for the diverse menu. In winter, you can eat in one of two rooms with high ceilings, and, in summer, you can sit outside and admire the scenery. **Known for:** Tuscan favorites; outdoor seating on a quaint piazza; funky food combinations. [$] *Average main: €19* ✉ *Via dei Vellutini 1/r, Piazza della Passera, Palazzo Pitti* ☎ *055/218562* 🌐 *www.4Leoni.it.*

Zeb

$$ | **TUSCAN** | "Zeb" stands for *zuppa e bollito* (soup and boiled things), but you can't go wrong with anything at this small *alimentari* (delicatessen). It's home-style Tuscan cuisine at its very best, served in unpretentious, intimate surroundings: there's room for only about 15 guests. **Known for:** lovely wine list; terrific pasta; fantastic soup. [$] *Average main: €17* ✉ *Via San Miniato 2, Oltrarno* ☎ *055/234–2864* 🌐 *www.zebgastronomia.com* 🕒 *Closed Wed. Nov.–Mar.: no dinner Sun.–Tues. Apr.–Oct.: no dinner Sun.*

Coffee and Quick Bites

Formaggioteca Terroir

$ | **ITALIAN** | This little wine bar combines the best of Italian and French cheeses with wine from the same places to create true gustatory pleasure. The list of crostini is creative and offers some unusual pairings (like French Brie with Italian Speck, which is dotted with a spicy tomato chutney). **Known for:** creative menu; charming staff; gorgeous wines by the glass. [$] *Average main: €11* ✉ *Via dei Renai 19, Oltrarno* ☎ *055/215901* 🌐 *www.formaggiotecaterroir.it.*

★ Fuori Porta

$ | **WINE BAR** | What is, perhaps, the oldest and best wine bar in Florence serves cured meats and cheeses, as well as daily specials. *Crostini* and *crostoni*—grilled breads topped with a mélange of cheeses and meats—are the house specialty, but the verdure sott'olio are divine, too. The lengthy wine list offers great options by the glass and terrific bottles from all over Italy and beyond. **Known for:** changing daily specials; crostini and crostoni; lengthy wine list. [$] *Average main: €11* ✉ *Via Monte alle Croci 10/r, San Niccolò* ☎ *055/234–2483* 🌐 *www.fuoriporta.it.*

Gelateria la Carraia

$ | **ICE CREAM** | **FAMILY** | Although it's a bit of a haul to get here (it's at the foot of Ponte Carraia, two bridges down from the Ponte Vecchio), you'll be well rewarded for doing so, with standard gelato flavors or creative options such as *limone con biscotti* (lemon sorbet with cookies). **Known for:** every flavor is delicious; generous €1 tasting cones; super-creamy gelato. [$] *Average main: €3* ✉ *Piazza Nazario Sauro 2, Santo Spirito* ☎ *055/280695* 🌐 *www.lacarraiagroup.eu.*

★ Il Santino

$ | **WINE BAR** | Though it has only four tables and four small stools at an equally small bar, Il Santino is blessed with a big wine list and superior cheeses, cured meats, and other delicacies. It's the perfect place to have a snack or a light lunch. **Known for:** great daily specials; great prices; knowledgeable staff. [$] *Average main: €6* ✉ *Via Santo Spirito 60/r, Santo Spirito* ☎ *055/230–2820* 🌐 *www.ilsantobevitore.com.*

★ Le Volpi e l'Uva

$ | **WINE BAR** | An oenophile's dream, this spot—whose name translates as "the foxes and the grape" and is based on one of Aesop's fables—is off Piazza Santa Felicita. Here, affable, knowledgeable "*volpi*" (foxes), pour wines by the glass and serve equally impressive cheeses and bite-size sandwiches. **Known for:** French wines (in addition to Italian); outdoor seating; a great cheese selection (including French cheeses). [$] *Average main: €10* ✉ *Piazza de' Rossi 1, Palazzo Pitti* ☎ *055/239–8132* 🌐 *www.levolpieluva.com* 🕓 *Closed Sun.*

Pitti Gola

$ | **WINE BAR** | At Pitti Gola you can order tasty tidbits to accompany your choices from the extensive and impressive wine list. The outdoor seats have a view of Palazzo Pitti. **Known for:** interesting crostini combinations; a wine-tasting lunch; vegetarian options. [$] *Average main: €11* ✉ *Piazza Pitti 16, Palazzo Pitti* ☎ *55/212704* 🌐 *www.pittigolaecantina.com* 🕓 *Closed Tues.*

🛏 Hotels

Hotel La Scaletta

$$ | **HOTEL** | In addition to a tremendous view of the Boboli Gardens, this cozy pensione near the Ponte Vecchio and Palazzo Pitti has simply furnished but large rooms and a sunny breakfast room. **Pros:** in-house restaurant with stunning views; wonderful, multilingual staff; in a lively neighborhood. **Cons:** books up quickly; neighborhood can be noisy; small elevator, many steps. [$] *Rooms from: €152* ✉ *Via Guicciardini 13, Palazzo Pitti* ☎ *055/283028* 🌐 *www.hotellascaletta.it* 🛏 *36 rooms* 🍴 *Free Breakfast.*

Hotel Lungarno

$$$$ | **HOTEL** | Many rooms and suites here have private terraces that jut out over the Arno, granting stunning views of the Palazzo Vecchio and the Lungarno; a studio suite in a 13th-century tower preserves details like exposed stone walls and old archways, and looks over a little square with a medieval tower covered in jasmine. **Pros:** upscale without being stuffy; Borgo San Jacopo, its attached restaurant; lovely views of the Arno. **Cons:** walls can be thin; street noise happens; rooms without Arno views feel less special. [$] *Rooms from: €680* ✉ *Borgo*

San Jacopo 14, Oltrarno ☎ *055/27261* 🌐 *www.lungarnocollection.com* 🛏 *67 rooms* 🍴 *Free Breakfast.*

Hotel Silla

$$ | HOTEL | Rooms in this 15th-century palazzo, entered via a courtyard with potted plants and sculpture-filled niches, are simply furnished; some have Arno views, others have stuccoed ceilings. **Pros:** in the middle of everything except the crowds; great breakfast; cordial, friendly staff. **Cons:** could use an update; small rooms; street noise. [$] *Rooms from: €130* ✉ *Via de' Renai 5, San Niccolò* ☎ *055/234–2888* 🌐 *www.hotelsilla.it* 🛏 *36 rooms* 🍴 *Free Breakfast.*

Nightlife

Montecarla

BARS | People sip cocktails against a backdrop of exotic flowers, leopard-print chairs and chintz, surrounded by red walls on the two crowded floors at Montecarla. ✉ *Via de' Bardi 2, San Niccolò* ☎ *055/294778.*

Zoe

BARS | Though it's called a *caffetteria,* and coffee is served (as well as terrific salads and burgers at lunchtime), Zoe's fine cocktails are the real draw for elegant Florentines who come here to see and be seen. ✉ *Via de' Renai 13/r, San Niccolò* ☎ *055/243111* 🌐 *www.zoebar.it.*

Performing Arts

Accademia Bartolomeo Cristofori

MUSIC | Also known as the Amici del Fortepiano (Friends of the Fortepiano), the Accademia Bartolomeo Cristofori sponsors fortepiano concerts throughout the year. ✉ *Via di Camaldoli 7/r, Santo Spirito* ☎ *055/221646* 🌐 *www.accademiacristofori.it.*

Shopping

★ **Giulio Giannini e Figlio**

STATIONERY | One of Florence's oldest paper-goods stores is *the* place to buy the marbleized stock, which comes in many shapes and sizes, from flat sheets to boxes and even on pencils. ✉ *Piazza Pitti 37/r, Oltrarno* ☎ *055/212621* 🌐 *www.giuliogiannini.com.*

★ **Il Torchio**

STATIONERY | Photograph albums, frames, diaries, and other objects dressed in handmade paper are high quality, and the prices lower than usual. ✉ *Via dei Bardi 17, San Niccolò* ☎ *055/234–2862* 🌐 *www.legatoriailtorchio.com.*

Maçel

WOMEN'S CLOTHING | Browse collections by lesser-known Italian designers, many of whom use the same factories as the A-list, at this women's clothing shop. ✉ *Via Guicciardini 128/r, Palazzo Pitti* ☎ *055/287355.*

★ **Madova**

HATS & GLOVES | Complete your winter wardrobe with a pair of high-quality leather gloves, available in a rainbow of colors and a choice of linings (silk, cashmere, and unlined), from Madova. It's been in business for 100 years. ✉ *Via Guicciardini 1/r, Palazzo Pitti* ☎ *055/239–6526* 🌐 *www.madova.com.*

Pitti Mosaici

HOUSEWARES | Stones are worked into exquisite tables, pictures, and jewelry at Pitti Mosaici, which continues the pietre dure tradition that was all the rage of 16th-century Florence. ✉ *Piazza dei Pitti 23/r, Palazzo Pitti* ☎ *055/282127* 🌐 *www.pittimosaici.com.*

Santo Spirito Flea Market

MARKET | FAMILY | The second Sunday of every month brings the Santo Spirito flea market. On the third Sunday of the month, vendors at the Fierucola organic fest sell such delectables as honeys, jams, spice mixes, and fresh vegetables. ✉ *Piazza Santo Spirito, Santo Spirito.*

Tiziana Alemanni
WOMEN'S CLOTHING | This dressmaker creates beautiful bespoke clothing. ✉ *Sdrucciolo de'Pitti 20/r, Santo Spirito* ☎ *327/674–5143* ⊕ *tizianaalemanni.it.*

Side Trips from Florence

Fiesole

10 km (6 miles) northeast of Florence city center.

A half-day excursion to Fiesole, in the hills above Florence, gives you a pleasant respite from museums and a wonderful view of the city. Fiesole began life as an ancient Etruscan and later Roman village that held some power until it succumbed to barbarian invasions. Eventually it gave up its independence in exchange for Florence's protection. The medieval cathedral, ancient Roman amphitheater, and lovely old villas behind garden walls are clustered on a series of hilltops. A walk around Fiesole can take from one to two or three hours.

GETTING HERE AND AROUND
The trip from Florence by car takes 20 to 30 minutes. Drive to Piazza Liberta, and cross the Ponte Rosso heading in the direction of the SS65/SR65. Turn right on to Via Salviati and continue on to Via Roccettini. Make a left turn to Via Vecchia Fiesolana, which will take you directly to the center of town.

There are several possible routes for the two-hour walk from central Florence to Fiesole. One route begins in the residential area of Salviatino (Via Barbacane, near Piazza Edison, on the Bus 7 route), and, after a short time, offers peeks over garden walls of beautiful villas, as well as the view over your shoulder at the panorama of Florence in the valley. A city bus can also get you to Fiesole with much greater ease.

VISITOR INFORMATION
CONTACTS Fiesole Tourism Office. ✉ *Via Portigiani 3* ☎ *055/596–1311* ⊕ *www. fiesoleforyou.it.*

Sights

Anfiteatro Romano (*Roman Amphitheater*)
RUINS | The beautifully preserved, 2,000-seat Anfiteatro Romano, near the Duomo, dates from the 1st century BC and is still used for summer concerts. To the right of the amphitheater are the remains of the Terme Romani (Roman Baths), where you can see the gymnasium, hot and cold baths, and rectangular chamber where the water was heated.

A beautifully designed Museo Archeologico, its facade evoking an ancient Roman temple, is built amid the ruins and contains objects dating from as early as 2000 BC. The nearby Museo Bandini is filled with the private collection of Canon Angelo Maria Bandini (1726–1803); he fancied 13th- to 15th-century Florentine paintings, terra-cotta pieces, and wood sculpture, which he later bequeathed to the Diocese of Fiesole. ✉ *Via Portigiani 1, Fiesole* ☎ *055/596–1293* ⊕ *www. museidifiesole.it* 🖾 *€12, includes access to archaeological park and museums* ⊙ *Museo Bandini closed Mon.–Thurs.*

Badia Fiesolana
CHURCH | From the church of San Domenico it's a five-minute walk northwest to Fiesole's original cathedral. Dating from the 11th century, it was first the home of the Camaldolese monks. Thanks to Cosimo il Vecchio de'Medici, the complex was substantially restructured. The facade, never completed owing to Cosimo's death, contains elements of its original Romanesque decoration. ✉ *Via della Badia dei Roccettini 11, Fiesole* ☎ *055/46851* ⊕ *www.eui.eu* ⊙ *Closed Sat. afternoon and Sun.*

Duomo
CHURCH | A stark medieval interior yields many masterpieces. In the raised

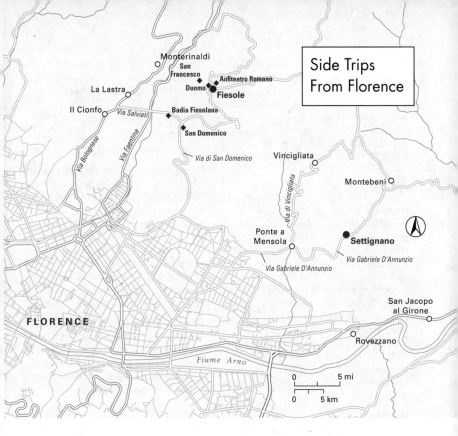

Monterinaldi
San
Francesco
Anfiteatro Romano
La Lastra
Duomo
Fiesole
Il Cionfo
Via Salviati
Badia Fiesolana
San Domenico
Via di San Domenico
Vincigliata
Montebeni
Ponte a
Mensola
Settignano
Via Gabriele D'Annunzio
Via Gabriele D'Annunzio
San Jacopo
al Girone
FLORENCE
Rovezzano
Fiume Arno

0   5 mi
0   5 km

Via Bolognese
Via Faentina
Via di Vincigliata

presbytery, the Cappella Salutati was frescoed by 15th-century artist Cosimo Rosselli, but it was his contemporary, sculptor Mino da Fiesole (1430–84), who put the town on the artistic map. The Madonna on the altarpiece and the tomb of Bishop Salutati are fine examples of the artist's work. ⊠ *Piazza Mino da Fiesole, Fiesole.*

San Domenico

CHURCH | If you really want to stretch your legs, walk 4 km (2½ miles) toward the center of Florence along Via Vecchia Fiesolana, a narrow lane in use since Etruscan times, to the church of San Domenico. Sheltered in the church is the *Madonna and Child with Saints* by Fra Angelico, who was a Dominican friar here before he moved to Florence. ⊠ *Piazza San Domenico, off Via Giuseppe Mantellini, Fiesole* ♥ *Closed Sun.*

San Francesco

CHURCH | This lovely hilltop church has a good view of Florence and the plain below from its terrace and benches. Off the little cloister is a small, eclectic museum containing, among other things, two Egyptian mummies. Halfway up the hill you'll see sloping steps to the right; they lead to a fragrant wooded park with trails that loop out and back to the church. ⊠ *Via San Francesco 13, Fiesole* ☎ *055/59175* ⊕ *www.fratifiesole. it* ⊠ *Free.*

Restaurants

La Reggia degli Etruschi

$$$ | **ITALIAN** | Atop a steep hill, en route to the church of San Francesco, this lovely little eatery is certainly worth the trek. Indulge in inventive reworkings of Tuscan classics, like the *mezzaluna di pera a* pecorino (little half-moon pasta stuffed with pear and pecorino) sauced with Roquefort and poppy seeds. **Known for:** small terrace with outdoor seating; good wine list and friendly service; out-of-the-way location. $ *Average main: €25* ✉ *Via San Francesco 18, Fiesole* ☎ *333/355–6126* ⊕ *www.lareggiadeglietruschi.com.*

Hotels

Fattoria di Maiano

$$ | **HOTEL** | **FAMILY** | In the foothills between Florence and Fiesole are these lovely apartments, which sleep 4 to 11 people and which are generally rented by the week. **Pros:** great way to have a country experience with the city nearby; beautiful views and clean air; the pool when it's hot. **Cons:** gets groups; minimum stay of at least three nights; a car is an absolute necessity. $ *Rooms from: €132* ✉ *Via Benedetto da Maiano 11, Fiesole* ☎ *055/599600* ⊕ *www.fattoriadimaiano.com* 🛏 *8 rooms, 12 apartments* ◯| *Free Breakfast.*

Villa San Michele

$$$$ | **HOTEL** | The cypress-lined driveway provides an elegant preamble to this incredibly gorgeous (and very expensive) hotel nestled in the hills of Fiesole. **Pros:** exceptional convent conversion; shuttle bus makes frequent forays to and from Florence; stunning views. **Cons:** you must either depend on the shuttle bus or have a car; some rooms are small; money must be no object. $ *Rooms from: €1715* ✉ *Via Doccia 4, Fiesole* ☎ *055/567–8200* ⊕ *www.belmond.com/hotels/europe/italy* ◷ *Closed Nov.–Easter* 🛏 *45 rooms* ◯| *Free Breakfast.*

🎭 Performing Arts

Estate Fiesolana

FESTIVALS | From June through August, Estate Fiesolana, a festival of theater, music, dance, and film, takes place in Fiesole's churches and in the Roman amphitheater—demonstrating that the ancient

Romans knew a thing or two about acoustics. ✉ *Teatro Romano, Fiesole* ☎ *055/59611* ⊕ *www.estatefiesolana.it.*

Settignano

8 km (5 miles) east of Florence city center.

When Florence is overcrowded and hot, this village, a 20-minute car or bus trip east of Florence, is particularly appealing. It was the birthplace of many artists, including the sculptors Desiderio di Settignano (circa 1428–64), Antonio (1427–79), Bernardo (1409–64), Rossellino, and Bartolomeo Ammannati (1511–92). Michelangelo's wet nurse was the wife of a stonecutter in Settignano, and to her he attributed his later calling in life.

GETTING HERE AND AROUND

Take Bus 10, from the station at Santa Maria Novella or at Piazza San Marco, all the way to the end of the line—the *capolinea.* It will put you in the middle of Settignano's piazzetta.

 Restaurants

Osvaldo

$ | **TUSCAN** | If you're making the trip to Settignano, get off Bus 10 at the stop called Ponte a Mensola for a meal at this small, unassuming, family-run trattoria situated along a street and a tiny stream. The food is terrific, and though it is described as *cucina casalinga* (home cooking), only the portions are home style. **Known for:** zuppa inglese (Italian-style trifle); locals love the place; fantastic pasta made in-house. $ *Average main: €12* ✉ *Via G. D'Annunzio 51/r, Settignano* ☎ *055/602168* ⊕ *www.trattoriaosvaldo.it* ◷ *Closed Wed. No lunch Tues.*

Chapter 4

PISA, LUCCA, AND NORTHWEST TUSCANY

4

Updated by
Patricia Rucidlo

 Sights
★★★★★

 Restaurants
★★★★★

 Hotels
★★★★☆

 Shopping
★★★☆☆

 Nightlife
★★★☆☆

WELCOME TO PISA, LUCCA, AND NORTHWEST TUSCANY

TOP REASONS TO GO

★ **Leaning Tower of Pisa:** It may be touristy, but it's still a whole lot of fun to climb to the top and admire the view.

★ **Olive-oil tasting in and around Lucca:** Italian olive oil is justifiably world famous, and cognoscenti insist that the best is found here.

★ **Cappella Maggiore, Duomo, Prato:** Filippo Lippi's solemn frescoes depicting scenes from the lives of John the Baptist and St. Stephen positively glow.

★ **Bagni di Lucca:** This sleepy little town attracted the English Romantics, among others, who were drawn to its salubrious waters and air.

★ **Tomb of Ilaria del Carretto, Duomo, Lucca:** Check out this moving sculpture by Jacopo della Quercia commemorating a young woman who died in childbirth.

1 **Montelupo.** A town noted for its ceramics.

2 **Empoli.** Of Dante's *Inferno* fame.

3 **Vinci.** Namesake of Leonardo.

4 **San Miniato.** A well-preserved hill town.

5 **Pisa.** There's more than just its leaning tower.

6 **Prato.** Famous for its wool industry.

7 **Pistoia.** Known for its plant nurseries.

8 **Montecatini Terme.** As seen in Fellini's 8½.

9 **Lucca.** Historic town with 99 churches.

10 **San Marcello Pistoiese.** A ski destination.

11 **Abetone.** A mountain vacation spot.

12 **Bagni Di Lucca.** Former home of poet Percy Shelley.

13 **Barga.** The Buffalo Soldiers defended this region in World War II.

14 **Castelnuovo Di Garfagnana.** Visit its busy historic center.

15 **Livorno.** A stopover for Britons in 19th century.

16 **Viareggio.** A popular summer beach town.

17 **Forte Dei Marmi.** The East Hampton of Italy.

18 **Carrara.** Famed for its marble.

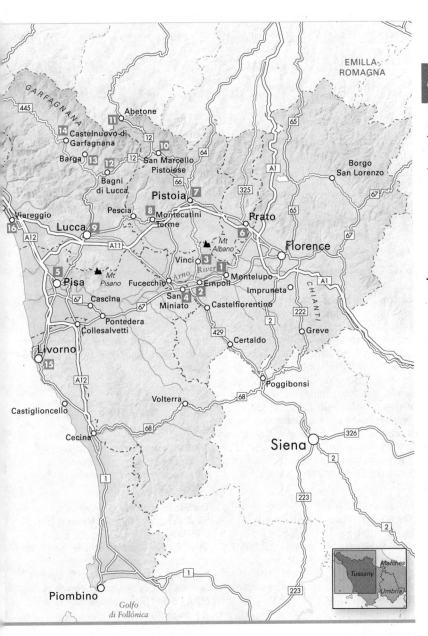

GARFAGNANA

EMILIA-ROMAGNA

445

Abetone

11 Castelnuovo di
Garfagnana

14

12

Barga

13 **12**

12

Bagni
di Lucca

10 San Marcello
Pistoiese

64

66

Pistoia **7**

Borgo
San Lorenzo

A1

325

65

67

Viareggio

Pescia

8 Montecatini
Terme

Prato **6**

65

67

16

Lucca **9**

A12

A11

Mt
Albano

Florence

5

Mt
Pisano

Pisa

Vinci **3**

1

Montelupo

A1

Fucecchio

Arno River

Empoli

Impruneta

CHIANTI

Cascina

67

San
Miniato

4 **2**

Castelfiorentino

67

Pontedera

Collesalvetti

2

222

Greve

Livorno

429

Certaldo

15

A12

Castiglioncello

Volterra

Poggibonsi

68

Cecina

68

326

Siena

2

1

223

2

Piombino

223

Golfo
di Follónica

Tuscany   Marches
Umbria

Lucca and Pisa are the most-visited cities of northwest Tuscany, and with good reason: Lucca has a charming historic center within its 16th-century walls, and Pisa is home to what may be the world's most famous tower. Both cities are due west of Florence, and although the landscape along the way isn't Tuscany's finest, several smaller cities offer good restaurants, a few noteworthy sights, and a taste of Italian life away from the main tourism centers.

Farther north the setting gets more impressive. Craggy, often snowcapped mountains rise above sparsely populated valleys, accessed by narrow winding roads. This is the Garfagnana, Tuscany's most mountainous territory, cut through by the majestic Alpi Apuane. The steep terrain rolls down into pine-forested hills and eventually meets the wide, sandy beaches of the Ligurian Sea. Along this stretch, known as the Versilian Coast, are the resort towns of Viareggio and Forte dei Marmi, both of which pack in Italian and other European beachgoers in the summer.

MAJOR REGIONS

Towns west of Florence. At industrial centers from the Middle Ages such as **Prato** and **Pistoia,** you can relax far from Florence's throngs and savor fine food and some art gems. Fragrant white truffles adorn many a restaurant menu in **San Miniato.**

Pisa. Thanks to an engineering mistake, the name Pisa is recognized the world over. The Leaning Tower, the baptistery, the Camposanto, and the cathedral make an impressive foursome on the Piazza del Duomo.

Lucca. This laid-back yet elegant town is surrounded by tree-bedecked 16th-century ramparts that are now a delightful promenade.

The Garfagnana. Sports enthusiasts and nature addicts flock to **Abetone** to ski in winter and refresh themselves with cool, mountain air in summer.

The Northwest Coast. Experience Italian beach culture at **Forte dei Marmi,** a crowded and expensive place to see and be seen. Farther west, a hop over the border from Tuscany into Liguria brings you to the Cinque Terre—five tiny, cliff-hugging, seaside villages that have become some of Italy's most popular destinations and are worth a side trip.

Planning

Getting Here and Around

BUS

Many of the region's cities have bus stations, served by two primary companies, but bus travel is often complicated; it's easier to take the train to Pisa, Prato, Pistoia, Lucca, Montecatini Terme, Livorno, and Empoli, where service is regular and trains run frequently. San Miniato and environs are best reached by car, as service is limited.

It's possible to take a bus from Pistoia or Florence to Abetone. A car is necessary to see Carrara and the rest of the Versilian Coast because bus service is dicey. For side trips to the Cinque Terre, buses will get you to La Spezia, and from there you can take the train to Riomaggiore.

COPIT. This bus service connects Empoli, Montelupo, Florence, Prato, and Pistoia; it also has Florence–Abetone service. ☎ *0573/3630 in Pistoia* ⊕ *www.copitspa.it.*
SITA. This bus service connects Florence and Empoli. ☎ *055/47821 in Florence* ⊕ *www.busitalia.it.*

CAR

The best way to explore the region is by car—and part of the fun is stopping to take in the scenery. In the northern part of the region, towns are spread out, and driving the winding mountain roads adds to your travel time.

The A1 autostrada connects Florence to Prato. For Pistoia, Montecatini, and Lucca, follow signs for Firenze Nord, which connects to the A11. For Empoli, Pisa, and hill towns west, take the Strada Grande Communicazione Firenze-Pisa-Livorno, commonly known as the Fi-Pi-Li and sometimes indicated on signage as S.G.C. Firenze-Pisa-Livorno, from Scandicci, just outside Florence. (Note that the Fi-Pi-Li is notorious for its frequent delays due to accidents and construction.)

The A12 will take you from near Pisa along the Versilian Coast to La Spezia, entryway to the Cinque Terre. The Cinque Terre itself is impractical for car travel because of the narrow roads and lack of parking (although better access and parking are available at the northern and southern towns of Monterosso al Mare and Riomaggiore). From La Spezia you can take the train, which is the main means of access to the area.

TRAIN

Two main train lines run from Florence's Santa Maria Novella station into northwest Tuscany—one traveling through Prato, Pistoia, Montecatini, and Lucca; the other through Empoli and Pisa. The two lines meet up on the coast with a line that runs through Livorno, Viareggio, and La Spezia.

Trains are a viable option if you're going to any of these cities. For the rest of northwest Tuscany, train connections are extremely limited or nonexistent.

To reach the Cinque Terre, you can take a train to La Spezia, and then pick up a local train to any of the five towns.

Making the Most of Your Time

The majority of first-time visitors to Tuscany start out by exploring Florence, and then are lured south by the Chianti district and Siena. Heading west instead is an appealing alternative. Pisa is the main attraction, and it certainly isn't short on tourists. If that's all you want (or have time) to see here, you're probably best off doing it as a day trip from Florence. If you want to stick around for a while, consider making Lucca your base. It's a tremendously appealing town, with fine food and an easygoing atmosphere.

From Lucca you can discover the rest of the area on day trips. The Garfagnana has gorgeous mountain peaks and excellent hiking opportunities (as well as skiing in winter).

You may not think of Tuscany as a beach destination, but its long coastline is popular with Italian vacationers. From June through August the resort towns of Viareggio, Forte dei Marmi, and Marina di Massa are packed with beachgoers. Bagni (bathhouses) open, and the sands fill with colorful umbrellas and beach chairs; you can rent your own for about €20 a day and upward.

Note that you can readily follow a day in the mountains of the Garfagnana with a day along the coast, continuing from Tuscany's resort towns all the way to those that make up the Cinque Terre.

Hotels

Excluding the beach resort towns, lodging is generally a better deal here than elsewhere in Tuscany, and some real bargains can be found in off-the-beaten-path towns. Consider staying at an *agriturismo*, a farm or vineyard with guest accommodations, which can range from rustic to stately.

Many area hotel restaurants serve excellent food, and meal plans are usually available as supplements to your room rate. In summer, when Florence is hot and crowded, it's not a bad plan to base yourself in one of the surrounding towns and use the train to make day trips into the city.

Hotel and restaurant reviews have been shortened. For full information, visit Fodors.com. Hotel prices are the lowest cost of a standard double room in high season. Restaurant prices are the average cost of a main course at dinner or, if dinner is not served, at lunch.

WHAT IT COSTS in Euros			
$	$$	$$$	$$$$
RESTAURANTS			
under €15	€15–€24	€25–€35	over €35
HOTELS			
under €125	€125–€200	€201–€300	over €300

Montelupo

30 km (19 miles) southwest of Florence, 6 km (4 miles) east of Empoli.

This small town, which straddles the Arno, and its surrounding villages have been producing ceramics for centuries. A ceramics museum proudly displays the work of the past, but the finest tribute to the tradition is the fact Montelupo's *centro storico* (historic center) is filled with shops selling top-quality ceramics that are still handmade in the region.

GETTING HERE
Train service does run from Florence's Santa Maria Novella to Montelupo. It's also an easy drive on the Fi-Pi-Li highway.

VISITOR INFORMATION
CONTACTS Montelupo Tourism Office.
✉ *Piazza Vittorio Veneto 10, Montelupo Fiorentino* ☎ *0571/51352* ⊕ *www.museo-montelupo.it.*

 Sights

Museo della Ceramica (*Museum of Archaeology and Ceramics*)
ART MUSEUM | The Museo della Ceramica has some 3,000 pieces of majolica, a type of glazed pottery made in this region since the early 14th century. The museum is beautifully lighted, and objects dating from the early 14th century to the late 18th century are well labeled and arranged, providing a good overview of the region's ceramics-making history. There's also an interesting display of the

Going Local at Festivals

A great way to get a feel for the region and its people is to attend a local *sagra* (festival). In summer, there's one taking place nearly every weekend in some small town or village, usually with a food theme, such as a *sagra dei funghi* (mushroom festival) or *sagra della zuppa* (soup festival). Held at night, the events dish out plenty to eat and drink, and there's usually dancing, sometimes with live music. Old-school ballroom moves are the norm; you're likely to see couples fox-trotting or doing the tango.

These are village affairs, with few people speaking English. There are no numbers to call for information. The festivals are advertised only by crudely printed signs on the side of the road. Attending a sagra is a unique opportunity to experience small-town Italian culture.

coats of arms of important Renaissance families such as the Medici and Strozzi. ✉ *Piazza Vittorio Veneto 10, Montelupo Fiorentino* ☎ *0571/51352* ⊕ *www.museo-montelupo.it* 🎟 *€5* ⊙ *Closed Mon.*

Performing Arts

FESTIVALS

Festa della Ceramica

FESTIVALS | FAMILY | Every June, Montelupo hosts the weeklong ceramics festival that includes exhibitions of local and international art, demonstrations of techniques new and ancient, and street theater and music. Of course, ceramics from around the world are for sale, too. Additional information about the ceramics festival is available from the Montelupo Fiorentino tourist office. ✉ *Montelupo Fiorentino* ☎ *0571/51352 tourist office.*

🛍 Shopping

Many of the pieces for sale at Montelupo's ceramics shops follow traditional styles, but some artists bring modern inspiration to their wheels. Note that not all of the stores will ship items home for you.

Bartoloni: La Ceramica Tradizionale di Montelupo

CERAMICS | Down the road from the Museo della Ceramica, this shop produces objects in a range of styles. ✉ *Corso Garibaldi 36, Montelupo Fiorentino* ☎ *0571/913569* ⊕ *www.ceramicabartoloni.it/sito/dove_siamo.htm.*

Ceramica ND Dolfi

CERAMICS | Run by the same family for three generations, this ceramics-making compound is 3 km (2 miles) from Montelupo on the road heading east toward Florence. Here you'll find a sun-drenched *spazio aziendale* (selling floor), a factory workshop, the family residence, and a yard where terra-cotta planters are displayed. The ceramics, all priced reasonably given the high-quality handcrafted work, include large vases, plates suitable for hanging, and brightly colored serving pieces for the table. ✉ *Via Toscoromagnola 1, Località Antinoro, Montelupo Fiorentino* ☎ *0571/51264* ⊕ *www.nddolfi.it.*

Le Ceramiche del Borgo

CERAMICS | Le Ceramiche del Borgo sells the work of Eugenio Taccini (among others), which includes bowls, platters, tiles, and plates. The store's proprietor (and artist's daughter), Lea Taccini, speaks English. ✉ *XX Settembre 30, Empoli* ☎ *0571/518856* ⊕ *www.galleriartigianato.it.*

Empoli

33 km (21 miles) west of Florence, 50 km (31 miles) east of Pisa.

Empoli, roughly halfway between Florence and Pisa, is a small town with a long history. References to the city first appear in documents from the 800s. By the late 12th century, it was under the control of Florence. It was here, in 1260, after the Battle of Montaperti, that Farinata degli Uberti, leader of the Ghibellines, decided not to burn Florence to the ground. Dante immortalized this decision in Canto X of his *Inferno.*

Now Empoli is a sleepy little town that's a quick train ride from Florence. If you're traveling in summer, when Florence is at its hottest and most crowded, you might consider staying here and hopping on the train for day trips into the city. But don't overlook the sights of Empoli itself—they're worth seeing.

GETTING HERE

Empoli is an easy 20-minute train ride from Florence's Santa Maria Novella station. If you're driving, take the Fi-Pi-Li—and head out armed with patience. The road is regularly under construction, and there are often delays due to accidents. Lazzi provides bus service from Florence to Empoli.

VISITOR INFORMATION

CONTACTS Empoli Tourism Office.
✉ *Piazza Farinata degli Uberti 3, Empoli* ☎ *0571/55671,* ⊕ *www.toscananelcuore. it.*

 Sights

Collegiata di Sant'Andrea

ART MUSEUM | The Collegiata di Sant'Andrea is a jewel of a museum, filled with terra-cotta sculptures from the della Robbia school, including one by Andrea della Robbia. There's also a magnificent 15th-century fresco pietà by Masolino (circa 1383–1440), as well as a small work by Fra Filippo Lippi (1406–69) and a wonderful tabernacle attributed to Francesco Botticini (circa 1446–97) and Antonio Rossellino (1427–79). On Sunday afternoon, entrance to the museum is free. ✉ *Just off Piazza Farinata degli Uberti, Empoli* ☎ *0571/76284* ⊕ *www. collegiatasantandreaempoli.it* 🎟 *From €5* ⊘ *Closed Mon.*

San Michele in Pontorme

CHURCH | A short but not very scenic walk from the center of town brings you to the little church of San Michele in Pontorme, chiefly notable for the gorgeous *St. John the Baptist* and *St. Michael the Archangel,* two works dating from about 1519 by native son Jacopo Carrucci (1494–1556), better known as Pontormo. Opening hours are erratic, so it's best to check with the tourist information office to see what's what. ✉ *Piazza San Michele, Empoli* 🎟 *Free.*

Santo Stefano

CHURCH | Originally founded by Augustinians in the 11th century, the church of Santo Stefano can be visited only by requesting a tour in the Collegiata di Sant'Andrea. It's worth the walk around the corner and down the street to see the *sinopie* (preparatory drawings) by Masolino depicting scenes from the *Legend of the True Cross.* He left without actually frescoing them; it may be that the Augustinian friars were late in making payment. ✉ *Via de' Neri, Empoli* ☎ *0571/76284* 🎟 *Free with admission to the Collegiata* ⊘ *Closed Mon.*

Villa di Cerreto Guidi

HISTORIC HOME | On the night of July 15, 1576, Isabella de' Medici, daughter of the all-powerful Cosimo I, grand duke of Tuscany, was murdered by her husband in the Villa Medicea in the town of Cerreto Guidi for "reasons of honor"—that is, she was suspected of adultery. These days, although the villa's formal garden is in somewhat imperfect condition, the vast halls and chambers within remain majestic. Copies of portraits of various

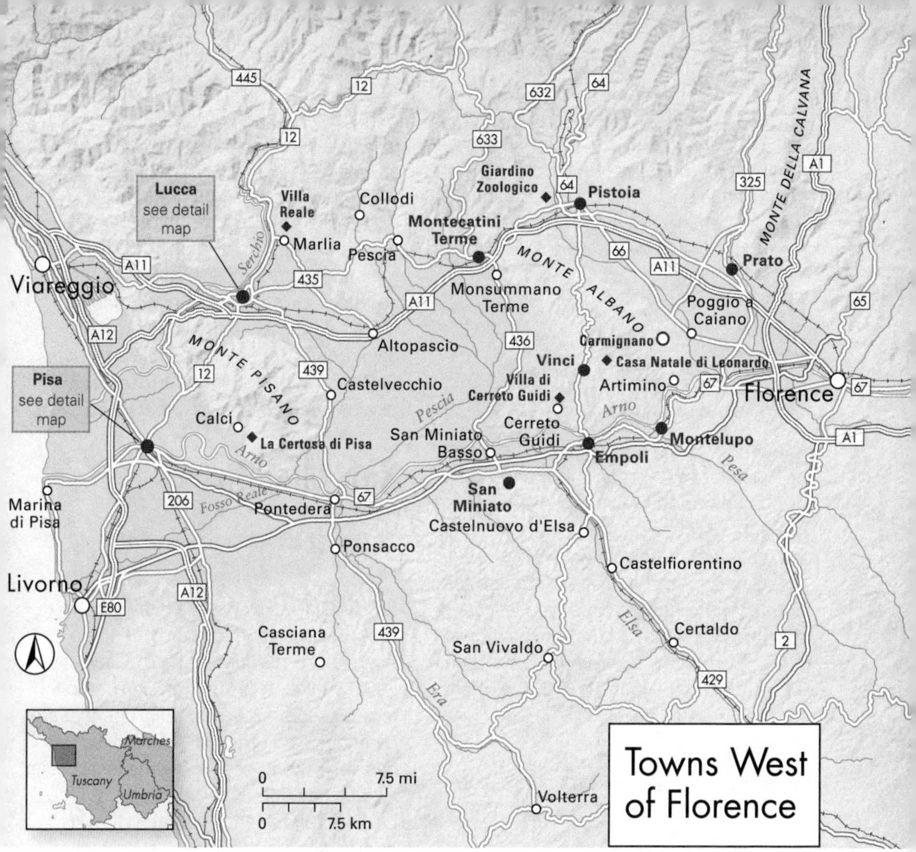
Towns West of Florence
Lucca
see detail map
Pisa
see detail map
Viareggio
Marina di Pisa
Livorno
Villa Reale
Marlia
Collodi
Pescia
Montecatini Terme
Giardino Zoologico
Pistoia
Prato
Monsummano Terme
MONTE ALBANO
MONTE DELLA CALVANA
Poggio a Caiano
Carmignano
Casa Natale di Leonardo
Artimino
Florence
Vinci
Villa di Cerreto Guidi
Cerreto Guidi
Empoli
Montelupo
Altopascio
MONTE PISANO
Castelvecchio
Calci
La Certosa di Pisa
San Miniato Basso
San Miniato
Pontedera
Castelnuovo d'Elsa
Ponsacco
Castelfiorentino
Certaldo
Casciana Terme
San Vivaldo
Volterra
Serchio
Arno
Pescia
Pesa
Fosso Reale
Elsa
Era
Tuscany
Marches
Umbria
0
7.5 mi
7.5 km

Medici, including Isabella, cover the walls. The villa sits atop the highest point in Cerreto Guidi, encircled by two narrow streets where the daily business of the town goes on. As you stand on the wide, flat front lawn, high above the streets of the town, with the villa behind you and terraced hillsides of olive groves and vineyards stretching into the distance, you can imagine what it was like to be a Medici. To see the villa, ring the bell for the custodian. ✉ *8 km (5 miles) west of Empoli, Via di Ponte Medicee, Cerreto Guidi* ☎ *0571/55707* 🌐 *www.polomuseale.firenze.it* 🎫 *Free* 🕑 *Closed 2nd and 3rd Mon. of month.*

🍴 Restaurants

Bar Leonardo

$ | ITALIAN | FAMILY | It's a most unassuming bar a stone's throw away from a massive Medici villa up the hill, and you might be tempted to walk right past it. Besides serving the usual array of coffees, spritzes, panini, and wines by the glass, it turns out terrific pizzas. **Known for:** outdoor seating; sumptuous pizzas; kind staff. [$] *Average main: €9* ✉ *Piazza Leonardo da Vinci 11, Cerreto Giudi.*

Schiacciavineria

$ | ITALIAN | Panini are the order of the day here, and they come with historic names (bearing no relation to what's actually contained between those two pieces of bread). Cured Italian pork products figure heavily, but there are vegetarian and pescatarian options, too. **Known for:** great list of wines by the glass; tasty sandwiches (including dessert options); outdoor seating in a lively piazza. [$] *Average main: €12* ✉ *Via Paladini 2, Empoli.*

Vinci

10 km (6 miles) north of Empoli, 45 km (28 miles) west of Florence.

The small hill town from which Leonardo da Vinci derived his name is a short drive or bus ride north of Empoli. At the church of Santa Croce, near the town square, you can see the font in which Leonardo was baptized. But if you want to see the house where he was born, you'll have to travel to Anchiano, 3 km (2 miles) north of Vinci. Though it's somewhat of a tourist trap, a trip to Vinci is worth the effort for the views alone.

GETTING HERE

To get to Vinci via public transportation, take the train to Empoli, then catch a PiuBus bus to Vinci.

VISITOR INFORMATION

CONTACTS Vinci Tourism Office. ✉ *Via delle Torre 11, Vinci* ☎ *0571/568012* 🌐 *www.toscananelcuore.it.*

Sights

Casa Natale di Leonardo

HISTORIC HOME | FAMILY | No one knows the precise location of Leonardo da Vinci's birthplace, but this typical 15th-century Tuscan house is in the general vicinity and probably shares much in common with the house where he was born. It's in Anchiano, 3 km (2 miles) from Vinci, and can be reached easily on foot or by car. It has a primitive interior—it hasn't been gussied up for tourists. Note the printed inventory of Leonardo's library. His tastes in literature were wide-ranging, from the ancients to contemporary (15th-century) authors. ✉ *Località Anchiano, Vinci* ☎ *0571/933285* 🌐 *www.museoleonardiano.it* 🎫 *€5.*

Museo Leonardiano

ART MUSEUM | FAMILY | Museo Leonardiano, atop the castle belonging to the Guidi family in the historic center of Vinci, has replicas of many of Leonardo's machines and gadgets. The stunning country views most likely influenced the artist, as some of his painted backgrounds suggest the hills of Vinci. ✉ *Via della Torre 2, Vinci* ☎ *0571/933251* 🌐 *www.museoleonardiano.it* 🎫 *€8.*

San Miniato

20 km (12 miles) southwest of Vinci, 43 km (27 miles) west of Florence.

San Miniato, which has a history dating from Etruscan and Roman times, is a tiny, pristine hill town of narrow streets lined with austere 13th- to 17th-century facades, some covering buildings that are centuries older. The Holy Roman Empire had very strong ties here—the local castle was built in 962 under the aegis of Otto I (912–973). Eventually the town, with its Ghibelline (pro-imperial) sympathies, passed into the hands of the Florentines.

San Miniato's artistic treasures are limited by Tuscan standards, but the town's prettiness makes a visit worthwhile. On three weekends in November an annual truffle festival adds to San Miniato's allure; it's well worth visiting if you're in the area. The food stalls teem with fantastic local stuff, while restaurants are crammed with locals and visitors chowing down on truffled things.

GETTING HERE

The easiest way to get to San Miniato is by car via the Fi-Pi-Li. The San Miniato train station is far from the centro storico.

VISITOR INFORMATION

CONTACTS San Miniato Tourism Office. ✉ *Piazza del Popolo 3, San Miniato* ☎ *0571/42745* 🌐 *www.sanminiatopromozione.it.*

Continued on page 161

SIMPLY PERFECT
The Basic Goodness of Tuscan Food

The cuisine of Tuscany isn't complicated. In fact, every dish follows the same basic recipe:

■ Begin with fresh, high-quality ingredients, preferably produced within walking distance of the kitchen.

■ Prepare them using techniques that have been refined over centuries, ideally by members of the chef's family.

■ Serve the finished dish unpretentiously ("plate" is not a verb here), accompanied by a glass of good local wine.

The recipe looks simple, but executing it is not so easy. Some of the staples of "fine dining" that chefs elsewhere depend upon are pointedly missing.

There's nothing exotic: it would violate the "walking distance" principle of fresh, local ingredients. There's nothing ostentatious: showiness would distract from the basic beauty of the food. And innovation is looked on with a skeptical eye: if a new recipe or a new technique were really so good, surely someone in the preceding ten generations would have already thought of it.

The result is a cuisine that's inextricably tied to the place where it's made. There may now be Tuscan restaurants all over the globe, but you can still only eat genuine Tuscan food in Tuscany. It's home cooking that's worth traveling halfway around the world to taste.

EXPLORING THE TUSCAN MENU

Menu Basics

A meal in Tuscany (and elsewhere in Italy) traditionally consists of five courses, and every menu you encounter will be organized along this five-course plan:

First up is the antipasto (appetizer), often consisting of cured meats or marinated vegetables. Next to appear is the primo, usually pasta or soup, and after that the secondo, a meat or fish course with, perhaps, a contorno (vegetable dish) on the side. A simple dolce (dessert) rounds out the meal.

This, you've probably noticed, is a lot of food. Italians have noticed as well—a full, five-course meal is an indulgence usually reserved for special occasions. Instead, restaurant meals are a mix-and-match affair: you might order a primo and a secondo, or an antipasto and a primo, or a secondo and a contorno.

■ TIP ➜ The crucial rule of restaurant dining is that you should **order at least two courses**. It's a common mistake for tourists to order only a secondo, thinking they're getting a "main course" complete with side dishes. What they wind up with is one lonely piece of meat.

After you've eaten at a couple of restaurants, you may feel you're experiencing déjà vu: many of the same dishes are served almost everywhere. This is a by-product of the devotion to local, traditional cuisine, and part of the pleasure of dining in Tuscany is seeing how preparations vary from region to region and restaurant to restaurant.

What follows is a rundown, course by course, of classic dishes. The ones highlighted as "quintessential" are the epitome of Tuscan cooking. They shouldn't be missed.

Clockwise from bottom left: A well-worn menu; preparing ribollita; a typical food shop.

ANTIPASTI: APPETIZERS

The quintessential antipasto

Affettati misti

The name, roughly translated, means "mixed cold cuts," and it's something Tuscans do exceptionally well. The platter of cured meats is sure to include prosciutto crudo (ham, cut paper thin) and salame (dry sausage, prepared in dozens of ways, some spicy, some sweet). The most distinctly Tuscan affettati are made from cinta senese (a once nearly extinct pig found only in the heart of the region) and cinghiale (wild boar, which roam all of central Italy). You can eat these delicious slices unadorned or layered on a piece of bread.

From left: A typical affettati misti plate; tuscan butcher; artichokes cured in olive oil

Other classics

Crostini

Toasted slices of bread with toppings—most commonly fegatini (chicken liver pâté), though other meat and vegetable concoctions also appear

Verdure sott'olio

Peppers, carrots, artichokes, and other vegetables cured in olive oil

Lardo di Colonnata

Not to be confused with lard (rendered fat), lardo is pig back fat that's seasoned with herbs, soaked in brine, and cured for months. Sliced thin and served over bread, it's a melt-in-your-mouth delicacy.

A WELL-OILED CUISINE

Olive oil is far and away the most important ingredient in Tuscan kitchens: it's a condiment, a cooking oil, a marinade, a salad dressing, a bread topping—one way or another, it makes its way into every meal.

The oil from Tuscany is frequently lauded as the best in the world. Open a bottle and you'll immediately know why: the aroma reaches out and grabs you. Like wine connoisseurs, oil lovers struggle for words to describe the experience—"spicy," "fruity," "herby," "redolent of artichokes"—but the sensual character of Tuscan oils defies description.

Which area in Tuscany produces the best oil is the subject of a never-ending debate. Sample as you go and decide for yourself—or simply enjoy the fact that there is no right answer. It's all good.

PRIMI: FIRST COURSES

The quintessential primo
Ribollita

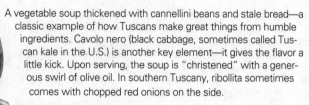

A vegetable soup thickened with cannellini beans and stale bread—a classic example of how Tuscans make great things from humble ingredients. Cavolo nero (black cabbage, sometimes called Tuscan kale in the U.S.) is another key element—it gives the flavor a little kick. Upon serving, the soup is "christened" with a generous swirl of olive oil. In southern Tuscany, ribollita sometimes comes with chopped red onions on the side.

Other classics

Panzanella
A summer salad made of bread, tomatoes, basil, cucumbers, and olive oil

Pappa al pomodoro
Pureed tomato soup, thickened with bread

Zuppa alla frantoiana
Another bean, bread, and vegetable soup, this time run through a food mill

Pappardelle col sugo di cinghiale
Fresh pasta cut in wide strips with wild boar sauce

Ravioli di ricotta e spinaci
Spinach and cheese ravioli

Local specialties
(and the town or region where they're found)

Pici all'aglione
Hand-rolled pasta with garlic sauce (Siena and Montalcino)

Linguine alla granseola
Linguine with stone crab (a staple on Elba)

Minestra al farro
Soup made with farro, a barley-like grain (Lucca and the Garfagnana)

Ignudi
"Naked" ravioli-spinach and cheese dumplings minus the pasta (Florence and Chianti)

Crespelle
Crepe-like pancakes, stuffed with spinach and cheese and topped with a bechamel sauce (Florence)

Polenta di castagne
Chestnut polenta (the Garfagnana)

Acquacotta
"Cooked water"—thick vegetable soup (a specialty of the Maremma)

Tordelli di carne al ragù
Meat-stuffed tortelli pasta with a meat sauce (Lucca, where they prefer the spelling with a "d")

SECONDI: SECOND COURSES

The quintessential secondo

Bistecca alla fiorentina

You can get grilled steak everywhere from Texas to Tokyo, but in Tuscany they've found a way to make it their own. Bistecca alla fiorentina is an extra-thick T-bone that comes from ox-like Chianina cattle, a carefully nurtured Tuscan breed. It's seasoned with salt, pepper, and olive oil, and always served rare; cooking it longer is considered a travesty. Maybe it's the high quality of the beef, maybe it's the wonderful oil—whatever the reason, bistecca alla fiorentina truly is exceptional.

Other classics

Arista di maiale
Roast pork with sage and rosemary

Calamari all'inzimino
Squid and spinach stew

Tagliata di manzo
Thin slices of roasted beef, drizzled with oil

Fritto di pollo e coniglio
Fried chicken and rabbit

Salsiccia e fagioli
Pork sausage with beans

Local specialties

Frittura di paranza
Mixed fish fry (found all along the coast, but best in Livorno)

Piccione
Pigeon—it can be roasted, stuffed, or baked (southern Chianti)

Baccalà con ceci
Salt cod with chickpeas (much beloved by the Livornesi)

Peposo
A peppery beef stew (Impruneta)

Trippa alla fiorentina
Tripe stewed in a tomato sauce (Florence)

Ricotta cheese, Vitereta, Tuscany

A TASTE OF THE TYPICAL

While "typical" can be a disparaging term in English, its Italian equivalent, "tipico," is high praise. Whether you're talking about a type of cheese, a variety of wine, or a particular cut of pasta, "tipico" indicates something that's traditional to the location where you find it. Which means it's been perfected over the course of centuries. And that means, whatever it is, you won't get it better anywhere else.

CONTORNI: VEGETABLES

The quintessential contorno
Fagioli all'olio

Tuscans are known among fellow Italians as "mangiafagioli" (bean eaters), and with good reason. White cannellini beans are the standard, usually boiled with fresh sage, drained, and liberally laced with olive oil. Another preparation is fagioli all'uccelletto, in which the beans are cooked with tomato and sage. Fagioli al fiasco are slow-cooked in a glass bottle.

Other classics

Virtually any fresh vegetable, either briefly boiled or sautéed in oil, possibly with a touch of garlic. Greens are especially popular—look for cime di rape (turnip greens) as well as spinaci (spinach). Other seasonal favorites are carciofi (artichokes), asparagi (asparagus) piselli (peas), zucchini, peperoni (peppers), and fave (fava beans).

DOLCI: DESSERTS

The quintessential dolce
Cantuccini con vin santo

These hard little almond cookies, also known as biscotti di Prato, are virtually inedible when dry, but dip them into sweet vin santo wine, and the result is delectable.

From left: Castagnaccio; cantucci and vin santo; buccellato

Other classics

Tuscan cuisine is not particularly noted for its desserts. Meals often end with an unadorned piece of fruit. Here and there, though, you'll find exceptions.

Local specialties

Buccellato
An anise-flavored sweet bun (Lucca)

Ricciarelli
Delicate almond cookies (Siena)

Brigidini
Sugary wafers, best when topped with gelato (Montecatini)

Castagnaccio
A flat chestnut-flour cake (Lucca)

Panforte
Candied fruit and nut cake (Siena)

👁 Sights

Convento di San Francesco (*Convent and Church of St. Francis*)

CHURCH | In 1211 St. Francis founded the Convento di San Francesco, which contains two cloisters and an ornate wooden choir. For a dose of monastic living, you can stay overnight. ✉ *Piazza San Francesco, San Miniato* ☎ *0571/43051* 🖃 *Free to visit; to stay overnight: €10 suggested donation, €35 for half-pension.*

Convento e Chiesa di Santi Jacopo e Lucia (*Convent and Church of Sts. Jacob and Lucia*)

CHURCH | The Convento e Chiesa di Santi Jacopo e Lucia is also oddly known as the church of San Domenico, which refers to the fact that the Dominicans took over the church in the 14th century. Most of the interior suffers from too much baroque, but there is a lovely sculpted tomb by Bernardo Rossellino for Giovanni Chellini, a doctor who died in 1461. You'll find it on the right-hand nave close to the high altar. ✉ *Piazza del Popolo, San Miniato* ☎ *0571/43150.*

Duomo

CHURCH | San Miniato's Duomo, set in a lovely piazza, has a simple yet pretty 13th-century facade, which has been restored. It also has a lovely pulpit designed by Giovanni Duprè, which was executed by his daughter Amalia (1845–1928). The interior is largely uninteresting, though there's a poignant plaque commemorating the 55 citizens who were killed in this church in July 1944 by German occupying forces. ✉ *Piazza del Castello, San Miniato.*

Museo Diocesano

ART MUSEUM | Although the Museo Diocesano is small, its modest collection incorporates a number of subtle and pleasant local works of art. Note the rather odd *Crucifixion* by Lorenzo Lippi, *Il Redentore*, probably by a follower of Verrocchio (1435–88), and the small but exquisite *Education of the Virgin*

by Tiepolo (1696–1770). ✉ *Piazza del Castello, San Miniato* ☎ *342/686–0873* ⊕ *sanminiato.chiesacattolica.it* 🖃 *€3* 🕑 *Closed Mon.–Wed.*

Torre di Federico II

NOTABLE BUILDING | Dating from the time of Frederick II (1194–1250), the Torre di Federico II was destroyed during World War II. A point of civic pride for San Miniatans and visible for miles, the tower was rebuilt and reopened in 1958. The hapless, ill-fated Pier della Vigna, chancellor and minister to Frederick II, leaped to his death from the tower, earning a mention in Dante's *Inferno*. The hill on which the tower stands—a surprisingly large oval of green grass—is one of the loveliest places in the area to have a picnic, enjoy the 360-degree view, and perhaps join local children in a pickup game of *calcio* (soccer). ✉ *Piazza la Torre, San Miniato* ☎ *0571/42745* ⊕ *www.valdarnomusei.it* 🖃 *€4* 🕑 *Closed Mon.*

🍴 Restaurants

Bar Cantini

$ | ITALIAN | FAMILY | At lunch and dinner time, this social hub for San Miniatans turns into a full-blown trattoria serving up local specialties. You can't go wrong with any of the wonderful panini, which are made with bread baked on-site and which you can eat seated at a table with a splendid valley view. **Known for:** good sandwiches at great prices; the view; lively, convivial atmosphere. 💲 *Average main: €10* ✉ *Via Conti 1, San Miniato* ☎ *0571/43030* 🖃 *No credit cards.*

Il Convio

$$ | TUSCAN | A short drive down a steep, serpentine road from San Miniato brings you to this rustic country ristorante with sponged walls, stenciled decorations, and checkered tablecloths. The main courses are mostly Tuscan classics, such as *bistecca fiorentina* (a generous cut of grilled steak), but white truffles, the local specialty, are also showcased, and you can get them with pasta, *crespelle* (thin pancakes filled with ricotta), tripe, eggs, beef fillet—there's even a postprandial truffled grappa. **Known for:** tranquil country setting; the wine list; truffled specialties. $ *Average main: €21* ✉ *Via San Maiano 2, San Miniato* ☎ *0571/408113* ⊘ *Closed Tues.*

La Prosciutteria
$ | **ITALIAN** | The very unassuming decor (wooden tables, wooden chairs) sets the scene for terrific Tuscan food. Though there's not a truffle dish to be found on the menu, there's lots to satisfy the palate. **Known for:** lampredotto (tripe) with salsa verde and hot sauce; adherence to Tuscan classics; apple crostata (tart). $ *Average main: €11* ✉ *Via Ser Ridolfo 8, San Miniato* ⊘ *Closed Mon.*

Sergio Falaschi dal 1925
$$ | **ITALIAN** | **FAMILY** | It's a butcher shop in the front and, on weekends, a great lunch restaurant in the back. Since 1925, the place has been in the hands of the Falaschi family, who source locally and put four generations' worth of experience into turning out excellent food. **Known for:** pork products and pork dishes; sunny staff; beef fillet with a creamy, green-peppercorn sauce. $ *Average main: €18* ✉ *Via Augusto Conti 18/20, San Miniato* ☎ *0571/43190* ⊕ *www. sergiofalaschi.it* ⊘ *Restaurant closed weekdays; no dinner.*

 ## Hotels

Convento di San Francesco
$ | **B&B/INN** | For a complete change of pace, you can stay in the company of five Franciscan friars at this 13th-century convent, where the simple, quiet guest rooms have en suite baths. **Pros:** great price; tranquillity; no curfew (guests are given their own key). **Cons:** most of staff speaks only Italian; quite removed from the historic center; rooms are rather spartan. $ *Rooms from: €50* ✉ *Piazza San Francesco, San Miniato* ☎ *0571/43051* ▭ *No credit cards* 🛏 *30 rooms* ⦿ *No Meals.*

Pisa

50 km (31 miles) west of San Miniato, 116 km (72 miles) west of Florence.

If you can get beyond the kitsch of the stalls hawking cheap souvenirs around the Leaning Tower, you'll find that Pisa has much to offer. Its treasures aren't as abundant as those of Florence, to which it is inevitably compared, but the cathedral-baptistery-tower complex of Piazza del Duomo, known collectively as the Campo dei Miracoli (Field of Miracles), is among the most dramatic settings in Italy.

Pisa may have been inhabited as early as the Bronze Age. It was certainly populated by the Etruscans and, in turn, became part of the Roman Empire. In the early Middle Ages, it flourished as an economic powerhouse—along with Amalfi, Genoa, and Venice, it was one of the four maritime republics.

The city's economic and political power ebbed in the early 15th century as it fell under Florence's domination, though it enjoyed a brief resurgence under Cosimo I in the mid-16th century. Pisa sustained heavy damage during World War II, but the Duomo and Tower were spared, along with some other grand Romanesque structures.

GETTING HERE
Pisa is an easy hour's train ride from Florence. By car it's a straight shot on the Fi-Pi-Li autostrada. The Pisa–Lucca train runs frequently and takes about 30 minutes.

VISITOR INFORMATION
CONTACTS Pisa Tourism Office. ✉ *Piazza del Duomo 7, Pisa* ☎ *050/550100* ⊕ *www. turismo.pisa.it.*

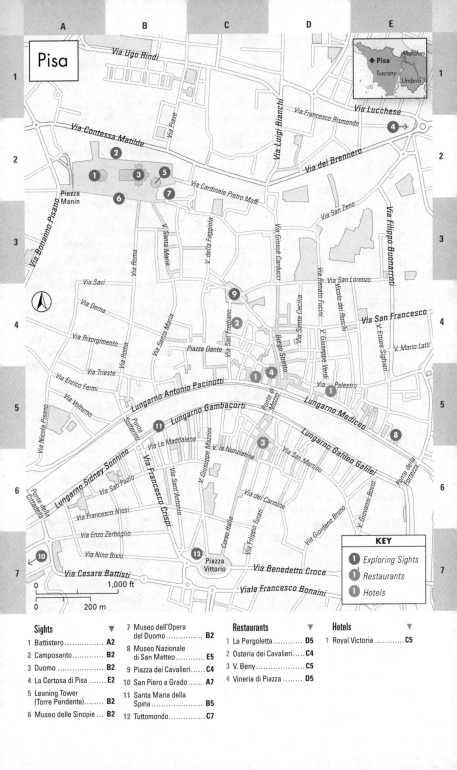

Pisa

Sights ▼

1 Battistero **A2**
2 Camposanto **B2**
3 Duomo **B2**
4 La Certosa di Pisa **E2**
5 Leaning Tower
   (Torre Pendente)........ **B2**
6 Museo delle Sinopie ... **B2**
7 Museo dell'Opera
   del Duomo **B2**
8 Museo Nazionale
   di San Matteo **E5**
9 Piazza dei Cavalieri...... **C4**
10 San Piero a Grado **A7**
11 Santa Maria della
   Spina **B5**
12 Tuttomondo.............. **C7**

Restaurants ▼

1 La Pergoletta **D5**
2 Osteria dei Cavalieri..... **C4**
3 V. Beny.................. **C5**
4 Vineria di Piazza **D5**

Hotels ▼

1 Royal Victoria **C5**

KEY

1 *Exploring Sights*
1 *Restaurants*
1 *Hotels*

Sights

Pisa, like many Italian cities, is best explored on foot, and most of what you'll want to see is within walking distance. The views along the Arno River are particularly grand and shouldn't be missed—there's a feeling of spaciousness that isn't found along the Arno in Florence.

As you set out, note that there are various combination-ticket options for sights on the Piazza del Duomo.

Battistero

NOTABLE BUILDING | This lovely Gothic baptistery, which stands across from the Duomo's facade, is best known for the pulpit carved by Nicola Pisano (circa 1220–84; father of Giovanni Pisano) in 1260. Every half hour, an employee will dramatically close the doors, then intone, thereby demonstrating how remarkable the acoustics are in the place. ⊠ *Piazza del Duomo, Pisa* ☎ *050/835011* ⊕ *www. opapisa.it* ✆ *From €7, discounts available if bought in combination with tickets for other monuments.*

Camposanto

CEMETERY | According to legend, the cemetery—a walled structure on the western side of the Piazza dei Miracoli—is filled with earth that returning Crusaders brought back from the Holy Land. Contained within are numerous frescoes, notably *The Drunkenness of Noah,* by Renaissance artist Benozzo Gozzoli (1422–97), and the disturbing *Triumph of Death* (14th century; artist uncertain), whose subject matter shows what was on people's minds in a century that saw the ravages of the Black Death. ⊠ *Piazza del Duomo, Pisa* ☎ *050/835011* ⊕ *www. opapisa.it* ✆ *From €7.*

Duomo

CHURCH | Pisa's cathedral brilliantly utilizes the horizontal marble-stripe motif (borrowed from Moorish architecture) that became common on Tuscan cathedrals. It is famous for the Romanesque panels on the transept door facing the tower that depict scenes from the life of Christ. The beautifully carved 14th-century pulpit is by Giovanni Pisano. ⊠ *Piazza del Duomo, Pisa* ☎ *050/835011* ⊕ *www.opapisa.it.*

La Certosa di Pisa

SCIENCE MUSEUM | **FAMILY** | A *certosa* is a monastery whose monks belong to the strict Carthusian order. This vast and sprawling complex, begun in 1366, was suppressed by Napoléon in the early 1800s and then again in 1866. Most of the art and architecture you see dates from the 17th and 18th centuries. The Carthusians returned here only to leave it permanently in 1969. Also within it is the Museo di Storia Naturale e del Territorio. This museum of natural history contains fossils, 24 whale skeletons that serve to trace the mammal's development over the millennia, and some exhibits of local minerals. Guided tours are given every hour and a half: unfortunately, there are given only in Italian. ⊠ *Via Roma 79, Pisa* ✈ *10 km (6 miles) east of Pisa via road north of Arno, through Mezzana and then toward Calci and Montemagno* ☎ *050/221–2970* ⊕ *www.msn.unipi.it* ✆ *From €8.*

★ Leaning Tower (Torre Pendente)

NOTABLE BUILDING | **FAMILY** | Legend holds that Galileo conducted an experiment on the nature of gravity by dropping metal balls from the top of the 187-foot-high Leaning Tower of Pisa. Historians, however, say this legend has no basis in fact—which isn't quite to say that it's false. Work on this tower, built as a campanile (bell tower) for the Duomo, started in 1173. The lopsided settling began when construction reached the third story.

The architects attempted to compensate through such methods as making the remaining floors slightly taller on the leaning side, but the extra weight only made the problem worse. The settling continued, and, by the late 20th century, it had accelerated to such a point that many feared the tower would simply

topple over, despite all efforts to prop it up. The structure has since been firmly anchored to the earth. Work to restore the tower to its original tilt of 300 years ago was launched in early 2000 and finished two years later. This involved removing some 100 tons of earth from beneath the foundation.

Reservations, which are essential, can be made online or by calling the Museo dell'Opera del Duomo. It's also possible to arrive at the ticket office and book for the same day. Note, though, that children under eight aren't allowed to climb. ⊠ Piazza del Duomo, Pisa ☎ 050/835011 ⊕ www.opapisa.it ⚒ €20.

Museo delle Sinopie
ART MUSEUM | The well-arranged museum on the south side of the Piazza del Duomo holds the sinopie (preparatory drawings) for the Camposanto frescoes. Though the exhibits are mostly of interest to specialists, some audiovisual material provides a good introduction to the whole religious complex. ⊠ Piazza del Duomo, Pisa ☎ 050/835011 ⊕ www.opapisa.it ⚒ €7.

Museo dell'Opera del Duomo
ART MUSEUM | At the southeast corner of the sprawling Piazza dei Miracoli, this museum holds a wealth of medieval sculptures and the ancient Roman sarcophagi that inspired Nicola Pisano's figures. ⊠ Piazza del Duomo, Pisa ☎ 050/835011 ⊕ www.opapisa.it ⚒ €7, discounts available if bought in combination with tickets for other monuments.

Museo Nazionale di San Matteo
ART MUSEUM | On the north bank of the Arno, this museum contains some beautiful examples of local Romanesque and Gothic art. Despite the fact that it has stunning works by Donatello and Benozzo Gozzoli (among others), here you'll find very few other visitors. ⊠ Piazza Matteo in Soarta 1, Pisa ☎ 050/541865 ⊕ www.polomusealetoscana.beniculturali.it ⚒ €5 ⊗ Closed Mon.

Piazza dei Cavalieri
PLAZA/SQUARE | The piazza, with its fine Renaissance Palazzo dei Cavalieri, Palazzo dell'Orologio, and Chiesa di Santo Stefano dei Cavalieri, was laid out by Giorgio Vasari in about 1560. The square was the seat of the Ordine dei Cavalieri di San Stefano (Order of the Knights of St. Stephen), a military and religious institution meant to defend the coast from possible invasion by the Turks.

Also in this square is the prestigious Scuola Normale Superiore, founded by Napoléon in 1810 on the French model. Here graduate students pursue doctorates in literature, philosophy, mathematics, and science. In front of the school is a large statue of Ferdinando I de' Medici dating from 1596. On the extreme left is the tower where the hapless Ugolino della Gherardesca (died 1289) was imprisoned with his two sons and two grandsons—legend holds that he ate them. Dante immortalized him in Canto XXXIII of his Inferno. Duck into the Church of Santo Stefano (if you're lucky enough to find it open) and check out Bronzino's splendid Nativity of Christ (1564–65). ⊠ Piazza dei Cavalieri, Pisa.

San Piero a Grado
CHURCH | Built over remnants of two earlier churches is this 11th-century basilica, situated on the Arno about 8 km (5 miles) southwest of Pisa. According to legend, it was here that St. Peter the Apostle stepped off the boat in AD 42—his first step on Italian soil. (It would have made more sense for him to land on the Adriatic Coast, as he was coming from Antioch.)

The structure is a lovely example of Romanesque architecture, and it's not without its quirks: it has two apses, one at each end. On the walls are some crumbling, but still vibrant, frescoes dating from the 12th and 13th centuries. Thirty-one of these frescoes depict scenes from the lives of saints Peter and Paul, an uncommon subject in Tuscan wall painting. A car is a necessity to get to this lovely church. ⊠ *Via Vecchia di Marina, Pisa* ☎ *050/960065* ⊕ *www. sanpieroagrado.it* 🎫 *Free.*

Santa Maria della Spina

CHURCH | Originally an oratory dating from the 13th century, this delicate, tiny church is a fine example of Tuscan Gothic architecture. It has been restored several times, including in 1996–98, after having been damaged by a flood. The results of a recent face-lift are grand. ⊠ *Lungarno Gambacorti, Pisa* 🎫 *Free.*

Tuttomondo

PUBLIC ART | Street/graffiti artist Keith Haring (1958–90) created this joyous work of art shortly before he died. It's on the southern wall of the church of Sant'Antonio Abate (originally dating from the mid-14th century but largely destroyed and rebuilt after World War II). "Tuttomondo" literally means "All World," and you can see figures dancing in harmony. ⊠ *Pizza Vittorio Emanuele II, 18, Pisa.*

🍽 Restaurants

La Pergoletta

$$ | TUSCAN | FAMILY | On an old town street named for its beautiful towers, this small, simple restaurant is in one such tower itself and is a place where Pisans come to celebrate. Three intimate rooms, one particularly charming with a pergola, are usually filled with locals eating dishes laced with imagination (curry and ginger often appear on the menu). **Known for:** gracious waitstaff; festive atmosphere; inventive, seasonal menu. $ *Average main: €16* ⊠ *Via delle Belle Torri 36, Pisa* ☎ *050/542458* ⊕ *www.ristorantelapergoletta.com* ☉ *Closed Mon. and 1 wk in Aug. No lunch Sat.*

Osteria dei Cavalieri

$$ | ITALIAN | This charming, white-walled restaurant, a few steps from Piazza dei Cavalieri, is reason enough to come to Pisa. They can do it all here—serve up exquisitely grilled fish dishes, please

vegetarians, and prepare *tagliata* for meat lovers. **Known for:** vegetable tasting menu; sea tasting menu; land tasting menu. $ *Average main: €16* ⊠ *Via San Frediano 16, Pisa* ☎ *050/580858* ⊕ *www. osteriacavalieri.pisa.it* ☉ *No lunch Sat. Closed Sun., 2 wks in Aug., and Dec. 29–Jan. 7.*

★ V. Beny

$$$ | TUSCAN | Apricot walls hung with etchings of Pisa make this small, single-room restaurant warmly romantic. Husband and wife Damiano and Sandra Lazzerini have been running the place for two decades, and it shows in their obvious enthusiasm while talking about the menu (fish is a focus) and daily specials, which often astound. **Known for:** terrific wine list; gracious service; superb fish dishes. $ *Average main: €27* ⊠ *Piazza Gambacorti 22, Pisa* ☎ *050/25067* ☉ *Closed Sun. and 2 wks in mid-Aug. No lunch Sat.*

★ Vineria di Piazza

$$ | ITALIAN | It's set in a lively, historic market square and frequented by locals. The menu adheres to Tuscan tradition, including high-quality bistecca fiorentina, but also indulges in some flights of fantasy, as evidenced by a whimsical dessert that riffs on a liquid Livornese classic. **Known for:** baccalà (salt cod) served in inventive ways; charming, energetic staff; inventive pasta dishes. $ *Average main: €20* ⊠ *Piazza delle Vettovaglie 13–15, Pisa* ☎ *330/441–6721.*

🛏 Hotels

Royal Victoria

$ | HOTEL | In a pleasant palazzo facing the Arno, a 10-minute walk from the Campo dei Miracoli, this hotel has room styles that range from the 1800s, complete with frescoes, to the 1920s; the most charming are in the old tower. **Pros:** friendly staff; old-world charm; lovely views of the Arno from many rooms. **Cons:** not all rooms have views of the

Arno; rooms a little worn; rooms vary significantly in size. $ *Rooms from: €95* ✉ *Lungarno Pacinotti 12, Pisa* ☏ *050/940111* ⊕ *www.royalvictoria.it* ⇨ *38 rooms* ⦿ *Free Breakfast.*

 Performing Arts

Fondazione Teatro di Pisa

THEATER | Pisa has a lively performing-arts scene, most of which happens at the 19th-century Teatro Verdi. Music and dance performances are presented from September through May. Contact Fondazione Teatro di Pisa for schedules and information. ✉ *Via Palestro 40, Lungarni, Pisa* ☏ *050/941111* ⊕ *www.teatrodipisa.pi.it.*

Luminaria

FESTIVALS | Pisa is at its best during the Luminaria feast day, on June 16. The day honors St. Ranieri, the city's patron saint. Palaces along the Arno are lit with white lights, and there are plenty of fireworks. ✉ *Pisa.*

Prato

19 km (12 miles) northwest of Florence, 60 km (37 miles) east of Lucca.

The wool industry in this city, one of the world's largest producers of cloth, was famous throughout Europe as early as the 13th century. Business was further stimulated in the late 14th century by a local cloth merchant, Francesco di Marco Datini.

One thing that distinguishes Prato from other Italian towns of its size is the presence of modern public art—most notably Henry Moore's enormous marble sculpture *Square Form with Cut* in Piazza San Marco.

GETTING HERE

Prato is a quick train ride from Florence. By car it's a 45-minute trip on the A11/E76 toll road.

VISITOR INFORMATION

CONTACTS Prato Tourism Office. ✉ *Piazza Buonamici 7, Prato* ☏ *0574/24112* ⊕ *www.pratoturismo.it.*

Sights

Carmignano

CHURCH | Pontormo's *Visitation* is in this small village a short drive from Poggio a Caiano. The Franciscan church of San Michele, dedicated in 1211, houses the work. The painting dates 1527–30, and it may well be Pontormo's masterpiece. The luminous colors, flowing drapery, and steady gaze shared between the Virgin and St. Elizabeth are breathtaking. The church's small cloister, shaded by olive trees, is always open, and offers a quiet place to sit. ✉ *Prato* ✛ *15 km (9 miles) south of Prato, through Poggio a Caiano, up Mt. Albano.*

Castello (*Castle*)

CASTLE/PALACE | This formidable structure, near Santa Maria delle Carceri, is an impressive sight. The (Sicilian) Holy Roman Emperor Frederick II (1194–1250) built the seat of his authority in Tuscany in this somewhat unlikely spot. Frederick's castles were designed to echo imperial Rome, and the many columns, lions, and porticoes testify to his ambition. This is the only castle he built outside southern Italy (other examples may be found in Sicily and Puglia). ✉ *Piazza Santa Maria delle Carceri, Prato* ☏ *0574/38207* ⬚ *Free* ☉ *Closed Tues.*

Centro per l'Arte Contemporanea Luigi Pecci (*Luigi Pecci Center of Contemporary Art*)

ART MUSEUM | Prato's Center for Contemporary Art Luigi Pecci contains works of artists from around the world completed after 1965. The exhibitions constantly change, and often feature debut presentations. ✉ *Viale della Repubblica 277, Prato* ☏ *0574/531915* ⊕ *centropecci.it* ⬚ *€7.*

Duomo

CHURCH | Prato's Romanesque Duomo, reconstructed from 1211, is famous for its Pergamo del Sacro Cingolo (Chapel of the Holy Girdle), which is to the left of its entrance and which enshrines the sash of the Virgin Mary. It is said that the girdle was given to the apostle Thomas by the Virgin Mary when she miraculously appeared after her Assumption into heaven. The Duomo also contains 15th-century frescoes by Prato's most famous son, Fra Filippo Lippi. His scenes from the life of St. Stephen are on the left wall of the Cappella Maggiore (Main Chapel); those from the life of John the Baptist are on the right. ⊠ *Piazza del Duomo, Prato* ☎ *0574/29339* ⊕ *www.diocesiprato.it* 🖭 *€5 to visit Cappella Maggiore.*

Museo del Tessuto (*Textile Museum*)

OTHER MUSEUM | Preserved in the Museo del Tessuto is what made this city a Renaissance economic powerhouse. The collection includes clothing, fabric fragments, and the machines used to make them—all dating from the 14th to the 20th century. Check out the 15th-century fabrics with pomegranate prints, a virtuoso display of Renaissance textile wizardry. The well-designed museum (objects are clearly labeled in English) is within the medieval walls of the city in the old Cimatoria, a 19th-century factory that finished raw fabrics. ⊠ *Via Puccetti 3, Prato* ☎ *0574/611503* ⊕ *www.museodeltessuto.it* 🖭 *€8* ☉ *Closed Mon.*

Museo dell'Opera del Duomo

ART MUSEUM | A sculpture by Donatello (circa 1386–1466) that originally adorned the Duomo's exterior pulpit is now on display in the Museo dell'Opera del Duomo. The museum also includes such 15th-century gems as Fra Filippo Lippi's *Madonna and Child,* Giovanni Bellini's (circa 1432–1516) *Christ on the Cross,* and Caravaggio's (1571–1610) *Christ Crowned with Thorns.* ⊠ *Piazza del Duomo 49, Prato* ☎ *0574/29339* ⊕ *www.diocesiprato.it* 🖭 *€8* ☉ *Closed Tues.*

Poggio a Caiano

HISTORIC HOME | For a look at gracious country living Renaissance style, take a detour to the Medici villa in Poggio a Caiano. Lorenzo "il Magnifico" (1449–92) commissioned Giuliano da Sangallo (circa 1445–1516) to redo the villa, which was lavished with frescoes by important Renaissance painters such as Pontormo (1494–1556), Franciabigio (1482–1525), and Andrea del Sarto (1486–1531). You can walk around the austerely ornamented grounds while waiting for one of the villa tours, which start on the half hour. The guides do not speak; rather, they follow you around the place. ⊠ *Piazza dei Medici 14, 7 km (4½ miles) south of Prato (follow signs), Prato* ☎ *055/877012* ⊕ *villegiardinimedicei.it* 🖭 *Free* ☉ *Closed Mon., Thurs., and 1st, 4th, and 5th Sun. of month.*

Santa Maria delle Carceri

CHURCH | The church of Santa Maria delle Carceri was built by Giuliano Sangallo in the 1490s and is a landmark of Renaissance architecture. ⊠ *Piazza Santa Maria delle Carceri, Prato* ⊹ *Off Via Cairoli and southeast of cathedral* ☎ *0574/39259* ⊕ *www.diocesiprato.it.*

🍽 Restaurants

★ Baghino

$$ | TUSCAN | In the heart of the historic center, Prato's best restaurant has been serving since 1870, capably run by five generations of the Pacetti family (daughters Guja and Silvia are presently in charge). The food lives up to the building's colorful history—part of the structure dates from the 15th century, when it was a convent; it was later the seat of the Freemasons. **Known for:** filetto al pepe verde (beef fillet in a creamy peppercorn sauce); superb wine list; sedano ripieno (a Pratese specialty). $ *Average main: €18* ⊠ *Via dell'Accademia 9, Prato* ☎ *0574/27920* ⊕ *ristorantebaghino. business.site* ☉ *Closed Sun. and Aug. No lunch Mon.*

★ Da Delfina

$$ | **TUSCAN** | Delfina Cioni began cooking many years ago for hungry hunters in the town of Artimino, 20 km (12 miles) south of Prato. Dishes celebrate Tuscan food, with an emphasis on fresh local ingredients. **Known for:** gorgeous view; fine wine list; delicious grilled meats cooked on a roaring fireplace. [$] *Average main: €17* ✉ *Via della Chiesa 1, Artimino* ☎ *055/871–8074* 🌐 *www.dadelfina.it* 🕒 *Closed Mon. No lunch Tues. No dinner Sun.*

La Vecchia Cucina di Soldano

$ | **TUSCAN** | This place could be mistaken for a grandmother's kitchen—it's completely unpretentious, with red-and-white-checked tablecloths and a waitstaff who treat you like an old friend. The restaurant teems with locals who appreciate the rock-bottom prices for well-prepared Tuscan specialties that include a superb *tagliolini sui fagioli* (thin noodles with beans). **Known for:** superb tagliolini sui fagioli; very reasonably priced; Tuscan specialties. [$] *Average main: €10* ✉ *Via Pomeria 23, Prato* ☎ *0574/34665* 🌐 *www.trattoriasoldano.it* 💳 *No credit cards* 🕒 *Closed Sun.*

Osteria da i'Peruzzi

$$ | **TUSCAN** | If you've just visited the Medici Villa at Poggio a Caiano, wander down the street to this intimate restaurant, the rooms of which date from the 16th century, where you'll find hearty, wonderful food, a great wine list, and lovely staff. The osteria's version of *peposo,* a local specialty, is a small masterpiece: a beef stew, laced with black pepper and a little bit of red wine, served on creamy polenta. **Known for:** adherence to Tuscan cuisine; charming dining room; creative menu. [$] *Average main: €16* ✉ *Via Cancellieri 29, Poggio a Caiano, Prato* ☎ *055/879–8692* 🕒 *Closed Mon.*

🛏 Hotels

Hotel Paggeria Medicea

$$ | **HOTEL** | Ferdinando I de'Medici loved to hunt, and he erected his villa to accommodate this whim, with his servants bunking in what is now this lovely, tranquil hotel in the middle of lush countryside. **Pros:** peace and tranquillity; spectacular views; a welcoming pool. **Cons:** often hosts wedding parties; rooms could use an update; a car is essential. [$] *Rooms from: €172* ✉ *Viale Papa Giovanni XXIII 1, Prato* ☎ *055/875–1426* 🌐 *www.tenutadiartimino.com* 🛏 *37 rooms* 🍴 *No Meals.*

🛍 Shopping

★ Antonio Mattei

FOOD | Prato's *biscotti* (literally "twice-cooked" cookies) have an extra-dense texture, lending themselves to submersion in your caffè or vin santo. The best biscotti in town are at Antonio Mattei, which has been around since 1858. Its *brutti ma buoni* (ugly but good) almond-laced cookies are especially delicious. ✉ *Via Ricasoli 20/22, Prato* ☎ *0574/25756* 🌐 *www.antoniomattei.it.*

Pistoia

18 km (11 miles) northwest of Prato, 37 km (23 miles) northwest of Florence, 43 km (27 miles) east of Lucca.

Founded in the 2nd century BC as a support post for Roman troops, Pistoia grew over the centuries into an important trading center. In the Middle Ages, it was troubled by civic strife and eventually fell to the Florentines, who imposed a pro-Guelph government in 1267. It lost its last vestiges of independence to Florence in 1329.

Reconstructed after heavy bombing during World War II, it has preserved some fine Romanesque architecture. Modern-day Pistoia's major industries include the manufacture of rail vehicles (including the cars for Washington, D.C.'s Metro) and tree and plant nurseries, which flourish on the alluvial plain around the city.

GETTING HERE
From Florence or Lucca, Pistoia is an easy train ride; trains run frequently. By car, take the A11/E76.

VISITOR INFORMATION
CONTACTS Pistoia Tourism Office. ⊠ *Palazzo dei Vescovi, Pistoia* ☎ *0573/21622* ⊕ *www.pistoia.turismo.toscana.it.*

Sights

Duomo
CHURCH | The Romanesque Duomo, the Cattedrale di San Zeno, dates from as early as the 5th century. It houses a magnificent silver altar dedicated to St. James. The two half-figures on the left are by Filippo Brunelleschi (1377–1446), the first Renaissance architect and the designer of Florence's magnificent Duomo cupola. ⊠ *Piazza del Duomo, Pistoia* ☎ *0573/25095* 🎫 *Free; access to altarpiece €2.*

Fondazione Marino Marini
ART MUSEUM | Lest you think that Tuscany produced only Renaissance artists, the Fondazione Marino Marini presents many works from its namesake modern native Pistoian (1901–80). Sculpture, etchings, paintings, engravings, and mixed media have all been installed in the elegantly renovated 14th-century Convento del Tau. Note that this museum has experienced temporary closures, so check on its status before visiting. ⊠ *Corso Silvano Fedi 30, Pistoia* ☎ *0573/30285* ⊕ *fondazionemarinomarini.it* 🎫 *From €4* ⊙ *Check ahead on opening days and times.*

Giardino Zoologico
ZOO | **FAMILY** | A 20-minute drive out of town brings you to the Giardino Zoologico, a small zoo laid out to accommodate

the wiles of both animals and children. ⊠ *Via Pieve a Celle 160/a, Pistoia* ⊹ *Take Bus 29 from train station* ☎ *0573/911219* ⊕ *www.zoodipistoia.it* 🎫 *€17.*

Museo dell'Antico Palazzo dei Vescovi
(*Old Bishop's Palace*)
HISTORY MUSEUM | At the end of the 11th century, the bishop of Pistoia began construction on this palace. One thousand years later, it houses several collections. The Museo della Cattedrale di San Zeno contains spectacular items from Pistoia's cathedral, including ornate pieces in gold, rings with jewels the size of small eggs, and solemn, powerful statuary. The Museo Tattile lets you touch various local buildings built to scale. The Percorso Archeologico contains Roman, medieval, and Etruscan archaeological finds uncovered during a 1970s renovation. Its treasures are showcased with simple elegance in a warren of corridors and caves below and austere rooms above. Note that a guide accompanies you while you wander the complex, and wandering days and times are limited. ⊠ *Piazza del Duomo, Pistoia* ☎ *0573/28782* ⊕ *www.pistoiamusei.it* 🎫 *€10.*

Museo Civico
ART MUSEUM | The Palazzo del Comune, begun around 1295, houses the Museo Civico, containing works by local artists from the 13th to 19th century. The courtyard (which is free) houses an equestrian sculpture by native son Marino Marini: it takes awhile to figure it out, and it's worth taking the time to do so. ⊠ *Piazza del Duomo 1, Pistoia* ☎ *0573/371296* ⊕ *www.musei.comune.pistoia.it* 🎫 *€4* ⊙ *Closed Mon.*

Ospedale del Ceppo
HOSPITAL | Founded in the 13th century, this still-functioning hospital has a facade with a superb early-16th-century exterior terra-cotta frieze. It was begun by Giovanni della Robbia (1469–1529) and completed by the workshop of Santi and Benedetto Buglioni between 1526

Pistoia's medieval skyline

and 1528. Don't miss the 17th-century graffiti on the columns outside. ⊠ *Piazza Giovanni XIII, Pistoia* ✛ *Down via Pacini from Piazza del Duomo.*

San Giovanni Fuorcivitas

CHURCH | An architectural gem in green-and-white marble, the medieval church of San Giovanni Fuorcivitas holds a *Visitation* by Luca della Robbia (1400–82), a painting attributed to Taddeo Gaddi, and a holy-water font that may have been made by Fra Guglielmo around 1270. ⊠ *Via Cavour, Pistoia* 🖾 *€2* ⊘ *Closed Mon.*

Sant'Andrea

CHURCH | In the 12th-century church of Sant'Andrea, the fine pulpit by Giovanni Pisano (circa 1250–1314) depicts scenes from the life of Christ in a series of high-relief, richly sculpted marble panels. ⊠ *Piazzetta Sant'Andrea, Via Sant'Andrea, Pistoia* 🕿 *0573/21912* 🖾 *€4 (includes admission to San Giovanni Fuoricivitas).*

🍴 Restaurants

Dan's Dumpling Lab

$ | **FUSION** | If you're tired of Tuscan food (it can happen), this place on a side street near the Duomo serves up typical Asian dumplings, as well as those that are completely Italian, such as *manzo e porcini* (beef with porcini mushrooms). The *insalatina di trippa piccante* (spicy tripe salad) pays homage to both Asian and Italian cuisine. **Known for:** wantons di maiale condito in salsa piccante (pork wantons in a spicy sauce); congenial host; dumplings pecorino e n'duja (sheep's milk cheese with spicy Calabrian pork). 🖫 *Average main: €12* ⊠ *Via Castel Cellesi 3, Pistoia* 🕿 *0573/178–3527* ⊘ *No lunch Mon.*

La BotteGaia

$$ | **WINE BAR** | Jazz plays softly in the background as you sip wine and dine either indoors, at rustic tables amid exposed brick-and-stone walls, or alfresco with a splendid view of the Piazza del Duomo. Typical wine-bar fare, such as plates of cured ham and cheese, shares the menu with a surprisingly sophisticated list of daily specials. **Known for:** fine wine list; splendid desserts; a menu that dares to be different. [$] *Average main: €15* ✉ *Via del Lastrone 17, Pistoia* ☎ *0573/365602* 🌐 *www.labottegaia.it* 🕒 *Closed Mon.*

MagnoGaudio
$$ | **ITALIAN** | It bills itself as a caffetteria/ristorante, which means it opens at 7 in the morning for coffee, serves lunch and dinner, and then closes well after dinner is over. Warm-color, sponged walls and simple wooden tables and chairs provide the backdrop for some tasty fare. **Known for:** satisfying lasagna; local wine list; fish dishes. [$] *Average main: €15* ✉ *Via Curtatone e Montanara 12, Pistoia* ☎ *0573/26905* 🌐 *www.magnogaudiopistoia.it.*

Performing Arts

La Giostra dell'Orso (*Bear Joust*)
FESTIVALS | **FAMILY** | Pistoia's patron saint, St. James, is honored during this festival held on July 25. One of the highlights is when three knights—one from each area of the city—on horseback do "battle" with a "bear," meaning that they must strike a bear-shaped target while riding. The visitor center has more information on the event. ✉ *Pistoia.*

Pistoia Blues
FESTIVALS | In mid-July, this event brings international blues artists and rock-and-rollers to town for performances in the main square. ✉ *Pistoia* ☎ *0573/994659* 🌐 *pistoiablues.com.*

Montecatini Terme

15 km (9 miles) west of Pistoia, 49 km (30 miles) west of Florence, 29 km (18 miles) northeast of Lucca.

Immortalized in Fellini's film *8½*, Montecatini Terme is one of Italy's premier *terme* (spas). Known for their curative powers—and, at least once upon a time, for their great popularity among the wealthy—the mineral springs flow from five sources and are taken for a variety of ailments, including liver and skin disorders. Those "taking the cure" report each morning to one of the town's *stabilimenti termali* (thermal establishments) to drink their prescribed cupful of water. Afterward, they can enjoy a leisurely breakfast, read the newspaper, recline and listen to music, or walk in the parks that surround these grand old spas.

Montecatini Terme's wealth of art nouveau buildings dates from the town's most active period of development at the beginning of the 20th century. Like most other well-heeled resort towns, Montecatini attracts the leisure traveler, conventioneer, and senior citizen on a group tour and is trimmed with a measure of neon and glitz. Aside from taking the waters and people-watching in Piazza del Popolo, there's not a whole lot to do here, but it is a good base from which to explore the region.

GETTING HERE

Montecatini Terme is one of the stops on the Florence–Lucca train line, and it's an easy walk from the station to the centro storico. The A11/E76 will get you here by car.

VISITOR INFORMATION

CONTACTS Montecatini Terme Tourism Office. ✉ *Viale Verdi 66–68, Montecatini Terme* ☎ *0572/772244* 🌐 *www.provincia.pistoia.it.* **Terme di Montecatini.** ✉ *Viale Verdi 43, Montecatini Terme* ☎ *0572/7781* 🌐 *www.termemontecatini.it.*

Sights

Montecatini Alto
PLAZA/SQUARE | The older town, Montecatini Alto, sits atop a hill nearby, and is reached by a funicular from Viale Diaz. Though there isn't much to do once you get up there, the medieval square is lined

with restaurants and bars, the air is crisp, and the views of the Nievole, the valley below, are gorgeous. ✉ *Montecatini Terme.*

Piazza del Popolo

PLAZA/SQUARE | The town's main square teems with cafés and bars. It's an excellent spot for people-watching; in the evening and on weekends it seems like everyone is out walking, seeing, and being seen. ✉ *Montecatini Terme.*

Terme Tettuccio

NOTABLE BUILDING | The most attractive art nouveau structure in town, Terme Tettuccio, has lovely colonnades. Here fountains set up on marble counters dispense mineral water, bucolic scenes painted on tiles decorate walls, and an orchestra plays under a frescoed dome. ✉ *Viale Verdi 71, Montecatini Terme* ☎ *0572/778501* 🌐 *www.termemontecatini.it* 🎟 *€15 to take the waters.*

Coffee and Quick Bites

★ Bargilli

$ | **ITALIAN** | *Cialde,* a local specialty, are circular wafers made with flour, sugar, eggs, and almonds from Puglia. The Bargilli family has been serving them with their equally delicious ice cream since 1936. **Known for:** arguably the best gelateria in town; terrific brigidini (they go well with gelato); nice wait staff. $ *Average main: €10* ✉ *Viale Grocco 2, Montecatini Terme* ☎ *0572/79459* 🌐 *www.cialdedimontecatini.it* 💳 *No credit cards.*

Hotels

Grand Hotel Croce di Malta

$$$ | **HOTEL** | Rooms at this 1911 hotel—a short walk on tree-lined streets from the center of town and even closer to the thermal baths—are spacious, with high ceilings. **Pros:** many rooms have deep bathtubs with water jets; in-house spa; rooftop terrace. **Cons:** service can be inconsistent; somewhat removed from the main drag; attracts many tour groups. $ *Rooms from: €221* ✉ *Viale IV Novembre 18, Montecatini Terme* ☎ *0572/9201* 🌐 *www.grandhotelcrocedimaltamontecatini.com* 🛏 *98 rooms* 🍴 *Free Breakfast.*

Lucca

33 km (21 miles) west of Montecatini Terme, 95 km (59 miles) west of Florence.

Ramparts built in the 16th and 17th centuries enclose this charming town filled with churches (99 of them), terra-cotta–roofed buildings, and narrow cobblestone streets, along which locals maneuver bikes to do their daily shopping. Here Caesar, Pompey, and Crassus agreed to rule Rome as a triumvirate in 56 BC. Lucca was later the first Tuscan town to accept Christianity, and the town still has a mind of its own. When most of Tuscany was voting communist, Lucca's citizens rarely followed suit.

The famous composer Giacomo Puccini (1858–1924) was born here and is celebrated during the summer Opera Theater and Music Festival of Lucca. The ramparts circling the centro storico are the perfect place to stroll, bicycle, or just admire the view.

GETTING HERE

You can reach Lucca easily by train from Florence; the historic center is a short walk from the station. If you're driving, take the A11/E76.

VISITOR INFORMATION

CONTACTS Lucca Tourism Office. ✉ *Piazzale Verdi, Lucca* ☎ *0583/583150* 🌐 *www.luccaturismo.it.*

4

Pisa, Lucca, and Northwest Tuscany LUCCA

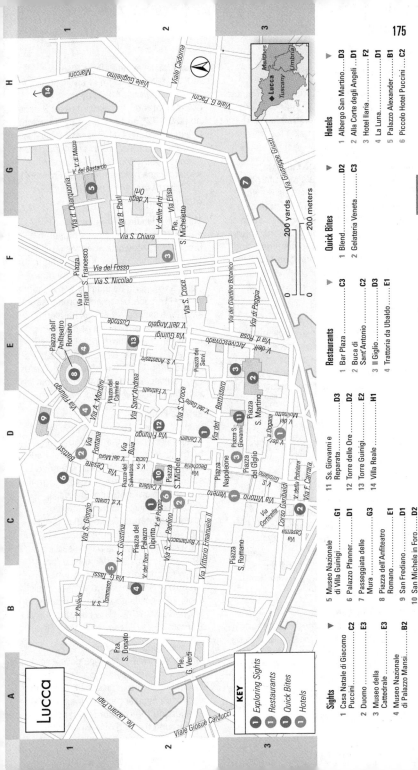

Lucca

KEY

- 1 Exploring Sights
- 1 Restaurants
- 1 Quick Bites
- 1 Hotels

Sights

1 Casa Natale di Giacomo Puccini......................**C2**
2 Duomo..................................**E3**
3 Museo della Cattedrale...........**E3**
4 Museo Nazionale di Palazzo Mansi.............**B2**
5 Museo Nazionale di Villa Guinigi.............**G1**
6 Palazzo Pfanner.................**D1**
7 Passeggiata delle Mura..........................**G3**
8 Piazza dell'Anfiteatro Romano....................**E1**
9 San Frediano....................**D1**
10 San Michele in Foro......**D2**
11 Ss. Giovanni e Reparata.........................**D3**
12 Torre delle Ore................**D2**
13 Torre Guinigi...................**E2**
14 Villa Reale.......................**H1**

Restaurants

1 Bar Plaza **C3**
2 Buca di Sant'Antonio **C2**
3 Il Giglio **D3**
4 Trattoria da Ubaldo.........**E1**

Quick Bites

1 Blend **D2**
2 Gelateria Veneta.............**C3**

Hotels

1 Albergo San Martino....**D3**
2 Alla Corte degli Angeli....**D1**
3 Hotel Ilaria........................**F2**
4 La Luna...............................**D1**
5 Palazzo Alexander........**B1**
6 Piccolo Hotel Puccini....**C2**

200 yards

200 meters

Sights

Traffic (including motorbikes) is restricted in the walled historic center of Lucca. Walking is the most enjoyable way to get around. Biking here is also recommended, as the center is quite flat.

Casa Natale di Giacomo Puccini

HISTORIC HOME | Lucca's most famous musical son was born in this house. It includes the piano on which Puccini composed *Turandot,* as well as scores of important early compositions, letters, costumes and costume sketches, and family portraits. ⊠ *Corte San Lorenzo 9, Via di Poggio, Lucca* ☎ *0583/584028* ⊕ *www.puccinimuseum.org* 🎫 *€9.*

Duomo

CHURCH | The blind arches on the cathedral's facade are a fine example of the rigorously ordered Pisan Romanesque style, in this case happily enlivened by an extremely varied collection of small, carved columns. Take a closer look at the decoration of the facade and that of the portico below; they make this one of the most entertaining church exteriors in Tuscany.

The Gothic interior contains a moving Byzantine crucifix—called the Volto Santo, or Holy Face—brought here, according to legend, in the 8th century (though it probably dates from between the 11th and early 13th century). The masterpiece of the Sienese sculptor Jacopo della Quercia (circa 1371–1438) is the marble *Tomb of Ilaria del Carretto* (1407–08). ⊠ *Piazza San Martino 8, Lucca* ☎ *0583/490530* ⊕ *www.museocattedralelucca.it* 🎫 *€3.*

Museo della Cattedrale

ART MUSEUM | The cathedral museum exhibits many items too precious to be in the church, most notably the finely worked golden decorations of the Volto Santo, the Byzantine crucifix that remains in the Duomo. ⊠ *Piazza Antelminelli, Lucca* ☎ *0583/490530* ⊕ *www.museocattedralelucca.it* 🎫 *From €4.*

Museo Nazionale di Palazzo Mansi

ART MUSEUM | Highlights here include the lovely *Portrait of a Youth* by Pontormo; portraits of the Medici painted by Bronzino (1503–72); and paintings by Tintoretto, Vasari, and others. ⊠ *Palazzo Mansi, Via Galli Tassi 43, near west walls of old city, Lucca* ☎ *0583/55570* ⊕ *www.polomusealetoscana.beniculturali.it* 🎫 *From €4* ☺ *Closed Mon. and 2nd, 4th, and 5th Sun. of month.*

Museo Nazionale di Villa Guinigi

ART MUSEUM | Although this museum presents a noteworthy overview of Lucca's artistic traditions up through the 17th century, you might find few other visitors exploring its extensive collections of local Etruscan, Roman, Romanesque, and Renaissance art. It's all housed in the 15th-century former villa of the Guinigi family, on the eastern end of the historic center. ⊠ *Via della Quarquonia 4, Lucca* ☎ *0583/496033* ⊕ *www.polomusealetoscana.beniculturali.it* 🎫 *€4* ☺ *Closed Mon. and 2nd, 4th, and 5th Sun. of month.*

Palazzo Pfanner

GARDEN | Here you can rest your feet and let time pass, surrounded by a harmonious arrangement of sun, shade, blooming plants, water, and mysterious statuary. The palazzo's well-kept formal garden, which abuts the city walls, centers on a large fountain and pool. Allegorical statues line pebbled paths that radiate outward. The palazzo, built in the 17th century, was purchased in the 19th century by the Pfanners, a family of Swiss brewers. The family, which eventually gave the town a mayor, still lives here. ⊠ *Via degli Asili 33, Lucca* ☎ *0583/954029* ⊕ *www.palazzopfanner.it* 🎫 *From €5* ☺ *Closed Dec.–Mar.*

★ Passeggiata delle Mura

CITY PARK | **FAMILY** | On nice days, the citizens of Lucca cycle, jog, stroll, or kick a soccer ball in this green, beautiful, and very large circular park. It's neither inside nor outside the city but rather right atop and around the ring of ramparts that defines Lucca. Sunlight streams through two rows of tall plane trees to dapple the *passeggiata delle mura* (walk on the walls), which is 4.2 km (2½ miles) long. Ten bulwarks are topped with lawns, many with picnic tables and some with play equipment for children. Be aware at all times of where the edge is—there are no railings, and the drop to the ground outside the city is a precipitous 40 feet. ✉ *Lucca.*

Piazza dell'Anfiteatro Romano

PLAZA/SQUARE | FAMILY | Here's where the ancient Roman amphitheater once stood. Some of the medieval buildings built over the amphitheater retain its original oval shape and brick arches. ✉ *Piazza Anfiteatro, Lucca.*

San Frediano

CHURCH | A 14th-century mosaic decorates the facade of this church just steps from the Anfiteatro. Inside are works by Jacopo della Quercia (circa 1371–1438) and Matteo Civitali (1436–1501), as well as the lace-clad mummy of St. Zita (circa 1218–78), the patron saint of household servants. ✉ *Piazza San Frediano, Lucca* ☎ *349/844–0290* ⊕ *www.sanfredianolucca.com* ⊠ *€3.*

San Michele in Foro

CHURCH | The facade here is even more fanciful than that of the Duomo. Its upper levels have nothing but air behind them (after the front of the church was built, there were no funds to raise the nave), and the winged Archangel Michael, who stands at the very top, seems precariously poised for flight. The facade, heavily restored in the 19th century, displays busts of such Italian patriots as Garibaldi and Cavour. Check out the superb Filippino Lippi (1457/58–1504) panel painting of Saints Jerome, Sebastian, Rocco, and Helen in the right transept. ✉ *Piazza San Michele, Lucca* ⊕ *www.luccatranoi.it.*

Ss. Giovanni e Reparata

CHURCH | The unusual element at this church is an archaeological site where five layers of Luccan history were revealed when it was discovered in 1969. Paths and catwalks suspended above the delicate sites in the grottoes under the church enable you to wander from one era to another—from the 2nd-century-BC site of a Roman temple through the 5th, 8th, 9th, and 11th centuries. After leaving the underground sights, the 12th-century church feels almost modern. ✉ *Piazza San Giovanni, Lucca* ☎ *0583/490530* ⊕ *www.museocattedralelucca.it* ⊠ *From €4.*

Torre delle Ore (*Tower of the Hours*)

OTHER ATTRACTION | FAMILY | The highest spot in Lucca is the top of this tower, which had its first mechanical clock in 1390. It's since contained several clocks over the centuries; the current timepiece was installed in 1754. The reward for climbing 207 steps to the top is a panoramic view of the town. ✉ *Via Fillungo at Via dell'Arancio, Lucca* ☎ *0583/316846* ⊕ *www.comune.lucca.it* ⊠ *€4* ⊙ *Closed Nov.–Mar.*

Torre Guinigi

NOTABLE BUILDING | FAMILY | The tower of the medieval Palazzo Guinigi contains one of the city's most curious sights: a grove of ilex trees has grown at the top of the tower, and their roots have pushed their way into the room below. From the top you have a magnificent view of the city and the surrounding countryside. (Only the tower is open to the public, not the palazzo.) ✉ *Via Sant'Andrea, Lucca* ☎ *0583/48090* ⊕ *www.comune.lucca.it* ⊠ *€5.*

Villa Reale

GARDEN | Eight kilometers (5 miles) north of Lucca in Marlia, this villa was once the home of Napoléon's sister, Princess Elisa. Restored by the Counts Pecci-Blunt, the estate is celebrated for its spectacular gardens, laid out in the 16th century and redone in the middle of the 17th. Gardening buffs adore the legendary *teatro di verdura*, a theater carved out of hedges and topiaries; concerts are occasionally held here. In summer, performances are held in the gardens of other famous Lucca villas as well. Contact the Lucca tourist office for details. ✉ *Marlia* ✥ *North of Lucca along river Serchio, in direction of Barga and Bagni di Lucca* ☎ *0583/30108* 🌐 *villarealedimarlia.it* 🎫 *From €10* 🕒 *Closed Nov.–Feb.*

🍴 Restaurants

Bar Plaza

$ | **ITALIAN** | This is a busy bistro that does just about everything. In this case, that means expertly mixed cocktails, wines by the glass, and light meals at lunch and dinner. **Known for:** on the city's largest and prettiest square; open early and late most days; great bacon and eggs. [$] *Average main: €12* ✉ *Piazza Napoleone 35, Lucca* ☎ *0583/467561* 🌐 *www.plazalucca.it* 🕒 *Closed Wed.*

★ **Buca di Sant'Antonio**

$$ | **TUSCAN** | The staying power of Buca di Sant'Antonio—it's been around since 1782—is the result of superlative Tuscan food brought to the table by waitstaff who don't miss a beat. The menu includes the simple but blissful *tortelli lucchesi al sugo* (meat-stuffed pasta with a tomato-and-meat sauce), as well as more daring dishes such as roast *capretto* (kid goat) with herbs. **Known for:** classy, family-run ambience; excellent sommelier; superlative pastas. [$] *Average main: €20* ✉ *Via della Cervia 3, Lucca* ☎ *0583/55881* 🌐 *www.bucadisantantonio.com* 🕒 *Closed Mon., 1 wk in Jan., and 1 wk in July. No dinner Sun.*

★ **Il Giglio**

$$$ | **TUSCAN** | Divine, cutting-edge food and Tuscan classics are served in this one-room space, where in winter, there's a roaring fireplace and, in warmer months, there's outdoor seating on a pretty little piazza. If mushrooms are in season, try the *tacchoni con funghi*, a homemade pasta with mushrooms and a native herb called *nepitella*. A local favorite during winter is the *coniglio con olive* (rabbit stew with olives). **Known for:** the wine list, especially its selection of local wines; fine service; creative menu with seasonal ingredients. [$] *Average main: €35* ✉ *Piazza del Giglio 2, Lucca* ☎ *0583/494508* 🌐 *www.ristorantegiglio.com* 🕒 *Closed Wed. and 15 days in Nov. No dinner Tues.*

Trattoria da Ubaldo

$ | **ITALIAN** | The macabre decor is not for the faint of heart, but any lover of seriously good food can look beyond the disembodied dolls (among other things) adorning the dining room's walls. The menu is strong on local dishes, served in generous portions. **Known for:** copious portions of pasta; fine, well-priced wine list; grilled meats. [$] *Average main: €13* ✉ *Via dell'Anfiteatro 67, Lucca* ☎ *347/500–4848.*

☕ Coffee and Quick Bites

Blend

$ | **ITALIAN** | Blend is open 10 am to 9:30 pm (after most places are closed) and serves sandwiches, pasta, and creative salads. It's on a quiet little piazza right around the corner from the Duomo. **Known for:** vegetarians and vegans will be happy; happy hour with tasty snacks; creative sandwiches. [$] *Average main: €10* ✉ *Piazza San Giusto 8, Lucca* ☎ *0583/050442.*

Gelateria Veneta

$ | **ITALIAN** | **FAMILY** | The outstanding gelato, sorbet, and ices, some of which are sugar-free, served here are prepared three times a day according to the same recipes used by the Arnoldo brothers when they opened the place in 1927. The pièces de résistance are frozen fruits stuffed with creamy filling: don't miss the apricot sorbet–filled apricot. **Known for:** delicious ices on a stick; sorbet-stuffed frozen fruits; longtime local favorite. [$] *Average main: €3 ✉ Via V. Veneto 74, Lucca ☎ 0583/467037 🌐 www.gelateria-veneta.net 🕑 Closed Nov.–Mar.*

Hotels

★ Albergo San Martino

$ | **HOTEL** | **FAMILY** | The brocade bedspreads of this inn in the heart of the centro storico are fresh and crisp; the proprietor is friendly; and the breakfast, served in a cheerful apricot room, is more than ample. **Pros:** comfortable beds; friendly staff; tucked away on a small, sunny square. **Cons:** slightly noisy during Lucca Music Festival; pleasant and stylish but not luxurious; parking is difficult. [$] *Rooms from: €81 ✉ Via della Dogana 9, Lucca ☎ 0583/469181 🌐 www.albergosanmartino.it 🛏 18 rooms 🍴 No Meals.*

Alla Corte degli Angeli

$$ | **B&B/INN** | This charming hotel with a friendly staff is right off the main shopping drag, Via Fillungo. **Pros:** many rooms are connecting, making them good for families; fantastic on-site restaurant; great location. **Cons:** books up quickly; not all rooms are created equal; some rooms have tubs but no showers. [$] *Rooms from: €180 ✉ Via degli Angeli 23, Lucca ☎ 0583/469204 🌐 www.allacortedegliangeli.it 🛏 21 rooms 🍴 Free Breakfast.*

Hotel Ilaria

$$ | **HOTEL** | The former stables of the Villa Bottini have been transformed into a modern hotel with stylish rooms done in a warm wood veneer with blue-and-white fittings. **Pros:** modern; multilingual, pleasant staff; free bicycles. **Cons:** books up quickly; some find it overpriced; though in the city center, it's a little removed from main attractions. [$] *Rooms from: €161 ✉ Via del Fosso 26, Lucca ☎ 0583/47615 🌐 www.hotelilaria.com 🛏 44 rooms 🍴 Free Breakfast.*

La Luna

$$ | **B&B/INN** | On a quiet, airy courtyard close to the Piazza del Mercato, this hotel, run by the Barbieri family for more than four decades, occupies two renovated wings of an old building. **Pros:** professional staff; central location; the annex has wheelchair-accessible rooms. **Cons:** may be too central for some; street noise can be a bit of a problem; some rooms feel dated. [$] *Rooms from: €175 ✉ Corte Compagni 12, at Via Fillungo, Lucca ☎ 0583/493634 🌐 www.hotellaluna.it 🕑 Closed Jan. 7–31 🛏 29 rooms 🍴 Free Breakfast.*

Palazzo Alexander

$$ | **HOTEL** | This hotel, in a building dating from the 12th century, has public rooms with timbered ceilings, warm yellow walls, and brocaded chairs and guest rooms with high ceilings and still more of that glorious damask. **Pros:** intimate feel; a short walk from San Michele in Foro; gracious staff. **Cons:** might be too quiet for some; books up quickly; some complain of too-thin walls. [$] *Rooms from: €160 ✉ Via S. Giustina 48, Lucca ☎ 0583/583571 🌐 www.hotelpalazzoalexander.it 🛏 13 rooms 🍴 Free Breakfast.*

Piccolo Hotel Puccini

$ | **HOTEL** | Steps from the busy square and church of San Michele al Foro, this tranquil, affordable little hotel has rooms with hardwood floors and cheerfully patterned fabrics. **Pros:** upbeat, English-speaking staff; quiet, central location; good value. **Cons:** many wish the breakfast was more copious; some rooms are on the dark side; books up quickly. [$] *Rooms from: €120 ✉ Via di Poggio 9, Lucca ☎ 0583/55421 🌐 www.hotelpuccini.com 🛏 14 rooms 🍴 No Meals.*

 Performing Arts

Estate Musicale Lucchese

FESTIVALS | FAMILY | Throughout the summer there are jazz, pop, and rock concerts in conjunction with the Estate Musicale Lucchese music festival. It happens in the large, beautiful Piazza Napoleone. Ask the tourist information office for more information. ⊠ Lucca ⊕ www.turismo.lucca.it.

Lucca Comics and Games

FESTIVALS | FAMILY | During the first weekend of November, the city's piazzas are filled with tents featuring exhibitions and games, and the streets are invaded with comic-book fans and gamers for Lucca Comics and Games. During the last week of October, and continuing through the Comics festival, a mostra mercato (market show) takes place as well. ⊠ Lucca ☎ 0583/401711 ⊕ www.luccacomicsandgames.com.

Opera Theater and Music Festival of Lucca

FESTIVALS | Sponsored by the Opera Theater of Lucca and the music college of the University of Cincinnati, the Opera Theater and Music Festival of Lucca runs from mid-June to mid-July; performances are staged in open-air venues. Call the Lucca tourist office or the Opera Theater of Lucca (☎ 0583/46531) for information. ⊠ Lucca ⊕ www.turismo.lucca.it.

Teatro del Giglio

THEATER | From September through April you can see operas, plays, and concerts staged at the Teatro del Giglio. ⊠ Piazza del Giglio, Duomo ☎ 0583/46531 ⊕ www.teatrodelgiglio.it.

Shopping

Lucca is known for its farro, an ancient barleylike grain that has found its way into regional specialties such as zuppa (or minestra) di farro (farro soup). It's available in food shops all over town.

The city is, however, most famous for its olive oil, which is exported throughout the world. Look for bottles of extra-virgin with labels clearly indicating that the oil is entirely from Tuscany or, better yet, entirely from a local fattoria, or farm.

Olio nuovo (new oil) is available for a few weeks in November, when the olive-picking season begins. This oil is strong-flavored and peppery—great for drizzling on soup, pasta, and bread—and it's also nearly impossible to find in North America. Wine from small Lucca producers is also difficult to find abroad, so be sure to pick some up while you're here.

CLOTHING

Mode Mignon Donna

WOMEN'S CLOTHING | Come here for one-stop high-end designer shopping, including Prada, Miu-Miu, Gucci, Dolce e Gabbana, Jil Sander, and Tod's—among others. (Modo Mignon Uomo is at another location in the center.) ⊠ Piazza Bernardini 1-2-3, Lucca ☎ 0583/491217.

FOOD

★ Antica Bottega di Prospero

FOOD | Stop by this shop for top-quality local food products, including farro, dried porcini mushrooms, olive oil, and wine. ⊠ Via San Lucia 13, Lucca ☎ 0583/494875.

★ Caniparoli

CHOCOLATE | FAMILY | Chocolate lovers will be pleased with the selection of artisanal chocolates, marzipan delights, and gorgeous cakes. Creations become even more fanciful during two big Christian holidays: Christmas and Easter. ⊠ Via San Paolino 44, Lucca ☎ 0583/53456 ⊕ www.caniparoliccioccolateria.it.

Pasticceria Pinelli

FOOD | FAMILY | For a broad selection of scrumptious pastries, visit this favorite haunt of Lucca's senior citizens, who frequently stop in after Sunday Mass. ⊠ Via Beccheria 28, Lucca ☎ 0583/496119 ⊕ www.pasticceriapinelli.it.

⭐ Pasticceria Taddeucci

FOOD | FAMILY | A particularly delicious version of *buccellato*—the sweet, anise-flavored bread with raisins that is a Luccan specialty—is baked at Pasticceria Taddeucci. ✉ *Piazza San Michele 34, Lucca* ☎ *0583/494933* ⊕ *www.buccellatotaddeucci.com.*

MARKETS

Antiques Market

MARKET | FAMILY | On the third weekend of the month, an antiques market happens in and around Piazza San Martino. Vendors unveil their wares around 8:30, and start packing up around dusk. There's something for everyone, including old-fashioned glassware, ancient coins, and furniture—some items are antique, some are just old. ✉ *Piazza del Duomo, Lucca.*

Bookstalls

MARKET | FAMILY | Just behind the church of San Giusto (off Via Beccheria, which runs for about two blocks between Piazza Napoleone and Piazza San Michele) are bookstalls that open their cupboard doors on clement days (including Sunday), from about 10 am to 7 pm. You may discover anything from hand-tinted prints of orchids to back issues of *Uomo Ragno* (Spider-Man looks and acts just the same even when he's speaking Italian). ✉ *Piazza Napoleone, Lucca.*

WINE

⭐ Enoteca Vanni

WINE/SPIRITS | A huge selection of wines, as well as an ancient cellar, make this place worth a stop. For the cost of the wine only, tastings can be organized through the shopkeepers and are held in the cellar or outside in a lovely little piazza. All of this can be paired with *affettati misti* (sliced cured meats) and cheeses of the highest caliber. ✉ *Piazza San Salvatore 7, Lucca* ☎ *0583/491902* ⊕ *www.enotecavanni.com.*

Massei Ugo

WINE/SPIRITS | This small shop offers great wine prices and assorted local delicacies. The owner, Ugo Massei, doesn't speak English, but he's friendly and helpful. ✉ *Via S. Andrea 19, Lucca* ☎ *0583/467656.*

Activities

A good way to spend the afternoon is to go biking around the large path atop the city's ramparts. There are two good spots right next to each other where you can rent bikes. The prices are about the same (about €15 for the day and €3 per hour for city bikes) and they are centrally located, just beside the town wall.

Poli Antonio Biciclette

BIKING | FAMILY | This is the best option for bicycle rental on the east side of town. ✉ *Piazza Santa Maria 42, Lucca East* ☎ *0583/493787* ⊕ *www.biciclettepoli.com.*

San Marcello Pistoiese

33 km (21 miles) northwest of Pistoia, 66 km (41 miles) northwest of Florence.

This small town—small, but still the largest in the area—bustles in summer and winter (when it's one of Tuscany's few ski destinations), but calms down in spring and fall. It's set amid spectacular scenery; you can drive across a dramatic suspension bridge over the Lima River.

GETTING HERE

By car, you're likely to approach San Marcello Pistoiese from Pistoia; take the SS435 to the SS66, which takes you right into town (follow the signs). COPIT provides frequent bus service as well. There is no train service.

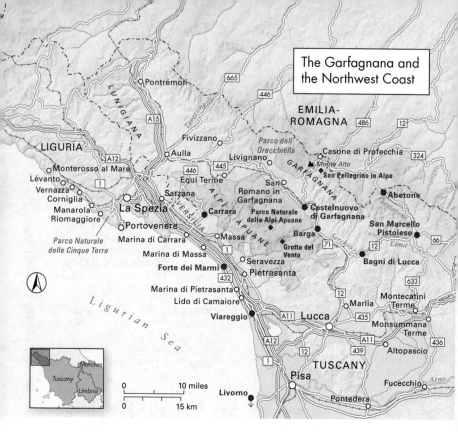

The Garfagnana and the Northwest Coast

👁 Sights

Pieve di San Marcello

CHURCH | This church dates from the 12th century, though the interior was redone in the 18th century and most of the art inside is from that period. ✉ *Piazza Arcangeli, San Marcello Pistoiese* 🎟 *Free.*

Abetone

20 km (12 miles) northwest of San Marcello Pistoiese, 53 km (33 miles) northwest of Pistoia, 86 km (53 miles) northwest of Florence.

Abetone is one of the most-visited vacation spots in the Apennine Mountains, where Tuscans, Emilia-Romagnans, and others come to ski. Set above two valleys, the resort town is on the edge of a lush and ancient forest of more than 9,000 acres.

The numerous ski trails are mostly for beginners and intermediate skiers (the entire area has only two expert slopes). Summer is the time to trek or mountain bike in and around the beautiful hills and mountains.

GETTING HERE

By car from Pistoia, take the SS435/SR436 and follow signs for Abetone-Modena. You'll exit onto the SS66/SR66; continue for some 30 km (18 miles) to the SS12, which will take you into Abetone. COPIT buses run to Abetone, but there is no train service.

Sights

San Pellegrino in Alpe

CHURCH | Stop at the San Pellegrino in Alpe monastery en route from Abetone to Castelnuovo di Garfagnana to see the staggering view and the large wooden cross. The story goes that a 9th-century Scot, Pellegrino ("Little Pilgrim") by name, came to this spot to repent. ✉ *Via del Voltone 14, San Pellegrino in Alpe* ✣ *Off SR12, 16 km (10 miles) northeast of Castelnuovo di Garfagnana, 28 km (17 miles) northwest of Abetone* ☎ *0583/649072* 🌐 *www.sanpellegrino.org* 🎟 *€3.*

Restaurants

Ciuste

$ | **ITALIAN** | Come here for a finely crafted sandwich (they have 18 different varieties on the menu), or something more substantial like the *crostone ai funghi* (a very large portion of toasted bread topped with local, fragrant porcini mushrooms). Tiny local blueberries, in season, appear in numerous guises on the dessert menu. **Known for:** fantastic sandwiches; youthful atmosphere; eating while breathing fine mountain air. [$] *Average main: €13* ✉ *Via dell'Uccellaria 22, Abetone* ☎ *0573/172–0114* 🌐 *www.weloveabetone.it.*

Hotels

Hotel Bellavista

$ | **HOTEL** | Originally a 19th-century villa belonging to Marchesa Guendalina Strozzi—her ancestors were powerful bankers in Renaissance Florence—this is now a contemporary inn. **Pros:** you can ski from hotel to chairlift; pretty views; some rooms have a whirlpool tub. **Cons:** a car is a necessity; some complain of noise in the halls; attracts a rowdy crowd. [$] *Rooms from: €110* ✉ *Via Brennero 383, Abetone* ☎ *0573/60028* 🌐 *www.abetone-bellavista.it* 🕒 *Closed May, Oct., and Nov.* 🛏 *40 rooms* 🍴 *Free Breakfast.*

Activities

SKIING

Consorzio Impianti

SKIING & SNOWBOARDING | This group manages the ski facilities in Abetone and has information on the Multipass, as well as maps, directions, and area information. ✉ *Via Brennero 429, Abetone* ☎ *0573/60557* 🌐 *www.multipassabetone.it.*

Pistoiese ski area

SKIING & SNOWBOARDING | The area has 37 ski slopes, amounting to about 50 km (31 miles) of ski surface, all accessible through the purchase of a single Multipass. You can check the Abetone section of the Pistoiese ski area website for details on the Multipass, or call the Tourist Information office in Pistoia. ✉ *Abetone.*

Bagni di Lucca

36 km (22 miles) southwest of Abetone, 27 km (17 miles) north of Lucca, 101 km (63 miles) northwest of Florence.

Pretty Bagni di Lucca was a fashionable spa town in the early 19th century—in part because of its thermal waters. The Romantic poet Percy Bysshe Shelley (1792–1822) installed his family here during the summer of 1818. He wrote to a friend in July of that year that the waters here were exceedingly refreshing: "My custom is to undress and sit on the rocks, reading Herodotus, until perspiration has subsided, and then to leap from the edge of the rock into this fountain." In 1853, Robert and Elizabeth Browning spent the summer in a house on the main square. Its heyday behind it, the town is now a quiet, charming place where elegant thermal spas still soothe on temperate summer days.

GETTING HERE

By car from Florence, take the A11 and exit at Capannori. Take the SS439 in the direction of Lucca. From Lucca, take the SS12/Via del Brennero. This leads to the SP18, which takes you directly into Bagni di Lucca. Lazzi bus lines also operate from Lucca and Florence. Trains run nearly every hour from Lucca and take about 25 minutes.

VISITOR INFORMATION

CONTACTS Bagni di Lucca Tourism Office. ✉ *Via Umberto I 139, Bagni di Lucca* ☎ *0583/805754* 🌐 *www.turismobagnididilucca.com.*

Sights

Centro Termale Bagni di Lucca
HOT SPRING | Here you'll find two natural steam-room caves, as well as spa services such as mud baths, massage, hydrotherapy, and facials. ✉ *Piazza San Martino 11, Bagni di Lucca* ☎ *0583/87221* 🌐 *www.termebagnidilucca.it* 🎫 *€15 for thermal pool; spa services vary.*

Il Ponte della Maddalena (*The Magdalen's Bridge*)
BRIDGE | **FAMILY** | Il Ponte della Maddalena is, oddly, also known as the Devil's Bridge. Commissioned in all likelihood by Matilde di Canossa (1046–1115), it was restructured by the petty despot Castruccio Castracani in the early 14th century. It's worth the climb to the middle—the bridge is narrow, steep, and pedestrians-only—to check out the view. Despite 1836 flood damage and early-20th-century alterations, it seems little changed from the Middle Ages. If you're heading north along the Serchio from Lucca to Bagni di Lucca, you will see the bridge on your left. ✉ *Bagni di Lucca.*

🍴 Restaurants

Osteria i Macelli
$$ | **TUSCAN** | Honest Tuscan cooking prevails at this simple trattoria next to a large parking lot. No matter that there's no view: the terrific food and pleasing service—all of it served in a typical Tuscan dining room with high timbered ceilings—make a stop here well worth the detour. **Known for:** creative pasta dishes; adherence to seasonal ingredients; its chef/sommelier. [$] *Average main: €18* ✉ *Piazza i Macelli, Bagni di Lucca* ✣ *Borgo a Mozzano, 21 km (13 miles) north of Lucca on the SS12* ☎ *0583/88700* 🌐 *www.osteriaimacelli.com* 🕒 *Closed 2 wks in Mar.*

Barga

17 km (11 miles) northwest of Bagni di Lucca, 111 km (69 miles) northwest of Florence.

Barga is a lovely little city (one of Italy's smallest under that classification) with a finely preserved medieval core. It produced textiles—mostly silk during the Renaissance and wool in the 18th century. You won't find textiles here today; now the emphasis is on tourism. Here the African-American troops known as the Buffalo Soldiers are remembered by the locals for their bravery in defending this mountainous area during World War II.

Walking around Barga is not for the faint of heart: it's one steep uphill after another to reach the tiny centro storico, followed by steps to get to Piazza del Duomo.

GETTING HERE

By car from Lucca, take the SS12/Via del Brennero directly to Barga. Though there is train service to Barga, the station is far away from the centro storico. The only bus option is the small CLAP line (✉ *Via Roma 7* ☎ *0583/723050*), which runs between here and Castelnuovo di Garfagnana.

VISITOR INFORMATION

CONTACTS Barga Tourism Office. ✉ *Via di Mezzo 45, Barga* ☎ *0583/724791* ⊕ *www.comune.barga.lu.it.*

Sights

Duomo

CHURCH | Dedicated to St. Christopher, the Romanesque cathedral is made from elegant limestone (quarried from nearby caves) and saw four separate periods of construction. The first began in the 9th century; the last was finished in the 15th. Inside, the intricately carved pulpit, one of the finest examples of mid-12th-century Tuscan sculpture, commands center stage. The view from the litte piazza outside the Duomo is incredible: Tuscan mountains have never looked so good. ✉ *Via del Duomo, Barga.*

Grotta del Vento

NATURE SIGHT | FAMILY | About 14 km (9 miles) southwest of Barga, after following a winding road flanked by both sheer cliffs and fantastic views, you come to Tuscany's Cave of the Wind. As the result of a steady internal temperature of 10.7°C (about 51°F), the wind is sucked into the cave in the winter and blown out in the summer. It has a long cavern with stalactites, stalagmites, "bottomless" pits, and subterranean streams. One-, two-, and three-hour guided tours of the cave are given. (The one-hour tour is offered only from November through March.) ✉ *SP 39, west at Galliciano, Vergemoli* ☎ *0583/722024* ⊕ *www.grottadelvento.com* 💰 *From €10.*

🎭 Performing Arts

Barga Jazz

FESTIVALS | Listen to the newest music during Barga Jazz, a jazz orchestra competition (in July and August). The scores presented each year are selected by a special committee, and a winner is selected by an international jury. ✉ *Teatro dell'Accademia dei Differenti, Via Nerici 176, Barga* ⊕ *bargajazz.it.*

Opera Barga

FESTIVALS | From mid-July to mid-August, the stony streets of Barga come alive as opera fans come to Opera Barga. This highly regarded festival takes place at the Teatro dell'Accademia dei Differenti (Theater of the Academy of the Different). The Opera Barga began in 1967 as a workshop for young singers and musicians. Now it stages lesser-known baroque operas, as well as contemporary works. ✉ *Teatro dell'Accademia dei Differenti, Piazza Angelio 4, Barga* ☎ *0583/711068* ⊕ *www.operabarga.it.*

Castelnuovo di Garfagnana

13 km (8 miles) northwest of Barga, 47 km (27 miles) north of Lucca, 121 km (75 miles) northwest of Florence.

Castelnuovo di Garfagnana might be the best base for exploring the Garfagnana because it's central with respect to the other towns. During the Renaissance, the town's fortunes were frequently tied to those of the powerful Este family of Ferrara. It's now a bustling town with a lovely historic center.

GETTING HERE

By car from Lucca, take the SS12/Via del Brennero, follow signs to Borgo a Mozzano; then take the SS445, which leads directly into town.

Buses run between Castelnuovo di Garfagnana and Barga. You can purchase tickets at Paolini, the tobacconist's shop in Piazza della Repubblica. (Note that the journey must make all stops, so many of the buses take more than one hour, whereas the journey by car takes about a half hour.) There is no train service.

VISITOR INFORMATION

CONTACTS Castelnuovo di Garfagnana Tourism Office. ✉ *Piazza della Erbe, Castelnuovo di Garfagnana* ☎ *0583/641007* 🌐 *www.castelnuovogarfagnana.org.*

Sights

Duomo

CHURCH | Dedicated to St. Peter, the Duomo was begun in the 11th century and was reconstructed in the early 1500s. Inside is a crucifix dating from the 14th to 15th century. There's also an early-16th-century terra-cotta attributed to the school of the della Robbia. ✉ *Piazza del Duomo, Castelnuovo di Garfagnana* ☎ *0583/62170.*

La Rocca (*The Fortress*)

MILITARY SIGHT | Dating from the 13th century, La Rocca (The Fortress) has a plaque commemorating writer Ludovico Ariosto's brief tenure here as commissar general for the Este. Ariosto (1474–1533) wrote the epic poem *Orlando Furioso* (1516), among other works. You can only see the impressive walls and great entryway of the fort from the outside. ✉ *Piazza Umberto, Castelnuovo di Garfagnana.*

Parco Naturale delle Alpi Apuane

NATIONAL PARK | **FAMILY** | The Parco Regionale delle Alpi Apuane (Regional Park of the Apuan Alps) straddles the hills of coastal Versilia and spreads mostly across the mountainous Garfagnana inland. It includes caves, grottoes, peaks, and valleys. Hiking, riding, and mountain bike trails crisscross the park. There are various points of access for various types of excursions, and all are clearly indicated on the interactive park map. The park's visitor center is in the town of Castelnuovo Garfagnana. ✉ *Castelnuovo di Garfagnana* ☎ *0583/644242* 🌐 *www.parcapuane.it* 🎟 *Free.*

Restaurants

★ Osteria Vecchio Mulino

$$ | **TUSCAN** | "The old mill" has an antique marble serving counter filled with free nibbles and two large wooden tables in a room lined with wine bottles. The enthusiastic host, Andrea Bertucci, proudly touts local products on his simple menu, which usually consists of superior cheese and *affettati misti* (mixed sliced cured meats); traditional local dishes with farro grain, polenta, pecorino cheese, trout from the many local streams, and salami round out the selections. **Known for:** exceptional wine list; exuberant host; commitment to local ingredients. [$] *Average main: €20* ✉ *Via Vittorio Emanuele 12, Castelnuovo di Garfagnana* ☎ *0583/62192* 🌐 *www.vecchiomulino.info* 🕒 *Closed Mon.*

Activities

HIKING AND CLIMBING

Centro Accoglienza Parco

HIKING & WALKING | **FAMILY** | Stop here for help with hiking information, particularly for the Parco Naturale delle Alpi Apuane. ✉ *Piazza Erbe 1, Castelnuovo di Garfagnana* ☎ *0583/644242* 🌐 *www.turismo.garfagnana.eu.*

Club Alpino Italiano

HIKING & WALKING | **FAMILY** | For detailed maps and information about trekking in the mountains surrounding Castelnuovo di Garfagnana, contact the Club Alpino Italiano. ✉ *Via Vittorio Emanuele, Castelnuovo di Garfagnana* ☎ *02/205–7231* 🌐 *www.cai.it.*

Livorno

24 km (15 miles) south of Pisa, 187 km (116 miles) west of Florence.

Livorno is a gritty city with a long and interesting history. In the early Middle Ages, it alternately belonged to Pisa and Genoa. In 1421, Florence, seeking access to the sea, bought it. Cosimo I de'Medici (1519–74) started construction of the harbor in 1571, putting Livorno on the map.

After Ferdinando I de' Medici (1549–1609) proclaimed Livorno a free city, it became a haven for people suffering from religious persecution; Roman Catholics from England and Jews and Moors from Spain and Portugal, among others, settled here. The *Quattro Mori* (Four Moors), also known as the Monument to Ferdinando I, commemorates this. (The statue of Ferdinando I dates from 1595, the bronze Moors by Pietro Tacca from the 1620s.)

In the following centuries, and particularly in the 18th, Livorno boomed as a port. In the 19th century, the town drew a host of famous Brits passing through on their grand tours. Its prominence continued up to World War II, when it was heavily bombed. Much of the town's architecture, therefore, postdates the war, and it's somewhat difficult to imagine what it might have looked like before. Livorno has recovered from the war, however, as it's become a huge point of departure for container ships, as well as the only spot in Tuscany for cruise ships to dock for the day.

Most of Livorno's artistic treasures date from the 17th century and aren't all that interesting unless you dote on obscure baroque artists. Livorno's most famous native artist, Amedeo Modigliani (1884–1920), was of a much more recent vintage. Sadly, there's no notable work by him in his hometown.

There may not be much in the way of art, but it's still worth strolling around the city. The Mercato Nuovo, which has been around since 1894, sells all sorts of fruits, vegetables, grains, meat, and fish. Outdoor markets nearby are also chock-full of local color. The presence of Camp Darby, an American military base just outside town, accounts for the availability of many American products.

If you have time, Livorno is worth a stop for lunch or dinner at the very least.

GETTING HERE

Livorno is easily reached by rail; trains from Florence run hourly. By car, it's about an hour west of Florence on the Fi-Pi-Li.

VISITOR INFORMATION

CONTACTS Livorno Tourism Office. ✉ *Via Pieroni 18/20, Livorno* ☎ *0586/894236* 🌐 *www.comune.livorno.it.*

🍴 Restaurants

★ Cantina Nardi
$ | ITALIAN | It's open only for lunch and it's well off the beaten path (even if it is in the center of Livorno's shopping district), but getting here is worth the trouble: this tiny place has a short menu that changes daily, a superb wine list, and a gregarious staff. Its *baccalà alla livornese* (deep-fried salt cod served with chickpeas) is succulent and crisp; soups, such as ribollita, are very soothing. **Known for:** tiny sandwiches stuffed with tasty things; worth the detour; to-die-for wines. [$] *Average main: €11* ✉ *Via Cambini 6/8, Livorno* ☎ *0586/808006* 🌐 *cantinanardi.com* 🕒 *Closed Sun. No dinner.*

L'Ostricaio
$$ | TUSCAN | Locals crowd into this tiny place with a lovely view at lunch and dinner to feast on treats from the sea. Antipasti such as raw oysters or *code di manzancolle* (deep-fried shrimp) are perfect starters, followed by delicious pasta dishes or succulent mixed fry. **Known for:** creative pasta dishes; lively, convivial atmosphere; raw oysters and shrimp. [$] *Average main: €15* ✉ *Viale Italia 100, Livorno* ☎ *0586/581345.*

Osteria del Mare
$$ | SEAFOOD | Husband and wife Claudio and Marila run this fish restaurant across the (busy) street from the docks. The

decor's nothing to write home about (paneled walls with framed prints and navigational coats of arms)—here, it's all about the creative dishes and desserts. **Known for:** fish of the day; Marila's cheesecake; inventive dishes. $ *Average main: €17* ⊠ *Borgo Cappuccini 5, Livorno* ☎ *0586/881027* ⊘ *Closed Thurs.*

Ristorante Gennarino

$$ | **ITALIAN** | Lovers of seafood fill this unpretentious trattoria, where the unremarkable decor (yellowed walls, fluorescent lights) can be taken as a testament to the singular focus here on high-quality cuisine. Start with the *insalata di mare tiepida* (seafood antipasti), and follow with the flavorful spaghetti *all'ammiraglia* (admiral-style, laden with mussels, baby clams, squid, and fresh tomatoes). **Known for:** excellent wine list; fine waitstaff; fish of the day. $ *Average main: €19* ⊠ *Via Santa Fortunata 11, Livorno* ☎ *0586/888093* ⊘ *Closed Wed. and 15 days in June.*

Viareggio

25 km (15 miles) northwest of Lucca, 97 km (60 miles) northwest of Florence.

Tobias Smollett (1721–71), the English novelist, wrote in the 1760s that Viareggio was "a kind of sea-port on the Mediterranean … The roads are indifferent and the accommodation is execrable." Much has changed here since Smollett's time. For one, this beach town becomes very crowded in summer, so accommodations are plentiful. It can also be loud and brassy at the height of the season, though there's peace and quiet in the autumn and early spring.

Viareggio has numerous buildings decorated in the 1920s Liberty style, characterized by colorful wood and, in some instances, ornate exterior decoration. Locals and tourists alike stroll along the town's wide seaside promenade lined with bars, cafés, and some very fine restaurants.

If you can't make it to Venice for *Carnevale* (Carnival), come here, where the festivities are in some ways more fun than in Venice. The city is packed with revelers from all over Tuscany, taking part in the riot of colorful parades with giant floats. Book lodging far in advance, and be aware that hotels charge top prices during Carnevale.

GETTING HERE

Trains run frequently from Florence on the Lucca line. By car from Lucca, take the A11 and follow the signs for Viareggio. Exit at Massarosa and take the SS439 to the SP5, which goes into the center of town.

VISITOR INFORMATION

CONTACTS Viareggio Tourism Office. ⊠ *Viale, Carducci 10, Viareggio* ☎ *0584/962233* ⊕ *www.luccaturismo.it.*

 Restaurants

e.dai

$ | **SEAFOOD** | The fish that's served here comes off the boats each morning, which partly explains why the food is so good. Creativity abounds in the "kitchen" (the place is very small); offerings, which change daily, are scrawled on a board; and the young staff is only too happy to explain the menu. **Known for:** the tuna sandwich; the freshness of its fish; the fritto misto (mixed fish fry). $ *Average main: €10* ⊠ *Viale Regina Margherita 148/B, Viareggio* ☎ *392/431–6705* ⊕ *www.edaifish.it.*

★ Pino Ristorante

$$$ | **SEAFOOD** | Locals swear by this small, unpretentious trattoria a couple of blocks from the beach, where the Artizzu family has been serving specialties from the sea since 1979. The house specialty *aragosta alla catalana con verdure* (Mediterranean lobster with steamed and raw vegetables) is pricey but divine, and the *spiedino di sogliola* (sole kebab) arrives with silken mashed potatoes topped with bottarga (a smoked-tuna product).

Outrageous is the rule at Viareggio's Carnevale festivities.

Known for: crunchy fritto misto; Patrizia's must-try desserts; dishes vary depending on conditions at sea. *Average main: €35 ⊠ Via Matteotti 18, Viareggio ☎ 0584/961356 ⊕ www.ristorantepino. it ⊗ Closed Wed. No lunch Mon., Tues., and Thurs.*

Romano

$$$$ | **SEAFOOD** | The Franceschini family has been running this swank seafood eatery since the 1970s. Ebullient host Romano Franceschini is justifiably proud of the food formerly produced by his wife, Franca (she still oversees the kitchen); son Roberto, an accomplished sommelier, presides over the floor.
Known for: phenomenal wine list; Romano and Roberto; fish brought daily from the docks.  *Average main: €48 ⊠ Via Mazzini 120, Viareggio ☎ 0584/31382 ⊕ www. romanoristorante.it ⊗ Closed Mon. and Jan. No lunch Tues. in July and Aug.*

🛏 Hotels

Hotel Plaza e de Russie

$$$$ | **HOTEL** | Viareggio's first hotel opened in 1871—hosting those on the Grand Tour, as well as many Russians who stayed for extended periods—and still exudes old-world charm, even though it's been completely updated to suit 21st-century tastes. **Pros:** proximity to beach; excellent restaurant; wonderful staff. **Cons:** maybe too trendy for some; fills up quickly in high season; some rooms facing street can get street noise. $ *Rooms from: €420 ⊠ Piazza d'Azeglio 1, Viareggio ☎ 0584/31714 ⊕ www. plazaederussie.com ⇄ 53 rooms ⦿⎮ Free Breakfast.*

🎭 Performing Arts

Carnevale

FESTIVALS | **FAMILY** | For four Sundays and Shrove Tuesday preceding Lent, this little seaside town produces its world-famous Carnevale, with intricate floats, or *carri*, representing Italy's most influential celebrities and politicians and sometimes the famous and infamous from around the world. Started in the late 1800s, the Viareggio Carnevale differs from that held in Venice because of its parades of huge and fantastical floats. Traditionally, they were put together by Viareggio's shipbuilders, and the masked celebrants were civil and political protesters. Today, the floats still used as a vehicle to lampoon popular figures. Other events—music, parties, and art displays—also take place during Carnevale. The crowds are huge, with many attending in costume. ✉ *Viareggio* ☎ *0584/962568* ⊕ *viareggio.ilcarnevale.com.*

🏃 Activities

Club Nautico Versilia

SAILING | Sailors who wish to tour the coastal waters should contact Club Nautico Versilia for assistance with maps, port and docking information, charter and craft-rental resources, and information about craft repair and refueling. ✉ *Piazza Palombardi dell'Artiglio, Viareggio* ☎ *0584/31444* ⊕ *www.clubnauticoversilia.it.*

Forte dei Marmi

14 km (9 miles) north of Viareggio, 37 km (27 miles) northwest of Lucca, 106 km (66 miles) northwest of Florence.

Forte dei Marmi is a playground for wealthy Italians and equally well-heeled visitors. Its wide, sandy beaches—strands are 6 km (4 miles) long—have the Alpi Apuane as a dramatic backdrop. The town was, from Roman times, the port for marble quarried in Carrara.

In the 1920s the Agnelli family (of Fiat fame) began summering here, and other tycoons followed suit. It remains the East Hampton of Italy; everyone seems to be dripping in gold, and prices are very high. In winter the town's population is about

7,000; in summer, it swells to about 150,000 people, most of whom stay in their own private villas.

GETTING HERE

By car from Florence, take the A11, following signs for Viareggio. From there, take the A12/E80 following signs for Genova. Exit at Versilia, and take the SP70 directly into town. Taking a train here is not recommended as the station is far from town.

VISITOR INFORMATION

CONTACTS Forte dei Marmi Tourism Office. ✉ *Piazza Garibaldi 1, Forte dei Marmi* ☎ *0584/280292.*

🍽 Restaurants

La Magnolia

$$$ | TUSCAN | Part of the elegant Hotel Byron but open to the public, La Magnolia is helmed by chef Marco Bernardo, who knows his basics and allows flights of fantasy to take over. The games begin with amuse-bouches; his take on *fegatini* (a typical Tuscan chicken liver spread) with a gelatin made from Aleatico (a serious red wine) sets the stage for what's to follow. **Known for:** fantastic wine list; the serenity of the place; creative menu. Ⓢ *Average main: €31* ✉ *Viale Morin 46, Forte dei Marmi* ☎ *0584/787052* ⊕ *www.hotelbyron.net* ⊗ *Closed Nov.–Mar.*

★ Lorenzo

$$$$ | SEAFOOD | The affable Lorenzo Viani has presided here for more than 30 years, and his restaurant still draws a well-heeled, sophisticated crowd. The menu relies heavily on creatures from the sea; a typical starter is spaghetti *versiliese*, served with shellfish and fresh tomato as is done in the northern Tuscan coastal town of Versilia. **Known for:** tasting menus with the freshest ingredients; stellar service; sophisticated dishes in an equally sophisticated space. Ⓢ *Average main: €40* ✉ *Via Carducci 61, Forte dei Marmi* ☎ *0584/874030* ⊕ *www.ristorantelorenzo.com* ⊗ *Closed Mon. No lunch Tues. or June–mid.-Sept.*

Pesce Baracca

$$ | **ITALIAN** | The first things you'll see upon entering this *mercato e cucina* (market and kitchen) are a row of dazzling, just-caught fish on ice and a display case with prepared foods to go. Select from a large array of *crudi* (including several raw oyster options) before opting for the fry (either mixed, anchovies, zucchini with squid, or fish croquettes) or the very tasty fish burger. **Known for:** seaside views; fine staff; the fine relationship of quality to price. $ *Average main: €15* ✉ *Viale Franceschi 2, Forte dei Marmi* 🕾 *0584/1716337* 🌐 *www.pescebaracca.it.*

 Hotels

★ Byron

$$$$ | **HOTEL** | The pale yellow exterior only hints at the elegance inside this hotel created by joining two Liberty villas dating from 1899 and 1902. **Pros:** golf and tennis privileges; fantastic hotel bar; free bikes. **Cons:** expensive, with a minimum seven-night stay; hard to get a reservation during high season; not open year-round. $ *Rooms from: €860* ✉ *Viale Morin 46, Forte dei Marmi* 🕾 *0584/787052* 🌐 *www. hotelbyron.net* ☾ *Closed Oct.–Easter* 🛏 *47 rooms* ⏱ *Free Breakfast.*

 Nightlife

Almarosa Art Music and Bar

BARS | After a day at the beach, the place to see and be seen is Almarosa Art Music and Bar. The clientele during high season frequently includes Italian soccer players, celebrities, and politicians. ✉ *Viale Morin 89/a, Forte dei Marmi* 🕾 *0584/82503* 🌐 *www.almarosa.it.*

 Activities

BIKING

Claudio Maggi Cicli

BIKING | **FAMILY** | This shop has been selling bicycle equipment and renting bikes since 1906. From May through September, it's open daily 8 to 1 and 3 to 8; from October through April, it's closed Wednesday and Sunday. ✉ *Viale Ammiraglio Morin 85, Forte dei Marmi* 🕾 *0584/89529* 🌐 *www.ciclimaggi.it.*

Coppa Bikes

BIKING | Right on the beach, Coppa rents bicycles and keeps late hours: 8 am to midnight daily from May through August, 8 to 8 daily the rest of the year. ✉ *Via A. Franceschi 4/d, Forte dei Marmi* 🕾 *0584/83528.*

HIKING AND CLIMBING

Forte dei Marmi Club Alpino Italiano

HIKING & WALKING | **FAMILY** | This group can provide guided tours, as well as information on area hiking, spelunking, and rock climbing. ✉ *Via Buonarroti 47, Forte dei Marmi* 🕾 *0584/789095* 🌐 *www. caifortedeimarmi.it.*

SCUBA DIVING

Associazione Subacquei Versilia

SCUBA DIVING | For information about the best places to scuba dive on the Versilian and Ligurian coasts, contact the Associazione Subacquei Versilia. ✉ *Via S. Allende 38, Forte dei Marmi* 🕾 *347/594–7951* 🌐 *www.subversilia.it.*

Carrara

40 km (25 miles) northeast of Viareggio, 126 km (79 miles) northwest of Florence.

Carrara, from which the famous white marble takes its name, lies in a beautiful valley midway up a spectacular mountain in the Apuane Alps. The surrounding peaks are free of foliage and white as snow, even in summer, because they are full of marble stone.

Marble has been quarried in the area for the past 2,000 years. The art historian Giorgio Vasari (1511–74) recorded that Michelangelo came to Carrara with two apprentices to quarry the marble for the never-completed tomb of Julius

II (1443–1513). According to Vasari, Michelangelo spent eight months among the rocks conceiving fantastical ideas for future works.

GETTING HERE

By car, take the A11, following signs for Lucca, then at Viareggio take the A12. Trains run frequently from Florence, but a change of trains is almost always required, and the Carrara station is not centrally located. Coming from Lucca, you usually have to change trains at Viareggio.

VISITOR INFORMATION

CONTACTS Carrara Tourism Office. ⊠ *Lungomare A. Vespucci 24, Marina di Massa* ☎ *0585/240063* ⊕ *www.turismomassa-carrara.it.*

Sights

Accademia di Belle Arti

COLLEGE | During the 19th and 20th centuries, Carrara became a hotbed for anarchism, and, during World War II, it fiercely resisted the Nazis. The town is still lively thanks to its art institute: the Accademia di Belle Arti, founded by Maria Teresa Cybo Malaspina d'Este in 1769, draws studio art students from all over Italy. This may explain why there's a good number of bars and cafés in many of the town's squares. ⊠ *Via Roma 1, Carrara* ☎ *0585/71658* ⊕ *www.accademi-acarrara.it.*

Marble Quarries

VISITOR CENTER | The area around Carrara has a lot of still-active quarries—well over 100 at last count. Most of them are not open to the public for safety reasons. However, it is possible to tour specific marble caves. The Carrara tourism office, 7 km (4½ miles) away in Marina di Massa, has details about which areas you can visit. ⊠ *Carrara Tourism Office, Lungomare A. Vespucci 24, Marina di Massa* ☎ *0585/240063* ⊕ *www.turismo-massacarrara.it.*

Duomo

CHURCH | Work began on the Duomo in the 11th century and continued into the 14th. The cathedral, dedicated to St. Andrew, is the first church of the Middle Ages constructed entirely of marble. Most of it comes from the area (the white, light blue-gray, black, and red). The tremendous facade is a fascinating blend of Pisan Romanesque and Gothic influences. Note the human figures and animals on Corinthian capitals. ⊠ *Piazza del Duomo, Carrara.*

Museo Civico del Marmo (*Marble Museum*)

ART MUSEUM | Carrara's history as a marble-producing center is well documented in the Museo del Marmo, beginning with early works from the 2nd century. Exhibits detail the working of marble, from quarrying and transporting it to sculpting it. ⊠ *Viale XX Settembre 85, Carrara* ☎ *0585/845746* ⊕ *museomarmocarrara.it* ⊠ *€5* ۞ *Closed Mon. and Tues.*

San Francesco

CHURCH | The lovely baroque church of San Francesco is a study in understated elegance. It dates from the 1620s to 1660s, and, even though it was built during the peak years of the baroque, the only excess can be found in the twisting marble columns embellishing the altars. ⊠ *Piazza XXVII Aprile, Carrara.*

Restaurants

Ristorante Venanzio

$$$ | TUSCAN | *Lardo di colonnata*, treated pork fat, is a gastronomic specialty in Tuscany, and there's no place better to try it than the place from which it hails. From the center of Carrara, the restaurant is a 15-minute drive up winding roads cut through marble-filled mountains. **Known for:** local ingredients; terrific semifreddi (chilled desserts); succulent primi. $ *Average main: €25* ⊠ *Piazza Palestro 3, Colonnata Carrara, 1 mile from Carrara, Carrara* ☎ *0585/758033* ۞ *Closed Thurs. and Dec. 23–Jan. 21.*

CHIANTI, SIENA, AND CENTRAL TUSCANY

Updated by
Patricia Rucidlo

👁 Sights	🍴 Restaurants	🛏 Hotels	🛍 Shopping	🍸 Nightlife
★★★★★	★★★★★	★★★★☆	★★☆☆☆	★☆☆☆☆

WELCOME TO CHIANTI, SIENA, AND CENTRAL TUSCANY

TOP REASONS TO GO

★ **The Piazza del Campo, Siena:** Sip a cappuccino or enjoy some gelato as you take in this spectacular shell-shape piazza.

★ **San Gimignano:** Grab a spot at sunset on the steps of the Collegiata as flocks of swallows swoop in and out of the famous medieval towers.

★ **Cheering the Palio in Siena:** Vie for a spot among thousands to salute the winners of this race, which takes over Siena's main square twice each year.

Undulating hills blanketed with vineyards, groves of silver-green olive trees, and enchanting towns perched on hilltops are the essence of central Tuscany. Siena, with its extraordinary piazza and magnificent cathedral, anchors the southern end of the region. Cypress-lined roads wind their way west to San Gimignano and Volterra, and north through the Chianti district.

1 Chianti. The heart of Italy's most famous wine region.

2 Greve in Chianti. Medieval town 30 km from Florence.

3 Passignano. A tiny, beautiful hamlet.

4 Panzano. Hilltop churches and river views.

5 Castellina in Chianti. Bucolic panoramas abound.

6 Radda in Chianti. Tiny village perfect for strolling.

7 Gaiole in Chianti. A market town since 1200.

8 Castelnuovo Berardenga. Southernmost village in Chianti.

9 Siena. Charming medieval town.

10 Monteriggioni. Served as Siena's northernmost defense in the 13th century.

11 Colle di Val d'Elsa. Modern town producing glass and crystal.

12 San Gimignano. Hilltown with medieval "skyscrapers."

13 Volterra. Handicrafts made with alabaster can be purchased here.

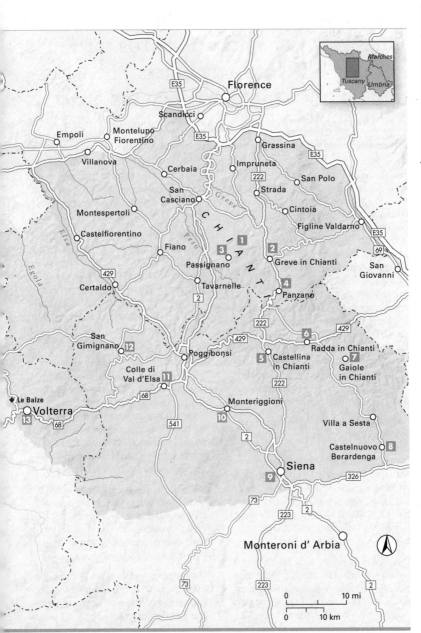

Country roads wind around cypress trees on hilltops that often appear to catch and hold onto the clouds. Planted vineyards, fields, and orchards turn those curving hills into a patchwork of colors and textures that have inspired artists and delighted travelers for centuries.

Sitting majestically in the midst of all this natural splendor is Siena, longtime rival of Florence and one of Italy's best-preserved medieval cities. Other hilltop towns will beckon you as well: San Gimignano, with its lofty towers; the ancient city of Volterra, once capital of a flourishing Etruscan state; and myriad charming villages dotting the rolling hills of Chianti. The rolling hills are the region's most famous geographic feature, and you can expect to do a lot of winding up and down on panoramic roads that link the area's hill towns. The narrow medieval streets of these old town centers are mostly closed to traffic. Park outside the city walls and walk in. Just keep in mind that roads often lack shoulders in these parts.

Siena fills to the brim in the weeks surrounding the running of the Palio on July 2 and August 16, when prices, crowds, and commotion are at their highest. Between May and late September, hotels and restaurants throughout the region fill up, and foreign license plates and rental cars cram the roads. There's a reason for the crush: summer is a glorious time to be driving in the hills and sitting on terraces.

If you want fewer crowds, try visiting during spring or fall. Spring can be especially spectacular, with blooming poppy fields, bursts of yellow broom, and wild irises growing by the side of the road.

Fall is somewhat more soothing, when all those colors typically associated with Tuscany—oranges, warm ocher, mossy forest greens—predominate.

In the winter months, you may have towns mostly to yourself, although the choices for hotels and restaurants can be a bit more limited than when the season is in full swing. From November through mid-March it's fairly difficult to find a room in San Gimignano and Volterra: plan accordingly.

MAJOR REGIONS

Chianti. The heart of Italy's most famous wine region is dotted with appealing towns. The largest, **Greve,** comes alive with a bustling local market in its town square every Saturday, while **Radda** sits on a hilltop in classic Tuscan style, ringed by a 14th-century walkway. Cutting through the region is the **Strada Chiantigiana,** one of Italy's most scenic drives.

Siena. Throughout the Middle Ages, Siena competed with Florence for regional supremacy. Today, it remains one of Italy's most enchanting medieval towns, with an exceptional Gothic cathedral and a main square that has magical charm.

Monteriggioni and Colle di Val d'Elsa. These two sleepy hill towns are pleasing, laid-back stops on the road between Siena and San Gimignano.

The classic rolling hills of central Tuscany

San Gimignano. From miles away you can spot San Gimignano's soaring medieval "skyscrapers"—towers that were once the ultimate status symbols of the aristocracy.

Volterra. Etruscan artifacts and Roman ruins are highlights of this city set in a rugged moonscape of a valley.

Planning

Getting Here and Around

BICYCLE

In spring, summer, and fall, cyclists are as much a part of the landscape as the cypress trees. Many are on weeklong tours, but it's also possible to rent bikes or to join afternoon or day tours.

I Bike Italy. I Bike Italy leads one-day rides through the Chianti countryside. ⊠ *Via del Campuccio 88, Florence* ☎ *342/935–2395* ⊕ *www.ibikeitaly.com.*

Marco Ramuzzi. Marco Ramuzzi rents bikes by the day or week from his shop in Greve.

He also organizes tours in the surrounding area. ⊠ *Via Stecchi 23, Greve in Chianti* ☎ *055/853037* ⊕ *www.ramuzzi.com.*

BUS

Buses are a reliable but time-consuming means of getting around the region because they often stop in every town.

Busitalia. From Florence, these buses serve Siena (one hour) and numerous towns in the Chianti region. ⊠ *Siena* ☎ *055/47821* ⊕ *www.fsbusitalia.it.*

CPT. ☎ *050/884111* ⊕ *www.cttnord.it.*

Tra.In SpA. This bus company covers much of the territory south of Florence as well as the province of Siena. ⊠ *Strada Statale Levante 73, Località Due Ponti, Siena* ☎ *0577/204111* ⊕ *www.trainspa.it.*

CAR

The best way to discover central Tuscany is by car, as its beauty often reveals itself along the road less traveled. The Certosa exit from the A1 highway (the Autostrada del Sole, running between Rome and Florence) provides direct access to the area. The Florence–Siena Superstrada (no number) is a four-lane, divided road with exits onto smaller country roads.

The Via Cassia (SR2) winds its way south from Florence to Siena, along the western edge of the Chianti region. The superstrada is more direct, but much less scenic, than the SR2, and it can have a lot of traffic, especially on Sunday evening. The Strada Chiantigiana (SR222) cuts through Chianti, east of the superstrada, in a curvaceous path past vineyards and countryside.

From Poggibonsi, a modern town to the west of the superstrada, you can quickly reach San Gimignano and then take the SR68 toward Volterra. The SR68 continues westward to join the Via Aurelia (SR1), linking Pisa with Rome.

TRAIN

Traveling between Florence and Siena by train is quick and convenient. Trains make the 80-minute trip several times a day, with a change in Empoli sometimes required. Train service also runs between Siena and Chiusi–Chianciano Terme, where you can make Rome–Florence connections. Siena's train station is 2 km (1 mile) north of the centro storico, but cabs and city buses are readily available.

Other train service within the region is limited. For instance, the nearest station to Volterra is at Saline di Volterra, 10 km (6 miles) to the west. From Siena, trains run north to Poggibonsi and southeast to Sinalunga. Trains run from Chiusi–Chianciano Terme to Siena (one hour) with stops in Montepulciano Scalo, Sinalunga, and Asciano. There are no trains to San Gimignano, Monteriggioni, or the Chianti wine region.

Trenitalia ☎ *892021 toll-free in Italy* ⊕ *www.trenitalia.com.*

Making the Most of Your Time

Central Tuscany has an enticing landscape, one that invites you to follow its meandering roads to see where they might lead. Perhaps you'll come to a farmhouse selling splendid olive oil or one of the superb wines produced in the region; or perhaps you'll arrive at a medieval *pieve* (country church), an art-filled abbey, a *castello* (castle), or a restaurant where a flower-bedecked terrace looks out on a spectacular panorama.

Whatever road you take, Siena, Italy's most enchanting medieval city, is the one stop that's mandatory. The perfectly preserved *centro storico* (historic center), with its medieval palaces, is a delight to walk around; vehicle traffic is banned.

Once in the region, however, there are plenty of other places to explore: San Gimignano is known as the "medieval Manhattan" because of its enormous towers, built by rival families, that still stand today. Like Siena, it benefited from commerce and trade along the pilgrimage routes, as the wonderful art in its churches and museums attests. With additional time, consider venturing farther afield to Volterra, with a stop in Colle di Val d'Elsa along the way.

Hotels

Siena, San Gimignano, and Volterra are among the most-visited towns in Tuscany, so there's no lack of choice for hotels across the price ranges. You can often stay right on the main square. The best accommodations, however, are often a couple of miles outside town.

If you're staying a week, you have enough time to rent an *agriturismo* (working farm) apartment. Stock up your refrigerator with local groceries and wines, go for hikes in the hills, and take leisurely day trips to the main towns of the region.

Hotel and restaurant reviews have been shortened. For full information, visit Fodors.com. Hotel prices are the lowest cost of a standard double room in high season. Restaurant prices are the average cost of a main course at dinner or, if dinner is not served, at lunch.

WHAT IT COSTS in Euros			
$	$$	$$$	$$$$
RESTAURANTS			
under €15	€15–€24	€25–€35	over €35
HOTELS			
under €125	€125–€200	€201–€300	over €300

Visitor Information

The tourist information office in Greve is an excellent source for general information about the Chianti wine region and its hilltop towns. In Siena, the centrally located tourist office in Piazza del Campo has information about the city and its province. Both offices book hotel rooms for a nominal fee. Offices in smaller towns can also be a good place to check if you need last-minute accommodations.

Tourist bureaus in larger towns are typically open from 8:30 to 1 and 3:30 to 6 or 7; bureaus in villages are generally open from Easter until early November, but usually remain closed Saturday afternoon and Sunday.

Chianti

This is the heartland: both sides of the Strada Chiantigiana, or SR222, are embraced by glorious panoramic views of vineyards, olive groves, and castle towers. Traveling south from Florence, you first reach the aptly named one-street-town of Strada in Chianti. Farther south, the number of vineyards on either side of the road dramatically increases—as do the signs inviting you in for a free tasting of wine. Beyond Strada lies Greve in Chianti, completely surrounded by wineries and filled with wineshops. There's art to be had as well: Passignano, west of Greve, has an abbey that shelters a 15th-century *Last Supper* by Domenico and Davide Ghirlandaio. Farther still, along the Strada Chiantigiana, are Panzano and Castellina in Chianti, both hill towns. It's from near Panzano and Castellina that branch roads head to the other main towns of eastern Chianti: Radda in Chianti, Gaiole in Chianti, and Castelnuovo Berardenga.

The Strada Chiantigiana gets crowded during the high season, but no one is in a hurry. The slow pace gives you time to soak up the beautiful scenery.

Greve in Chianti

40 km (25 miles) north of Siena, 28 km (17½ miles) south of Florence.

If there is a capital of Chianti, it is Greve, a friendly market town with no shortage of cafés, *enoteche* (wine bars), and crafts shops lining its streets.

GETTING HERE
Driving from Florence or Siena, Greve is easily reached via the Strada Chiantigiana (SR222). SITA buses travel frequently between Florence and Greve. Tra-In and SITA buses connect Siena and Greve, but a direct trip is virtually impossible. There is no train service to Greve.

VISITOR INFORMATION
CONTACTS Greve in Chianti Tourism Office. ✉ *Piazza Matteotti 11* ☎ *055/854–6299* ⊕ *www.greve-in-chianti.info.*

Central Tuscany, Past and Present

It may be hard to imagine that much of central Tuscany was once the battleground of warring Sienese and Florentine armies, but until Florence finally defeated Siena in 1555, the enchanting walled cities of this gentle area were strategic-defensive outposts in a series of seemingly endless wars.

Since the 1960s, many British and northern Europeans have relocated here: they've been drawn to the unhurried life, balmy climate, and old villages. They've bought and restored farmhouses, many given up by the young heirs who decided not to continue life on the farm and instead found work in cities. There are so many Britons, in fact, that the area has been nicknamed Chiantishire. Nevertheless, the whole area still proudly exerts its strongly Tuscan character.

Sights

★ Castello di Verrazzano
WINERY | FAMILY | Tours here take you down to the cellars, through the gardens, and into the woods in search of wild boar (though why you'd want to meet a wild boar is anyone's guess). You can also have a delicious crostino on a terrace with latticed grape leaves forming a beautiful bower above; the view from the terrace stretches for miles. Lunch and dinner are also available, and all the food pairs beautifully with their wines—which they've been making since 1170. ⊠ *Via S. Martino in Valle 12, Greve in Chianti* ☎ *055/854243* ⊕ *www.verrazzano.com* ⚲ *Reservations essential.*

Chiesa di San Donato a Lamole
CHURCH | The tiny village of Lamole contains this Romanesque church, which was greatly modified in 1860; the only remnant of its earlier incarnation can be found in its simple facade. Inside is a 14th-century altarpiece, as well as a curious side chapel on the right that is decorated with rather garish 20th-century religious works. From Greve in Chianti, drive south on SR222 for about 1 km (½ mile); take a left and follow signs for Lamole. It's about 10 km (6 miles) southeast of Greve. ⊠ *Località Lamole in Chianti 1, Greve in Chianti.*

Montefioralle
TOWN | A tiny hilltop hamlet, about 2 km (1 mile) west of Greve in Chianti, Montefioralle is the ancestral home of Amerigo Vespucci (1454–1512), the mapmaker, navigator, and explorer who named America. (His cousin-in-law, Simonetta, may have been the inspiration for Sandro Botticelli's *Birth of Venus*, painted sometime in the 1480s.) ⊠ *Greve in Chianti.*

Piazza Matteotti
PLAZA/SQUARE | Greve's gently sloping and asymmetrical central piazza is surrounded by an attractive arcade with shops of all kinds. In the center stands a statue of the discoverer of New York harbor, Giovanni da Verrazzano (circa 1480–1527). Check out the lively market held here on Saturday morning. ⊠ *Greve in Chianti.*

Restaurants

Enoteca Fuoripiazza
$$ | TUSCAN | Detour off Greve's flower-strewn main square for food that relies heavily on local ingredients (like cheese and salami produced nearby). The lengthy wine list provides a bewildering array of choices to pair with *affettati misti* (cured meats) or one of the *primi* (appetizers)—the *pici* (a thick, hand-rolled spaghetti) are deftly prepared here. **Known for:** attentively prepared food; local cheese

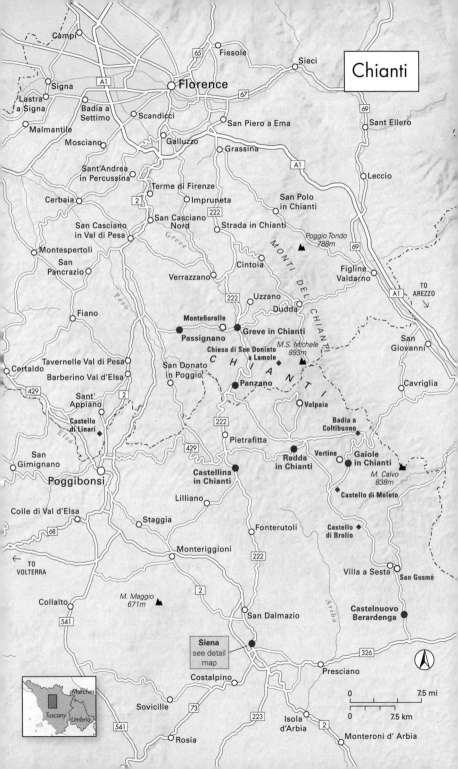

and salami; alfresco dining. $ *Average main: €15* ✉ *Via I Maggio 2, Greve in Chianti* ☎ *055/854–6313* ⊕ *www.enotecaristorantefuoripiazza.it* ⊗ *Closed Mon.*

★ Falorni
$ | **ITALIAN** | This institution—it's been around since 1806—began life as a butcher shop and, indeed, it still is. But it also has a little restaurant inside the shop which serves great *taglieri* (plates of mixed cured pork products, usually, though cheese does prominently figure as well). **Known for:** cured meats using centuries' old recipes; outdoor seating; great wines by the glass. $ *Average main: €10* ✉ *Piazza G. Matteotti 66, Greve in Chianti* ☎ *055/853029* ⊕ *falorni.it.*

★ Ristoro di Lamole
$$ | **TUSCAN** | Up a winding road lined with olive trees and vineyards, this place is worth the effort it takes to find. The view from the outdoor terrace is divine, as is the simple, exquisitely prepared Tuscan cuisine—start with the bruschetta drizzled with olive oil or the sublime *verdure sott'olio* (marinated vegetables) before moving on to any of the fine *secondi*. **Known for:** your hosts Paolo and Filippo; sweeping view from the terrace; coniglio (rabbit) is a specialty. $ *Average main: €20* ✉ *Via di Lamole 6, Località Lamole, Greve in Chianti* ☎ *055/854–7050* ⊕ *www.ristorodilamole.it* ⊗ *Closed Wed. and Nov.–Apr.*

 ## Hotels

Albergo del Chianti
$$ | **B&B/INN** | **FAMILY** | Simple but pleasantly decorated bedrooms with plain modern cabinets and wardrobes and wrought-iron beds have views of the town square or out over the tile rooftops toward the surrounding hills. **Pros:** central location; swimming pool; best value in Greve. **Cons:** remote: a car is a necessity; small bathrooms; rooms facing the piazza can be noisy. $ *Rooms from: €145*

✉ *Piazza Matteotti 86, Greve in Chianti* ☎ *055/853763* ⊕ *www.albergodelchianti.it* ⊗ *Closed Jan.–early Mar.* ⌁ *16 rooms* ⦿| *Free Breakfast.*

Castello Vicchiomaggio
$$ | **B&B/INN** | **FAMILY** | Stay in a fortified castle, which was built more than a millennium ago, was rebuilt during the Renaissance, and is now a charming inn and a prestigious wine estate where you can taste local vintages. **Pros:** spacious rooms; spectacular views; very helpful staff. **Cons:** might be too remote for some; you need a car to get around; some rooms lack air-conditioning. $ *Rooms from: €185* ✉ *Via Vicchiomaggio 4, Località Vicchiomaggio, Greve in Chianti* ☎ *055/854079* ⊕ *www.vicchiomaggio.it* ⊗ *Closed Dec.–mid Mar.* ⌁ *15 rooms* ⦿| *Free Breakfast.*

★ Villa Bordoni
$$$ | **B&B/INN** | Scottish expats David and Catherine Gardner transformed a ramshackle, 16th-century villa into a stunning retreat where no two rooms are alike—all have stenciled walls; some have four-poster beds, others small mezzanines. **Pros:** splendidly isolated in the hills above Greve; wonderful hosts; beautiful decor. **Cons:** books up quickly; need a car to get around; on a long and bumpy dirt road. $ *Rooms from: €240* ✉ *Via San Cresci 31/32, Greve in Chianti* ☎ *055/854–6230* ⊕ *www.villabordoni.com* ⊗ *Closed Dec.–Feb.* ⌁ *12 rooms* ⦿| *Free Breakfast.*

★ Villa Il Poggiale
$$ | **B&B/INN** | **FAMILY** | Renaissance gardens, beautiful rooms with high ceilings and elegant furnishings, a panoramic pool, and expert staff are just a few of the things that make a stay at this 16th-century villa memorable. **Pros:** beautiful gardens and panoramic setting; exceptionally professional staff; elegant historical building. **Cons:** it may be too isolated for some; some rooms face a country road and may be noisy during the day; private transportation necessary.

Eating Well in Central Tuscany 🍴

Chianti restaurants serve Tuscan dishes similar to those in Florence, but they also have local specialties, such as pasta creations made with *pici* (a long, thick, hand-rolled spaghetti). You'll find other pasta dishes, like *pappardelle alla lepre* (a long, flat type of pasta noodle with hare sauce), and soups, such as *pappa al pomodoro* (a thick tomato soup) and *ribollita* (Tuscan bread soup), on most menus.

Panzanella, a salad of tomato, basil, bread, and onion, is a common first course on summer menus.

The so-called *tonno del Chianti* (Chianti tuna) is really a dish of tender flakes of pork that looks and, believe it or not, tastes like tuna. Pecorino, a sheep's-milk cheese, makes it onto many menus in pasta dishes and appetizers.

The Sienese often add a subtle flair of extra herbs and garlic to their rendition of traditional Tuscan fare. *Antipasti* (starters, usually made of the simplest ingredients) are extremely satisfying.

A typical starter might be a plate of excellent locally cured meats, such as those made from *cinta senese*, a species of domestic pig rescued from near extinction. *Verdure sott'olio* (marinated vegetables) are usually artichokes, red peppers, carrots, celery, cauliflower, olives, and capers marinated in olive oil. Second courses are traditionally game meats, and *piccione* (pigeon), served either roasted or stuffed and baked, is commonly on the menu.

After your meal, try some delicious amber-color *vin santo*, a sweet dessert wine with *cantuccini* (hard almond cookies), which are dunked once or twice in the glass. The wine is made from choice white Trebbiano Toscano, or Malvasia del Chianti grapes and is aged in small, partially filled oak barrels. Other favorite Sienese sweets include *ricciarelli*, succulent almond-flavored cookies.

Excellent extra-virgin olive oil is produced throughout the region, and the best way to taste it is in the form of a *fettunta* (oily slice), a thick slice of toasted Tuscan bread rubbed with garlic, sprinkled with salt, and dripping with olive oil. Asking for a plate or bowl to sample olive oil with bread before a meal is a dead giveaway that you're a tourist—it's the invention of American restaurateurs.

[$] Rooms from: €142 ✉ Via Empolese 69, San Casciano Val di Pesa ✥ 20 km (12 miles) northwest of Greve ☎ 055/828311 🌐 www.villailpoggiale.it ⏲ Closed Jan. and Feb. 🛏 26 rooms 🍴 Free Breakfast.

Passignano

8 km (5 miles) west of Greve in Chianti, 29 km (18 miles) south of Florence.

Other than its Romanesque abbey and the few houses clustered around it, there is very little to actually see in this tiny hamlet. But the panoramic setting and the beautiful natural surroundings do make a short side trip recommendable.

GETTING HERE

By car, take the Tavernelle exit from the Florence–Siena Superstrada. Direct bus or train service is not available.

Sights

Badia a Passignano
(*Abbey of Passignano*)
RELIGIOUS BUILDING | The dining hall of the towering 11th-century Abbey of Passignano houses a stunningly massive, 21-foot-wide *Last Supper* (1476) by Domenico and Davide Ghirlandaio, and the monastery's church has a 13th-century sculpture of St. Michael slaying the dragon. ✉ *Via Passignano 20, Tavarnelle Val di Pesa* ☎ *055/807–1171* 🕒 *Closed Sun. and Thurs.*

Restaurants

La Cantinetta di Rignana
$ | **ITALIAN** | On Sunday afternoon, this old-fashioned farmhouse-esque trattoria is teeming with lively Italian families. Grilled meats are the specialty of the house, and if you have room for dessert, the kitchen whips up a mean tiramisu. **Known for:** generous portions; dine in the garden overlooking the vineyards; bistecca fiorentina. [$] *Average main: €13* ✉ *Via di Rignana 15, Greve in Chianti* ☎ *055/852601* 🌐 *www.lacantinettadirignana.com* 🕒 *Closed Tues.*

★ **Osteria di Passignano**
$$$$ | **ITALIAN** | In an ancient wine cellar owned by the Antinori family—who also happen to own much of what you see in the area—is a sophisticated restaurant ably run by chef Marcello Crini and his attentive staff. The menu changes seasonally; traditional Tuscan cuisine is given a delightful twist through the use of unexpected herbs. **Known for:** extensive wine list with local and international vintages; daylong cooking courses; dedication to local products. [$] *Average main: €41* ✉ *Via Passignano 33, Badia a Passignano, Tavarnelle Val di Pesa* ☎ *055/807–1278* 🌐 *www.osteriadipassignano.com* 🕒 *Closed Sun., mid-Jan.–mid-Feb., and 1 wk in Aug.*

Panzano

7 km (4½ miles) south of Greve in Chianti, 36 km (22 miles) south of Florence.

The magnificent views of the valleys of the Pesa and Greve rivers easily make Panzano one of the prettiest stops in Chianti. The triangular Piazza Bucciarelli is the heart of the new town. A short stroll along Via Giovanni da Verrazzano brings you up to the old town, Panzano Alto, which is still partly surrounded by medieval walls. The town's 13th-century castle is now almost completely absorbed by later buildings (its central tower is now a private home).

GETTING HERE

From Florence or Siena, Panzano is easily reached by car along the Strada Chiantigiana (SR222). SITA buses travel frequently between Florence and Panzano. From Siena, the journey by bus is extremely difficult because SITA and Tra-In do not coordinate their schedules. There is no train service to Panzano.

Sights

San Leolino
CHURCH | Ancient even by Chianti standards, this hilltop church probably dates from the 10th century, but it was completely rebuilt in the Romanesque style sometime in the 13th century. It has a 14th-century cloister worth seeing. The 16th-century terra-cotta tabernacles are attributed to Giovanni della Robbia, and there's also a remarkable triptych (attributed to the Master of Panzano) that was executed sometime in the mid-14th century. Open days and hours are unpredictable; check with the tourist office in

Dario Cecchini

Dario Cecchini is not your typical butcher. He calls himself *un' artigiano* (an artisan)—an indication of the pride he takes in his work. His shop has been in the family since the late 1700s, and his father trained Dario in the craft. "At 13," he says, "my grandmother made me a butcher's jacket. My mother began to cry. I guess she hoped I'd choose something else."

Dario is perhaps the world's greatest devotee of *bistecca fiorentina*, the definitive Tuscan steak, which you can sample at one of his Panzano eateries—Soloccicia and the aptly named Officina della Bistecca. About its preparation, Dario brooks no compromises. "It must be very thick, seared on both sides, and very, very rare in the middle." If you prefer your steak well done? "You shouldn't order it."

This is not to say that Dario is an unwavering traditionalist. One of his prized creations is sushi del Chianti, which took him five years to develop. After a taste of the coarsely ground raw beef, it can be difficult to stop eating.

What wine does Dario pair with his bistecca? "A young, simple, unstructured Chianti." If—heaven forbid—such a Chianti is not on the wine list, "Any young, honest red will do—no dallying in oak casks. Anything disliked by the *Wine Spectator*."

Greve in Chianti for the latest information. ⊠ *Località San Leolino, Panzano* ✛ *3 km (2 miles) south of Panzano.*

Santa Maria Assunta
CHURCH | Situated next to the castle in the upper part of town, this church was completely rebuilt in the 19th century. In the small chapel to the right of the nave is an *Annunciation* attributed to Michele di Ridolfo del Ghirlandaio (1503–77). ⊠ *Via Castellana 6, Panzano.*

Restaurants

Enoteca Baldi
$ | **WINE BAR** | Sample the local *vino* while satisfying your appetite with simply prepared and presented bruschetta, soups, and pastas. In summer, a few tables are set in the shade under the trees in the town's main square. **Known for:** fun atmosphere; great staff; fine wine list. Ⓢ *Average main: €10* ⊠ *Piazza Bucciarelli 26, Panzano* ☎ *055/852843* ⏱ *Closed Tues.*

★ Officina della Bistecca
$$$$ | **ITALIAN** | **FAMILY** | Local butcher and restaurateur, Dario Cecchini, has extended his empire of meat to include this space above his butcher's shop. In addition to two tasting menus—one heavily meat laden, the other with none—you'll find a house-made version of *giardiniera sott'olio* (pickled and preserved vegetables) that's second to none. **Known for:** enormously popular, especially in summer; performing waitstaff; convivial atmosphere. Ⓢ *Average main: €50* ⊠ *Via XX Luglio 11, Panzano* ☎ *055/852020* ⊕ *www.dariocecchini.com/officina* ⏱ *Closed Sun.*

★ Solociccia
$$$$ | **TUSCAN** | **FAMILY** | As at his other eateries, Dario Cecchini, Panzano's local merchant of meat, offers two set menus—one where beef products dominate every course and the other vegetarian. The *musetto al limone e brodo vero* (an interesting salame served with stunning beef broth) kicks off the proceedings. **Known for:** party atmosphere; great

service; choice of two set menus. [$] *Average main: €40* ⊠ *Via XX Luglio 11, Panzano* ☎ *055/852020* ⊕ *www. dariocecchini.com/solociccia* ☉ *No dinner Mon.–Thurs.*

 ## Hotels

★ **Villa Le Barone**

$$$ | B&B/INN | Once the home of the Viviani della Robbia family, this 16th-century villa in a grove of ancient cypress trees retains many aspects of a private country dwelling, complete with homey guest quarters. **Pros:** beautiful location; great base for exploring the region; wonderful restaurant. **Cons:** a car is a must; 15-minute walk to nearest town; some rooms are a bit small. [$] *Rooms from: €271* ⊠ *Via San Leolino 19, Panzano* ☎ *055/852621* ⊕ *villalebarone. com* ☉ *Closed Oct.–Easter* ⇆ *28 rooms* ⏶*Free Breakfast.*

 ## Shopping

★ **Antica Macelleria Cecchini**

FOOD | This just might be the world's most dramatic butcher shop. Here, amid classical music and lively conversation, owner Dario Cecchini holds court: while quoting Dante, he serves samples of his very fine *sushi di Chianina* (raw slices of Chianina beef gently salted and peppered). He has researched recipes from the 15th century, and sells pâtés and herb concoctions found nowhere else. Serious food enthusiasts should not miss the place. ⊠ *Via XX Luglio 11, Panzano* ☎ *055/852020* ⊕ *www.dariocecchini.com.*

Castellina in Chianti

13 km (8 miles) south of Panzano, 59 km (35 miles) south of Florence, 22 km (14 miles) north of Siena.

Castellina in Chianti—or simply Castellina—is on a ridge above three valleys: the Val di Pesa, Val d'Arbia, and Val d'Elsa.

No matter which direction you turn, the panorama is bucolic.

The strong 15th-century medieval walls and fortified town gate hint at the history of this village, which was an outpost during the continuing wars between Florence and Siena. In the main square, the Piazza del Comune, there's a 15th-century palace and a 15th-century fort constructed around a 13th-century tower. It now serves as the town hall.

GETTING HERE

As with all the towns along the Strada Chiantigiana (SR222), Castellina is an easy drive from either Siena or Florence. From Siena, Castellina is well served by the local Tra-In bus company. However, only one bus a day travels here from Florence. The closest train station is at Castellina Scalo, some 15 km (9 miles) away.

VISITOR INFORMATION

CONTACTS Castellina in Chianti Tourism Office. ⊠ *Via Ferruccio 40, Castellina in Chianti* ☎ *0577/741392.*

 ## Sights

Castello di Fonterutoli

WINERY | Seven different wine tours are on offer here, including a few that involve some very good food. In the capable hands of the Mazzei family since the 11th century, this gorgeous estate is a perfect place to taste some very fine wines, which pair well with items on the Tuscan menu in the osteria. ⊠ *Castellina in Chianti* ☎ *0577/73571* ⊕ *www.fonterutoli.it.*

Rocca delle Macìe

WINERY | At this family-run and-operated establishment, you can do a simple wine tasting, or taste while eating lunch or dinner at the rather fine restaurant. It's also possible to stay on the estate in restored farmhouses. ⊠ *Località Le Macìe 45, Castellina in Chianti* ☎ *0577/732236* ⊕ *www.roccadellemacie.com.*

🍴 Restaurants

Albergaccio

$$$ | **TUSCAN** | The fact that the dining room can seat only 35 guests makes a meal here an intimate experience, and the ever-changing menu mixes traditional and creative dishes. In late September and October, *zuppa di funghi e castagne* (mushroom and chestnut soup) is a treat; grilled meats and seafood are on offer throughout the year. **Known for:** marvelous waitstaff; superb wine list; creative menu. [$] *Average main: €25* ✉ *Via Fiorentina 63, Castellina in Chianti* ☎ *0577/741042* 🌐 *www.ristorantealbergaccio.com* 🕒 *Closed Tues. and Wed.*

Osteria alla Piazza

$$ | **ITALIAN** | Relax amid vineyards on a countryside terrace with one of Chianti's most spectacular views, namely that of vineyards in the valley of the River Pesa. Enjoy the sophisticated menu, which pairs perfectly with the wine list (many of its selections are from what's growing around you). **Known for:** gracious service; inventive menu; beautiful views. [$] *Average main: €20* ✉ *Località La Piazza, Castellina in Chianti* ☎ *331/926–7403* 🌐 *www.osteriaallapiazza.com* 🕒 *Closed Mon.; Jan. and Feb.; and weekdays Mar., Nov., and Dec.*

Ristorante Le Tre Porte

$$ | **TUSCAN** | Grilled meat dishes are the specialty at this popular restaurant, with a bistecca fiorentina (served very rare, as always) taking pride of place; paired with grilled fresh porcini mushrooms when in season (spring and fall), it's a heady dish. The panoramic terrace is a good choice for dining in summer. **Known for:** fine wine list with lots of local bottles; their way with mushrooms; views from the terrace. [$] *Average main: €18* ✉ *Via Trento e Trieste 4, Castellina in Chianti* ☎ *0577/741163* 🌐 *www.treporte.com* 🕒 *Closed Mon.–Wed.*

Sotto Le Volte

$$ | **TUSCAN** | As the name suggests, you'll find this small restaurant under the arches of Castellina's medieval walkway, and the eatery's vaulted ceilings make for a particularly romantic setting. The menu is short and eminently Tuscan, with typical soups and pasta dishes. **Known for:** attentive waitstaff; flair for Tuscan classics; unique setting. [$] *Average main: €17* ✉ *Via delle Volte 14–16, Castellina in Chianti* ☎ *0577/741299* 🌐 *www.ristorantesottolevolte.it* 🕒 *Closed Wed. and Jan.–Mar.*

🛏 Hotels

Colle Etrusco Salivolpi

$$ | **B&B/INN** | The family that owns this farmhouse took special care not to change too much when they began accepting guests—faded family photos and bric-a-brac of all kinds decorate the common areas, and each room is simply furnished with antiques that are typical of the late 18th and early 19th centuries in Chianti, including heavy wooden wardrobes, marble-top chests, and woven straw–seat chairs. **Pros:** tranquil location; large pool with valley views; beautiful garden. **Cons:** a car is a must; books up quickly; some stairs to climb. [$] *Rooms from: €143* ✉ *Via Fiorentina 89, Castellina in Chianti* ☎ *0577/740484* 🌐 *hotelsalivolpi.com* 🕒 *Closed Jan. 7–Easter* 🛏 *19 rooms* 🍴 *Free Breakfast.*

Hotel Belvedere di San Leonino

$$ | **B&B/INN** | **FAMILY** | Stroll around the wonderful gardens on this restored country estate dating from the 14th century, where guest rooms with arched windows and oak-beam ceilings are in two houses that look out on vineyards to the north and Siena to the south. **Pros:** great family atmosphere; lovely old house; central location. **Cons:** need a car to get around; expensive breakfast; stairs to climb. [$] *Rooms from: €130* ✉ *Località San Leonino, Castellina in Chianti* ☎ *0577/740887* 🌐 *hotelsanleonino.com* 🕒 *Closed mid-Nov.–mid-Apr.* 🛏 *28 rooms* 🍴 *No Meals.*

Locanda Le Piazze

$$$ | B&B/INN | This old farmhouse has been transformed into a marvelous hotel in the midst of vineyards. **Pros:** pastoral setting; fun cooking classes; luxurious bathrooms. **Cons:** need a car to get around; hosts weddings; children under 14 not welcome. $ *Rooms from: €235 ✉ Località Le Piazze 41, Castellina in Chianti ☎ 0577/743190 ⊕ locandalepiazze.com ⊙ Closed Nov.–Apr. ⌻ 20 rooms ❍ Free Breakfast.*

★ Palazzo Squarcialupi

$$ | B&B/INN | In this lovely, 15th-century palace, spacious rooms have high ceilings, tile floors, and 18th-century furnishings, and many have views of the valley below. **Pros:** great location in town center; nice spa, pool, and grounds; elegant public spaces. **Cons:** rooms facing the street can experience some noise; across from a busy restaurant; on a street with no car access. $ *Rooms from: €140 ✉ Via Ferruccio 22, Castellina in Chianti ☎ 0577/741186 ⊕ www.squarcialupirelaxinchianti.com ⊙ Closed Nov.–Mar. ⌻ 17 rooms ❍ Free Breakfast.*

🛍 Shopping

Most of Castellina's shops are either along Via Ferruccio or on the Piazza del Comune. But don't miss the specialty stores hidden away on Via delle Volte, which runs inside the eastern medieval walls of the town—you can reach it from either end of Via Ferruccio.

La Bottega

ART GALLERIES | Mario Cappelletti carries interesting prints and reproductions of well-known Renaissance artworks, as well as contemporary paintings of the Tuscan countryside. ✉ *Via Ferruccio 34/36, Castellina in Chianti ☎ 0577/740980 ⊕ www.tuscanantiques.com.*

Le Volte Enoteca

WINE/SPIRITS | On Castellina's main street, Aleandro and Gilles stock an ample and well-chosen supply of local wines produced by small estates. On request, they can also organize visits to nearby wineries. ✉ *Via Ferruccio 12, Castellina in Chianti ☎ 0577/740308 ⊕ www.enoteca-levolte.com.*

Lucia Volontieri

CERAMICS | You'll find a delightful selection of delicately hand-painted ceramics in Lucia's studio and shop near the center of Castellina. ✉ *Via Trento e Trieste 24, Castellina in Chianti ☎ 0577/741133 ⊕ www.luciavolontieri.com.*

Radda in Chianti

10 km (6 miles) east of Castellina in Chianti, 55 km (34 miles) south of Florence.

Radda in Chianti, which sits on a ridge stretching between the Val di Pesa and Val d'Arbia, is another of those tiny villages with steep streets for strolling. Follow the signs that point you toward the *camminamento medioevale,* a covered 14th-century walkway that circles part of the city inside the walls.

GETTING HERE

Radda can be reached by car from either Siena or Florence along the SR222 (Strada Chiantigiana), and from the A1 highway. From Castellina, it is easily reached via the SR429.

Three Tra-In buses make their way from Siena to Radda. One morning SITA bus travels from Florence to Radda. There is no train service convenient to Radda.

VISITOR INFORMATION

CONTACTS **Radda in Chianti Tourism Office.** ✉ *Piazza Castello 6,* ☎ *0577/738494 ⊕ www.chianti.com.*

Continued on page 216

GRAPE ESCAPES
THE PLEASURES OF TUSCAN WINE

The vineyards stretching across the landscape of Tuscany may look like cinematic backdrops, but in fact they're working farms, and they produce some of Italy's best wines. No matter whether you're a wine novice or a connoisseur, there's great pleasure to be had from exploring this lush terrain, visiting the vineyards, and uncorking a bottle for yourself.

GETTING TO KNOW TUSCAN WINE

Most of the wine produced in Tuscany is red (though there are some notable whites as well), and most Tuscan reds are made primarily from one type of grape, *Sangiovese*. That doesn't mean, however, that all wines here are the same. God (in this case Bacchus) is in the details: differences in climate, soil, and methods of production result in wines with several distinct personalities.

Chianti

Chianti is the most famous name in Tuscan wine, but what exactly the name means is a little tricky. It once identified wines produced in the region extending from just south of Florence to just north of Siena. In the mid-20th century, the official Chianti zone was expanded to include a large portion of central Tuscany. That area is divided into eight subregions. Chianti Classico is the name given to the original zone, which makes up 17,000 of the 42,000 acres of Chianti-producing vineyards.

Classico wines, which bear the *gallo nero* (black rooster) logo on their labels, are the most highly regarded Chiantis (with Rùfina running second), but that doesn't mean Classicos are always superior. All Chiantis are strictly regulated (they must be a minimum 75% to 80% Sangiovese, with other varieties blended in to add nuance), and they share a strong, woodsy character that's well suited to Tuscan food. It's a good strategy to drink the local product—Colli Senesi Chianti when in Siena, for example. The most noticeable, and costly, difference comes when a Chianti is from *riserva* (reserve) stock, meaning it's been aged for at least two years.

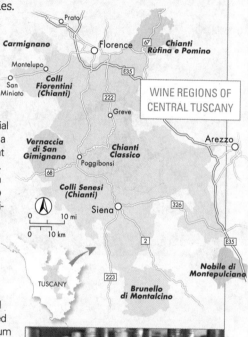

WINE REGIONS OF CENTRAL TUSCANY

Prato
Carmignano
Florence
67 Chianti Rùfina e Pomino
Montelupo
Colli Fiorentini (Chianti)
San Miniato
E35
222
Greve
Arezzo
Vernaccia di San Gimignano
Chianti Classico
Poggibonsi
68
Colli Senesi (Chianti)
326
Siena
0   10 mi
0   10 km
2
E35
Nobile di Montepulciano
TUSCANY
223
Brunello di Montalcino

DOC & DOCG. The designations "DOC" and "DOCG"—Denominazione di Origine Controllata (e Garantita)—mean a wine comes from an established region and adheres to rigorous standards of production. Ironically, the esteemed Super Tuscans are labeled *vini da tavola* (table wines), the least prestigious designation, because they don't use traditional grape blends.

Brunello di Montalcino

The area surrounding the hill town of Montalcino, to the south of Siena, is drier and warmer than the Chianti regions, and it produces the most powerful of the Sangiovese-based wines. Regulations stipulate that Brunello di Montalcino be made entirely from Sangiovese grapes (no blending) and aged at least four years. **Rosso di Montalcino** is a younger, less complex, less expensive Brunello.

The Super Tuscans

Beginning in the 1970s, some winemakers, chafing at the regulations imposed on established Tuscan wine varieties, began blending and aging wines in innovative ways. Thus were born the so-called Super Tuscans. These pricey, French oak–aged wines are admired for their high quality, led by such star performers as **Sassicaia**, from the Maremma region, and **Tignanello**, produced at the Tenuta Marchesi Antinori near Badia a Passignano. Purists, however, lament the loss of local identity resulting from the Super Tuscans' use of nonnative grape varieties such as Cabernet Sauvignon and Merlot.

Vino Nobile di Montepulciano

East of Montalcino is Montepulciano, the town at the heart of the third, and smallest, of Tuscany's top wine districts.

Blending regulations aren't as strict for Vino Nobile as for Chianti and Brunello, and as a result it has a wider range of characteristics. Broadly speaking, though, Vino Nobile is a cross between Chianti and Brunello—less acidic than the former and softer than the latter. It also has a less pricey sibling, **Rosso di Montepulciano**.

The Whites

Most whites from Tuscany are made from Trebbiano grapes, which produce a wine that's light and refreshing but not particularly aromatic or flavorful—it may hit the spot on a hot afternoon, but it doesn't excite connoisseurs.

Golden-hued **Vernaccia di San Gimignano** is a local variety with more limited production but greater personality—it's the star of Tuscan whites. Winemakers have also brought Chardonnay and Sauvignon grapes to the region, resulting in wines that, like some Super Tuscans, are pleasant to drink but short on local character.

TOURING & TASTING IN TUSCAN WINE COUNTRY

Strade del Vino di Toscana

Tuscany has visitor-friendly wineries, but the way you go about visiting is a bit different here from what it is in California or France. Many wineries welcome drop-ins for a tasting, but for a tour you usually need to make an appointment a few days in advance. There are several approaches you can take, depending on how much time you have and how serious you are about wine.

PLAN 1: FULL IMMERSION. Make an appointment to tour one of the top wineries (see our recommendations on the next page), and you'll get the complete experience: half a day of strolling through vineyards, talking grape varieties, and tasting wine, often accompanied by food. Groups are small; in spring and fall, it may be just you and the winemaker. The cost is usually €10 to €20 per person, but can go up to €40 if a meal is included. Remember to specify a tour in English.

PLAN 2: SEMI-ORGANIZED. If you want to spend a few hours going from vineyard to vineyard, make your first stop one of the local tourist information offices—they're great resources for maps, tasting itineraries, and personalized advice about where to visit. The offices in **Greve, Montalcino,** and **Montepulciano** are the best equipped. Enoteche can also be good places to pick up tips about where to go for tastings.

PLAN 3: SPONTANEOUS. Along Tuscany's country roads you'll see signs for wineries offering *vendita diretta* (direct sales) and *degustazioni* (tastings). For a taste of the local product with some atmosphere thrown in, a spontaneous visit is a perfectly viable approach. You may wind up in a simple shop or an elaborate tasting room; either way, there's a fair chance you'll sample something good. Expect a small fee for a three-glass tasting.

THE PICK OF THE VINEYARDS

Within the Chianti Classico region, these wineries should be at the top of your to-visit list, whether you're dropping in for a taste or making a full tour. (Tours require reservations unless otherwise indicated.)

Badia a Coltibuono (✉ Gaiole in Chianti ☎ 0577/74481 ⊕ www.-coltibuono.com). Along with an extensive prelunch tour and tasting, there are shorter afternoon tours, no reservation required, starting on the hour from 2 to 5.

Castello di Fonterutoli (✉ Castellina in Chianti ☎ 0577/741385 ⊕ mazzei.it). Hour-long tours include a walk through the neighboring village.

Castello di Volpaia (✉ Radda in Chianti ☎ 0577/738066 ⊕ www.volpaia.com). The tour here includes a visit to the olive oil press and a tour of the town.

Castello di Verrazzano (✉ Greve in Chianti ☎ 055/854243 ⊕ www.verrazzano.com). Tours here take you down to the cellars, through the gardens, and into the woods in search of wild boar.

Rocca delle Màcie (✉ Castellina in Chianti ☎ 0577/732236 ⊕ www.rocca dellemacie.-com). A full lunch or dinner can be incorporated into your tasting here.

Castello di Brolio (✉ Gaiole in Chianti ☎ 0577/7301 ⊕ www.ricasoli.com). One of Tuscany's most impressive castles also has a centuries-old winemaking tradition.

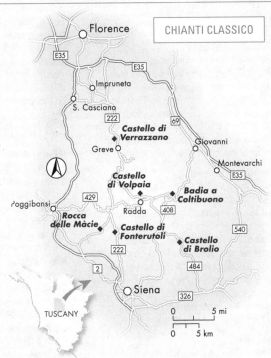

CHIANTI CLASSICO

REMEMBER ⚠

Always have a designated driver when you're touring and tasting. Vineyards are usually located off narrow, curving roads. Full sobriety is a must behind the wheel.

Sights

Castello di Volpaia

WINERY | At this small enoteca on Piazza della Cisterna, you can sample and purchase the fine wines, olive oil, and flavored vinegars made by Castello di Volpaia. Booked in advance, tours in English of the winery and olive press are also available. ✉ *Piazza della Cisterna 1, Radda in Chianti* ⊕ *www.volpaia.it.*

Palazzo del Podestà

GOVERNMENT BUILDING | Radda's town hall (aka Palazzo Comunale), in the middle of town, was built in the second half of the 14th century and has always served the same function. The 51 coats of arms (the largest is the Medici's) embedded in the facade represent the past governors of the town, but unless you have official business, the building is closed to the public. ✉ *Piazza Ferrucci 1, Radda in Chianti.*

Volpaia

TOWN | This tiny town, with a population of roughly 40, is perched on a hill 10 km (6 miles) north of Radda. During the wars between Florence and Siena, it served as a key castle and military outpost, but lost its importance when the Florentines defeated Siena in 1555. Approximately three-quarters of the town is now given over to the production of wine and olive oil. ✉ *Radda in Chianti.*

 Restaurants

Osteria Le Panzanelle

$ | **TUSCAN** | Silvia Bonechi's experience in the kitchen—with the help of a few precious recipes handed down from her grandmother—is one of the reasons for the success of this small restaurant in the tiny hamlet of Lucarelli; the other is the front-room hospitality of Nada Michelassi. These two *panzanelle* (women from Panzano) serve a short menu of tasty and authentic dishes at what the locals refer to as *il prezzo giusto* (the right

price). **Known for:** unpretentious atmosphere; good wine list; fine home cooking. **$** *Average main: €13* ✉ *Località Lucarelli 29, Radda in Chianti* ✛ *8 km (5 miles) northwest of Radda on road to Panzano* ☎ *0577/733511* ⊕ *www.lepanzanelle.it* ☉ *Closed Mon. and Jan. and Feb.*

Hotels

Il Borgo di Vescine

$$ | **B&B/INN** | The grounds of this former Etruscan settlement—a series of low-slung medieval stone buildings with barrel-tile roofs—feature cobbled paths and cypress trees; the interior has unfussy rooms with terra-cotta tile floors, attractive woodwork, and elegant but comfortable furnishings. **Pros:** set in a lovely park; cozy public rooms; tranquillity prevails. **Cons:** isolated location; a car is a must; long walk to nearest town. **$** *Rooms from: €200* ✉ *Località Vescine, Radda in Chianti* ✛ *5 km (3 miles) west of Radda in Chianti* ☎ *0577/741144* ⊕ *www.vescine.it* ☉ *Closed Nov.–Apr., except at Christmas* 🛏 *27 rooms* 🍴 *Free Breakfast.*

La Bottega di Giovannino

$ | **B&B/INN** | This is a fantastic place for the budget-conscious traveler, as rooms are immaculate and most have a stunning view of the surrounding hills. **Pros:** great location in the center of town; super value; close to restaurants and shops. **Cons:** basic decor; books up quickly; some rooms are small. **$** *Rooms from: €65* ✉ *Via Roma 6–8, Radda in Chianti* ☎ *0577/735601* ⊕ *www.labottegadigiovannino.it* 🛏 *9 rooms* 🍴 *No Meals.*

★ La Locanda

$$$ | **B&B/INN** | At an altitude of more than 1,800 feet, this converted farmhouse is probably the loftiest luxury inn in Chianti. **Pros:** idyllic setting; wonderful host; panoramic views. **Cons:** need a car to get around; isolated location; on a very rough gravel access road. **$** *Rooms from: €220* ✉ *Località Montanino di Volpaia, Radda in Chianti* ✛ *Off Via della Volpaia,*

Tuscany in its autumn gold

13 km (8 miles) northwest of Radda ☎ *0577/738833* 🌐 *www.lalocanda.it* 🕑 *Closed mid-Oct.–mid-Apr.* 🛏 *7 rooms* 🍴 *Free Breakfast.*

Palazzo San Niccolò

$ | **HOTEL** | The wood-beam ceilings, terra-cotta floors, and some of the original frescoes of a 19th-century town palace remain, but the marble bathrooms have all been updated, some with Jacuzzi tubs. **Pros:** central location; pool (though a car is necessary to get there); friendly staff. **Cons:** some street noise in some rooms; room sizes vary; some rooms face a main street. [$] *Rooms from: €91* ✉ *Via Roma 16, Radda in Chianti* ☎ *0577/735666* 🌐 *www.hotelsanniccolo.com* 🕑 *Closed Nov.–Mar.* 🛏 *18 rooms* 🍴 *Free Breakfast.*

Podere Terreno

$ | **HOTEL** | People come from all over the world to enjoy the quiet country life in this 16th-century farmhouse, where rooms are furnished with unadorned wooden furniture. **Pros:** historic setting; comfortable accommodations; great home-cooked meals. **Cons:** need a car to get around; books up quickly; isolated location. [$] *Rooms from: €98* ✉ *Via della Volpaia, Volpaia* ✥ *5 km (3 miles) north of Radda in Chianti* ☎ *0577/738312* 🌐 *www.podereterreno.it* 🕑 *Closed Christmas wk* 🛏 *5 rooms* 🍴 *Free Breakfast.*

★ **Relais Fattoria Vignale**

$$$ | **B&B/INN** | A refined and comfortable country house offers numerous sitting rooms with terra-cotta floors and attractive stonework, as well as wood-beamed guest rooms filled with simple wooden furnishings and handwoven rugs. **Pros:** intimate public spaces; nice grounds and pool; excellent restaurant. **Cons:** a car is necessary; annex across a busy road; single rooms are small. [$] *Rooms from: €170* ✉ *Via Pianigiani 9, Radda in Chianti* ☎ *0577/738300 hotel, 0577/738094 restaurant* 🌐 *www.vignale.it* 🕑 *Closed Nov.–Mar.* 🛏 *41 rooms* 🍴 *No Meals.*

🛍 Shopping

Studio Rampini

CERAMICS | This kiln and painting studio, 5 km (3 miles) south of Radda in Chianti, produces exquisite (and expensive) hand-painted ceramic objects, including plates, bowls, and candlesticks. The firm ships anywhere in the world and keeps its customers' information on file. If you break a plate or want to buy more, they'll know exactly what your pattern is. ✉ *Località Casa Beretone di Vistarenni, Radda in Chianti* ☎ *0577/738043* ⊕ *www.rampiniceramics.com.*

Tecno-Casa

HOUSEWARES | Locals come here to buy their nuts, bolts, and small tools, but visitors will also find a surprisingly varied assortment of traditional Italian household items, including coffeemakers and cups, wine decanters, and decorative bottle stoppers. ✉ *Via Roma 20/22, Radda in Chianti* ☎ *334/6210-0456.*

Gaiole in Chianti

9 km (5½ miles) southeast of Radda in Chianti, 69 km (43 miles) south of Florence.

A market town since 1200, Gaiole is now a central destination for touring southern Chianti. A stream runs through its center, and flowers adorn many of its window boxes. The surrounding area is dotted with castles perched on hilltops (the better to see the approaching enemy): they were of great strategic importance during the Renaissance, and still make dazzling lookout points.

GETTING HERE

To get here by car from the A1, take the Val d'Arno exit and follow signs for Gaiole on the SR408. Gaiole is relatively well connected to Siena by Tra-In buses, but cannot be reached by train.

👁 Sights

Badia a Coltibuono (*Abbey of the Good Harvest*)

WINERY | This Romanesque abbey has been owned by internationally acclaimed cookbook author Lorenza de' Medici's family for more than a century and a half (the family isn't related to the Florentine Medici). Wine has been produced here since the abbey was founded by Vallombrosan monks in the 11th century. Today, the family continues the tradition, making wines, cold-pressed olive oil, and various flavored vinegars. Don't miss the jasmine-draped courtyard and the inner cloister with its antique well. ✉ *Località Badia a Coltibuono, Gaiole in Chianti* ✛ *4 km (2½ miles) north of Gaiole* ☎ *0577/74481 tours* ⊕ *www.coltibuono.com* ✉ *Abbey €7* ⊗ *Closed Jan. 7–mid-Mar.*

★ Castello di Brolio

CASTLE/PALACE | If you have time for only one castle in Tuscany, this is it. At the end of the 12th century, when Florence conquered southern Chianti, Brolio became Florence's southernmost outpost, and it was often said, "When Brolio growls, all Siena trembles." It was built about AD 1000 and owned by the monks of the Badia Fiorentina. The "new" owners, the Ricasoli family, have been in possession since 1141. Bettino Ricasoli (1809–80), the so-called Iron Baron, was one of the founders of modern Italy and is said to have invented the original formula for Chianti wine.

Brolio, one of Chianti's best-known labels, is still justifiably famous. The grounds are worth visiting, and some of the guided tours do provide a glimpse of the castle's interior. The entrance fee includes a wine tasting in the enoteca. A small museum, where the Ricasoli Collection is housed in a 12th-century tower, displays objects that relate the long history of the family and the origins of Chianti wine. There are various options for an overnight here. ✉ *Località Madonna a Brolio, Gaiole in Chianti* ⊕ *2 km (1 mile) southeast of Gaiole* ☎ *0577/7301* ⊕ *www.ricasoli.com* 🎫 *€7 gardens* ⊗ *Closed Dec. Museum closed Mon.*

Castello di Meleto

WINERY | It's a pretty drive up winding roads to this 13th-century fortress. Attached is an 18th-century villa; a wineshop serves tastes of the locally produced wine as well as honeys and jams. It's worth visiting the castle, which is possible by guided-tour only (reservations required), to get a sense of how 18th-century aristocrats lived; the tour also includes a visit to the cellar and to the gardens. If that doesn't interest you, proceed directly to the enoteca for a tasting. Apartments clustered near the castle are available for rent. ✉ *Località Meleto, Gaiole in Chianti* ⊕ *5 km (3 miles) south of Gaiole* ☎ *0577/749217 castle, 0577/749129 enoteca* ⊕ *www.castellomeleto.it* 🎫 *€35* 🍴 *Reservations essential.*

Vertine

TOWN | Dating from the 10th century, this walled town is oval in shape and has a tall watchtower guarding the entrance gate. A walk along the unspoiled streets gives you a glimpse of life in a Tuscan hill town as it once was, and the views of the undulating countryside from the occasional opening in the walls are simply spectacular. ✉ *Località Vertine, Gaiole in Chianti* ⊕ *2 km (1 mile) west of Gaiole.*

🍴 Restaurants

Badia a Coltibuono

$$ | ITALIAN | Outside the walls of Badia a Coltibuono is the abbey's pleasant restaurant, with seating on a terrace teeming with flowers or in soft-yellow rooms divided by ancient brick arches. The menu is schooled in Tuscan flavors, but has twists and flights of fantasy. **Known for:** the wine list, sourced mostly from its own backyard; gracious waitstaff; its use of seasonal ingredients. $ *Average main: €19* ✉ *Località Badia a Coltibuono, Gaiole in Chianti* ⊕ *4 km (2½ miles) north of Gaiole* ☎ *0577/749031* ⊕ *www.coltibuono.com.*

La Grotta della Rana

$$ | ITALIAN | A perfect stop for lunch while exploring the region's wineries, this trattoria offers *cucina casalinga* (home cooking) that can be eaten in the dining room or on a lovely outdoor patio. Outstanding primi include *maccheroni alla nonna* (macaroni with asparagus in a light cream sauce dotted with truffle oil). **Known for:** outstanding primi; succulent grilled meats; views. $ *Average main: €15* ✉ *Località San Sano 32/33, Gaiole in Chianti* ⊕ *8 km (5 miles) south of Gaiole* ☎ *0577/746020* ⊕ *www.lagrottadellarana.it* ⊗ *Closed Wed. and Feb.–mid-Mar.*

Lo Sfizio di Bianchi

$$ | ITALIAN | This pleasant restaurant, with outdoor seating on Gaiole's main square, is as popular with the locals as it is with travelers. The menu, presented on small blackboards, has the occasional unexpected item, like the plate of perfectly grilled vegetables that is listed as an antipasto but is practically a meal in itself. **Known for:** delicious grilled meats; house-made pastries and ice cream; honest Tuscan food without frills. $ *Average main: €15* ✉ *Via Ricasoli 44/46, Gaiole in Chianti* ☎ *0577/749501* ⊕ *www.losfiziodibianchi.it.*

Hotels

Agritoursimo San Sano

$ | B&B/INN | An open-hearth fireplace and hand-hewn stone porticoes hark back to the 13th century, when this was a fortress, and although it's now a small hotel with modern amenities, including a beautiful outdoor pool, the traditional tone is maintained by the wood-beamed ceilings and simple, country-style furniture. **Pros:** good base for exploring Chianti; great family atmosphere; warm and friendly hosts. **Cons:** furnishings, in true Tuscan style, are very plain; books up quickly; need a car to get around. $ *Rooms from: €109* ⊠ *Località San Sano 21, Gaiole in Chianti* ⊹ *10 km (6 miles) south of Gaiole* ☎ *0577/169–8022* ⊕ *www.agriturismosansano.it* ⊘ *Closed Jan. and Feb.* ⤿ *16 rooms* ⏺ *Free Breakfast.*

★ Borgo Argenina
$$$ | **B&B/INN** | Elena Nappa, a former interior designer, is now the consummate hostess at this centuries-old villa, which has old-fashioned guest rooms that are lovingly decorated with antique quilts and handmade wooden furnishings yet are also equipped with modern appliances. **Pros:** homemade buffet breakfasts; off-the-beaten-path feel; two highly affable canines on site. **Cons:** need a car to get around; three-night minimum stay; no pool. $ *Rooms from: €190* ⊠ *Località Borgo Argenina, Gaiole in Chianti* ⊹ *15 km (9 miles) south of Gaiole* ☎ *345/353–7673* ⊕ *www.borgoargenina.it* ⊘ *Closed mid-Nov.–Easter* ⤿ *15 rooms* ⏺ *Free Breakfast.*

★ Castello di Spaltenna
$$$$ | **B&B/INN** | This rustic yet elegant lodging consists of a former convent (dating from the 1300s) and a Romanesque church; inside you'll find rooms with canopy beds, chiseled-stone fireplaces, and massage-jet tubs (in suites). **Pros:** excellent service; first-class restaurant on site; views of hills, woods, and vineyards. **Cons:** some rooms look over the interior courtyard; a car is a necessity; access to some rooms is via narrow stairways. $ *Rooms from: €360* ⊠ *Pieve di Spaltenna 13, Gaiole in Chianti* ☎ *0577/749483* ⊕ *www.spaltenna.it* ⊘ *Closed Nov.–Easter* ⤿ *37 rooms* ⏺ *Free Breakfast.*

Castelnuovo Berardenga

20 km (12 miles) southeast of Gaiole in Chianti, 90 km (56 miles) southeast of Florence, 23 km (14 miles) east of Siena.

The southernmost village in Chianti has a compact center with hilly, curving streets. A plethora of piazzas invite wandering.

GETTING HERE
Castelnuovo is easily reached by car from Siena via the SS73. Tra-In buses run infrequently from Siena. Castelnuovo's train station, Castelnuovo Berardenga Scalo, is 8 km (5 miles) away.

VISITOR INFORMATION
CONTACTS Castelnuovo Berardenga Tourism Office. ⊠ *Via del Chianti 60/65, Castelnuovo Berardenga* ☎ *0577/351335* ⊕ *www.terresiena.it.*

Sights

San Giusto e San Clemente
CHURCH | Built in the 1840s on a Greek-cross plan, this neoclassical church contains a Madonna and Child with angels by an anonymous 15th-century master. Also inside is the *Holy Family with St. Catherine of Siena,* attributed to Arcangelo Salimbeni (1530/40–79). ⊠ *Piazza Matteotti 4, Castelnuovo Berardenga.*

San Gusmè
TOWN | The oldest and most interesting of the hilltop medieval villages that surround Castelnuovo Berardenga retains its early 1400s layout, with arched passageways, gates topped with coats of arms, narrow squares, and steep streets. You can walk through the entire village in 20 minutes, but in those 20 minutes you may feel as if you have stepped back in time some 600 years. ⊠ *Castelnuovo Berardenga* ⊹ *SR484 5 km (3 miles) north of Castelnuovo Berardenga.*

Villa Chigi
GARDEN | Peek at the gardens of Villa Chigi, a 19th-century villa built on the site of a 14th-century castle (actually the "new castle" from which Castelnuovo got its name). The villa is closed to the public, but its manicured gardens are open on Sunday and holidays. ⊠ *Via Berardenga 20, Castelnuovo Berardenga.*

Hotels

Borgo San Felice

$$$$ | B&B/INN | Spread across five buildings, this elegant lodging used to be a small medieval town, but now it's given over to luxury, which is immediately apparent upon entering the reception area—white walls, high vaulted ceilings, and furniture covered in exquisite chintz prints mingle with tasteful etchings and watercolors. **Pros:** beautiful buildings; romantic setting; heated pool and on-site spa. **Cons:** may be too remote for some; need a car to get around; service is sometimes lax. Ⓢ *Rooms from: €552* ✉ *Località San Felice, Castelnuovo Berardenga* ✚ *8 km (5 miles) northwest of Castelnuovo Berardenga* ☎ *0577/3964* ⊕ *www.borgosanfelice.com* ⊘ *Closed Nov.–Mar.* ⊯ *60 rooms* ❑ *All-Inclusive.*

Siena

20 km (12 miles) southwest of Castelnuovo Berardenga, 78 km (48 miles) south of Florence.

With its narrow streets and steep alleys, a Gothic Duomo, a bounty of early Renaissance art, and the glorious Palazzo Pubblico overlooking its magnificent Campo, Siena is often described as Italy's best-preserved medieval city. It is also remarkably modern.

Sienese mythology holds that the city shares common ancestry with Rome: the legendary founder, Senius, was said to be the son of Remus, the twin brother of Rome's founder, Romulus. The city emblem—a she-wolf and suckling twin boys—promulgates the claim. Archaeological evidence suggests there were prehistoric as well as Etruscan settlements here, which undoubtedly made way for Saena Julia, the Roman town established by Augustus in the 1st century BC.

Siena rose to prominence as an essential stop on that most important of medieval roads, the Via Francigena (or Via Romea), prospering from the yearly flow of thousands of Christian pilgrims coming south to Rome from northern Europe. Siena developed a banking system—one of Europe's oldest banks, the Monte dei Paschi, is still in business—and dominated the wool trade, thereby establishing itself as a rival to Florence. The two towns became regional powers and bitter enemies, each taking a different side in the struggle that divided the peninsula between the Guelphs (loyal to the Pope) and Ghibellines (loyal to the Holy Roman Emperor). Siena aligned itself with the latter.

Victory over Florence in 1260 at Montaperti marked the beginning of Siena's golden age. Even though Florentines avenged the loss 29 years later, Siena continued to prosper. During the following decades, Siena erected its greatest buildings (including the Duomo); established a model city government presided over by the Council of Nine; and became a great art, textile, and trade center. All of these achievements came together in the decoration of the Sala della Pace in Palazzo Pubblico.

In 1348, a plague decimated the population, brought an end to the Council of Nine, and left Siena economically vulnerable. It succumbed to Florentine rule in the mid-16th century, when a year-long siege virtually eliminated the local population. Ironically, it was this decline that, along with Sienese pride, prevented further development, to which we owe the city's marvelous medieval condition today.

Although it looks much as it did in the early 14th century, Siena is no museum. Walk through the streets and you can see that the medieval *contrade*, 17 neighborhoods into which the city has been historically divided, are a vibrant part of modern life. You may see a contrada's symbol—turtle (Tartuca), goose (Oca), porcupine (Istrice), tower (Torre)—emblazoned on banners and engraved on building walls.

The Sienese still strongly identify themselves by the contrada where they were born and raised; loyalty and rivalry run deep. At no time is this more visible than during the centuries-old Palio, a twice-yearly horse race held in the Piazza del Campo, but you need not visit then to experience the city's rich culture. Make a point of catching the *passeggiata serale* (evening stroll), when locals throng the Via di Città, Banchi di Sopra, and Banchi di Sotto, the city's three main streets.

GETTING HERE

From Florence, the quickest way to Siena is via the Florence–Siena Superstrada. Otherwise, take the Via Cassia (SR2), for a scenic route. Coming from Rome, leave the A1 at Valdichiana, and follow the Siena–Bettole Superstrada.

SITA provides excellent bus service between Florence and Siena. Because buses are direct and speedy, they're preferable to the train, which sometimes involves a change in Empoli.

Tra-In. ☎ 0577/204111 ⊕ *www.trainspa. it.*

VISITOR INFORMATION

CONTACTS Siena Tourism Office. ⊠ *Piazza del Duomo 2,* ☎ 0577/280551 ⊕ *www. terresiena.it.*

Sights

Driving is prohibited in most of the city center and impractical elsewhere. If you come by car, park it in one of the lots around the perimeter of town.

Practically unchanged since medieval times, Siena is laid out in a "Y" over the slopes of three hills, which divide the city into *terzi* (thirds). The most interesting sites are in a fairly compact area in the center of town. Be sure to see the Piazza del Campo, considered by many to be

the finest public square in Italy, and its Palazzo Pubblico. The Duomo and the Cripta are also must-sees.

Hills notwithstanding, it's a joy to walk through this medieval city. Although, with minimal stops, you can see Siena in a day, give yourself two days to tour the church building and museums, to wander the narrow streets that rise and fall steeply from the main thoroughfares, and to enjoy the cityscape itself.

Battistero

RELIGIOUS BUILDING | The Duomo's 14th-century Gothic Baptistery was built to prop up the apse of the cathedral. There are frescoes throughout, but the highlight is a large bronze 15th-century baptismal font designed by Jacopo della Quercia (1374–1438). It's adorned with bas-reliefs by various artists, including two by Renaissance masters: the *Baptism of Christ* by Lorenzo Ghiberti (1378–1455) and the *Feast of Herod* by Donatello. ⊠ *Piazza San Giovanni, Città* ☎ *0577/286300* ⊕ *operaduomo.siena. it* 🎟 *€13 combined ticket includes the Duomo, Cripta, and Museo dell'Opera.*

Casa di Santa Caterina

HISTORIC HOME | Caterina Benincasa, born here in 1347, had divine visions and received the stigmata, but she is most famous for her words and her argumentative skills. Her letters—many of which are preserved in the Biblioteca Comunale—were dictated because she did not know how to write. She is credited with convincing Pope Gregory XI (1329–78) to return the papacy to Rome after 70 years in Avignon and French domination, ending the Western Schism. Caterina died in Rome in 1380 and was canonized in 1461.

In subsequent centuries, the rooms of the house, including her cell and the kitchen, were converted into a series of chapels and oratories and decorated by noteworthy artists with scenes from Caterina's life. In 1939, she was made a patron saint of Italy, along with

St. Francis of Assisi. In 1970, she was elevated to Doctor of the Church, the highest possible honor in Christendom. She has been named a patron saint of Europe but, strangely enough, never of her hometown. ⊠ *Costa di Sant'Antonio 6, Camollìa* ☎ *0577/288175* ⎘ *Free.*

★ **Cripta**

CEMETERY | Routine excavation work revealed this crypt, which had been hidden for centuries under the grand *pavimento* (floor) of the Duomo and was opened to the public in 2003. In the late 13th century, an unknown master executed the crypt's breathtaking frescoes, which have sustained remarkably little damage and have retained their original colors. The *Deposition/Lamentation* proves that the Sienese school could paint emotion just as well as the Florentine school—and that it did so some 20 years before Giotto. ⊠ *Scale di San Giovanni, Città* ✢ *Down steps to right side of cathedral* ☎ *0577/286300* ⊕ *operaduomo.siena.it* ⎘ *€13 combined ticket includes the Duomo, Battistero, and Museo dell'Opera.*

★ **Duomo**

CHURCH | Siena's cathedral is one of the finest Gothic churches in Italy. The multicolor marbles and painted decoration are typical of the Italian approach to Gothic architecture—lighter and much less austere than the French. The amazingly detailed facade has few rivals. It was completed in two brief phases at the end of the 13th and 14th centuries. The statues and decorative work were designed by Nicola Pisano and his son Giovanni, although much of what's seen today are copies, the originals having been removed to the adjacent Museo dell'Opera Metropolitana. The gold mosaics are 18th-century restorations. The Campanile (no entry) is among central Italy's finest, the number of windows increasing with each level, a beautiful and ingenious way of reducing the weight of the structure as it climbs to the heavens.

With its dark-green-and-white striping throughout and its illusionistic coffered and gilded dome, the Duomo's interior is simply striking. Look up at copies of Duccio's (circa 1255–1319) stained-glass panels; the originals, finished in 1288, are in the Museo dell'Opera and are the oldest examples of stained glass in Italy. The Duomo is most famous, though, for its inlaid-marble floors, which took almost 200 years to complete. More than 40 artists contributed to the magnificent work of 56 compositions depicting biblical scenes, allegories, religious symbols, and civic emblems. Although conserving the floors requires keeping them covered for much of the year, they are unveiled during September and October.

Also noteworthy is the Duomo's carousel pulpit, carved by Nicola Pisano (circa 1220–84) around 1265; the Life of Christ is depicted on the rostrum frieze. In striking contrast to the nave's Gothic decoration are the well-preserved Renaissance frescoes in the Biblioteca Piccolomini, off the left aisle. Painted by Pinturicchio (circa 1454–1513) and completed in 1509, they depict events from the life of Aeneas Sylvius Piccolomini (1405–64), who became Pope Pius II in 1458.

The Duomo is grand, but the medieval Sienese people had even grander plans, namely, to use the existing church as a transept and build a new nave running toward the southeast, creating what would have been the world's largest church. Alas, only the side wall and part of the new facade were completed when the Black Death struck in 1348. The city subsequently fell into decline, funds dried up, and the plans were never carried out.

Indeed, the grand church project was actually doomed from the start—subsequent attempts to get it going revealed that the foundation was insufficient to bear the weight of the proposed structure. In any event, the unfinished new nave extending from the right side of the

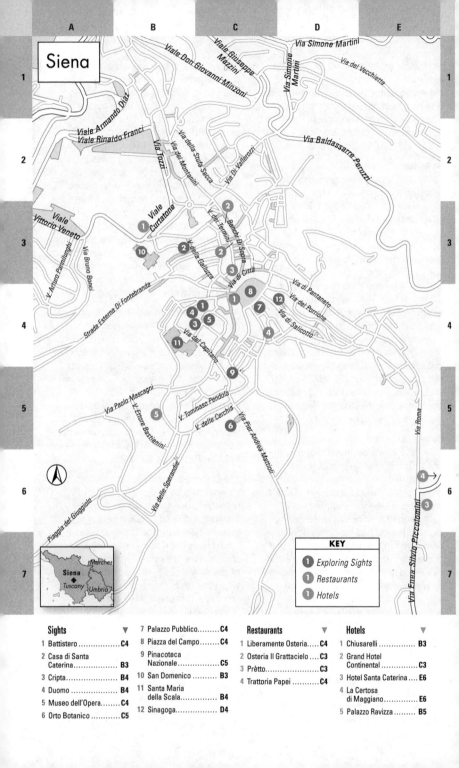

Siena

A **B** **C** **D** **E**

Via Simone Martini
Viale Giuseppe Mazzini
Viale Don Giovanni Minzoni
Via del Vecchietta
Viale Armando Diaz
Viale Rinaldo Franci
Via della Sturä Socca
Via dei Montanini
Via Tozzi
Via Baldassarre Peruzzi
Via Di Vallerozzi
Viale Vittorio Veneto
V. Arturo Famiglunghi
Via Bruno Bonci
Viale Curtatone
V. dei Termini
V. della Galluzza
Banchi Di Sopra
Via di Città
Via di Pantaneto
Strada Esterna Di Fontebranda
Via del Capitano
Via del Porrione
Via di Salicotto
Via Paolo Mascagni
V. Ettore Bastianini
V. Tommaso Pendola
V. delle Cerchia
Via Pier Andrea Mattioli
Via delle Sperandie
Via delle Sperandie
Via Roma
Via Enea Silvio Piccolomini
Piaggia del Giuggiolo

KEY

- **1** Exploring Sights
- **1** Restaurants
- **1** Hotels

Siena — Tuscany, Marches, Umbria

Sights ▼

1 Battistero **C4**
2 Casa di Santa Caterina **B3**
3 Cripta **B4**
4 Duomo **B4**
5 Museo dell'Opera **C4**
6 Orto Botanico **C5**
7 Palazzo Pubblico **C4**
8 Piazza del Campo **C4**
9 Pinacoteca Nazionale **C5**
10 San Domenico **B3**
11 Santa Maria della Scala **B4**
12 Sinagoga **D4**

Restaurants ▼

1 Liberamente Osteria **C4**
2 Osteria Il Grattacielo **C3**
3 Prètto **C3**
4 Trattoria Papei **C4**

Hotels ▼

1 Chiusarelli **B3**
2 Grand Hotel Continental **C3**
3 Hotel Santa Caterina **E6**
4 La Certosa di Maggiano **E6**
5 Palazzo Ravizza **B5**

Duomo was ultimately enclosed to house the Museo dell'Opera. The Cripta was discovered during routine preservation work on the church. ⊠ *Piazza del Duomo, Città* ☎ *0577/286300* ⊕ *operaduomo. siena.it* 🎟 *€13 combined ticket includes Cripta, Battistero, and Museo dell'Opera* ☞ *Last entrance is 30 mins before closing.*

★ **Museo dell'Opera**

ART MUSEUM | Part of the unfinished nave of what was to have been a new cathedral, the museum contains the Duomo's treasury and some of the original decoration from its facade and interior. The first room on the ground floor displays weather-beaten 13th-century sculptures by Giovanni Pisano (circa 1245–1318) that were brought inside for protection and replaced by copies, as was a tondo of the *Madonna and Child* (now attributed to Donatello) that once hung on the door to the south transept.

The masterpiece is unquestionably Duccio's *Maestà,* one side with 26 panels depicting episodes from the Passion, the other side with a *Madonna and Child Enthroned.* Painted between 1308 and 1311 as the altarpiece for the Duomo (where it remained until 1505), its realistic elements, such as the lively depiction of the Christ child and the treatment of interior space, proved an enormous influence on later painters. The work originally decorated the Duomo's high altar, before being displaced by Duccio's *Maestà.* There is a fine view from the tower inside the museum. ⊠ *Piazza del Duomo 8, Città* ☎ *0577/286300* ⊕ *operaduomo. siena.it* 🎟 *€13 combined ticket includes the Duomo, Cripta, and Battistero.*

Orto Botanico

GARDEN | Siena's botanical garden is a great place to relax and enjoy views onto the countryside below. Guided tours in English are available by reservation. ⊠ *Via Pier Andrea Mattioli 4, Città* ☎ *0577/235407* ⊕ *www.ortobotanicoitalia.it* 🎟 *€5.*

Palazzo Pubblico

GOVERNMENT BUILDING | The Gothic Palazzo Pubblico, the focal point of the Piazza del Campo, has served as Siena's town hall since the 1300s. It now also contains the Museo Civico, with walls covered in early Renaissance frescoes. The nine governors of Siena once met in the Sala della Pace, famous for Ambrogio Lorenzetti's frescoes called *Allegories of Good and Bad Government*, painted in the late 1330s to demonstrate the dangers of tyranny. The good government side depicts utopia, showing first the virtuous ruling council surrounded by angels and then scenes of a perfectly running city and countryside. Conversely, the bad government fresco tells a tale straight out of Dante. The evil ruler and his advisers have horns and fondle strange animals, and the town scene depicts the seven mortal sins in action.

The Torre del Mangia, the palazzo's famous bell tower, is named after one of its first bell ringers, Giovanni di Duccio (called Mangiaguadagni, or earnings eater). The climb up to the top is long and steep, but the view makes it worth every step. ⊠ *Piazza del Campo 1, Città* ☎ *0577/292232* ⊕ *www.comune.siena.it* 🎟 *Museum €10, ticket sales end 30 mins before closing; tower €10, ticket sales end 45 mins before closing.*

★ **Piazza del Campo**

PLAZA/SQUARE | The fan-shape Piazza del Campo, known simply as Il Campo (The Field), is one of the finest squares in Italy. Constructed toward the end of the 12th century on a market area unclaimed by any contrada, it's still the heart of town. Its brickwork is patterned in nine different sections—representing each member of the medieval Council of Nine.

Continued on page 230

Climbing the 400 narrow steps of the Torre del Mangia rewards you with unparalleled views of Siena's rooftops and the countryside beyond.

The Palazzo Pubblico, Siena's town hall since the 14th century.

Something about the fan-shaped, sloping design of Il Campo encourages people to sit and relax (except during the Palio, when they stand and scream). The communal atmosphere here is unlike that of any other Italian piazza.

PIAZZA DEL CAMPO

Fodor's Choice ★

The fan-shaped **Piazza del Campo**, known simply as Il Campo (The Field), is one of the finest squares in Italy. Constructed toward the end of the 12th century on a market area unclaimed by any contrada, it's still the heart of town. The bricks of the Campo are patterned in nine different sections—representing each member of the medieval Council of Nine. At the top of the Campo is a copy of the Fonte Gaia, decorated in the early 15th century by Siena's greatest sculptor, Jacopo della Quercia, with 13 sculpted reliefs of biblical events and virtues. Those lining the rectangular fountain are 19th-century copies; the originals are in the Spedale di Santa Maria della Scala. On Palio horse race days (July 2 and August 16), the Campo and all its surrounding buildings are packed with cheering, frenzied locals and tourists craning their necks to take it all in.

The Gothic **Palazzo Pubblico**, the focal point of the Piazza del Campo, has served as Siena's town hall since the 1300s. It now also contains the Museo Civico, with walls covered in early Renaissance frescoes. The nine governors of Siena once met in the Sala della Pace, famous for Ambrogio Lorenzetti's frescoes called *Allegories of Good and Bad Government,* painted in the late 1330s to demonstrate the dangers of tyranny. The good government side depicts utopia, showing first the virtuous ruling council surrounded by angels and then scenes of a perfectly running city and countryside. Conversely, the bad government fresco tells a tale straight out of Dante. The evil ruler and his advisers have horns and fondle strange animals, and the town scene depicts the seven mortal sins in action. Interestingly, the bad government fresco is severely damaged, and the good government fresco is in terrific condition. The **Torre del Mangia**, the palazzo's famous bell tower, is named after one of its first bell ringers, Giovanni di Duccio (called Mangiaguadagni, or "*Earnings Eater*"). The climb up to the top is long and steep, but the view makes it worth every step.

THE PALIO

The three laps around a makeshift racetrack in Piazza del Campo are over in less than two minutes, but the spirit of Siena's Palio—a horse race held every July 2 and August 16—lives all year long.

The Palio is contested between Siena's *contrade*, the 17 neighborhoods that have divided the city since the Middle Ages. Loyalties are fiercely felt. At any time of year you'll see on the streets contrada symbols—turtle (Tartuca), goose (Oca), porcupine (Istrice), tower (Torre)—emblazoned on banners and engraved on building walls. At Palio time, simmering rivalries come to a boil.

It's been that way since at least August 16, 1310, the date of the first recorded running of the Palio. At that time, and for centuries to follow, the race went through the streets of the city. The additional July 2 running was instituted in 1649; soon thereafter the location was moved to the Campo and the current system for selecting the race entrants established. Ten of the contrade are chosen at random to run in the July Palio. The August race is then contested between the seven contrade left out in July, plus three of the 10 July participants, again chosen at random. Although the races are in theory of equal importance, Sienese will tell you that it's better to win the second and have bragging rights for the rest of the year.

The race itself has a raw and arbitrary character—it's no Kentucky Derby. There's barely room for the 10 horses on the makeshift Campo course, so falls and collisions are inevitable. Horses are chosen at random three days before the race, and jockeys (who ride bareback) are mercenaries hired from surrounding towns. Almost no tactic is considered too underhanded. Bribery, secret plots, and betrayal are commonplace—so much so that the word for "jockey," *fantino*, has come to mean "untrustworthy" in Siena. There have been incidents of drugging (the horses) and kidnapping (the jockeys); only sabotaging a horse's reins remains taboo.

Above: The tension of the starting line.
Top left: The frenzy of the race.
Bottom left: A flag-bearer follows in the footsteps of his ancestors.

AQUILA

BRUCO

CHIOCCIOLA

MEDIEVAL CONTRADE

Festivities kick off three days prior to the Palio, with the selection and blessing of the horses, trial runs, ceremonial banquets, betting, and late-night celebrations. Residents don their contrada's colors and march through the streets in medieval costumes. The Campo is transformed into a racetrack lined with a thick layer of sand. On race day, each horse is brought to the church of the contrada for which it will run, where it's blessed and told, "Go little horse and return a winner." The Campo fills through the afternoon, with spectators crowding into every available space until bells ring and the piazza is sealed off. Processions of flag wavers in traditional dress march to the beat of tambourines and drums and the roar of the crowds. The palio itself—a banner for which the race is named, dedicated to the Virgin Mary—makes an appearance, followed by the horses and their jockeys.

The race begins when one horse, chosen to ride up from behind the rest of the field, crosses the starting line. There are always false starts, adding to the frenzied mood. Once underway, the race is over in a matter of minutes. The victorious rider is carried off through the streets of the winning contrada (where in the past tradition dictated he was entitled to the local girl of his choice), while winning and losing sides use television replay to analyze the race from every possible angle. The winning contrada will celebrate into the night, at long tables piled high with food and drink. The champion horse is guest of honor.

CIVETTA

DRAGO

GIRAFFA

ISTRICE

LEOCORNO

LUPA

NICCHIO

OCA

ONDA

PANTERA

SELVA

TARTUCA

TORRE

VALDIMONTONE

At the top of the Campo is a copy of the early 15th-century Fonte Gaia by Siena's greatest sculptor, Jacopo della Quercia. The 13 sculpted reliefs of biblical events and virtues that line the fountain are 19th-century copies; the originals are in the museum complex of Santa Maria della Scala. On Palio horse-race days (July 2 and August 16), the Campo and all its surrounding buildings are packed with cheering, frenzied locals and tourists craning their necks to take it all in. ⊠ *Piazza del Campo, Città.*

Pinacoteca Nazionale

ART MUSEUM | The superb collection of five centuries of local painting in Siena's national picture gallery can easily convince you that the Renaissance was by no means just a Florentine thing. Accordingly, the most interesting section of the collection, chronologically arranged, has several important firsts. Room 1 contains a painting of the *Stories of the True Cross* (1215) by the so-called Master of Tressa, the earliest identified work by a painter of the Sienese school, and is followed in Room 2 by late-13th-century artist Guido da Siena's *Stories from the Life of Christ,* one of the first paintings ever made on canvas (earlier painters used wood panels).

Rooms 3 and 4 are dedicated to Duccio, a student of Cimabue (circa 1240–1302) and considered to be the last of the proto-Renaissance painters. Ambrogio Lorenzetti's landscapes in Room 8 are among the first truly secular paintings in Western art. Among later works in the rooms on the floor above, keep an eye out for the preparatory sketches used by Domenico Beccafumi (1486–1551) for the 35 etched marble panels he made for the floor of the Duomo. ⊠ *Via San Pietro 29, Città* ☏ *0577/286143* ⊕ *pinacotecanazionale.siena.it* 🎟 *€8* ⊘ *Closed Mon.*

★ Santa Maria della Scala

ART MUSEUM | For more than 1,000 years, this complex across from the Duomo was home to Siena's hospital, but it now serves as a museum containing, among other things, Sienese Renaissance treasures. Restored 15th-century frescoes in the Sala del Pellegrinaio (once the emergency room) tell the history of the hospital, which was created to give refuge to passing pilgrims and others in need and to distribute charity to the poor. Incorporated into the complex is the church of the Santissima Annunziata, with a celebrated *Risen Christ* by Vecchietta (also known as Lorenzo di Pietro, circa 1412–80). Down in the dark, Cappella di Santa Caterina della Notte is where St. Catherine went to pray at night.

The displays—including the *bucchero* (dark, reddish clay) ceramics, Roman coins, and tomb furnishings—are clearly marked and can serve as a good introduction to the history of regional excavations. Be sure to visit the subterranean archaeological museum to see della Quercia's original sculpted reliefs from the Fonte Gaia. Although the fountain has been faithfully copied for the Campo, there's something incomparably beautiful about the real thing. ⊠ *Piazza del Duomo 2, Città* ☏ *0577/534511* ⊕ *www.santamariadellascala.com* 🎟 *€9* ⊘ *Closed Tues.*

San Domenico

CHURCH | Although the Duomo is celebrated as a triumph of 13th-century Gothic architecture, this church, built at about the same time, turned out to be an oversize, hulking brick box that never merited a finishing coat in marble, let alone a graceful facade. Named for the founder of the Dominican order, the church is now more closely associated with St. Catherine of Siena. Just to the right of the entrance is the chapel in which she received the stigmata. On the wall is the only known contemporary portrait of the saint, made in the late 14th century by Andrea Vanni (circa 1332–1414). Farther down is the famous Cappella delle Santa Testa, the church's official shrine.

Revered throughout the country long before she was officially named a patron saint of Italy in 1939, Catherine was, quite literally, "distributed" across the nation—one of her feet is in Venice, most of her body is in Rome, and her head (kept in a reliquary on the chapel's altar) and her right thumb are here. On either side of the chapel are well-known frescoes by Sodoma (aka Giovanni Antonio Bazzi, 1477–1549) of *St. Catherine in Ecstasy*. Don't miss the view of the Duomo and town center from the apse-side terrace. ⊠ *Piazza San Domenico, Camollìa* 🕿 *0577/286848* 🌐 *www.basilica-cateriniana.it.*

Sinagoga
SYNAGOGUE | Down a small street around the corner from Il Campo, this synagogue is worth a visit simply to view the two sobering plaques that adorn its facade. One commemorates June 28, 1799, when 13 Jews were taken from their homes by a fanatic mob and burned in the square. The other memorializes the Sienese Jews who were deported during World War II. Visits are permitted every half hour, and guided tours in English are available by prior arrangement. ⊠ *Vicolo delle Scotte 14, San Martino* 🕿 *0577/271345* 🌐 *www.museisenesi.org* 🎟 *€4* 🕙 *Closed Sat.*

🍴 Restaurants

Liberamente Osteria
$ | **ITALIAN** | Though the food here is rather good, the real reasons to come are the exquisitely crafted cocktails and the view, which just happens to be of Il Campo, arguably the prettiest square in all of Italy. Tasty little nibbles accompany the generously proportioned aperitivi. **Known for:** opens early (9 am) and closes late (2 am); facility with rum-based drinks; variations on the spritz. 🟋 *Average main: €7* ⊠ *Il Campo 27, Siena* 🕿 *0577/274733* 🌐 *www.liberamenteosteria.it.*

Osteria Il Grattacielo
$ | **TUSCAN** | If you're wiped out from too much sightseeing, consider a meal at this hole-in-the-wall restaurant where

locals congregate for a simple lunch over a glass of wine. There's a collection of verdure sott'olio, a wide selection of affettati misti, and various types of frittatas—all of which can be washed down with the cheap, yet eminently drinkable, house red. **Known for:** usually filled with local men arguing about the Palio; earthy ambience; simple, good-value food. 🟋 *Average main: €10* ⊠ *Via Pontani 8, Camollìa* 🕿 *331/742–2835* 🕙 *Closed Wed.*

Prètto
$ | **ITALIAN** | This one-room *prosciutteria*, which opens late in the morning and closes late at night, serves salads and sandwiches featuring pork products in their various incarnations. The wine list is particularly strong with bottles from the area, and its prices are reasonable. **Known for:** porchetta; desserts; lampredotto. 🟋 *Average main: €10* ⊠ *Via dei Termini 4, Città* 🕿 *0577/289089* 🌐 *www.prettoprosciutteria.it.*

Trattoria Papei
$ | **TUSCAN** | The menu hasn't changed for years, and why should it? This place, which has been in the Papei family for three generations, attracts both locals and visitors with basic but fine Sienese specialties and reasonable prices. **Known for:** outdoor seating; lively atmosphere; great place to sample local specialties. 🟋 *Average main: €13* ⊠ *Piazza del Mercato 6, Città* 🕿 *0577/280894* 🌐 *anticatrattoriapapei.com.*

Hotels

Chiusarelli
$$ | **B&B/INN** | Caryatids stud the grounds of this well-kept neoclassical villa (it's been a hotel since 1870), where a small garden invites reading, and guest rooms are functional, airy, and reasonably quiet. **Pros:** near the main bus terminal and sights; spacious rooms; quiet garden. **Cons:** bland furnishings; hosts the occasional tour group; on a busy street. 🟋 *Rooms from: €131* ⊠ *Viale Curtatone 15, Camollìa* 🕿 *0577/280562*

⊕ *www.chiusarelli.com* ⬎ *48 rooms* ⏐◎⏐ *Free Breakfast.*

Grand Hotel Continental

$$$$ | **HOTEL** | Pope Alexander VII of the famed Sienese Chigi family gave this palace to his niece as a wedding present in 1600, and, through the centuries, it has been a private family home as well as a grand hotel—one that exudes elegance from its stately pillared entrance to its crisp-linen sheets. **Pros:** luxurious accommodations; first-rate concierge; great location on the main drag. **Cons:** breakfast costs extra; lots of noise if your room is street-side; sometimes stuffy atmosphere. $ *Rooms from: €530* ⊠ *Banchi di Sopra 85, Camollìa* ☎ *0577/56011* ⊕ *www.starhotelscollezione.com* ⬎ *51 rooms* ⏐◎⏐ *No Meals.*

Hotel Santa Caterina

$$ | **B&B/INN** | Manager Lorenza Capannelli and her fine staff are welcoming, hospitable, enthusiastic, and go out of their way to ensure a fine stay; rooms in the back look out onto the garden or the countryside in the distance. **Pros:** friendly staff; breakfast in the garden; a short walk to center of town. **Cons:** 15-minute (easy) walk into the historic center; outside city walls; on a busy intersection. $ *Rooms from: €134* ⊠ *Via Piccolomini 7, San Martino* ☎ *0577/221105* ⊕ *www. hotelsantacaterinasiena.com* ⬎ *22 rooms* ⏐◎⏐ *Free Breakfast.*

La Certosa di Maggiano

$$$$ | **B&B/INN** | A 14th-century monastery has been converted into this upscale country hotel, where rooms have the style and comfort of an aristocratic villa, with classic prints and bold colors such as daffodil yellow. **Pros:** far from the madding crowd; elegant service; luxurious rooms. **Cons:** a car is a necessity; located outside of town; some find the atmosphere too formal. $ *Rooms from: €345* ⊠ *Strada di Certosa 82, Siena* ✛ *½ km (¼ mile) east of Siena; Siena Sud exit off Superstrada* ☎ *0577/179–4006* ⊕ *www.lacertosadimaggiano.com* ⬎ *18 rooms* ⏐◎⏐ *Free Breakfast.*

★ **Palazzo Ravizza**

$$ | **HOTEL** | This charming palazzo exudes a sense of an age gone by; its guest rooms have high ceilings, antique furnishings, and bathrooms decorated with hand-painted tiles. **Pros:** 10-minute walk to the center of town; professional staff and delightful restaurant; pleasant garden with a view beyond the city walls. **Cons:** somewhat removed from the center of things; some rooms are a little cramped; not all rooms have views. $ *Rooms from: €129* ⊠ *Pian dei Mantellini 34, Città* ☎ *0577/280462* ⊕ *www.palazzoravizza.it* ⬎ *41 rooms* ⏐◎⏐ *Free Breakfast.*

Nightlife

Caffè del Corso

BARS | Enjoy *aperitivi* (apertifs) at this very popular bar, where aspiring local artists and savvy students hobnob until 2 am. ⊠ *Banchi di Sopra 25, Camollìa* ☎ *0577/226656.*

Sapordivino

BARS | This wine bar at the Grand Hotel Continental is a tranquil place to have a finely crafted cocktail. A well-stocked liquor collection includes a well-thought-out list of whiskeys. ⊠ *Banchi di Sopra 85, Città* ☎ *0577/56011* ⊕ *www.starhotelscollezione.com.*

Performing Arts

Estate Musicale Chigiana

MUSIC | Master classes and workshops held by internationally famous musicians result in top-notch performances in Siena between July and September. Age-old venues such as the Accademia Musicale Chigiana, the Spedale di Santa Maria della Scala, the church of Sant'Agostino, and Piazza Duomo are used for these exceptional concerts. It is best to book well in advance as tickets are usually in high demand. The ChigianArt Cafe is a perfect place for a light lunch or a cocktail. ⊠ *Accademia Musicale Chigiana, Via*

Ricciarelli, delicate almond cookies native to Siena

di Città 89, Città ☎ 0577/22091 ⊕ www.chigiana.org.

Settimane Musicali Senesi festival

CONCERTS | Performances by local and national classical musicians take place during a series of concerts held in churches and courtyards during the Settimane Musicali Senesi festival in July and August. ✉ *Siena* ⊕ *www.chigiana.org.*

 ## Shopping

Siena is known for a delectable variety of cakes and cookies with recipes dating from medieval times. Some Sienese sweets are *cavallucci* (sweet spice biscuits), *panforte* (literally "strong bread," with honey, hazelnuts, almonds, and spices), *ricciarelli* (almond-paste cookies), and *castagnaccio* (a baked Tuscan flat cake that's made in fall and winter using chestnut flour and is topped with pine nuts and rosemary).

ARTS AND CRAFTS

Bottega dell'Arte

CRAFTS | If you've always wanted a 14th- or 15th-century painting to hang on your wall, but the cost of acquiring one is prohibitive, consider purchasing one of the superb copies at this shop made by Chiara or her brother, Michelangelo Casoni. Their work in tempera and gold leaf is of the highest quality. ✉ *Via Stalloreggi 47, Città* ☎ *0577/40755* ⊕ *www.arteinsiena.it.*

Siena Ricama

CRAFTS | Siena has been famous for centuries for its fine embroidery work, and Bruna Brizza continues the tradition in her tiny shop. Hand stitching, usually on simple white and cream-color linen, adorns lamp shades, tablecloths, and other housewares. ✉ *Via di Città 61, Città* ☎ *0577/288339.*

Vetrate Artistiche Toscane

CRAFTS | Stained-glass artists create and sell contemporary secular and religious works here. If you want to learn the technique, they also offer workshops and

Siena's frenetic Palio

apprenticeship programs. ⊠ *Via della Galluzza 5, Camollia* ☎ *0577/48033* ⊕ *www.glassisland.com.*

FOOD AND DRINK

Antico Pizzicheria

FOOD | There has been a *salumeria* (delicatessen) here since 1889. The cheeses, cured meats, and made-to-order panini are top-notch. ⊠ *Via di Città 93–95, Città* ☎ *0577/289164.*

La Bottega dei Sapori Antichi

FOOD | Bruno De Miccoli stocks an impressive array of verdure sott'olio, local wines, and dried herbs in his food-and-wine bar. ⊠ *Via delle Terme 39–41, Camollia* ☎ *0577/285501.*

★ Nannini

FOOD | Locals flock to this central café to quaff a cappuccino and pick up panforte (the chocolate panforte is a real treat) and ricciarelli to go. ⊠ *Banchi di Sopra 24, Camollia* ☎ *0577/236009* ⊕ *www.caffetterienannini.com.*

 Activities

★ Palio

HORSE RACING | Siena's thrilling horse race takes place every year on July 2 and August 16. Three laps around the track in the Piazza del Campo earn the victor the *palio* (a hand-painted banner, unique to each event), and the respect or scorn of the remaining 16 contrade. Tickets usually sell out months in advance; call the Siena tourist office for more information. Note that some hotels reserve a number of tickets for guests. It's also possible you might luck out and get an unclaimed seat or two. The standing-room center of the piazza is free to all on a first-come, first-served basis, until just moments before the start. If you opt for standing-room, beware of the summer heat, and take water with you. The entry of the horses into the starting gate can sometimes be a lengthy process—they are easily spooked, and it can take several hours to get things ready—all-in-all, you might be better off finding a comfortable seat in front of a TV. ⊠ *Siena* *tourist office, Piazza del Campo 56, Città* ☎ *0577/280551* 🌐 *www.terresiena.it.*

Monteriggioni

19 km (12 miles) northwest of Siena, 55 km (34 miles) south of Florence.

Tiny Monteriggioni makes a nice stop on the way north to Colle di Val d'Elsa, San Gimignano, or Volterra. It's hard to imagine that this little town surrounded by poppy fields was ever anything but sleepy, but, in the 13th century, Monteriggioni served as Siena's northernmost defense against impending Florentine invasion. (It's likely that the residents of the town spent many a sleepless night.)

The town's formidable walls are in good condition, although the 14 square towers are not as tall as in Dante's (1265–1321) time, when the poet likened them to giants guarding the horrifying central pit of hell. The town empties of day-trippers at sundown, and this hamlet becomes very tranquil.

GETTING HERE

You can reach Monteriggioni by car on either the SR2 or the Florence–Siena Superstrada. Buses run frequently to and from Siena. The closest train station to Monteriggioni, with frequent service to and from Siena, is in Castellina Scalo. You will then have to reach Monteriggioni on foot—it's a 4-km (2½-mile) walk.

VISITOR INFORMATION

CONTACTS Monteriggioni Tourism Office. ✉ *Piazza Roma 23, Monteriggioni* ☎ *0577/304834* 🌐 *www.monteriggioniturismo.it.*

🍴 Restaurants

Bar dell'Orso

$ | **ITALIAN** | This spot just outside the walled town of Monteriggioni is the perfect stop on the way to Siena from Florence or vice versa. The bar serves excellent coffees and sweets, and the highly informal dining room serves up terrific local specialties. **Known for:** top-quality pork products with which to stuff a sandwich; pici (a local pasta) served in all its guises; lovely wines by the glass. [$] *Average main: €13* ✉ *Via Cassia Nord 23, Monteriggioni* ☎ *0577/305074* 🌐 *bardellorso.it.*

Il Pozzo

$ | **TUSCAN** | Famous for its preparation of a 16th-century recipe of *cinghiale al cioccolato* (wild boar stewed in chocolate sauce), this restaurant is a popular spot. Tamer specialties include a range of freshly made pastas, *filetto alla boscaiola* (fillet of beef with porcini mushrooms), *piccione ripieno* (stuffed squab), and a long list of homey desserts. **Known for:** great wine list; outdoor seating when it's warm; adherence to local cuisine. [$] *Average main: €13* ✉ *Piazza Roma 2, Siena* ☎ *0577/304127* ⏲ *Closed Mon., and Jan. 6–Feb. 14.*

🛏 Hotels

Borgo San Luigi

$$ | **HOTEL** | This 17th-century villa lined with lavender bushes and cypress trees sits just outside Monteriggioni. **Pros:** good base for exploring Siena; some rooms have kitchens; excellent gym and pool. **Cons:** few restaurants are within walking distance; a car is a must; somewhat isolated. [$] *Rooms from: €189* ✉ *Strada della Cerretta 7, Monteriggioni* ✣ *4 km (2½ miles) southwest of Monteriggioni* ☎ *0577/301055* 🌐 *www.borgosanluigi.it* 🛏 *74 rooms* 🍴 *Free Breakfast.*

Hotel Monteriggioni

$$$ | **B&B/INN** | A sense of freshness comes from the terra-cotta floors, high wood-beamed ceilings, and soothing whitewashed walls in this hotel's guest rooms. **Pros:** great location inside town walls; well-appointed rooms; peaceful setting. **Cons:** no nightlife to speak of; a car is a must; no views beyond the walls.

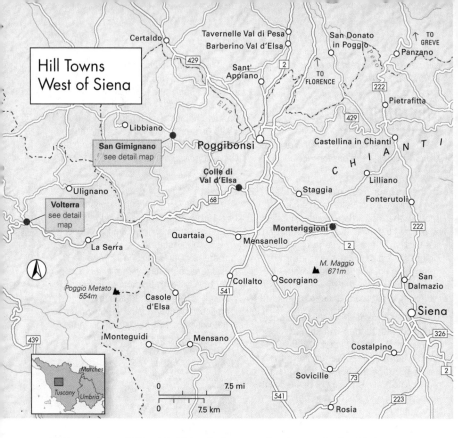

Hill Towns
West of Siena

Certaldo

Tavernelle Val di Pesa
Barberino Val d'Elsa

San Donato
in Poggio

↑ TO
GREVE

Panzano

429

Sant'
Appiano

2

↓ TO
FLORENCE

222

Pietrafitta

Libbiano

429

San Gimignano
see detail map

Poggibonsi

Castellina in Chianti

C H I A N T I

Colle di
Val d'Elsa

Lilliano

Ulignano

Volterra
see detail
map

68

Staggia

Fonterutoli

222

Quartaia

Mensanello

Monteriggioni

La Serra

2

M. Maggio
671m

Poggio Metato
554m

Collalto

Scorgiano

San
Dalmazio

Casole
d'Elsa

541

Siena

439

Monteguidi

Mensano

Costalpino

326

0   7.5 mi

Sovicille

73

2

0   7.5 km

541

223

Rosia

Marches

Tuscany *Umbria*

$ *Rooms from: €230* ✉ *Via I Maggio 4,
Siena* ☎ *0577/305009* ⊕ *www.hotelmon-
teriggioni.it* ⊗ *Closed Dec.–Feb.* ⇱ *12
rooms* ⊙ *Free Breakfast.*

Colle di Val d'Elsa

*12 km (7 miles) west of Monteriggioni,
25 km (16 miles) northwest of Siena, 51
km (32 miles) south of Florence.*

Most people pass through on their way
to and from popular tourist destinations
Volterra and San Gimignano—a shame,
because Colle di Val d'Elsa has a lot to offer.
It's another town on the Via Francigena that
benefited from trade along the pilgrimage
route to Rome. Colle got an extra boost in
the late 16th century when it was given a
bishopric, probably related to an increase in

trade when nearby San Gimignano was cut
off from the well-traveled road.

The town is arranged on two levels, and,
from the 12th century onward, the flat
lower portion was given over to a flourishing papermaking industry. Today, the
area is mostly modern, and efforts have
shifted toward the production of fine
glass and crystal.

Make your way from the newer lower town
(Colle Bassa) to the prettier, upper part of
town (Colle Alta). The best views of the valley are to be had from Viale della Rimembranza, the road that loops around the
western end of town, past the church of
San Francesco. The early-16th-century Porta Nuova was inserted into the preexisting
medieval walls, just as several handsome
Renaissance palazzos were placed into the
medieval neighborhood to create what is
now called the Borgo.

The Via Campana, the main road, passes through the facade of the surreal Palazzo Campana, an otherwise unfinished building that serves as a door connecting the two parts of the upper town. Via delle Volte, named for the vaulted arches that cover it, leads straight to Piazza del Duomo. There is a convenient parking lot off the SS68, with stairs leading up the hill. Buses arrive at Piazza Arnolfo, named after the town's favorite son, Arnolfo di Cambio (circa 1245–1302), the early-Renaissance architect who designed Florence's Duomo and Palazzo Vecchio (but sadly nothing here).

GETTING HERE
You can reach Colle di Val d'Elsa by car on either the SR2 from Siena or the Florence–Siena Superstrada. Bus service to and from Siena and Florence is frequent.

VISITOR INFORMATION
CONTACTS Colle di Val d'Elsa Tourism Office. ✉ *Piazza Arnolfo di Cambio 10* ☎ *0577/292222* ⊕ *www.terresiena.it.*

Sights

Chiesa di Santa Caterina
CHURCH | Visit this 15th-century church to view the excellent stained-glass window in the apse, executed by Sebastiano Mainardi (circa 1460–1513), as well as a haunting *Pietà* created by local artist Zacchia Zacchi (1473–1544). ✉ *Via Campana 35, Colle di Val d'Elsa.*

Duomo
CHURCH | Several reconstructions have left little to admire of the once-Romanesque Duomo. Inside is the Cappella del Santo Chiodo (Chapel of the Holy Nail), built in the 15th century to hold a nail allegedly from the cross upon which Christ was crucified. (Perhaps it inspired the locals to go into the nail-making business, which became another of the town's flourishing industries.) ✉ *Piazza del Duomo, Colle di Val d'Elsa.*

Museo San Pietro
ART MUSEUM | The museum of sacred art displays religious relics as well as triptychs from the Sienese and Florentine schools dating from the 14th and 15th centuries. It also contains the town's tribute to Arnolfo di Cambio, with photos of the buildings he designed for other towns. Down Via del Castello, at Number 63, is the house-tower where Arnolfo was born in 1245. (It's not open to the public.) ✉ *Via Gracco del Secco 102, Colle di Val d'Elsa* ☎ *0577/286300* ⊕ *www.museisenesi.org* 🎟 *€9, includes the Museo Archeologico.*

 Restaurants

L'Antica Trattoria
$$ | TUSCAN | Residents of Colle di Val d'Elsa hold this trattoria in high esteem, even though it's a little overpriced. Tuscan classics fill the large menu, which concentrates on game, particularly pheasant, pigeon, and quail, and pastas differ from the usual fare. **Known for:** pescatarians will be happy; fine wine list; tasting menus. 💲 *Average main: €22* ✉ *Piazza Arnolfo di Cambio 23, Colle di Val d'Elsa* ☎ *0577/923747* ⊕ *www.anticatrattoriaparadisi.it* ⊘ *Closed Tues.*

Molino il Moro
$$ | TUSCAN | The early-12th-century grain mill, now a romantic restaurant, is perched over a rushing river. The chef concocts sophisticated spins on traditional dishes, such as the divine *filetto di coniglio in crosta con purè di pruge* (rabbit loin with a prune puree). **Known for:** gorgeous setting; short but sweet wine list; inventive cuisine. 💲 *Average main: €21* ✉ *Via della Ruota 2, Colle di Val d'Elsa* ☎ *0577/920862* ⊘ *Closed Mon. No lunch Tues.*

★ Ristorante Arnolfo
$$$$ | MODERN ITALIAN | Food lovers should not miss Arnolfo, one of Tuscany's most highly regarded restaurants, where chef Gaetano Trovato sets high standards of

creativity; his dishes daringly ride the line between innovation and tradition, almost always with spectacular results. The menu changes frequently but you are always sure to find fish and lots of fresh vegetables in the summer. **Known for:** superb wine list; imaginative dishes; talented chef. $ *Average main: €70* ✉ *Via XX Settembre 50, Colle di Val d'Elsa* ☎ *0577/920549* 🌐 *www.arnolfo.com* 🕒 *Closed Tues. and Wed. and mid-Jan.–Feb.*

Hotels

Palazzo San Lorenzo

$ | **B&B/INN** | A 17th-century palace in the historic center of Colle has rooms that exude warmth and comfort, with light-color wooden floors, soothingly tinted fabrics, and large windows. **Pros:** central location; extremely well maintained; indoor pool. **Cons:** a car is a necessity; some of the public spaces feel rather sterile; caters to business groups. $ *Rooms from: €113* ✉ *Via Gracco del Secco 113, Colle di Val d'Elsa* ☎ *0577/923675* 🌐 *www.palazzosanlorenzo.it* 🛏 *48 rooms* 🍴 *Free Breakfast.*

San Gimignano

14 km (9 miles) northwest of Colle di Val d'Elsa, 38 km (24 miles) northwest of Siena, 54 km (34 miles) southwest of Florence.

When you're on a hilltop surrounded by soaring medieval towers silhouetted against the sky, it's difficult not to fall under the spell of San Gimignano. Its tall walls and narrow streets are typical of Tuscan hill towns, but it's the medieval "skyscrapers" that set the town apart from its neighbors.

Today, 14 towers remain, but at the height of the Guelph–Ghibelline conflict there was a forest of more than 70, and it was possible to cross the town by rooftop rather than by road. The towers were built partly for defensive purposes—they were a safe refuge and useful for hurling stones on attackers—and partly for bolstering the egos of their owners, who competed with deadly seriousness to build the highest tower in town.

The relative proximity of San Gimignano, arguably Tuscany's best-preserved medieval hill town, to Siena and Florence also makes it one of Italy's most-visited places. But the traffic is hardly a new problem: the Etruscans were encamped here, and the Romans made it an outpost. With the yearly flow of pilgrims to and from Rome in the Middle Ages, the town—then known as Castel di Selva—became a prosperous market center. When locals prayed to a martyred bishop from Modena for relief from invading barbarians, relief they got, and in gratitude they rechristened the town in his honor as San Gimignano.

Devastated by the Black Death of 1348, the town subsequently fell under Florentine control. Things got going again in the Renaissance, with some of the best and brightest painters—Ghirlandaio (1449–94), Benozzo Gozzoli (1420–97), and Pinturicchio (circa 1454–1513)—coming to work, but soon after, the main road was moved, cutting San Gimignano off from the main trade route and sending it into decline.

Today, San Gimignano isn't much more than a gentrified and touristy walled city, but, despite the profusion of cheesy souvenir shops lining the main drag, there's some serious Renaissance art to be seen here. Tour groups arrive early and clog the wine-tasting rooms—San Gimignano is famous for its light white Vernaccia—and art galleries for much of the day, but most sights stay open through late afternoon, when most tour groups have long since departed.

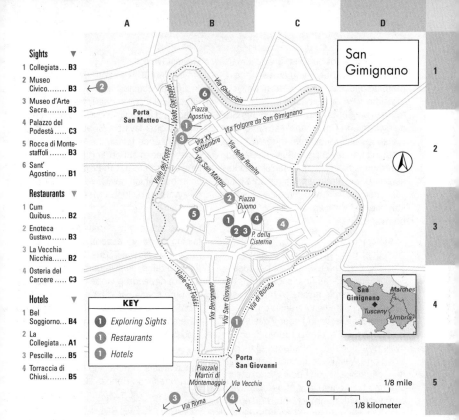

KEY
1 *Exploring Sights*
1 *Restaurants*
1 *Hotels*

San Gimignano

Porta San Matteo

Piazza Agostino

Via Ghiacciaia

Via Folgore da San Gimignano

Via XX Settembre

Via della Romite

Viale Garibaldi

Viale dei Fossi

Via San Matteo

Piazza Duomo

P. della Cisterna

Via Berganna

Via San Giovanni

Via di Bonda

Piazzale Martiri di Montemaggio

Porta San Giovanni

Via Vecchia

Via Roma

San Gimignano

Marches

Tuscany

Umbria

0 ___ 1/8 mile
0 ___ 1/8 kilometer

GETTING HERE

You can reach San Gimignano by car from the Florence–Siena Superstrada. Exit at Poggibonsi Nord and follow signs for San Gimignano. Although it involves changing buses in Poggibonsi, getting to San Gimignano by bus from Florence is a relatively straightforward affair. SITA operates the service between Siena or Florence and Poggibonsi. From Siena, Tra-In offers direct service to San Gimignano several times daily. You cannot reach San Gimignano by train.

VISITOR INFORMATION

CONTACTS San Gimignano Tourism Office.
✉ *Piazza Duomo 1* ☎ *0577/940008*
⊕ *www.sangimignano.com.*

◉ Sights

The center of San Gimignano is closed to traffic. If you arrive by car, park in lots next to the Parco della Rimembranza, near Porta San Giovanni (where all the buses from Florence and Siena stop), the main pedestrian entrance into town. Souvenir shops lining the way leave no doubt about the lifeblood of the town, but better things lie ahead.

Pass under Arco dei Becci, a leftover from the city's Etruscan walls, to Piazza della Cisterna, a square named for the cistern at its center. The Piazza del Duomo, where you'll find the Museo Civico, lies just beyond the two towers built by the Ardinghelli family. Continue along Via San Matteo and turn right just before Porta San Matteo to reach Sant'Agostino.

You can see all of San Gimignano's main sights in a day. But, if you arrive in the morning and leave in the afternoon, you miss the town at its best. From 9 to 5 tourists on jaunts from Florence and Siena swarm San Gimignano's streets, filling the shops and museums. In the evening, when all the day-trippers have departed, the town is transformed. Reclaiming its serenity, San Gimignano takes on a magically medieval air that, if you can possibly stay the night in or near town, is not to be missed.

★ Collegiata

CHURCH | The town's main church is not officially a duomo (cathedral), because San Gimignano has no bishop. But behind the simple facade of the Romanesque Collegiata lies a treasure trove of fine frescoes, covering nearly every wall. Bartolo di Fredi's 14th-century fresco cycle of Old Testament scenes extends along one wall. Their distinctly medieval feel, with misshapen bodies, buckets of spurting blood, and lack of perspective, contrasts with the much more reserved scenes from the Life of Christ (attributed to 14th-century artist Lippo Memmi) painted on the opposite wall just 14 years later.

Taddeo di Bartolo's otherworldly *Last Judgment* (late 14th century), with its distorted and suffering nudes, reveals the great influence of Dante's horrifying imagery in Inferno. Proof that the town had more than one protector, Benozzo Gozzoli's arrow-riddled St. Sebastian was commissioned in gratitude after the locals prayed to the saint for relief from plague. The Cappella di Santa Fina is decorated with a fresco cycle by Domenico Ghirlandaio illustrating the life of St. Fina. ⌧ *Piazza Pecori 1–2, entrance on left side of church, San Gimignano* ☎ *0577/286300* ⊕ *www.duomosangimignano.it* ⌨ *€5* ⊘ *Closed Jan. 1, 15–31, and Nov. 15–30.*

Museo Civico

CASTLE/PALACE | The impressive civic museum occupies what was the "new" Palazzo del Popolo; the Torre Grossa is adjacent. Dante visited San Gimignano for only one day as a Guelph ambassador from Florence to ask the locals to join the Florentines in supporting the pope—just long enough to get the main council chamber, which now holds a 14th-century *Maestà* by Lippo Memmi, named after him.

Off the stairway is a small room containing the racy frescoes by Memmo di Filippuccio (active 1288–1324), depicting the courtship, shared bath, and wedding of a young, androgynous-looking couple. That the space could have been a private room for the commune's chief magistrate may have something to do with the work's highly charged eroticism.

Upstairs, paintings by famous Renaissance artists Pinturicchio (*Madonna Enthroned*) and Benozzo Gozzoli (*Madonna and Child*), and two large *tondi* (circular paintings) by Filippino Lippi (circa 1457–1504) attest to the importance and wealth of San Gimignano. Admission includes the steep climb to the top of the Torre Grossa, which on a clear day has spectacular views. ⌧ *Piazza Duomo 2, San Gimignano* ☎ *0577/990312* ⊕ *www.sangimignanomusei.it* ⌨ *€9 cumulative ticket.*

Museo d'Arte Sacra

ART MUSEUM | Even with all the decoration in the Collegiata, the fine collection of religious articles in the church museum, across the pretty courtyard, is still worth a look. The highlight is a *Madonna and Child* by Bartolo di Fredi. Other pieces include several busts, wooden statues of Christ, the Virgin Mary, and the angel Gabriel, and several illuminated songbooks. ⌧ *Piazza Pecori 4, San Gimignano* ☎ *0577/286300* ⊕ *www.sangimignano.com* ⌨ *€5, includes the Collegiata* ⊘ *Closed Jan. 1, 15–31, Nov. 15–30, and Dec. 25.*

Palazzo del Podestà

CASTLE/PALACE | Across the piazza from the Collegiata is the "old" town hall built in 1239. Its tower was erected by the municipality in 1255 to settle the raging "my-tower-is-bigger-than-your-tower" contest—as you can see, a solution that just didn't last long. The palace is closed to visitors. ⊠ *Piazza Duomo, San Gimignano.*

Rocca di Montestaffoli

GARDEN | If you want to see more of that quintessential Tuscan landscape, walk up to the Rocca di Montestaffoli, which sits at the highest point in San Gimignano. Built after the Florentine conquest to keep an eye on the town, and dismantled a few centuries later, it's now a public garden. ⊠ *Via della Rocca, San Gimignano* ☒ *Free.*

Sant'Agostino

CHURCH | Make a beeline for Benozzo Gozzoli's superlative 15th-century fresco cycle depicting scenes from the life of St. Augustine. The saint's work was essential to the early development of church doctrine. As thoroughly discussed in his autobiographical *Confessions* (an acute dialogue with God), Augustine, like many saints, sinned considerably in his youth before finding God. But unlike the lives of other saints, where the story continues through a litany of deprivations, penitence, and often martyrdom, Augustine's life and work focused on philosophy and the reconciliation of faith and thought.

Benozzo's 17 scenes on the choir wall depict Augustine as a man who traveled and taught extensively in the 4th and 5th centuries. The 15th-century altarpiece by Piero del Pollaiolo (1443–96) depicts *The Coronation of the Virgin* and the various protectors of the city. On your way out of Sant'Agostino, stop in at the Cappella di San Bartolo, with a sumptuously elaborate tomb by Benedetto da Maiano (1442–97). ⊠ *Piazza Sant'Agostino 10, San Gimignano* ⊕ *www.sangimignano. com* ☒ *Free.*

⊗ Restaurants

★ Cum Quibus

$$$ | ITALIAN | This is, without a doubt, one of the region's most creative restaurants—an intimate place with a menu that's Tuscan but not (it's rare to see bok choy incorporated into any dish, but here it's done with élan). Not a step is missed, and although it's possible to order à la carte, most opt for one of the tasting menus. **Known for:** amazing wine list with prices to suit all budgets; incorporation of non-Tuscan ingredients into Tuscan food; two marvelous tasting menus. $ *Average main: €26* ⊠ *Via San Martino 17, San Gimignano* ☎ *0577/943199* ⊕ *www. mktn.it/cumquibus* ☉ *Closed Tues. and Jan. and Feb.*

Enoteca Gustavo

$ | WINE BAR | There's no shortage of places to try Vernaccia di San Gimignano, the justifiably famous white wine with which San Gimignano is often singularly associated. At this wine bar, run by energetic Maristella Becucci, you can buy a glass of Vernaccia di San Gimignano and sit down with a cheese plate or one of the fine crostini. **Known for:** quality products; fine list of wines by the glass; Maristella, who is a force of nature. $ *Average main: €10* ⊠ *Via San Matteo 29, San Gimignano* ☎ *0577/940057* ☉ *Closed Tues.*

La Vecchia Nicchia

$$ | ITALIAN | Though it's still very much in the center, it's far from the madding crowds. Wonderful wines pair beautifully with the tasty morsels served atop toasted bread. **Known for:** locally sourced ingredients; genial hosts; wines by the bottle. $ *Average main: €15* ⊠ *Via San Martino 12, San Gimignano* ☎ *0577/940803* ☉ *Closed Mon.–Thurs.*

Osteria del Carcere

$$ | ITALIAN | Although it calls itself an *osteria* (tavern), this place much more resembles a wine bar, with a bill of fare that includes several different types of pâtés and a short list of seasonal soups

and salads. The sampler of goat cheeses, which can be paired with local wines, should not be missed. **Known for:** housed in a former jail; inventive dishes; excellent chef-proprietor. $ *Average main: €18* ⊠ *Via del Castello 13, San Gimignano* ☎ *0577/941905* ⊘ *Closed Wed. and early Jan.–Mar. No lunch Thurs.*

Hotels

Bel Soggiorno
$$ | B&B/INN | If you're looking for a place within the town walls, this is a fine choice—one where contemporary furnishings in the guest rooms are softened by warm, umber-color walls and floral artwork. **Pros:** inside the ancient walls of San Gimignano; magnificent views; some rooms have small terraces facing the countryside. **Cons:** breakfast costs extra; can be a little noisy if you're street-side; plain decor. $ *Rooms from: €128* ⊠ *Via San Giovanni 91, San Gimignano* ☎ *0577/940375* ⊕ *hotelbelsoggiorno.it* ⊘ *Closed Jan. 7–Feb.* ⇆ *21 rooms* ⭗ *No Meals.*

La Collegiata
$$$ | HOTEL | After serving as a Franciscan convent and then the residence of the noble Strozzi family, the Collegiata has been converted into a fine hotel, with no expense spared in the process. **Pros:** gorgeous views from terrace; wonderful staff; elegant rooms in main building. **Cons:** some rooms are dimly lit; service can be impersonal; long walk into town. $ *Rooms from: €220* ⊠ *Località Strada 27, San Gimignano* ✛ *1 km (½ mile) north of San Gimignano town center* ☎ *0577/943201* ⊕ *www.lacollegiata.it* ⊘ *Closed Nov.–Mar.* ⇆ *20 rooms* ⭗ *Free Breakfast.*

Pescille
$ | B&B/INN | A rambling farmhouse has been transformed into a handsome hotel with understated contemporary furniture in the bedrooms and country-classic motifs such as farm implements hanging on the walls in the bar. **Pros:** splendid views; 10-minute walk to town; quiet atmosphere. **Cons:** a vehicle is a must; there's an elevator for luggage but not for guests; furnishings a bit austere. $ *Rooms from: €120* ⊠ *Località Pescille, San Gimignano* ✛ *4 km (2½ miles) south of San Gimignano* ☎ *0577/940186* ⊕ *www.pescille.it* ⊘ *Closed mid-Oct.– Easter* ⇆ *38 rooms* ⭗ *Free Breakfast.*

Torraccia di Chiusi
$$ | B&B/INN | FAMILY | A perfect retreat for families, this tranquil hilltop *agriturismo* (farm stay) offers simple, comfortably decorated accommodations on extensive grounds 5 km (3 miles) from the hubbub of San Gimignano. **Pros:** great walking possibilities; delightful countryside view; family-run hospitality. **Cons:** might be too remote for some; need a car to get here; 30 minutes from the nearest town on a winding gravel road. $ *Rooms from: €160* ⊠ *Località Montauto, San Gimignano* ☎ *0577/941972* ⊕ *www.torracciadichiusi.it* ⇆ *11 rooms* ⭗ *Free Breakfast.*

Performing Arts

Carnevale
FESTIVALS | San Gimignano is one of the few small towns in the area that make a big deal out of carnival festivities, with locals dressing up in colorful costumes and marching through the streets from 3:30 to 6:30 on the four Sundays preceding Shrove Tuesday. ⊠ *San Gimignano.*

San Gimignano Musica
MUSIC FESTIVALS | If you visit in summer, check with the tourist office about concerts and performances related to San Gimignano's music festival, one of Tuscany's oldest. It's held from late June to September each year. ⊠ *Piazza Duomo 1, San Gimignano* ☎ *0577/940008* ⊕ *www.sangimignano.com.*

🛍 Shopping

★ Antica Latteria di Maurizio e Tiziana
FOOD | FAMILY | Maurizio and Tiziana's shop has an arresting array of cheeses and perhaps the best array of verdure sott'olio in town. They also make top-notch panini, and killer sweets. ✉ Via San Matteo 19, San Gimignano ☎ 0577/941952 ⊕ enotecaanticalatteria. com.

Mercato
MARKET | As everywhere else, the town brightens on mercato (open-air market) mornings, every Thursday and Saturday, in Piazza del Duomo. It's the place to pick up fresh fruits and other snacks. ✉ San Gimignano.

Volterra

30 km (18 miles) southwest of San Gimignano.

As you approach through bleak, rugged terrain, you can see that not all Tuscan hill towns rise above rolling green fields. Volterra stands mightily over Le Balze, a stunning series of gullied hills and valleys formed by erosion that has slowly eaten away at the foundation of the town—now considerably smaller than it was during its Etruscan glory days 25 centuries ago.

Volterra began as the northernmost of the 12 cities that made up the Etruscan League, and excavations in the 18th century revealed a bounty of relics, which are on exhibit at the impressively overstocked Museo Etrusco Guarnacci. The Romans and later the Florentines laid siege to the town to secure its supply of minerals and stones, particularly alabaster, which is still worked into handicrafts on sale in many of the shops around town.

Note that if you happen to be in town on the first Sunday in September, you can experience the Astiludio festival, which celebrates a flag-throwing tradition that dates from 1406. Performances and processions are part of the festivities.

GETTING HERE
By car, the best route from San Gimignano follows the SP1 south to Castel San Gimignano and then the SS68 west to Volterra. Coming from the west, take the SS1, a coastal road to Cecina, then follow the SS68 east to Volterra. Either way, there's a long, winding climb at the end of your trip.

Traveling to Volterra by bus or train is complicated; avoid it if possible, especially if you have lots of luggage. From Florence or Siena the bus journey involves a change in Colle di Val d'Elsa. From Rome or Pisa, you can take a train to Cecina and then a bus to Volterra or a train to the Volterra-Saline station. The latter is 10 km (6 miles) from town.

VISITOR INFORMATION
CONTACTS Volterra Tourism Office. ✉ Piazza dei Priori 10 ☎ 0588/86150 ⊕ www. provolterra.it.

Sights

Driving in the old town is forbidden. There are several parking areas around the perimeter of the city walls, the most convenient of which is the underground lot at Piazza Martiri della Libertà. Begin your exploration of Volterra from Piazza Martiri della Libertà and take Via Marchesi to Piazza dei Priori. It's lined with an impressive collection of medieval buildings, including the imposing Palazzo dei Priori, the seat of city government for more than seven centuries.

Across the piazza is the Palazzo Pretorio topped by the Torre del Porcellino, named after the sculpted little boar mounted at the upper window. Walk down Via Turazza along the side of the Duomo to the triangular Piazza San Giovanni, and head out the left corner of the piazza to steal a look at the ancient Porta all'Arco Etrusco.

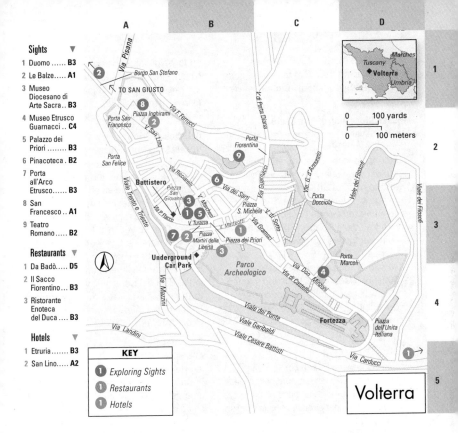

KEY

1 Exploring Sights
1 Restaurants
1 Hotels

Volterra

Although Volterra makes a good stopover, you can explore much of it in a half-day. Off-season, it's best to start early so there's time to see the museums before they close.

Duomo

CHURCH | Behind the textbook 13th-century Pisan–Romanesque facade is proof that Volterra counted for something during the Renaissance, when many important Tuscan artists came to decorate the church. Three-dimensional stucco portraits of local saints are on the gold, red, and blue ceiling (1580) designed by Francesco Capriani, including St. Linus, the successor to St. Peter as pope and claimed by the Volterrans to have been born here.

The highlight of the Duomo is the brightly painted, 13th-century, wooden, life-size *Deposition* in the chapel of the same name. The unusual Cappella dell'Addolorata (Chapel of the Grieved) has two terra-cotta Nativity scenes; the depiction of the arrival of the Magi has a background fresco by Benozzo Gozzoli. ✉ *Piazza San Giovanni, Volterra.*

Le Balze

NATURE SIGHT | Walk along Via San Lino, through Porta San Francesco, and out Borgo Santo Stefano into Le Balze—a haunting, undulating landscape of yellow earth drawn into crags and gullies that's thought to be the result of rainwater wearing down the soil substructure. This area was originally part of the Etruscan town of Velathri, as evidenced by walls that extend 1 km (½ mile) toward the old Porta Menseri. Toward the end of the road, on the right, is the church of San Giusto (with terra-cotta statues of the town's patron saints) built to replace an earlier church under which the earth had eroded. The bus for Borgo San Giusto, leaving from Piazza Martiri, goes through Le Balze (about 10 runs per day). ⊠ *Volterra.*

Museo Diocesano di Arte Sacra

ART MUSEUM | The religious-art collection housed in the Bishop's Palace was collected from local churches and includes an unusual reliquary by Antonio Pollaiolo with the head of St. Octavian in silver resting on four golden lions. There's also a fine terra-cotta bust of St. Linus by Andrea della Robbia (1435–1525/28). Two paintings are noteworthy: Rosso Fiorentino's (1495–1540) *Madonna di Villamagna* and Daniele da Volterra's (1509–66) *Madonna di Ulignano,* named for the village churches in which they were originally placed. ⊠ *Via Roma 13, Palazzo Vescovile, Volterra* ☎ *0588/87733* ⊕ *www.comune.volterra.pi.it* ✉ *€5* ⊘ *Closed Mon.*

★ Museo Etrusco Guarnacci

HISTORY MUSEUM | An extraordinary collection of Etruscan relics is made all the more interesting by clear explanations in English. The bulk of the collection is comprised of roughly 700 carved funerary urns. The oldest, dating from the 7th century BC, were made from tufa (volcanic rock). A handful are made of terra-cotta, but most—dating from the 3rd to 1st century BC—are done in alabaster. The urns are grouped by subject, and, taken together, they form a fascinating testimony about Etruscan life and death.

Some illustrate domestic scenes, others the funeral procession of the deceased. Greek gods and mythology, adopted by the Etruscans, also figure prominently. The sculpted figures on many of the covers may have been made in the image of the deceased, reclining and often holding the cup of life overturned. Particularly well known is *Gli Sposi* (Husband and Wife), a haunting, elderly duo in terra-cotta. The *Ombra della Sera* (Evening Shadow)—an enigmatic bronze statue of an elongated, pencil-thin male

nude—highlights the collection. Also on display are Attic vases, bucchero ceramics, jewelry, and household items. ⊠ *Via Don Minzoni 15, Volterra* ☎ *0588/86347* ⊕ *www.comune.volterra.pi.it* ✉ *From €8.*

Palazzo dei Priori

NOTABLE BUILDING | Tuscany's first town hall, built between 1208 and 1254, has a no-nonsense facade, fortress-like crenellations, and a five-sided tower. It later served as a model for other town halls throughout the region, including Florence's Palazzo Vecchio. The medallions that adorn the facade were added after the Florentines conquered Volterra. The town leaders still meet on the first floor in the Sala del Consiglio, which is open to the public and has a mid-14th-century fresco of the *Annunciation.* ⊠ *Piazza dei Priori 1, Volterra* ☎ *0588/86099* ✉ *€3.*

Pinacoteca

ART MUSEUM | One of Volterra's best-looking Renaissance buildings contains an impressive collection of Tuscan paintings arranged chronologically on two floors. Head straight for Room 12, with Luca Signorelli's (circa 1445–1523) *Madonna and Child with Saints* and Rosso Fiorentino's later *Deposition.* Though painted just 30 years apart, they illustrate the shift in style from the early 16th-century Renaissance ideals to full-blown mannerism: the balance of Signorelli's composition becomes purposefully skewed in Fiorentino's painting, where the colors go from vivid but realistic to emotively bright. Other important paintings in the small museum include Ghirlandaio's *Apotheosis of Christ with Saints* and a polyptych of the *Madonna and Saints* by Taddeo di Bartolo, which once hung in the Palazzo dei Priori. ⊠ *Via dei Sarti 1, Volterra* ☎ *0588/87580* ⊕ *www.comune. volterra.pi.it* ✉ *From €8.*

Porta all'Arco Etrusco

RUINS | Even if a good portion of the arch was rebuilt by the Romans, three dark, weather-beaten, 4th-century-BC heads (thought to represent Etruscan gods) still

Volterra's Porta all'Arco Etrusco

face outward to greet those who enter
here. A plaque on the outer wall recalls
the efforts of the locals who saved the
arch from destruction by filling it with
stones during the German withdrawal
at the end of World War II. ⊠ *Via Porta
all'Arco, Volterra.*

San Francesco

CHURCH | Look inside the church for the
celebrated early-15th-century frescoes of
the *Legend of the True Cross* by a local
artist. It traces the history of the wood
used to make the cross upon which
Christ was crucified. From Piazza San
Giovanni, take Via Franceschini (which
becomes Via San Lino) to the church.
⊠ *Piazza Inghirami, Volterra* ⊕ *Off Via San
Lino.*

Teatro Romano

RUINS | Just outside the walls, past Porta
Fiorentina, are the ruins of the 1st-cen-
tury-BC Roman theater, one of the best
preserved in Italy, with adjacent remains
of the Roman *terme* (baths). You can
enjoy an excellent bird's-eye view of the
theater from Via Lungo le Mura. ⊠ *Viale

Francesco Ferrucci, Volterra* 🎫 *€13
⊙ Closed weekdays Nov.–Mar.*

 **Restaurants**

Da Badò

$ | TUSCAN | Family-run Da Badò—with
Lucia in the kitchen and her sons, Giacomo and Michele, waiting tables—is the
best place in town to eat traditional food
elbow-to-elbow with locals. Lucia likes
to concentrate on just a few dishes, so
it won't take long to decide between the
standards, all prepared with a sure hand.
Known for: local favorite; small menu;
excellent traditional dishes. 💲 *Average
main: €14* ⊠ *Borgo San Lazzaro 9, Volterra* 🕾 *0588/80402* ⊕ *www.trattoriadabado.
com* ⊙ *Closed Wed.*

Il Sacco Fiorentino

$$ | TUSCAN | This lovely trattoria has been
around for a long time, and with good
reason. Here, they turn out Tuscan classics, relying heavily on the local cheese
(pecorino) and local meats (especially
wild boar, among others). **Known for:**

248

excellent wine list; tranquil setting; three well-priced tasting menus. $ *Average main: €16* ⊠ *Via Giusto Turazza 13, Volterra* ☎ *0588/88537* ☻ *Closed Wed.*

★ Ristorante Enoteca del Duca
$$ | **ITALIAN** | Although this restaurant is on a tiny side street and can be easy to miss, do try to find it, as it serves fantastic food, with dishes listed on the seasonal menu under "L'Innovazione" (Innovations, usually, on classics) or "La Tradizione" (Tradition). Adventurous eaters should try such flights of fancy *bavarese di fegato,* which comes adorned with pomegranate seeds and redefines chicken liver pâté. **Known for:** seasonal fare; superb staff; well-culled wine list. $ *Average main: €20* ⊠ *Via di Castello 2, Volterra* ☎ *0588/81510* ⊕ *www.enoteca-delduca-ristorante.it* ☻ *Closed Tues.*

Hotels

Etruria
$ | **B&B/INN** | The rooms are modest, and there's no elevator, but the central location, the ample buffet breakfast, and the modest rates make this a good choice for those on a budget. **Pros:** great central location; tranquil garden with rooftop views; friendly staff. **Cons:** no elevator; books up quickly as it's good value; some rooms can be noisy during the day. $ *Rooms from: €93* ⊠ *Via Matteotti 32, Volterra* ☎ *0588/87377* ⊕ *albergoetruria. it* ☻ *Closed Jan. and Feb.* 🛏 *15 rooms* ⭤ *Free Breakfast.*

San Lino
$ | **HOTEL** | Within the town's medieval walls, this convent-turned-hotel has wood-beam ceilings, graceful archways, and terra-cotta floors, with nice contemporary furnishings and ironwork in the rooms. **Pros:** steps from center of town; convenient parking; friendly and helpful staff. **Cons:** though in the center, somewhat removed from things; books up quickly; rooms facing the street can be noisy. $ *Rooms from: €89* ⊠ *Via San*

Lino 26, Volterra ☎ *0588/85250* ⊕ *www. hotelsanlino.net* ☻ *Closed Nov.–Feb.* 🛏 *43 rooms* ⭤ *No Meals.*

Shopping

Anna Maria Molesini
CRAFTS | A large loom dominates this tiny workshop and showroom where scarves, shawls, throws, and jackets are woven. Anna Maria's work, mostly in mohair, is done in lively hues. ⊠ *Via Gramsci 45, Volterra* ☎ *0588/88411* ⊕ *www.arteinbottegavolterra.it.*

Camillo Rossi
CRAFTS | At Camillo Rossi, which has been around since 1912, you can watch artisans create household items in alabaster and then buy their wares. ⊠ *Piazza della Peschiera 3, Volterra* ☎ *0588/86133* ⊕ *www.rossialabastri.com.*

Cooperativa Artieri Alabastro
CRAFTS | Since 1895, two large showrooms here are housed in medieval buildings and contain a large number of alabaster objects for sale, including bookends, ashtrays, and boxes. ⊠ *Piazza dei Priori 5, Volterra* ☎ *0588/87590* ⊕ *www. artierialabastro.it.*

Mercato (*Market*)
MARKET | Volterra's market is held on Saturday morning from November to April in Piazza dei Priori and from May through October on Viale Ferrucci (just outside the city walls). In addition to fresh fruits and vegetables, vendors selling everything from corkscrews to *intimi* (underwear). ⊠ *Volterra.*

Chapter 6

AREZZO, CORTONA, AND EASTERN TUSCANY

Updated by
Patricia Rucidlo

 Sights
★★★★★

 Restaurants
★★★★☆

 Hotels
★★★☆☆

 Shopping
★☆☆☆☆

 Nightlife
★☆☆☆☆

WELCOME TO AREZZO, CORTONA, AND EASTERN TUSCANY

TOP REASONS TO GO

★ **Driving through the Parco Nazionale Casentino:** The vistas along the winding road of this park in the Casentino will not disappoint.

★ **Piero della Francesca's True Cross frescoes:** If your Holy Grail is great Renaissance art, seek out these 12 silently enigmatic scenes in Arezzo's Basilica di San Francesco.

★ **Santa Maria al Calcinaio:** The interior of this Cortona church is much like that of Florence's Duomo, and it's a prime example of Renaissance architecture.

★ **Shopping for jewelry in Arezzo:** Gold has been part of Arezzo's economy since Etruscan times, and today the town is well known worldwide for jewelry design.

The hill towns of Arezzo and Cortona are the main attractions of eastern Tuscany; despite their appeal, this part of the region gets less tourist traffic than its neighbors to the west. You'll truly escape the crowds if you venture north to the Casentino, which is backwoods Tuscany—tiny towns and abbeys are sprinkled through beautiful forestland, some of which is set aside as a national park.

1 **Arezzo.** Tuscany's third-largest city.

2 **Cortona.** This ancient stone town was made famous by the book *Under the Tuscan Sun.*

3 **Sansepolcro.** The birthplace of Piero della Francesca.

4 **Parco Nazionale Casentino.** A stunning National Park.

5 **Sacro Eremo E Monastero Di Camaldoli.** Monks live in silence in 20 cottages at this hermitage.

6 **Santuario Della Verna.** This sanctuary was founded by Saint Francis.

Loro Ciufenn

San Giovanni

Montevarchi

Bucine

Siena

| 0 | | 10 mi |
| 0 | | 10 km |

Closer to Italy's rugged Apennines than any other part of the region, eastern Tuscany hides its secrets in the valleys of the upper Arno and Tiber rivers and among mountains covered with forests of chestnut, fir, and beech. This is where Michelangelo saw the first light of day and St. Francis founded a sanctuary and received the signs of Christ's wounds.

The region attracts those seeking an experience far from the madding crowd. One of Tuscany's best "off-the-beaten-path" experiences, Parco Nazionale Casentino beckons, with mountain scenery that has been safeguarded by monks for eight centuries. Anchoring the area are the hill towns of Arezzo and Cortona, both of which carry on age-old local traditions. Each June and September, for example, Arezzo's Romanesque and Gothic churches are enlivened by the Giostra del Saracino, a medieval pageant.

Since ancient times, Arezzo has been home to important artists: from the Etruscan potters who produced those fiery-red vessels to the poet Petrarch and the writer, architect, and painter Giorgio Vasari. Cortona, magnificently situated, with olive groves and vineyards creeping up to its walls, commands sweeping views over Lago Trasimeno and the plain of the Valdichiana. The medieval streets are a pleasure to wander, and the town has galleries and churches that are worth a visit.

MAJOR REGIONS

Arezzo. Tuscany's third-largest city feels a touch more cosmopolitan than the neighboring hill towns—meaning, among other things, that it has the best shopping in the region. The real draw, though, is the Basilica di San Francesco, adorned with frescoes by Piero della Francesca.

Cortona. This ancient stone town, made famous by the book *Under the Tuscan Sun,* sits high above the perfectly flat Valdichiana Valley, offering great views of beautiful countryside.

Sansepolcro. Lovers of Renaissance painting make pilgrimages to out-of-the-way Sansepolcro, birthplace of Piero della Francesca. He often worked in or near his hometown, finding inspiration for the landscapes in his often enigmatic paintings.

The Casentino. A short distance north of Arezzo, the Casentino region is highlighted by the Parco Nazionale Casentino—a drive through it reveals one gorgeous view after another. Dante, exiled here from Florence, recorded his love of the countryside in *The Divine Comedy.*

Planning

Getting Here and Around

BUS

Baschetti. The bus company provides regular service between Arezzo and Sansepolcro. ☎ *0575/749816 in Sansepolcro* ⊕ *www.baschetti.it.*

Etruria Mobilità. All bus service in the province of Arezzo is coordinated by Etruria Mobilità, a cooperative of seven different transport companies, including BUSITALIA and Baschetti; it's the best source for information about bus service to outlying towns in the region. ☎ *0575/39881 in Arezzo* ⊕ *www.etruria-mobilita.it.*

CAR

The best way to travel within the region, making it possible to explore tiny hill towns and country restaurants, is by car. The roads are better north–south than east–west, so allow time for excessively winding roads when heading east or west. Sometimes it's faster to go out of your way and get on one of the bigger north–south routes.

The A1 highway, which runs from Florence to Rome, passes close to Arezzo. Cortona is just off the main road linking Perugia to the A1, and Sansepolcro can be reached from Arezzo on the SR73, with Monterchi a short 3-km (2-mile) detour along the way.

Though Arezzo is the third-largest city in Tuscany (after Florence and Pisa), the old town is small, and is on a low hill almost completely closed to traffic. Look for parking along the roads that circle the lower part of town, near the train station, and walk up into town from there.

In Cortona, the city center is completely closed to traffic and the few parking areas sprinkled outside the city walls don't make it easy to park. The majority of Cortona's streets are steep. Fortunately, most of the main sights are grouped near the Duomo in the lower part of town, but if you want to visit the upper town, be prepared for a stiff climb.

For visits to the mountainous National Park of the Casentino and the smaller towns and villages farther to the east, such as Sansepolcro and Monterchi, a car is almost a necessity: bus schedules can be difficult to plan around, and train service is either infrequent or nonexistent. All make for rewarding day trips, though a fair part of your time will be spent on winding, beautiful, country roads. If you want time to explore, plan to stay the night.

TRAIN

Trenitalia. The national railway system provides frequent trains between Florence and Arezzo. A regular service also links Arezzo with Cortona, and with Poppi and the Casentino. ☎ *892021 within Italy* ⊕ *www.trenitalia.com.*

Making the Most of Your Time

Plan on allowing a good four days to tour the area. Arezzo and Cortona each merit a full day, and if you stay in the vicinity of either, you'll have a good base from which to explore the countryside. Both towns are close to the A1 (Autostrada del Sole) and are on main train lines.

Hotels

A visit to Tuscany is a trip to the country. There are good hotels in Arezzo and Cortona, but for a classic experience stay in one of the rural accommodations—often converted villas, sometimes working farms or vineyards (known as *agriturismi*).

Hotel and restaurant reviews have been shortened. For full information, visit Fodors.com. Hotel prices are the lowest cost of a standard double room in high season. Restaurant prices are the average cost of a main course at dinner or, if dinner is not served, at lunch.

WHAT IT COSTS in Euros

$	$$	$$$	$$$$
RESTAURANTS			
under €15	€15–€24	€25–€35	over €35
HOTELS			
under €125	€125–€200	€201–€300	over €300

Arezzo

71 km 44 miles) northwest of Siena, 77 km (48 miles) southeast of Florence.

Arezzo is best known for the magnificent Piero della Francesca frescoes in the church of San Francesco. It's also the birthplace of the poet Petrarch (1304–74), the Renaissance artist and art historian Giorgio Vasari, and Guido d'Arezzo (aka Guido Monaco), the inventor of contemporary musical notation.

The city dates from pre-Etruscan times: the first settlers erected a cluster of huts here in around 1000 BC. Arezzo thrived as an Etruscan capital from the 7th to the 4th century BC, and it was one of the most important cities in the Etruscans' anti-Roman 12-city federation, resisting Rome's rule to the last.

Arezzo eventually fell and, in turn, flourished under the Romans. In 1248, Guglielmino degli Ubertini, a member of the powerful Ghibellines, was elected bishop of Arezzo. This sent the city headlong into the enduring conflict between the Ghibellines (pro-emperor) and the Guelphs (pro-pope). In 1289, Florentine Guelphs defeated Arezzo in a famous battle at Campaldino. Among the Florentine soldiers was Dante Alighieri (1265–1321), who often referred to Arezzo in his *Divine Comedy*. Guelph–Ghibelline wars

continued to plague the city until the end of the 14th century, when it lost its independence to Florence.

GETTING HERE

Arezzo is easily reached by car from the A1, the main highway running between Florence and Rome. Direct trains connect Arezzo with Rome (2½ hours) and Florence (1 hour). Direct bus service is available from Florence but not from Rome.

VISITOR INFORMATION

CONTACTS Arezzo Tourism Office. ⊠ *Piazza Libertà 1* ☎ *0575/377678* ⊕ *www.arezzointuscany.it.*

Sights

Sitting on a low hill in a wide plain, Arezzo, especially the bell tower of its Duomo, is visible from afar. Surrounding the older town is an area of urban sprawl. As you begin to walk along the narrow pedestrian streets inside the walls, however, the standard stores of the lower town are gradually replaced by the exclusive antiques and jewelry shops for which Arezzo is known, and the anonymous buildings of the new town give way to Renaissance town palaces, Romanesque and Gothic churches, and the medieval squares of the upper town—all of which is crowned, quite naturally, by the Duomo itself.

Anfiteatro Romano

RUINS | Periodic excavations since 1950 have brought to light segments of Arezzo's Roman amphitheater, which was probably built during the early 2nd century AD. The entire perimeter has been exposed, and you can see some of the entrance passages and the structures that supported the amphitheater's central arena. The ticket price includes admission to the Museo Archeologico. ⊠ *Via Margaritone 10, Arezzo* ☎ *0575/20882* ⊕ *www. polomusealetoscana.beniculturali.it* 🎫 *€6* 🕐 *Closed Wed. and Thurs. and Sat.–Mon.*

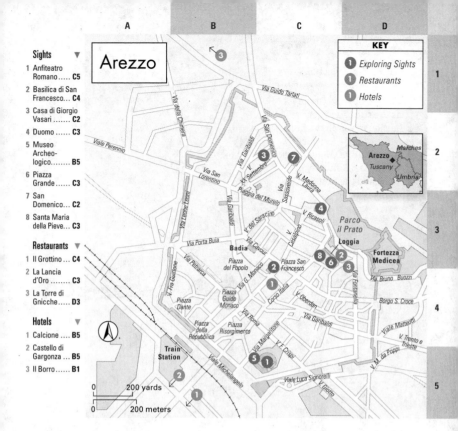

★ Basilica di San Francesco

CHURCH | The famous Piero della Francesca frescoes depicting *The Legend of the True Cross* (1452–66) were executed on the three walls of the Capella Bacci, the apse of this 14th-century church. What Sir Kenneth Clark called "the most perfect morning light in all Renaissance painting" may be seen in the lowest section of the right wall, where the troops of Emperor Maxentius flee before the sign of the cross. Reservations are recommended June through September. ⊠ Piazza San Francesco 2, Arezzo ☎ 0575/352727 ⊕ www.pierodellafrancesca-ticketoffice.it ⊠ €8.

Casa di Giorgio Vasari

HISTORIC HOME | Giorgio Vasari (1511–74), the region's leading Mannerist artist, architect, and art historian, designed and decorated this house after he bought it in 1540. He ended up not spending much time here, since he and his wife moved to Florence in 1554. Today, the building houses archives on Vasari, as well as works by the artist and his peers. In the first room, which Vasari called the "Triumph of Virtue Room," a richly ornamented wooden ceiling shows Virtue combating Envy and Fortune in a central octagon. ⊠ Via XX Settembre 55, Arezzo ☎ 0575/409048 ⊕ www.polomusealetoscana.beniculturali.it ⊠ €4.

Duomo

CHURCH | Arezzo's medieval cathedral at the top of the hill contains a fresco of a tender *Maria Maddalena* by Piero della Francesca (1420–92); look for it in the north aisle next to the large marble tomb near the organ. Construction of the Duomo began in 1278 but twice came to a halt, and the church wasn't completed

until 1510. The ceiling decorations and the stained-glass windows date from the 16th century. The facade, designed by Arezzo's Dante Viviani, was added later (1901–14). ⊠ *Piazza del Duomo 1, Arezzo* ⊕ *www.diocesi.arezzo.it.*

Museo Archeologico
HISTORY MUSEUM | The Archaeological Museum in the Convento di San Bernardo, just outside the Anfiteatro Romano, exhibits a fine collection of Etruscan bronzes. The ticket allows admission to the Anfiteatro Romano. ⊠ *Via Margaritone 10, Arezzo* ☎ *0575/20882* ⊕ *www.polomusealetoscana.beniculturali.it* 🔊 *€6* ⌚ *Closed Wed. and Fri.–Sun.*

Piazza Grande
PLAZA/SQUARE | With its irregular shape and sloping brick pavement, framed by buildings of assorted centuries, Arezzo's central piazza echoes Siena's Piazza del Campo. Though not quite so magnificent, it's lively enough during the outdoor antiques fair the first weekend of the month and when the Giostra del Saracino (Saracen Joust), featuring medieval costumes and competition, is held here on the third Saturday of June and on the first Sunday of September. ⊠ *Piazza Grande, Arezzo.*

San Domenico
CHURCH | Inside the northern city walls, this church was begun by Dominican friars in 1275 and completed in the 14th century. The walls were once completely frescoed and decorated with niches and chapels. Very little remains of the original works, but a famous 13th-century crucifix by Cimabue (circa 1240–1302) and frescoes by Spinello Aretino (1350–1410) still survive. ⊠ *Piazza San Domenico 7, Arezzo* ☎ *0575/22906.*

Santa Maria della Pieve (Church of Saint Mary of the Parish)
CHURCH | The curving, tiered apse on Piazza Grande belongs to a church that was originally an early Christian structure— itself constructed over the remains of a

Roman temple. The church was rebuilt in Romanesque style in the 12th century. The splendid facade dates from the early 13th century but includes granite Roman columns. A magnificent polyptych, depicting the Madonna and Child with four saints, by Pietro Lorenzetti (circa 1290–1348), embellishes the high altar. ⊠ *Corso Italia 7, Arezzo.*

Restaurants

Il Grottino
$ | **ITALIAN** | **FAMILY** | It's small, but the very cheery staff is only too happy to provide you with wonderful plates of typical Tuscan food. The kitchen stays open a little bit later than most, which makes this a perfect stop after seeing some of the amazing art that Arezzo has to offer. **Known for:** their soups (particularly the truffled potato/fungi); inventive desserts; surprisingly well-composed mixed salads. 🅂 *Average main: €14* ⊠ *Via della Madonna del Prato 1, Arezzo* ☎ *0575/302537.*

La Lancia d'Oro
$$$ | **ITALIAN** | Fantastic food is to be had at this cheery, intimate trattoria with a view of Piazza Grande. An inventive menu has Tuscan classics; other dishes have unusual flavor combinations, and a superb wine list offers great pairings with all the food. **Known for:** desserts; stellar staff; fantastic pastas. 🅂 *Average main: €26* ⊠ *Piazza Grande 18, Arezzo* ☎ *0575/21033* ⊕ *www.ristorantelanci-adoro.it/en* ⌚ *Closed Mon. No dinner Sun.*

La Torre di Gnicche
$ | **ITALIAN** | Wine lovers shouldn't miss this wine bar/eatery, which is just off Piazza Grande and has more than 700 labels on its list. Seasonal traditional dishes, such as *acquacotta del casentino* (porcini mushroom soup) or *baccalà in umido* (salt-cod stew), are served in the simply decorated, vaulted dining room. **Known for:** outdoor seating in warm weather; an ever-changing menu; the

extensive wine list, with many choices by the glass. $ *Average main: €9* ✉ *Piaggia San Martino 8, Arezzo* ☎ *0575/352035* ⊕ *www.latorredignicche.it* ⊘ *Closed Wed. and Jan.*

Hotels

★ Calcione
$ | B&B/INN | FAMILY | This six-century-old family estate (circa 1483) now houses sophisticated rustic lodgings; many of the apartments have open fireplaces, and the stone houses have a private pool (the rest share the estate pool). **Pros:** houses can sleep up to 17; quiet, beautiful, remote setting; private lakes for fishing and windsurfing. **Cons:** minimum two- to five-night stay in warmer months; no air-conditioning; private transportation is a must—nearest village is 8 km (5 miles) away. $ *Rooms from: €120* ✉ *Località Il Calcione 102, Lucignano* ✛ *26 km (15 miles) southwest of Arezzo* ☎ *0575/837153* ⊕ *www.castellodelcalcione.com* ⤳ *30 rooms* ⦿ *No Meals.*

★ Castello di Gargonza
$$ | HOTEL | FAMILY | Enchantment reigns at this tiny 13th-century countryside hamlet, part of the fiefdom of the aristocratic Florentine Guicciardini family and reinvented by the modern Count Roberto Guicciardini. **Pros:** romantic, one-of-a-kind accommodation in a medieval castle; on-site restaurant; peaceful, isolated setting. **Cons:** private transportation is a necessity; a little out of the way for exploring the region; standard rooms are extremely basic. $ *Rooms from: €180* ✉ *SR73, Monte San Savino* ✛ *32 km (19 miles) southwest of Arezzo* ☎ *0575/847021* ⊕ *gargonza.it* ⊘ *Closed 2nd week of Jan.–Mar.* ⤳ *47 rooms* ⦿ *No Meals.*

★ Il Borro
$$$$ | HOTEL | The location has been described as "heaven on earth," and a stay at this elegant Ferragamo estate—situated near a medieval village and with accommodations that include a 10-bedroom villa (rented out as a single unit) that was once a luxurious hunting lodge—is sure to bring similar descriptions to mind. **Pros:** exceptional service; unique setting and atmosphere; great location for exploring eastern Tuscany. **Cons:** very expensive; not all suites have country views; off the beaten track, making private transport a must. $ *Rooms from: €495* ✉ *Località Il Borro 1* ✛ *Outside village of San Giustino Valdarno, 20 km (12 miles) northwest of Arezzo* ☎ *055/977053* ⊕ *www.ilborro.it* ⊘ *Closed Dec.–Mar.* ⤳ *61 rooms* ⦿ *Free Breakfast.*

Shopping

Ever since Etruscan goldsmiths set up their shops here more than 2,000 years ago, Arezzo has been famous for its jewelry. Today the town lays claim to being one of the world's capitals of jewelry design and manufacture, and you can find an impressive display of big-time baubles in the town center's shops. Arezzo is also famous for its antiques dealers.

ANTIQUES
The first weekend of every month, between 8:30 and 5:30 each day, a colorful market selling antiques and not-so-antiques takes place in the town's main square, Piazza Grande.

JEWELRY
Mariasole Gioielli
JEWELRY & WATCHES | Precious gems, pearls, and coral in fanciful floral settings are offered here. ✉ *Corso Italia 51, Arezzo* ☎ *0575/24771* ⊕ *mariasolegioielli.com.*

Cortona

30 km (19 miles) southeast of Arezzo,
105 km (65 miles) southeast of Florence.

Made popular by Frances Mayes's book
Under the Tuscan Sun and film of the
same name, Cortona is no longer the
destination of just a few specialist art
historians and those seeking reprieve
from busier tourist venues. The main
street, Via Nazionale, is now lined with
souvenir shops and fills with crowds
during summer.

Though the main sights make braving Cortona's bustling center worthwhile, much of
the town's charm lies in its maze of quiet
backstreets. It's here that you will see laun-
dry hanging from windows, find children
playing, and catch the smell of simmering
pasta sauce. Wander off the beaten track
and you won't be disappointed.

Cortona is called "Mother of Troy and
Grandmother of Rome" in popular
speech, and it may be one of Italy's
oldest towns. Tradition claims it was
founded by Dardanus, the founder of Troy
(after whom the Dardanelles are named).
He was fighting a local tribe, the story
goes, when he lost his helmet (*corythos*
in Greek) on Cortona's hill. In time, a
town grew up that took its name (Corito)
from the missing headgear.

By the 4th century BC, the Etruscans
had built town walls, the traces of which
can still be seen in the 3-km (2-mile)
sweep of the present fortifications. As a
member of the Etruscans' 12-city league,
Cortona became one of the federation's
leading northern cities. The area's major
road, the Via Cassia, passed the foot of
Cortona's hill, maintaining the town's
importance under the Romans.

Medieval fortunes waned, however, as the
plain below reverted to marsh. After holding out against Perugia, Arezzo, and Siena,
Cortona was captured by King Ladislas of
Naples in 1409 and sold to the Florentines.

GETTING HERE

Cortona is easily reached by car from
the A1 highway. Take the Valdichiana exit
toward Perugia, then follow signs for
Cortona.

Regular bus service, provided by Etruria
Mobilità, is available between Arezzo
and Cortona (one hour). Train service to
Cortona is made inconvenient by the
location of the train station, in the valley
3 km (2 miles) steeply below the town
itself. From there, you have to rely on bus
or taxi service to get up to Cortona.

VISITOR INFORMATION

CONTACTS Cortona Tourism Office. ⊠ *Piaz-*
za Signorelli 9, Cortona ☎ *0575/637223*
⊕ *www.comunedicortona.it.*

Sights

Duomo

CHURCH | Cortona's cathedral stands on
an edge of the city, next to what's left of
the Etruscan and medieval walls. Built
on the site of a Romanesque church, the
present Renaissance church was begun
in 1480 and finished in 1507. An arcade
along the outside wall was erected in the
16th century. The interior, a mixture of
Renaissance and baroque styles, features
an exquisite 1664 baroque tabernacle
on the high altar by Francesco Mazzuoli.
⊠ *Piazza Duomo 1, Cortona.*

Museo Diocesano

ART MUSEUM | Housed in part of the orig-
inal cathedral structure, this nine-room
museum has an impressive number of
large, splendid paintings by native son
Luca Signorelli (1445–1523), as well as a
delightful *Annunciation* by Fra Angelico
(1387/1400–55). The church was built
between 1498 and 1505 and restructured by Giorgio Vasari in 1543. Frescoes depicting sacrifices from the Old
Testament by Doceno (1508–56), based
on designs by Vasari, line the walls. ⊠ *Pi-*
azza Duomo 1, Cortona ☎ *0575/62830*
⊕ *www.cortonamia.com* ✏ *€6* ☉ *Closed*
Mon.

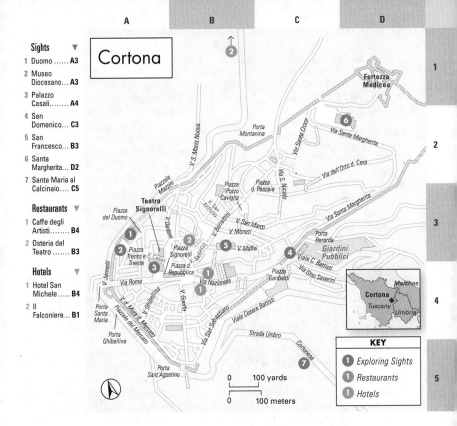

Sights ▼

1 Duomo **A3**
2 Museo Diocesano... **A3**
3 Palazzo Casali........ **A4**
4 San Domenico... **C3**
5 San Francesco... **B3**
6 Santa Margherita... **D2**
7 Santa Maria al Calcinaio.... **C5**

Restaurants ▼

1 Caffe degli Artisti........ **B4**
2 Osteria del Teatro **B3**

Hotels ▼

1 Hotel San Michele **B4**
2 Il Falconiere... **B1**

Palazzo Casali

ART MUSEUM | Built by the Casali family, who lived here until 1409, this palace is home to the Accademia Etrusca, with an extensive library, La Biblioteca Comunale, and the Museo dell'Accademia Etrusca e della Città di Cortona (aka MAEC). An eclectic mix of Egyptian objects, Etruscan and Roman bronzes and statuettes, and paintings is on display in the museum. Perhaps the most famous piece is the Tabula Cortonensis, an Etruscan contract written on bronze that was found in 1922 and dates from the second century BC. Look for work by Renaissance artists such as Luca Signorelli and Pinturicchio (circa 1454–1513). From May through September, guided tours are available in English with prior arrangement. ⊠ *Piazza Signorelli 9, Cortona* ☎ *0575/630415* ⊕ *www.cortonamaec.org* ⊜ *€10* ⊗ *Closed Mon. Nov.–Mar.*

San Domenico

CHURCH | Inside this rather nondescript 14th-century church, just outside Cortona's walls, is an altarpiece depicting the *Coronation of the Virgin* against a sparkling gold background by Lorenzo di Niccolò Gerini (active late 14th–early 15th century). Among the other works is a *Madonna and Child* by Luca Signorelli. ⊠ *Largo Beato Angelico 1, Cortona* ☎ *0575/603217.*

San Francesco

CHURCH | In the mid-13th century, this Gothic-style church was built on the site of Etruscan and Roman baths. It is decorated with frescoes that date from 1382 and a 17th-century crucifix by Giuseppe Piamontini of Florence. It also houses a relic of the Santa Croce, a vestige of the True Cross apparently given to Brother Elia when he served as an envoy for Federico II in Constantinople. The church's rather beautiful organ was unfortunately badly damaged during World War II. ✉ *Via Berrettini 4, Cortona* ☎ *0575/603205.*

Santa Margherita

CHURCH | The large 1897 basilica was constructed over the foundation of a 13th-century church dedicated to the same saint. What makes the 10-minute uphill walk worthwhile is the richly decorated interior. The body of the 13th-century St. Margherita—clothed but with skull and bare feet clearly visible—is displayed in a case on the main altar. ✉ *Piazzale Santa Margherita 1, Cortona* ☎ *0575/603116.*

Santa Maria al Calcinaio

CHURCH | Legend has it that the image of the Madonna appeared on a wall of a medieval *calcinaio* (lime pit used for curing leather), the site on which the church was then built between 1485 and 1513. The linear gray-and-white interior recalls Florence's Duomo. Sienese architect Francesco di Giorgio (1439–1502) most likely designed the sanctuary: the church is a terrific example of Renaissance architectural principles. ✉ *Località Il Calcinaio 227, Cortona* ✥ *3 km (2 miles) southeast of Cortona's center.*

🍴 Restaurants

Caffe degli Artisti

$ | **CAFÉ** | If you need a break from sightseeing, stop here for a cappuccino, sandwiches at lunchtime, or the array of appetizers set out during the cocktail hour. In summer, a few outdoor tables are set up directly on Via Nazionale, Cortona's main pedestrian street, and provide a great perch from which to people-watch. **Known for:** people-watching; perfect for cocktail hour; outdoor dining. [$] *Average main: €6* ✉ *Via Nazionale 18, Cortona* ☎ *0575/601237.*

Osteria del Teatro

$$ | **TUSCAN** | Photographs from theatrical productions spanning many years line the walls of this tavern off Cortona's large Piazza del Teatro. The food is simply delicious—try the *filetto al lardo di colonnata e prugne* (beef cooked with bacon and prunes); service is warm and friendly. **Known for:** pretty dining room; lively atmosphere; food that's in season. [$] *Average main: €20* ✉ *Via Maffei 2, Cortona* ☎ *0575/630556* 🌐 *www.osteria-del-teatro.it* 🕒 *Closed Wed. and 2 wks in Nov.*

🛏 Hotels

Hotel San Michele

$ | **HOTEL** | Cortona might tempt you to step back in time and stay there awhile, and the spacious, beamed, richly furnished rooms in a 15th-century palazzo in the center of town provide the perfect hideaway. **Pros:** lovely surroundings in perfect hill town location; character-filled rooms; excellent service, including valet parking. **Cons:** some street noise; some find it overpriced; limited views from some rooms. [$] *Rooms from: €120* ✉ *Via Guelfa 15, Cortona* ☎ *0575/604348* 🌐 *hotelsanmichele.net* 🛏 *40 rooms* 🍴 *Free Breakfast.*

★ **Il Falconiere**

$$$$ | **B&B/INN** | Accommodation options at this sumptuous property include rooms in an 18th-century villa, suites in the *chiesetta* (chapel, or little church), or for more seclusion, Le Vigne del Falco suites at the far end of the property. **Pros:** elegant, but relaxed; excellent service; attractive setting in the valley beneath Cortona. **Cons:** a car is a must; some find rooms in main villa a little noisy; might be too isolated for some. [$] *Rooms from: €500* ✉ *Località San Martino 370, Cortona* ✥ *3 km (2 miles) north of Cortona* ☎ *0575/612679* 🌐 *www.ilfalconiere.it* 🕒 *Closed Nov.–Jan.* 🛏 *33 rooms* 🍴 *Free Breakfast.*

Shopping

l'Antico Cocciaio
CERAMICS | For nice ceramics, with many pieces depicting the brilliant sunflowers that blanket local fields, check here. ⊠ *Via Benedetti 24, Cortona* ☎ *0575/605294* ⊕ *www.lanticocacciaio.com.*

Sansepolcro

40 km (25 miles) northeast of Arezzo.

Originally called Borgo San Sepolcro (City of the Holy Sepulchre), this sprawling agricultural town takes its name from relics brought here from the Holy Land by two pilgrims in the 10th century. Today, inside a circle of 15th-century walls, the gridded street plan hints at the town's ancient Roman origins. Known as the birthplace of Piero della Francesca—several of his paintings are displayed in the town's Civic Museum—the old center of Sansepolcro retains a distinctly medieval air, with narrow streets lined with churches and 15th-century palaces.

GETTING HERE
From Arezzo, it's better to travel to Sansepolcro by either car or bus than by train, which can take up to four hours. By car, follow the SS73; if traveling by bus (1 hour), check with Etruria Mobilità for the schedule; service is infrequent.

VISITOR INFORMATION
CONTACTS Sansepolcro Tourism Office. ⊠ *Via Matteotti 8, Sansepolcro* ☎ *0575/740536* ⊕ *www.valtiberinaintoscana.it.*

Sights

Duomo
CHURCH | In a combination of Romanesque and Gothic styles, Sansepolcro's cathedral, though somewhat austere, contains some significant works of art. These include the *Volto Santo,* a wooden sculpture of the 9th century, which is believed to be the earliest crucifix depicting a completely clothed Christ on the cross. The *Ascension of Christ,* by Perugino (circa 1448–1523), and its neighbor, an *Assumption of the Virgin,* by Jacopo Palma the Younger (circa 1550–1628) are also highlights. ⊠ *Via Matteotti 1–3.*

Monterchi
TOWN | This sleepy town, sitting on a small knoll about 15 km (9 miles) south of Sansepolcro, would probably attract little attention if not for the fact that, in the 1450s, Piero della Francesca painted one of his greatest masterpieces—the *Madonna del Parto,* a rare image of a pregnant Virgin Mary—here. ⊠ *Sansepolcro.*

Museo Civico
ART MUSEUM | Piero della Francesca is the star at this small provincial museum, where his works include the reassembled altarpiece of the *Misericordia* (1445–62) and frescoes depicting the *Resurrection* (circa 1460), *Saint Julian,* and the disputed *Saint Louis of Toulouse,* which is possibly the work of a close follower of the artist. Other works of interest are those by Santi di Tito (1536–1603), also from Sansepolcro, and Pontormo's *San Quintino* (1517–18). ⊠ *Via Aggiunti 65, Sansepolcro* ☎ *0575/732218* ⊕ *www. museociviscosansepolcro.it* ⊡ *€12.*

Museo della Madonna del Parto
ART MUSEUM | Not surprisingly, only one painting is displayed here, Piero's *Madonna del Parto* (circa 1455), a fresco depicting the expectant Virgin flanked by two angels. Originally painted for the small chapel of Santa Maria a Momentana in Monterchi's cemetery, the work was restored in 1992–93 and moved, shortly thereafter, into the museum. The iconography of the image is extremely rare and, emphasized by its static atmosphere and studied symmetry, the fresco achieves an extraordinary sense of enigmatic and monumental spirituality. ⊠ *Via Reglia 1, Sansepolcro* ☎ *0575/70713* ⊕ *www.*

madonnadelparto.it 🎟 *€7; pregnant women are admitted free of charge.*

Parco Nazionale Casentino

Pratovecchio: 55 km (34 miles) north of Arezzo, 50 km (31 miles) east of Florence.

The sparsely populated region of the Casentino—defined as the upper valley of the Arno, the Val d'Arno—contains enough castles, Romanesque parish churches, and unspoiled villages to keep you exploring for days. But the jewels in its crown are contained within the Parco Nazionale Casentino, a roughly 90,000-acre preserve.

The heart of the park, on an Apennine ridge between the Arno and the Tiber, is the ancient forest tended for eight centuries by the monks of the Abbazia Camaldoli, designers of the world's first forestry code. Every year they've plant thousands of saplings. Over time, they planted only firs, creating majestic stands of the trees whose 150-foot trunks were once floated down the Arno to be used for the masts of warships.

GETTING HERE
You'll need a car to explore this area. Getting here by bus, though surprisingly easier from Florence than it is from Arezzo, is still a complicated process; it's impossible by train.

VISITOR INFORMATION
Park Information Office. In addition to this office, there are branch offices at Camaldoli (✉ *Località Camaldoli 19*) and Stia (✉ *Piazza Tanucci*). ✉ *Via Giodo Brocchi*

7, Pratovecchio 🖃 *0543/50301* ⊕ *www. parcoforestecasentinesi.it.*

Sights

Foreste Casentinesi
NATIONAL PARK | A drive through the park, especially on the very winding 34-km (21-mile) road between the Monastero di Camaldoli and Santuario della Verna, passing through the lovely abbey town of Badia Prataglia, reveals one satisfying vista after another, from walls of firs to velvety pillows of pastureland where sheep or white cattle graze. In autumn, the beeches add a mass of red-brown to the palette, and, in spring, torrents of bright golden broom pour off the hillsides with an unforgettable profusion and fragrance.

Walking the forests—which also include sycamore, lime, maple, ash, elm, oak, hornbeam, and chestnut trees and abundant brooks and impressive waterfalls—is the best way to see some of the wilder creatures, from deer and mouflon (wild sheep imported from Sardinia in 1872) to eagles and many other birds, as well as 1,000 species of flora, including many rare and endangered plants and an orchid found nowhere else. The park organizes theme walks in summer and provides English-speaking guides anytime with advance notice. 🖃 *0575/503029* ⊕ *www. parcoforestecasentinesi.it.*

Sacro Eremo e Monastero di Camaldoli

20 km (12 miles) northeast of Pratovecchio, 55 km (34 miles) north of Arezzo.

GETTING HERE
As with the Casentino National Park in general, the only practical way to reach the hermitage and monastery is by car: take SP71 to Serravalle, then follow the signs.

Bus service is infrequent, and the schedule is tortuous; train service is nonexistent.

 ## Sights

Sacro Eremo e Monastero di Camaldoli

RELIGIOUS BUILDING | In 1012, four centuries after the founding of the Benedictine order, St. Romualdo—feeling that his order had become too permissive—came to the forests of the Casentino and found their remoteness, beauty, and silence more conducive to religious contemplation. He stayed and founded this hermitage, which was named for Count Maldoli, who donated the land, and which became the seat of a reformed Benedictine order. An important requirement of the new order was preserving its ascetic atmosphere: "If the hermits are to be true devotees of solitude, they must take the greatest care of the woods." When the flow of pilgrims began to threaten that solitude, Romualdo had a monastery and hospital built down the mountain to create some distance.

Today, you can view the hermitage—where the monks live in complete silence in 20 separate little cottages, each with its own walled garden—through gates and visit the church and original cell of Romualdo, the model for all the others. The church, rebuilt in the 13th century and transformed in the 18th to its present appearance, strikes an odd note in connection with such an austere order and the simplicity of the hermits' cells, because it's done up in gaudy baroque style, complete with gilt cherubs and a frescoed vault. Its most appealing artwork is the glazed terra-cotta relief *Madonna and Child with Saints* (including a large figure of Romualdo and a medallion depicting his fight with the devil) by Andrea della Robbia. The main entrance to the hermitage, the bronze *Porta Speciosa* (Beautiful Door) of 2013, by Claudio Parmiggiani

(born in 1943), has an inscription on its inner side that likens the monks' spirits to the trees that they tend.

Within the Monastero di Camaldoli, 3 km (1 mile) away, is a church (repeatedly restructured) containing 14th-century frescoes by Spinello Aretino, seven 16th-century panel paintings by Giorgio Vasari, and a quietly lovely monastic choir. The choir has 18th-century walnut stalls, more Vasari paintings, and a serene fresco (by Santi Pacini) of St. Romualdo instructing his white-robed disciples. In a hospital built for sick villagers in 1046, the 1543 Antica Farmacia (Old Pharmacy) contains original carved walnut cabinets. Here you can buy herbal teas and infusions, liqueurs, honey products, and toiletries made by the monks from centuries-old recipes as part of their daily routine balancing prayer, work, and study (the monastery is entirely self-supporting). In the back room is an exhibit of the early pharmacy's alembics, mortars, and other equipment with which the monks made herbs into medicines. You can attend short spiritual retreats organized by the monks throughout the year; contact the *foresteria* (visitors lodge) for details. ⊠ *Località Camaldoli 14, Poppi* ☎ *0575/556021 Eremo, 0575/556012 Monastero, 0575/556013 Foresteria* ⊕ *www.camaldoli.it* ✎ *Donation suggested.*

Santuario della Verna

34 km (21 miles) southeast of Monastero di Camaldoli and of Pratovecchio.

GETTING HERE

The only practical way to reach the sanctuary is by car—it's a winding, 21 km (13 miles) east of Bibbiena on SP208. There is no direct bus service, and train service is nonexistent.

Sights

Caprese Michelangelo

TOWN | Some 10 km (6 miles) south of La Verna on SR54 is the small hilltop town where Michelangelo Buonarroti, sculptor, painter, architect, and poet, was born on March 6, 1475. During two weekends in mid-October, Caprese Michelangelo's very lively Sagra della Castagna (Chestnut Festival) takes place. Among the many delights that feature in the fair, the freshly made *castagnaccia* (a typically Tuscan dessert made with chestnut flour, pine nuts, olive oil, and rosemary) is a must-try. ⊠ *La Verna* ☎ *0575/793912 town offices* ⊕ *capresemichelangelo.net.*

Museo Michelangiolesco

NOTABLE BUILDING | Opened in 1964 to honor the 400th anniversary of Michelangelo's death, the museum displays photographs, plaster casts, and documents relating to the artist's work. ⊠ *Via Capoluogo 1, La Verna* ☎ *0575/793776* ⊕ *www.casanatalemichelangelo.it* ⊠ *€4.*

Santuario della Verna

RELIGIOUS BUILDING | A few hills away from the Monastero di Camaldoli, dramatically perched on a sheer-walled rock surrounded by firs and beeches, is La Verna, founded by St. Francis of Assisi in 1214. Ten years later, after a 40-day fast, St. Francis had a vision of Christ crucified, and when it was over, Francis had received the stigmata, the signs of Christ's wounds, on his hands, feet, and chest. A stone in the floor of the 1263 Chapel of the Stigmata marks the spot.

A covered corridor through which the monks pass, chanting in a solemn procession each day at 3 pm on the way to Mass, is lined with simple frescoes of the *Life of St. Francis* by a late-17th-century Franciscan artist. The true artistic treasures of the place, though, are 15 della Robbia glazed terra-cottas. Most, like a heartbreakingly beautiful Annunciation, are in the 14th- to 15th-century basilica, which has a 5,000-pipe organ that sings out joyously at Masses.

Several chapels, each with its own story, can be visited, and some natural and spiritual wonders can also be seen. A walkway along the 230-foot-high cliff leads to an indentation where the rock is said to have miraculously melted away to protect St. Francis when the devil tried to push him off the edge. Most touching is the enormous Sasso Spicco (Projecting Rock), detached on three sides and surrounded with mossy rocks and trees, where St. Francis meditated. You can also view the Letto di San Francesco (St. Francis's Bed), a slab of rock in a cold, damp cave with an iron grate on which he prayed, did penance, and sometimes slept.

A 40-minute walk through the woods to the top of Mt. Penna passes some religious sites and ends in panoramic views of the Arno Valley, but those from the wide, cliff-edge terrace are equally impressive, including the tower of the castle in Poppi, the Prato Magno (great meadow), and the olive groves and vineyards on the lower slopes. Santuario della Verna's foresteria also has simple but comfortable rooms with or without bath. A restaurant with basic fare is open to the public, and a shop sells souvenirs and the handiwork of the monks.

As you leave La Verna, be glad you needn't do it as Edith Wharton (1862–1937) did on a 1912 visit during a drive across the Casentino. As she wrote, her car "had to be let down on ropes to a point about ¾ mile below the monastery, Cook [her chauffeur] steering down the vertical descent, and twenty men hanging on to a funa [rope] that, thank the Lord, didn't break." ⊠ *Via del Santuario 45, La Verna* ✛ *21 km (13 miles) east of Bibbiena on the Sp 208* ☎ *0575/5341* ⊕ *www.laverna.it.*

Chapter 7

SOUTHERN TUSCANY

Updated by
Patricia Rucidlo

TUSCANY

UMBRIA

⊙ Sights	🍴 Restaurants	🛏 Hotels	🛍 Shopping	🍸 Nightlife
★★★★★	★★★★☆	★★★★☆	★★★☆☆	★★★☆☆

WELCOME TO SOUTHERN TUSCANY

TOP REASONS TO GO

★ **Pienza's urban renewal:** A 15th-century makeover turned this otherwise unpretentious village into a model Renaissance town.

★ **Saturnia's hot water:** The gods themselves reportedly had a hand in creating the springs at this world-famous spa town.

★ **Napoléon's home in exile:** The island of Elba, where the French leader was once imprisoned, is among the prettiest islands in the Tuscan archipelago.

★ **Wine tastings in Montepulciano:** This gorgeous town also happens to be the home of one of Italy's finest wines—Vino Nobile di Montepulciano.

★ **A stroll through Abbazia di Sant'Antimo:** This 12th-century Romanesque abbey shows French, Lombard, and even Spanish influences.

Southeast of Siena, not far from the Umbrian border, the towns of Montepulciano, Montalcino, and Pienza are Tuscan classics—perched on hills, constructed during the Middle Ages and the Renaissance, and saturated with fine wine. Venture farther south and you encounter Tuscany with a rougher edge: the Maremma region is populated by cowboys, and a good portion of the landscape remains wild. But you won't forget you're in Italy here; the wine is still excellent, and some locals store their supply in Etruscan tombs.

1 Chiusi. Filled with 5th-century artifacts.

2 Chianciano Terme. Visitors flock to its healing waters.

3 Montepulciano. Its high altitude means cool summers.

4 Pienza. Planned by Pope Pius II.

5 San Quirico D'Orcia. See Romanesque churches here.

6 Bagno Vignoni. Famous for its sulfurous waters.

7 Montalcino. This town produces Brunello di Montalcino wine.

8 Abbazia Di Sant'Antimo. 12th-century Romanesque abbey.

9 Buonconvento. The death place of Holy Roman Emperor Henry VII.

10 Abbazia Di Monte Oliveto Maggiore. Most-visited abbey in Tuscany.

11 Asciano. A sleepy, bike-friendly town.

12 Monte Amiata. Ski its namesake slope, a dormant volcano.

13 Sorano. A former Etruscan citadel carved from tufa.

14 Pitigliano. A lively, trendy town.

15 Sovana. The area's former capital.

16 Saturnia. Relax in its thermal waters.

17 Parco Naturale Della Maremma. A nature preserve.

18 Monte Argentario. Come for beaches and views of the mountains.

19 Massa Marittima. Former mining town.

20 Abbazia Di San Galgano. A Gothic cathedral in beautiful ruins.

21 Giglio. A romantic isle.

22 Elba. The largest island of the Tuscan archipelago.

23 Capraia. An island frequented by sailors.

In landscapes that range from the green knolls of the Val d'Orcia to the sandy beaches at Punta Ala, this region contains some of Tuscany's wildest areas: the Maremma, once a malaria-ridden swampland where the *butteri*, Italy's cowboys, rounded up their cattle, now a peaceful woodland fringed with beaches; Monte Amiata, a scruffy mountain landscape where goats gnaw at clumps of brown grass among scattered rocks; and the still-wild islands of the Tuscan archipelago.

Some of Tuscany's best-kept secrets are here in the south, among them the Abbazia di San Galgano, which is open to the sky (it has no roof), and the cool mountain enclaves of Monte Amiata. This is Etruscan country, where the necropolis near Sovana hints at a rich and some-what mysterious pre-Roman civilization.

Apart from the occasional rocky prom-ontory, the coast of southern Tuscany is virtually one long stretch of fine-sand beach. Private beach areas are common near the resort towns south of Livorno and just north of Monte Argentario, where there are chairs and umbrellas for rent, shower facilities, and bars. Along the rest of the coast, the beaches are public. They're particularly pleasant in the nature reserve at Monti dell'Uccellina and along the sandbars that connect Monte Argentario to the mainland. On the islands, rocky shores predominate,

although Elba has a few sandy beaches on its southern side.

You can visit the whole region in about five days. Keep in mind that southern Tus-cany isn't well served by trains, so if you aren't renting a car, you'll have to plan around sometimes difficult bus sched-ules, and the going will be slow. The A1 (Autostrada del Sole), which runs from Florence to Rome, passes near the Val d'Orcia. The SS1 (Via Aurelia) follows the western coastline for much of the way, before jutting inland north of Grosseto.

MAJOR REGIONS

Val d'Orcia. In the area surrounding this lush valley you'll find some of southern Tuscany's most attractive towns. **Mon-talcino** and **Montepulciano** are famed for their wine, **Pienza** for its urban planning and pecorino cheese.

Le Crete. South of Siena, the stark clay landscape and unassuming towns are interrupted by **Abbazia di Monte Oliveto Maggiore,** the most-visited abbey in Tuscany.

The Maremma. Tuscany's deep south may not conform to your expectations for the region; it's best known for its cattle ranches and coastline. "Discovering" the Maremma has become popular with off-the-beaten-path travelers, though you hardly have to rough it here—you'll find exceptional food and wine, and the spa town of Saturnia is all about indulgence.

Elba and the Surrounding Islands. It's a short hop from the coast to the islands of the Tuscan archipelago. Several of them—most notably Elba—have long been vacation getaways.

Planning

Getting Here and Around

BUS

Although tortuous roads and circuitous routes make bus travel in southern Tuscany slow, it's a reliable way to get around if you don't have a car. Schedules are always changing, so plan your trip carefully with the aid of local tourist offices. (They're more likely to have an English-speaking staff than are bus stations.) The major bus stations for the region are in Siena and Grosseto, but most towns have bus service even if they don't have actual bus stations.

BUSITALIA. This bus company provides regular rapid service between Florence and Siena. ☎ 055/47827 in Florence ⊕ www.fsbusitalia.it.
CTT. With an office in Portoferraio, the company provides bus service around Elba. ☎ 050/88400 ⊕ www.livorno. cttnord.it.
RAMA. Based in Grosseto, the company provides bus service throughout the Maremma region. ☎ 0564/475111 ⊕ www.griforama.it.
Tra-In. Bus service throughout the province of Siena is provided by Tra-In. ☎ 0577/204111 ⊕ www.trainspa.it.

CAR

The area is easily reached by car on the A1 highway (Autostrada del Sole), which runs between Rome and Florence—take the Chiusi–Chianciano Terme exit for Montepulciano, Pienza, and San Quirico Val d'Orcia. From Florence the fastest route to southern Tuscany is via the Florence–Siena Superstrada and then the Via Cassia (SR2) from Siena for Buonconvento and Montalcino. There is also a good road, the SR223 linking Siena and Grosseto, for outings to the Parco Naturale della Maremma and Monte Argentario.

From Genoa or the northern Tuscan coast, follow the coastal highway (A12) to Livorno and its ferry service to Capraia. For direct ferry service to Elba, continue south on the SS1 (the Via Aurelia) to Piombino. Past Piombino, the SS1 passes Grosseto, the Parco Naturale della Maremma, and Monte Argentario, before continuing south toward Rome.

TRAIN

Trains do run from Chiusi–Chianciano Terme to Siena (one hour) with stops in Montepulciano and Asciano. That said, service within this region is slow; in many cases, buses are quicker.

Trenitalia
You can check the website of the state railway for train schedules. ☎ 06/6847–5475 ⊕ www.trenitalia.com.

Making the Most of Your Time

The towns in southern Tuscany are fairly close together, so it's possible to pick one of them as your base and take day trips to almost everywhere else in the region. Pienza, in the middle of the

Val d'Orcia, makes an excellent place to begin your trip. Other good choices include Montepulciano and Montalcino. From any of these it's only a short drive to all the other towns in the Val d'Orcia, as well as the famous abbeys in and around Le Crete.

If your main reason for visiting this region is a dip in the hot springs, you should stay in Saturnia or one of the surrounding villages. (Because so many people go there for a soak, Saturnia has the most luxurious lodgings.)

If your destination is the Tuscan archipelago, you'd do best to choose one island, as there is no ferry service between them. Elba is more famous, but it's hard to find a place to lay your towel in summer. Giglio has less-crowded beaches, including a few accessible on foot or by boat that you might have all to yourself.

Hotels

Southern Tuscany is a great place to enjoy the *agriturismo* (agrotourism) lifestyle: if you have a week to stay in one of these rural farmhouses, pick somewhere central, such as Pienza, and explore the region from that base. It may be so relaxing and the food so good that you might have trouble wandering away.

You will also find many hotels in this region: modern affairs in cities, surf-side beach resorts, and timeworn villas.

Hotel and restaurant reviews have been shortened. For full information, visit Fodors.com. Hotel prices are the lowest cost of a standard double room in high season. Restaurant prices are the average cost of a main course at dinner or, if dinner is not served, at lunch.

WHAT IT COSTS in Euros			
$	$$	$$$	$$$$
RESTAURANTS			
under €15	€15–€24	€25–€25	over €35
HOTELS			
under €125	€125–€200	€201–€300	over €300

Restaurants

The restaurant scene in this part of Tuscany has a split personality. Several towns that are popular vacation destinations for Italians—notably Monte Argentino, Saturnia, and the villages sprinkled across the island of Elba—have excellent upscale restaurants that serve elaborate dishes.

It's not in high-end places, though, that you can experience the diverse flavors of the cooking of this region. Instead, look for the family-run trattorias that can be found in every town. In classic Italian style, the service and setting are often basic, but the food can be great.

Few places serve lighter fare at midday, so be prepared to face heavy meals at lunch and dinner, especially in out-of-the-way towns. Hours for meals are fairly standard: lunch between 12:30 and 2, dinner between 7:30 and 10.

Chiusi

40 km (25 miles) south of Cortona, 84 km (50 miles) southeast of Siena, 126 km (78 miles) southeast of Florence.

Chiusi was once one of the most powerful of the ancient cities of the Etruscan League, and it's now a valuable source of information about that archaic civilization. Fifth-century BC tombs found in the nearby hills have provided archaeologists with a wealth of artifacts.

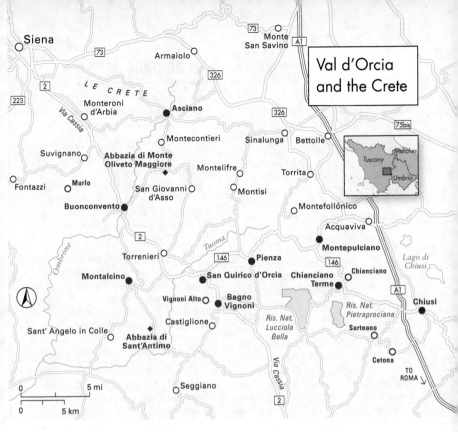

On the route of the ancient Via Cassia, Chiusi became a major Roman center and an important communication hub that linked Rome with the agriculturally rich Chiana Valley to the east, with Siena to the northwest, and with other major cities in central and northern Italy. When the Chiana Valley became a malaria-ridden swamp during the Middle Ages, Chiusi's importance declined, and it was not until the Medici devised a scheme to drain the valley (with plans supplied by Leonardo da Vinci) in the early 15th century that the town began to reestablish itself.

GETTING HERE

Chiusi is easily reached by car on the A1 highway (Autostrada del Sole), which runs between Rome and Florence. Tra-In buses link Chiusi with Siena, but train service is faster and more frequent.

Chiusi is on a main rail line between Florence and Rome, and can be reached from either city.

VISITOR INFORMATION

CONTACTS Chiusi Tourism Office. ⊠ *Via Porsena 79, Chiusi* ☎ *0578/227667* ⊕ *www.prolocochiusi.it.*

◉ Sights

Cattedrale di S. Secondiano

CHURCH | This beautiful cathedral, which practically abuts the Museo Nazionale Etrusco, is thought by many to be the among the oldest churches in Tuscany; parts of it date from the mid-6th century. It houses the remains of Santa Mustiola, the patron saint of the city. It has very little artificial light inside, so you can get a pretty good idea of how people experienced this space over the centuries. ✉ *Piazza Duomo 1, Chiusi.*

Museo Nazionale Etrusco

HISTORY MUSEUM | Most of the artifacts found during the excavations of Chiusi's Etruscan sites are now on display in this small but expertly laid out museum. Relics include elegant Etruscan and Greek vases, carved Etruscan tomb chests, and a number of the strange canopic jars with anthropomorphic shapes that are particular to this area.

The tombs themselves can be seen by arrangement with the museum—sometimes. (You're accompanied by museum personnel, and staff shortages have led to tomb closures.) These underground burial chambers are still evocative of ancient life, particularly in the Tomba della Scimmia (Tomb of the Monkey), where well-preserved frescoes depict scenes from ordinary life 2,500 years ago. The Tomba del Leone (Tomb of the Lion) and Tomba della Pellegrina (Tomb of the Pilgrim) might also be open at set times during museum hours. ✉ *Via Porsenna 93, Chiusi* ☎ *0578/20177* 🌐 *www.prolocochiusi.it* 🎟 *€6.*

🍴 Restaurants

★ La Solita Zuppa

$ | **ITALIAN** | The name means "the usual soup," but there's hardly anything usual about the soups on offer—as wait staffers often explain, this restaurant is committed to cooking seasonally, using what's currently available at the market. Expect wonderfully tasty soups and brilliant *secondi* (second course), all served in a room with high vaulted arches dating from the 17th century. **Known for:** cacio e pepe (pasta with cheese and black pepper); local favorite; seasonal soups and marvelous desserts. [$] *Average main: €14* ✉ *Via Porsenna 21, Chiusi* ☎ *0578/21006* 🌐 *www.lasolitazuppa.it* 🕒 *Closed Tues.*

Chianciano Terme

11 km (7 miles) northwest of Chiusi, 73 km (44 miles) southeast of Siena, 128 km (80 miles) south of Florence.

People from around the world come to the *città del fegato sano* (city of the healthy liver) to experience the curative waters. The area's mineral waters are reputed to restore and maintain the health of the skin, among other things, and you can experience them at a number of springs.

This is nothing new; as early as the 5th century BC Chianciano Terme was the site of a temple to Apollo the Healer. It's no secret, either—the Terme di Chianciano spa alone claims to draw 120,000 visitors a year, and Italian state health insurance covers visits to the baths and springs for qualified patients.

If you're not here for the waters, probably the most interesting part of Chianciano is the old town, which lies to the north. The modern town, stretching along a hillside to the south, is a series of hotels, shops, and restaurants catering to spa aficionados.

GETTING HERE

From Florence, Chiusi is easily reached by car on the A1 highway (Autostrada del Sole). Tra-In buses link Chianciano with Siena. The closest train station is in Chiusi, about 11 km (7 miles) away.

VISITOR INFORMATION

CONTACTS Chianciano Terme Tourism Office. ✉ *Piazza Italia 67, Chianciano Terme* ☎ *0578/671122* 🌐 *www.terresiena.it.*

👁 Sights

Cetona

TOWN | Follow SP19 past Sarteano and continue on SP21 to reach this delightful village. Time may seem to have stopped as you walk along the quiet, narrow,

Terme, Wrath of the Gods

In a country known for its seismic activity, Tuscany seems to have gotten a lucky break. Although Campania and Sicily have active volcanoes, and Umbria and the Marches stand on notoriously shaky ground, Tuscany's underground activity makes itself known in the form of steamy and sulfurous hot springs that have earned the region a name as a spa-goer's paradise. (Though the occasional minor earthquake has been known to happen.)

Tuscany is dotted throughout with small *terme* (thermal baths), where hot waters flow from natural springs deep under the earth's surface. Since the time of the Etruscans, these springs have been valued for their curative properties. The Romans attributed their origins to divine thunderbolts that split the earth open and let flow the miraculous waters. Regardless of their genesis, their appeal endures, as the presence of thousands of people taking the waters attests.

Each of the springs has different curative properties, attributable to the various concentrations of minerals and gases that individual water flows pick up on their way to the surface. Carbon dioxide, for example, is said to strengthen the immune system, and sulfur, its characteristic rotten-egg smell notwithstanding, is said to relieve pain and aid in relaxation.

At spas, you generally pay an admission fee to swim in baths that range from hot natural lakes and waterfalls (with accompanying mud) to giant limestone swimming pools filled with cloudy, bright blue, steaming water. Larger establishments have treatments that can range from mineral mud baths to steam inhalations.

Believers swear that Tuscany's hot springs have a positive effect on everything from skin disorders to back pain to liver function to stress. Whatever your opinion, a good soak in a Tuscan spring is a relaxing way to take a break, and as far as geological phenomena go, it beats an earthquake or a volcanic eruption any day.

The world-famous Montecatini Terme is well known outside Tuscany, but for the most part, the local establishments that run the springs are not well-publicized, which can mean a more local flavor, lower prices, and fewer crowds: Terme di Bagni di Lucca is near Lucca; Terme di Chianciano is near Chiusi; Bagno Vignoni is just south of San Quirico d'Orcia; and Terme di Saturnia is not too far from Grosseto.

medieval lanes and back alleys. Peer through the locked gate for a glimpse of the privately owned castle, and take in splendid views of olive orchards, cypress groves, and the quiet wooded slopes of Mt. Cetona from the town's terraced streets. ⊠ *Chianciano Terme* ✚ *20 km (12 miles) southeast of Chianciano Terme.*

Chianciano

TOWN | This walled medieval town, 3 km (2 miles) northeast of Chianciano Terme, is best known for its proximity to the nearby spas. Nevertheless, the well-preserved center has an appeal all of its own. ⊠ *Chianciano Terme.*

Museo Civico Archeologico

HISTORY MUSEUM | This museum contains Etruscan and Roman sculpture and pottery excavated from around the area. According to cognoscenti, the Etruscan collection is one of the best in Italy. ⊠ *Viale Dante, Chianciano Terme* ☎ *0578/30471* ⊕ *www.museoetrusco.it* 🎫 *€6* ⊗ *Closed Tues.–Thurs.*

San Martino in Foro

CHURCH | Don't miss this small church, which houses a striking *Annunciation* by the important Sienese painter Domenico Beccafumi (1486–1551). ⊠ *Piazza San Martino, Sarteano, Chianciano Terme.*

Sarteano

TOWN | To the southeast of Chianciano, 10 km (6 miles) along SP19, lies this relatively unspoiled village that dates from the 12th and 13th centuries. The town's narrow streets, which wind slowly up toward an imposing fortress, now privately owned, make for very pleasant strolling. ⊠ *Chianciano Terme* ⊕ *www. terresiena.it.*

Terme di Chianciano

HOT SPRING | This spa has two buildings with a large park in the middle and three types of water: Acqua Santa, Acqua Fucoli, and Acqua Sillene. Mud baths happen at the last, and the website lists the other varied spa treatments that are available. The all-important mineral water is served at long counters, where the spa staff is always ready to refill your glass. Be warned: The water can have a cleansing effect on your system that may come on suddenly. ⊠ *Via delle Rose 12, Chianciano Terme* ☎ *0578/68501* ⊕ *www. termechianciano.it.*

Montepulciano

10 km (6 miles) northeast of Chianciano Terme, 65 km (40 miles) southeast of Siena, 114 km (70 miles) southeast of Florence.

Perched on a hilltop, Montepulciano is made up of a pyramid of redbrick buildings set within a circle of cypress trees. At an altitude of almost 2,000 feet, it is cool in summer and chilled in winter by biting winds sweeping down its spiraling streets.

The town has an unusually harmonious look, the result of the work of three architects: Antonio da Sangallo "il Vecchio" (circa 1455–1534), Vignola (1507–73), and Michelozzo (1396–1472). The group endowed it with fine palaces and churches in an attempt to impose Renaissance architectural ideals on an ancient Tuscan hill town.

The town is also at the heart of the third and smallest of Tuscany's wine districts. The area is known for both Vino Nobile di Montepulciano (a cross between Chianti and Brunello) and Rosso di Montepulciano, which is often priced more affordably.

GETTING HERE

From Florence, take the Chiusi–Chianciano exit from the A1 highway (Autostrada del Sole). From Siena, take the SR2 south to San Quirico and then the SP146 to Montepulciano.

Tra-In offers bus service from Siena to Montepulciano several times a day. The town's train station is in Montepulciano Stazione, 10 km (6 miles) away.

VISITOR INFORMATION

CONTACTS Montepulciano Tourism Office. ⊠ *Piazza Don Minzoni 1, Montepulciano* ☎ *0578/757341* ⊕ *www.prolocomontepulciano.it.*

Summer in Val d'Orcia

Sights

Duomo

CHURCH | The unfinished facade of Montepulciano's cathedral doesn't measure up to the beauty of its neighboring palaces. On the inside, however, its Renaissance roots shine through. The high altar has a splendid triptych painted in 1401 by Taddeo di Bartolo (circa 1362–1422), and you can see fragments of the tomb of Bartolomeo Aragazzi, secretary to Pope Martin V, that was sculpted by Michelozzo between 1427 and 1436. ✉ *Piazza Grande, Montepulciano.*

Palazzo Comunale

CASTLE/PALACE | Montepulciano's town hall dates from the late 13th century, though it was restructured in the 14th century and again in the mid-15th century. Michelozzo oversaw this last phase, using the Palazzo Vecchio in Florence as his inspiration. From the tower, a commanding view of Siena, Mt. Amiata (the highest point in Tuscany) and Lake Trasimeno (the largest lake on the Italian peninsula) can be enjoyed on a clear day. ✉ *Piazza Grande 1, Montepulciano* ☎ *0578/757341* ✉ *Free.*

Piazza Grande

PLAZA/SQUARE | Filled with handsome buildings, this large square on the heights of the old historic town is Montepulciano's pièce de résistance. ✉ *Piazza Grande, Montepulciano.*

★ San Biagio

CHURCH | Designed by Antonio da Sangallo il Vecchio, and considered his masterpiece, this church sits on the hillside below the town walls and is a model of High Renaissance architectural perfection. Inside is a painting of the Madonna that, according to legend, was the only thing remaining in an abandoned church that two young girls entered on April 23, 1518. The girls saw the eyes of the Madonna moving, and that same afternoon so did a farmer and a cow, who knelt down in front of the painting. In 1963, the image was proclaimed the Madonna del Buon Viaggio (Madonna of the Good Journey), the protector of tourists in Italy. ✉ *Via di San Biagio, Montepulciano* ☎ *0578/286300* 🌐 *www.tempiosanbiagio.it* 🎫 *€4.*

Sant'Agostino

CHURCH | Michelozzo had a hand in creating the beautiful travertine facade on the church of Sant'Agostino, which was built in 1285 and renovated in the early 1400s. He also sculpted the terra-cotta relief of the Madonna and Child above the entrance. ✉ *Piazzale Pasquino da Montepulciano 6, Montepulciano* ☎ *0578/757341.*

🍴 Restaurants

La Dolce Vita

$$ | **WINE BAR** | An elegantly restored monastery in the upper part of Montepulciano is home to this excellent *enoteca* (wine bar), which has a wide selection of wines by the glass. **Known for:** graceful service; serene setting; exquisite food that pairs beautifully with its wines. [$] *Average main: €15* ✉ *Via di Voltaia nel Corso 80/82, Montepulciano* ☎ *0578/758760* 🌐 *www.enotecaladolcevita.it.*

★ **La Grotta**

$$ | **TUSCAN** | You might be tempted to pass right by the innocuous entrance across the street from San Biagio, but you'd miss some fantastic food. This tasty menu relies heavily on local classics turned out to perfection. **Known for:** stellar service; local wine list; creative menu. [$] *Average main: €22* ✉ *Via di San Biagio 15, Montepulciano* ☎ *0578/757479* 🌐 *www.lagrottamontepulciano.it* ⏲ *Closed Wed. and Jan. 15–Mar. 15.*

Osteria del Conte

$$ | **TUSCAN** | As high in Montepulciano as you can get, just behind the Duomo, this intimate restaurant is expertly run by the mother-and-son team of Lorena and Paolo Brachi, both of whom are passionate about the food they prepare and have a flair for the region's traditional dishes. Although the wine list is limited in range, it does have a decent selection of offerings from both Montepulciano and Montalcino. **Known for:** filetto ai funghi porcini (steak with porcini mushrooms); fresh fish served Friday; pici all'aglione (handmade spaghetti with garlic sauce). [$] *Average main: €15* ✉ *Via di San Donato 19, Montepulciano* ☎ *0578/756062* 🌐 *www.osteriadelconte.it* ⏲ *Closed Mon. No dinner Sun.*

🛏 Hotels

La Terrazza

$ | **B&B/INN** | **FAMILY** | On a quiet street in the upper part of town, these unpretentious lodgings are given sparkle by the welcoming and friendly service of the owners, Roberto and Vittoria Giardinelli. **Pros:** friendly family atmosphere; great value for money; quiet central location. **Cons:** books up quickly; no night porter; no air-conditioning. [$] *Rooms from: €95* ✉ *Via del Piè al Sasso 16, Montepulciano* ☎ *0578/757440* 🌐 *www.laterrazzadimontepulciano.it* 🛏 *14 rooms* 🍴 *Free Breakfast.*

★ **Podere Dionora**

$$$ | **B&B/INN** | At this secluded and serene country inn, earth-tone fabrics complement antiques in the individually decorated rooms, all of which have functioning fireplaces. **Pros:** great views; bathrooms have a sauna and a whirlpool tub; attentive service. **Cons:** books up quickly; need a car to get around; long walk to the nearest town. [$] *Rooms from: €280* ✉ *Via Vicinale di Poggiano 9, Montepulciano* ✣ *3 km (2 miles) east of Montepulciano town center* ☎ *0578/717496* 🌐 *www.dionora.it* ⏲ *Closed mid-Dec.–mid-Mar.* 🛏 *6 rooms* 🍴 *Free Breakfast.*

🎫 Performing Arts

Cantiere Internazionale d'Arte

MUSIC FESTIVALS | This festival of art, music, and theater takes place in a variety of venues during July and August, ending with a dramatic stage production in the Piazza Grande. ✉ *Via*

Fiorenzuola Vecchia 5, Montepulciano
☎ *0578/757089 ticket office* ⊕ *www.
fondazionecantiere.it.*

Pienza

*12 km (7 miles) west of Montepulciano,
52 km (31 miles) southeast of Siena, 120
km (72 miles) southeast of Florence.*

Pienza owes its appearance to Pope Pius
II (1405–64), who had grand plans to
transform his hometown of Corsignano—
its former name—into a compact model
Renaissance town. The man entrusted
with the transformation was Bernardo
Rossellino (1409–64), a protégé of the
great Renaissance architectural theorist
Leon Battista Alberti (1404–72). His man-
date was to create a cathedral, a papal
palace, and a town hall that adhered to
the vainglorious pope's principles.

Gothic and Renaissance styles were
fused, and the buildings were decorated
with Sienese paintings. The result was
a project that expressed Renaissance
ideals of art, architecture, and civilized
living in a single scheme: it stands as an
exquisite example of the architectural
canons that Alberti formulated in the early Renaissance and that were utilized by
later architects, including Michelangelo,
in designing many of Italy's finest buildings and piazzas. Today, the cool nobility
of Pienza's center seems almost surreal
in this otherwise unpretentious village,
renowned for its smooth sheep's-milk
pecorino cheese.

GETTING HERE
From Siena, drive south along the SR2
to San Quirico d'Orcia and then take the
SP146. The trip should take just over an
hour. Tra-In shuttles passengers between
Siena and Pienza. There is no train service to Pienza.

VISITOR INFORMATION
CONTACTS Pienza Tourism Office. ✉ *Piazza
Dante 18* ☎ *0578/748359* ⊕ *www.pienza.
info.*

Sights

Duomo
CHURCH | This 15th-century cathedral was
built by the architect Bernardo Rossellino
(1409–64) under the influence of Leon
Battista Alberti. The travertine facade is
divided into three parts, with Renaissance arches under the pope's coat
of arms encircled by a wreath of fruit.
Inside, the cathedral is simple but richly
decorated with Sienese paintings. The
building's perfection didn't last long—the
first cracks appeared immediately after
it was completed, and its foundations
have shifted slightly ever since as rain
erodes the hillside behind. You can see
this effect if you look closely at the base
of the first pier as you enter the church
and compare it with the last. ✉ *Piazza
Pio II, Pienza* ☎ *0578/749071* ⊕ *www.
pienza.org.*

Museo Diocesano
ART MUSEUM | This museum, which sits
to the left of Pienza's Duomo, is small
but has a few interesting papal treasures
and rich Flemish tapestries. The most
precious piece is a rare mantle that
belonged to Pope Pius II: it's woven in
gold and embellished with pearls and
embroidered religious scenes. ✉ *Corso
Il Rossellino 30, Pienza* ☎ *0578/749905*
⊕ *www.palazzoborgia.it* ⊡ *From €5*
⊘ *Closed Tues.*

Palazzo Piccolomini
CASTLE/PALACE | In 1459, Pius II commis-
sioned Bernardo Rossellino to design the
perfect palazzo for his papal court. The
architect took Florence's Palazzo Rucellai
by Alberti as a model and designed this
100-room palace. Three sides of the
building fit perfectly into the urban plan
around it, while the fourth, looking over
the valley, has a lovely loggia uniting it

with the gardens in back. Guided tours departing every 30 minutes take you to the papal apartments, including a beautiful library, the Sala delle Armi (with an impressive weapons collection), and the music room, with its extravagant wooden ceiling forming four letter Ps, for Pope, Pius, Piccolomini, and Pienza. The last tour departs 30 minutes before closing. ✉ *Piazza Pio II, Pienza* ☎ *0577/286300* 🌐 *www.palazzopiccolominipienza.it* 🎫 *€7* 🕒 *Closed Tues. and early Jan.–mid-Feb. and mid-Nov.–late Nov.*

🍴 Restaurants

★ Osteria Sette di Vino

$ | **TUSCAN** | Tasty dishes based on the region's cheeses are the specialty at this simple and inexpensive osteria on a quiet, pleasant, central square. Try versions of pici or the starter of radicchio baked quickly to brown the edges. **Known for:** awesome vegetable options; bean soup; pecorino tasting menu. [$] *Average main: €7* ✉ *Piazza di Spagna 1, Pienza* ☎ *0578/749092* 🕒 *Closed Wed., July 1–15, and Nov.*

San Quirico d'Orcia

9½ km (5½ miles) southwest of Pienza, 43 km (26 miles) southeast of Siena, 111 km (67 miles) southeast of Florence.

San Quirico d'Orcia, on the modern Via Cassia (SR2) south from Siena toward Rome, has almost-intact 15th-century walls topped with 14 turrets. The pleasantly crumbling appearance of the town recalls days of yore. It's well suited for a stop to enjoy a gelato or a meal and to see its Romanesque church.

GETTING HERE

From Siena, San Quirico d'Orcia is an hour-long drive on the SR2. Tra-In provides buses from Siena to San Quirico. There is no train service to San Quirico.

VISITOR INFORMATION

CONTACTS San Quirico d'Orcia Tourism Office. ✉ *Piazza Chigi 2, San Quirico d'Orcia* ☎ *0577/899711* 🌐 *www.comune-sanquirico.it.*

👁 Sights

Collegiata

CHURCH | The 13th-century Collegiata church has three majestic portals, one possibly the work of Giovanni Pisano (circa 1245/48–1318). Behind the high altar are some fine examples of inlaid woodwork by Antonio Barilli (1482–1502). In the floor of the left aisle, look for the tomb slab of Henry of Nassau, a pilgrim knight who died here in 1451. ✉ *Piazza Chigi, San Quirico d'Orcia.*

Horti Leonini

GARDEN | Against the walls of San Quirico d'Orcia, these Italian-style gardens retain merely a shimmer of their past opulence. They were planted in 1581 by Diomede Leoni—hence the name of the park. In the center there's a 17th-century statue of Cosimo III, the penultimate Medici grand duke of Tuscany. ✉ *Off Piazza della Libertà, San Quirico d'Orcia* 🎫 *Free.*

Palazzo Chigi

NOTABLE BUILDING | Near the Collegiata stands this splendid town palace, named after the family to whom the Medici bestowed San Quirico in 1667. Small art exhibitions are occasionally displayed in the palace courtyard, and the tourist office is here. The rest of the building is closed to the public. ✉ *Piazza Chigi 2, San Quirico d'Orcia.*

🍴 Restaurants

Trattoria al Vecchio Forno

$$ | **TUSCAN** | A meal here in this rustic place is always special; the menu offers Tuscan classics as well as other dishes with a hint of fantasy. Don't miss the dishes accented with porcini mushrooms, such as the excellent mushroom

soup. **Known for:** a divine dessert list; attentive staff; fine wine list featuring local wine (think Rosso and Brunello). [$] *Average main: €19* ✉ *Via Piazzola 8, San Quirico d'Orcia* ☎ *0577/897380* 🌐 *www.palazzodelcapitano.com/tuscany/trattoria-toscana* ⏲ *Closed Feb.*

Hotels

Palazzo del Capitano

$$ | **B&B/INN** | The guest rooms at this 14th-century palace are named for signs of the zodiac, but the astrological reference stops at the painted symbol on the door, as each elegant room is unique—an antique sewing-machine table serves as a nightstand, a medieval-looking chandelier with a forged-iron ring and a globe hangs from a ceiling, elegant striped silk covers a wooden settee. **Pros:** dogs are allowed; elegant furnishings; secluded garden. **Cons:** some street noise; a car is a must; rooms are on the small side. [$] *Rooms from: €150* ✉ *Via Poliziano 18, San Quirico d'Orcia* ☎ *0577/899028, 0577/899421* 🌐 *www.palazzodelcapitano.com* 🛏 *21 rooms* 🍴 *Free Breakfast.*

Bagno Vignoni

5 km (3 miles) south of San Quirico d'Orcia, 48 km (29 miles) southeast of Siena, 116 km (70 miles) southeast of Florence.

Bagno Vignoni has been famous since Roman times for the mildly sulfurous waters that come bubbling up into the large rectangular pool that forms the town's main square, Piazza delle Sorgenti (Square of the Springs). Medieval pilgrims and modern hikers alike have soothed their tired feet in the pleasantly warm water that flows through open channels on its way to the River Orcia. Of particular interest are the ruins of an 18th-century bathhouse on the edge of town and the Chapel of Saint Catherine, who, it seems, came here often.

GETTING HERE

Bagno Vignoni is off the SR2, about an hour from Siena. Tra-In provides bus service from Siena to Bagno Vignoni. There is no train station nearby.

VISITOR INFORMATION

CONTACTS Bagno Vignoni Tourism Office. ✉ *Località Bagno Vignoni 2, San Quirico d'Orcia* ☎ *0577/899711* 🌐 *www.comune-sanquirico.it.*

Sights

Vignoni Alto

TOWN | A steep gravel road leads north out of Bagno Vignoni for 2 km (1 mile) to the town's upper village, a tiny grouping of buildings huddled at the base of a 13th-century tower. The tower, now a private home, was built to watch over the Via Francigena. A spectacular view of the entire Val d'Orcia opens up from the eastern gate. ✉ *San Quirico d'Orcia.*

Restaurants

Bottega di Cacio

$ | **TUSCAN** | Lots of shaded outdoor seating makes this a pleasant place for lunch on a warm day. Pecorino cheese, spicy salami, and grilled vegetables *sott'olio* (preserved in olive oil) are served cafeteria-style. **Known for:** artisanal local products; fine wine list; great food at great prices. [$] *Average main: €10* ✉ *Piazza del Moretto 31, Bagno Vignoni* ☎ *0577/887477* 🌐 *labottegadicacio.com* 💳 *No credit cards* ⏲ *Closed Tues.*

Montalcino

19 km (12 miles) northeast of Bagno Vignoni, 41 km (25½ miles) south of Siena, 109 km (68 miles) south of Florence.

Tiny Montalcino, with its commanding view from high on a hill, can claim an Etruscan past. It saw a fair number of travelers, as it was directly on the road

from Siena to Rome. During the early Middle Ages, it enjoyed a brief period of autonomy before falling under the orbit of Siena in 1201.

Now, Montalcino's greatest claim to fame is that it produces Brunello di Montalcino, one of Italy's most esteemed reds. Driving to the town, you pass through the Brunello vineyards. You can sample the excellent but expensive red in wine cellars in town or visit a nearby winery, such as Fattoria dei Barbi (which has an on-site taverna), for a guided tour and tasting; you must call ahead for reservations.

GETTING HERE

By car, follow the SR2 south from Siena, then follow the SP45 to Montalcino. Several Tra-In buses travel between Siena and Montalcino daily, making a tightly scheduled day trip possible. There is no train service available.

VISITOR INFORMATION

CONTACTS Montalcino Tourism Office. ✉ *Costa del Municipio 1, Montalcino* ☎ *0577/849331* 🌐 *www.prolocomontalcino.com.*

Sights

★ La Fortezza

CASTLE/PALACE | **FAMILY** | Providing refuge for the last remnants of the Sienese army during the Florentine conquest of 1555, the battlements of this 14th-century fortress are still in excellent condition. Climb the narrow, spiral steps for the 360-degree view of most of southern Tuscany. An on-site enoteca serves delicious snacks that pair beautifully with the local wines. ✉ *Piazzale Fortezza, Montalcino* ☎ *0577/849221* 🎫 *Fortress free, walls €4* 🕒 *Closed Mon. Nov.–Mar.*

Museo Civico e Diocesano d'Arte Sacra

ART MUSEUM | This fine museum is in a building that once belonged to 13th-century Augustinian friars. The ticket booth is in the glorious refurbished cloister, and the sacred art collection, gathered from churches throughout the region, is displayed on two floors in former monastic quarters. Although the art here might be called B-list, a fine altarpiece by Bartolo di Fredi (circa 1330–1410), the *Coronation of the Virgin,* makes dazzling use of gold. In addition, there's a striking 12th-century crucifix that originally adorned the high altar of the church of Sant'Antimo. Also on hand are many wood sculptures, a typical medium in these parts during the Renaissance. ✉ *Via Ricasoli 31, Montalcino* ☎ *0577/846014* 🌐 *www.museisenesi.org* 🎫 *€10* 🕒 *Closed Mon.–Thurs. Nov. 2–Dec. 24 and Jan. 7–Mar. 31.*

Restaurants

Il Grappolo Blu

$$ | **ITALIAN** | Any one of this restaurant's *piatti tipici* (typical plates) is worth trying, though the local specialty, *pici all'aglione* (thick, long noodles served with sautéed cherry tomatoes and many cloves of garlic), is done particularly well. The chef also has a deft touch with vegetables; if there's fennel on the menu, make sure to order it. **Known for:** convivial atmosphere; kind, caring staff; great quality and price. [$] *Average main: €15* ✉ *Scale di Via Moglio 1, Montalcino* ☎ *0577/847150* 🌐 *www.grappoloblu.it* 🕒 *Closed Wed.*

Taverna dei Barbi

$ | **TUSCAN** | This rustic taverna with a large stone fireplace is amid vineyards that produce excellent Brunello—as well as its younger cousin, Rosso di Montalcino—a few minutes south of Montalcino, in the direction of Sant'Antimo. The estate farm produces many of the ingredients used in the various soups and other traditional specialties. **Known for:** the superb staff; fantastic wines; heavenly aromas coming from grilled meat on a spit. [$] *Average main: €12* ✉ *Podere Podernuovo 170, Montalcino* ☎ *0577/84111* 🌐 *www.fattoriadeibarbi.it* 🕒 *Closed Wed. and Dec.–Feb.*

Hotels

★ Castiglion del Bosco

$$$$ | **RESORT** | This estate, one of the largest still in private hands in Tuscany, was purchased at the beginning of this century and meticulously converted into a second-to-none resort that incorporates a medieval *borgo* (village) and surrounding farmhouses and has luxurious suites, as well as opulent three- to five-bedroom villas, each with its own pool. **Pros:** exclusive and tranquil location; acclaimed golf course; breathtaking scenery. **Cons:** truly exorbitant prices; private transportation required; well off the beaten track, the nearest town is 12 km (7½ miles) away. $ *Rooms from: €1852* ✉ *Località Castiglion del Bosco, Montalcino* ☎ *0577/191–3111* ⊕ *www.castigliondelbosco.com* ⌂ *53 units* ⦿ *Free Breakfast.*

Abbazia di Sant'Antimo

10 km (6 miles) south of Montalcino, 51 km (32 miles) south of Siena, 119 km (74 miles) south of Florence.

GETTING HERE

Abbazia di Sant'Antimo is a 15-minute drive from Montalcino. Tra-In bus service is extremely limited. The abbey cannot be reached by train.

Sights

★ Abbazia di Sant'Antimo

CHURCH | The exterior and interior sculpture of this Romanesque abbey, dating from the 12th-century, is outstanding, particularly the nave capitals, a combination of French, Lombard, and even Spanish influences. The sacristy (seldom open) forms part of the primitive Carolingian church (founded in AD 781), its entrance flanked by 9th-century pilasters. The small vaulted crypt dates from the same period. ✉ *Castelnuovo dell'Abate* ☎ *0577/286300* ⊕ *www.antimo.it.*

Buonconvento

27 km (17 miles) southeast of Siena, 80 km (50 miles) south of Florence.

Buonconvento dates from the 12th century, though it was surrounded by defensive walls in the later Middle Ages. Though the name means "happy place" in Latin, it was here that Holy Roman Emperor Henry VII died in 1313, cutting short his ill-fated attempt to establish imperial rule in Italy.

GETTING HERE

By car, Buonconvento is a 30-minute drive south from Siena on the SR2. Tra-In buses travel daily between Siena and Buonconvento several times a day, making a carefully scheduled day trip quite possible. A train connects Siena with Buonconvento, Monte Amiato Scalo, Asciano, and Arbia.

VISITOR INFORMATION

CONTACTS Buonconvento Tourism Office. ✉ *Santa Maria della Scala, Piazza del Duomo 1, Siena* ☎ *0577/280551* ⊕ *www.terresiena.it.*

Sights

Museo d'Arte Sacra

ART MUSEUM | Today, quiet Buonconvento is worth a stop for a look at its tiny museum, a two-room picture gallery with more than its fair share of works by Tuscan artists such as Duccio and Andrea di Bartolo. A triptych with the *Madonna and Saints Bernardino and Catherine* by Sano di Pietro stands out amid other gems by Sienese painters of the 14th and 15th centuries, and Donatello tops a list of the Renaissance sculptors also represented. ✉ *Via Soccini 18, Buonconvento* ☎ *0577/807181* ⊕ *www.museisenesi.org* 🎟 *€3* ⊘ *Closed Mon. and Tues. Oct.–Apr.*

Murlo

TOWN | If you're heading northwest to Siena, stray 9 km (5½ miles) west of the Via Cassia to Vescovado and then follow the signs 2 km (1 mile) south to this tiny fortified medieval *borgo* (village) that has been completely restored. ✉ *Buonconvento.*

Abbazia di Monte Oliveto Maggiore

9 km (5½ miles) northeast of Buonconvento, 37 km (23 miles) southeast of Siena.

GETTING HERE

From Siena, the abbey is a 45-minute drive on the SR2 south to Buonconvento and then the SP451 to Monte Oliveto. Bus and train service are not available.

Sights

★ **Abbazia di Monte Oliveto Maggiore**

RELIGIOUS BUILDING | Tuscany's most-visited abbey sits in an oasis of olive and cypress trees amid the harsh landscape of Le Crete. It was founded in 1313 by Giovanni Tolomei, a rich Sienese lawyer who, after miraculously regaining his sight, changed his name to Bernardo in homage to St. Bernard of Clairvaux. Bernardo then founded a monastic order dedicated to the restoration of Benedictine principles. The name of the order—the White Benedictines—refers to a vision that Bernardo had in which Christ, Mary, and his own mother were all clad in white. The monks are also referred to as Olivetans (the name of the hill where the monastery was built).

In the abbey's main cloister, frescoes by Luca Signorelli and Sodoma depict scenes from the life of St. Benedict. Signorelli began the cycle by painting scenes from the saint's adult life as narrated by St. Gregory the Great. Though these nine scenes are badly worn, the individual expressions pack some punch. Later, Sodoma completed scenes from the saint's youth and the last years of his life. Note the detailed landscapes, the rich costumes, and the animals (similar to those Sodoma was known to keep as pets). ✉ *Località Monteoliveto Maggiore 1, Chiusure, Asciano* ☎ *0577/707258* 🌐 *www.monteolivetomaggiore.it* 🎫 *Donation suggested.*

Restaurants

La Torre

$ | **TUSCAN** | You can enjoy straightforward Tuscan fare in the massive tower at the abbey's entrance, or, when it's warm, on a flower-filled terrace. The *pici ai funghi* (extra-thick handmade spaghetti with mushroom sauce) or *zuppa di funghi* (mushroom soup) take the sting out of a crisp winter day, and the grilled meats are a good bet at any time of year. **Known for:** pici all'aglione (a local specialty); simple food in historic setting; flavorful home cooking. [$] *Average main: €12* ✉ *Località Monteoliveto Maggiore 2, Chiusure, Asciano* ✢ *8 km (5 miles) south of Asciano on SS451* ☎ *0577/707022* 🌐 *www.facebook.com/ristorantelatorre-monteoliveto* 🕓 *Closed Tues.*

Hotels

Fattoria del Colle

$ | **B&B/INN** | Amid rolling vineyards and olive trees, this *fattoria* (farmhouse) produces fine wine and olive oil. **Pros:** great for families; beautiful location; dogs allowed. **Cons:** no phones in rooms; 30-minute walk to nearest town; no air-conditioning. [$] *Rooms from: €115* ✉ *Località Il Colle, Trequanda* ✢ *12 km (7 miles) east of Abbazia di Monte Oliveto Maggiore* ☎ *0577/662108* 🌐 *www.cinellicolombini.it* 🛏 *22 rooms* 🍴 *Free Breakfast.*

Asciano

8 km (5 miles) north of Abbazia di Monte Oliveto Maggiore, 25 km (16 miles) southeast of Siena, 124 km (77 miles) southeast of Florence.

Founded by the Etruscans around the 5th century BC, Asciano is now a sleepy little town surrounded by 13th-century walls. The tiny *centro storico* (historic center) is eminently bike-friendly; any serious cyclist should consider a pit stop here.

GETTING HERE

From Siena, driving to Asciano on the SP438 takes about 40 minutes. Tra-In has limited bus service, making the train, with five or six daily departures, a better option.

VISITOR INFORMATION

CONTACTS Asciano Tourism Office. ✉ *Via delle Fonti, Asciano* ☎ *0577/718811* ⊕ *www.terresiena.it.*

 Sights

★ Museo d'Arte Sacra e Archeologico Palazzo Corboli

ART MUSEUM | Palazzo Corboli, a magnificent palace dating from the 12th century, has been refurbished and houses the Museo d'Arte Sacra e Archeologico. The collection of Etruscan artifacts is worth a visit, though the real highlight is the collection of lesser-known 13th- and 14th-century paintings from the Sienese school. ✉ *Corso Matteotti 122, Asciano* ☎ *0577/714450* ⊕ *www.museisenesi.org* 🎫 *€5* ⏱ *Closed Mon. and Tues. Apr.–Oct. Closed weekdays Nov.–Mar.*

Monte Amiata

16 km (10 miles) south of Abbazia di Sant'Antimo, 86 km (52 miles) southeast of Siena, 156 km (94 miles) southeast of Florence.

At 5,702 feet, this benign volcano is one of Tuscany's few ski slopes, but it's no Mont Blanc. Come in warmer months to take advantage of an abundance of hiking trails that cross wide meadows full of wildflowers and slice through groves of evergreens. Panoramic views of all of Tuscany present themselves on the winding road up to the summit. Along the way, you pass through a succession of tiny medieval towns, including Castel del Piano, Arcidosso, Santa Flora, and Piancastagnaio, where you can pick up picnic supplies and sample the chestnuts and game for which the mountain is famous.

GETTING HERE

Monte Amiata can be reached by car from Siena on the SR2 (Via Cassia). Bus service is extremely limited. There is a train station at Monte Amiata Scalo, but it is at the base of the mountain and not well served by local buses.

VISITOR INFORMATION

CONTACTS Monte Amiata Tourism Office. ✉ *Via Adua 21, Abbadia San Salvatore* ☎ *0577/775811* ⊕ *www.terresiena.it.*

 Sights

Abbadia San Salvatore

TOWN | This 1,000-year-old village is worth a stop—skip the nondescript new town and head straight to the centro storico to explore winding stone streets with tiny churches around every corner. The abbey for which the town was named was founded in 743; its current appearance reflects an 11th-century renovation, but the original crypt remains intact.

In Search of Etruscan Artifacts

To fully appreciate the strangely quixotic relationship that the ancient Etruscan culture had with the tufa rock that provided the fabric of its civilization, you must visit southern Tuscany. The houses and tombs, and sometimes even the roads, were carved from this soft volcanic stone, making it impossible to think about the Etruscans without also imagining the dark sandy tufa that surrounded them.

Some of the best-preserved, and most mysterious, of all their monumental tombs are in the area of Pitigliano, Sorano, and Sovana. In the necropolis of the latter, you can actually walk on a section of Etruscan road that is almost 2,500 years old.

Chiusi should not be missed if you are interested in things Etruscan: several tombs that still retain their brightly colored decorations and a particularly fine and thoughtfully organized archaeological museum await you there.

The tourist office in town has hiking-trail maps for Monte Amiata. ✉ *Tourist office, Via Adua 21, Abbadia San Salvatore* ☎ *0577/775811* ⊕ *www.terresiena.it.*

Grosseto

TOWN | The largest town in southern Tuscany, Grosseto is the capital of the Maremma. First recorded in the 9th century as a *castellum* (small fort) built to defend a bridge and a port on the nearby River Ombrone, the town is now a thriving agricultural center. Badly damaged during World War II, it has been largely rebuilt since the 1950s, but a small centro storico, protected by defensive walls that follow a hexagonal plan, is worth a short visit on your way to the coast. ✉ *Grosseto.*

Sorano

38 km (23 miles) south of Abbadia San Salvatore on Monte Amiata, 138 km (86 miles) southeast of Siena, 208 km (130 miles) southeast of Florence.

Sorano's history follows the pattern of most settlements in the area: it was an ancient Etruscan citadel, built up in the 15th century and fortified by one of the many warring families of Tuscany (in this case, the Orsini). It's the execution that sets it apart. With its tiny, twisted streets and stone houses connected by wooden stairways and ramps, Sorano looks as if it was carved from the tufa beneath it—and that's because it was.

Underneath the town, visible as you approach, is a vast network of colombari, Etruscan-era rooms lined with hundreds of niches carved into stone walls, dating from the 1st century BC. The colombari aren't open to the public, but Sorano is worth a visit regardless, if only to walk its medieval alleyways and to watch old-style artisans at work. Views of the densely forested hills around town will have you reaching for your camera.

GETTING HERE

Being in the southern part of Tuscany, Sorano is most easily reached from Rome. From the A1 highway, take the Orvieto exit. There are no practical ways to arrive here by bus or train.

Hotels

Hotel della Fortezza

$$ | **B&B/INN** | High above Sorano, this austere-looking 11th-century Orsini castle has spectacular views of the town and surrounding countryside. **Pros:** no-smoking rooms; rooms have great views of Sorano; romantic location. **Cons:** might be too remote for some; not all rooms have air-conditioning; very basic decor. [$] *Rooms from: €159* ✉ *Piazza Cairoli 5, Sorano* ☎ *0564/632010* 🌐 *www.hoteldellafortezza.com* 🛏 *16 rooms* 🍴 *Free Breakfast.*

Pitigliano

10 km (6 miles) south of Sorano, 147 km (92 miles) southeast of Siena, 217 km (136 miles) southeast of Florence.

From a distance, the medieval stone houses of Pitigliano look as if they melt into the cliffs upon which they are perched. Etruscan tombs, which locals use to store wine, are connected by a network of caves and tunnels.

At the beginning of the 14th century, the Orsini family moved its base from Sovana to the better-fortified Pitigliano. They built up the town's defenses and fortified their home, Palazzo Orsini. Later, starting in 1543, Antonio da Sangallo the Younger added to the town's fortress, building bastions and towers throughout the town and adding the aqueduct as well.

Pitigliano has become a trendy locale for Italian vacation rentals, making the town center lively in summer. Restaurants serve up good meals that, as a result of the tourist boom, have inflated prices. Bianco di Pitigliano (Pitigliano white wine) is a fresh and light, dry wine produced from the vines that thrive in the tufa soil of the area.

GETTING HERE

Pitigliano is best reached by car along the SR74 from either the Via Aurelia to the west or the A1 highway to the east. Plan on a journey of about an hour. Pitigliano cannot be reached directly by train, but bus service is available from the train station in Grosseto.

VISITOR INFORMATION

CONTACTS Pitigliano Tourism Office. ✉ *Piazza Garibaldi 37, Pitigliano* ☎ *0564/616322* 🌐 *www.comune.pitigliano.gr.it.*

Sights

Duomo

CHURCH | This 18th-century Baroque cathedral has a single nave with chapels and paintings on the sides. There are two altarpieces by local artist Francesco Zuccarelli (1702–88), a Rococo landscape artist, a favorite of George III and one of the founders of the British Royal Academy. ✉ *Piazza S. Gregorio 1, Pitigliano.*

Museo di Arte Sacra

ART MUSEUM | The museum, housed in the Palazzo Orsini, has several rooms featuring paintings by Zuccarelli, who was born in Pitigliano in 1702. Other works include a Madonna carved in wood by Jacopo della Quercia (1371/74–1438), a 14th-century crucifix, period furniture, and a numismatic collection. ✉ *Piazza Fortezza Orsini 4, Pitigliano* ☎ *347/728–9656* 🌐 *www.palazzo-orsini-pitigliano.it* 🎟 *€5* 🕒 *Closed Mon.*

Restaurants

Il Tufo Allegro

$$ | **TUSCAN** | The name means Happy Tufa, and you will be happy, too, if you eat at this fine restaurant cut directly into the tufa rock plateau upon which old Pitigliano sits. The cuisine is local and regional: *pappardelle al ragù di cinghiale* (pappardelle pasta with wild boar sauce) is particularly tasty, and fish also figures

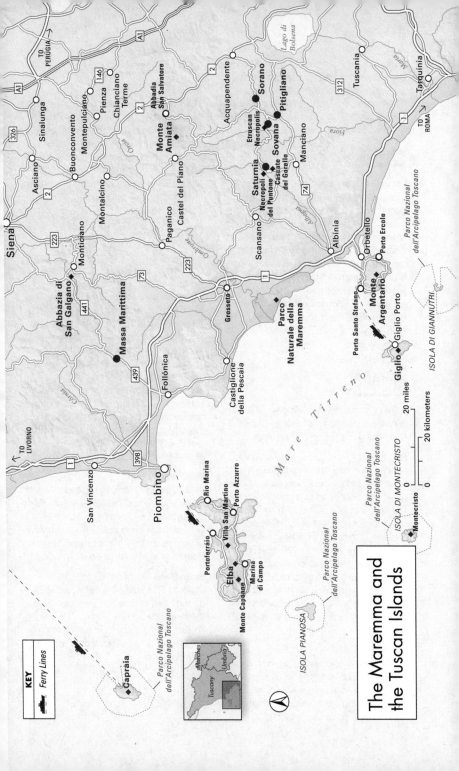

The Maremma and the Tuscan Islands

on the menu from time to time. **Known for:** local and regional cuisine; stunning setting; fixed-price menus available. $ *Average main: €25* ✉ *Vicolo della Costituzione 5, Pitigliano* ☎ *0564/616192* ⊘ *Closed Wed. No dinner Tues.*

 Hotels

Locanda Il Tufo Rosa

$ | **B&B/INN** | The space for part of this tiny guesthouse has been carved out of the tufa rock beneath the aqueduct at the entrance to the old town. **Pros:** excellent location; best value in town; kind and caring proprietors. **Cons:** getting here is difficult, narrow stairways to climb; some complain of traffic noise; rooms are small. $ *Rooms from: €85* ✉ *Piazza Petruccioli 97, Pitigliano* ☎ *0564/617019* ⊕ *iltuforosa.com* ⇌ *7 rooms* ⦿ *Free Breakfast.*

Sovana

5 km (3 miles) north of Pitigliano, 155 km (97 miles) southeast of Siena, 225 km (141 miles) southeast of Florence.

This town of Etruscan origin was once the capital of the area in southern Tuscany dominated by the Aldobrandeschi family, whose reign was at its height in the 11th and first half of the 12th centuries. One member of the family, Hildebrand, was the 11th-century Catholic reformer Pope Gregory VII (circa 1020–85). The 13th- to 14th-century Romanesque fortress known as the Rocca Aldobrandesca is now in ruins. Via di Mezzo, with stones arranged in a herringbone pattern, is the main street running the length of the town.

GETTING HERE

Like Sorano and Pitigliano, Sovana is best reached by car along the SR74, either from the Via Aurelia to the west or the A1 highway to the east. Sovana cannot be reached by train or easily by bus.

 Sights

Duomo

CHURCH | Sovana extends from the Rocca Aldobrandesca at the eastern end of town west to this imposing cathedral, built between the 10th and 14th century. The church, dedicated to Saints Peter and Paul, is Romanesque in style but, atypically, the main entrance is on the left-hand side of the building. ✉ *Piazza del Duomo, Sovana.*

Etruscan Necropolis

RUINS | Some of Italy's best-preserved monumental rock tombs, dating from the 2nd to the 3rd century BC, are found just outside the town at the Etruscan necropolis. Some of the tombs, such as the so-called Tomba Sirena (Siren's Tomb), preserve clear signs of their original and elaborately carved decorations. Others, like the Tomba Ildebranda (Hildebrand Tomb), are spectacular evidence of the architectural complexity sometimes achieved. Don't forget to walk along the section of an Etruscan road carved directly into the tufa stone. ✉ *Sovana* ⚓ *1½ km (1 mile) west of town center* ☎ *0564/488573* 🎟 *€5.*

Piazza del Pretorio

PLAZA/SQUARE | Here, in the central town square, you'll find the 13th-century Palazzo Pretorio, which has a facade adorned with coats of arms of Sovana's captains of justice, and the Renaissance Palazzo Bourbon dal Monte. ✉ *Sovana.*

Santa Maria Maggiore

CHURCH | This little 14th-century church on the main square has frescoes from the late-15th-century Sienese Umbrian school and a ciborium dating from the 8th century. ✉ *Piazza del Pretorio, Sovana.*

Restaurants

★ La Taverna Etrusca

$$ | TUSCAN | Elaborately prepared Tuscan fare is served at this elegant restaurant on Sovana's central square. For your starter, try the *tortino di pecorino maremmano con miele di castagno, gelatina di pere e cialda croccante* (local sheep cheese tart with chestnut honey, pear gelatine, and a Parmesan crisp); grilled meat and some fish dishes highlight the list of second courses, but a well-priced fixed menu might be a good way to go. **Known for:** tasty local dishes; attentive staff; outdoor seating. $ *Average main: €20 ⊠ Piazza del Pretorio 16, Sovana* ☎ *0564/616183* ⊕ *www.tavernaetrusca. com* ⊗ *Closed Wed. and Jan.–Easter.*

Saturnia

25 km (15 miles) of Pitigliano, 26 km (16 miles) northeast of Sovana, 129 km (77 miles) south of Siena, 199 km (119 miles) south of Florence.

Saturnia was settled even before the Etruscan period, but now it's best known not for what lies buried beneath the ground but for what comes up from it: hot, sulfurous water that supplies the town's world-famous spa. According to an oft-repeated legend, the thermal waters were created when Saturn, restless with Earth's bickering mortals, threw down a thunderbolt and created a hot spring whose miraculously calming waters created peace among them.

Today, these magnesium-rich waters bubble forth from the clay, drawing Italians and non-Italians alike seeking relief for skin and muscular ailments as well as a bit (well, a lot) of relaxation. Unlike better-known spa centers such as Montecatini Terme, nature still has its place here.

GETTING HERE

Saturnia is a 30-minute drive from Pitigliano. Follow the SS74 to Manciano, then the SS322 to Montemerano, and then turn right onto the Strada Saturnia–La Croce. The RAMA bus company travels from Grosseto to Saturnia, but three changes make the journey particularly arduous. There is no train service to Saturnia.

◉ Sights

Cascate del Gorello (*Gorello Falls*)
WATERFALL | Outside Saturnia, the hot, sulfurous waters cascade over natural limestone shelves at the Cascate del Gorello, affording bathers a sweeping view of the open countryside. The falls are on public land and can be enjoyed 24 hours a day. They get extremely crowded—day and night—during August. ⊠ *Saturnia ⊕ 2 km (1 mile) south of Saturnia, on road to Montemerano* ⊠ *Free.*

Necropoli del Puntone

RUINS | Pre-Etruscan tombs at this necropolis aren't kept up well, but they're interesting simply for their age, as they're even older than Saturnia's legendary baths. Access is free and at all hours. ⊠ *Saturnia ⊕ 1 km (½ mile) north of Saturnia, on road to Poggio Murello, turn left and follow signs.*

Terme di Saturnia

HOT SPRING | The swimming pools and treatments at Terme di Saturnia spa and resort are open to the public. You might make an appointment for a thermal mud therapy or rent a lounge chair and umbrella to sit by the pools. On weekends, the day price jumps a wee bit. ⊠ *Saturnia ⊕ 3 km (2 miles) east of Saturnia on road to Montemerano, after Gorello Falls* ☎ *0564/600111* ⊕ *www. termedisaturnia.it* ⊠ *From €26.*

🍴 Restaurants

★ Da Caino

$$$$ | **TUSCAN** | At this excellent restaurant not far from Saturnia, specialties include roast veal tongue with blueberry-flavored onions, saffron, and capers, *tortelli di cinta senese in brodetto di castagne e gallina* (pasta filled with Sienese pork in a chicken and chestnut broth), and such hearty dishes as *cinghiale lardolato con finocchi, arance e olive* (larded wild boar with fennel, orange, and olives). Prices are among the highest in the region; locals consider it a serious splurge. **Known for:** serious splurge; innovative cuisine; fine wine list. [$] *Average main: €50* ✉ *Via della Chiesa 4, Montemerano* ✣ *7 km (4½ miles) south of Saturnia on road to Scansano* ☎ *0564/602817* 🌐 *www.dacaino.it* ⏲ *Closed Wed., Jan., and 2 wks in July. No lunch Thurs.*

I Due Cippi

$$$ | **TUSCAN** | Alessandro Aniello and his brother, Lorenzo, carry on with the captivating food created by their late father. Local ingredients are emphasized, and the dishes are turned to perfection. **Known for:** duck and wild boar dishes; marvelous pastas; food with fantasy. [$] *Average main: €25* ✉ *Piazza Vittorio Veneto 26, Saturnia* ☎ *0564/601074* 🌐 *www.iduecippi.com* ⏲ *Closed Tues. No lunch.*

🛏 Hotels

Terme di Saturnia

$$$$ | **RESORT** | Spa living might not get any more top-notch than at this resort, where you can roam in a plush white bathrobe (waiting in your room) before dipping into the 37.5°C (100°F) sulfurous pools and where seemingly every possible health and beauty treatment is available. **Pros:** luxurious setting; excellent service; wide range of treatments. **Cons:** aseptic atmosphere; gets rather crowded on holidays; on the pricey side. [$] *Rooms from: €334* ✉ *Saturnia* ✣ *3 km (2 miles) east of Saturnia on road to Montemerano, past Gorello Falls* ☎ *0564/600111* 🌐 *www.termedisaturnia.it* 🛏 *114 rooms* 🍴 *Free Breakfast.*

Villa Acquaviva

$ | **B&B/INN** | An elegant villa painted antique rose appears at the end of a tree-lined driveway perched on top of a hill off the main road half a mile before Montemerano. **Pros:** near the hot springs; lovely views; some pets welcome. **Cons:** books up quickly; need a car to get around; attendants can be hard to find during the day. [$] *Rooms from: €108* ✉ *Strada Scansanese, Montemerano* ✣ *4 miles south of Saturnia* ☎ *0564/602890* 🌐 *www.villacquaviva.com* 🛏 *25 rooms* 🍴 *Free Breakfast.*

Parco Naturale della Maremma

10 km (6 miles) south of Grosseto, 88 km (55 miles) southwest of Siena, 156 km (97 miles) south of Florence.

GETTING HERE

The park is best reached by car from the Via Aurelia (SS1), which runs between Rome and Pisa. Local bus service connects the park with the train station in nearby Grosseto.

VISITOR INFORMATION

CONTACTS Parco Naturale della Maremma Tourism Office. ✉ *Via del Bersgliere 7/9, Alberese* ☎ *0564/393238* 🌐 *www.parco-maremma.it.*

👁 Sights

Parco Naturale della Maremma

STATE/PROVINCIAL PARK | **FAMILY** | The well-kept nature preserve at Monti dell'Uccellina is an oasis of green hills sloping down to small, secluded beaches on protected coastline. Wild goats and rabbits, foxes and wild boars, as well as horses and a domesticated long-horned white ox

A field of sunflowers in the Maremma

unique to this region, make their home among miles of sea pines, rosemary plants, and juniper bushes. The park also has scattered Etruscan and Roman ruins and a medieval abbey, the Abbazia di San Rabano.

Enter from the south at Talamone (turn right 1 km [½ mile] before town) or from Alberese, both reachable from the SS1 (Via Aurelia). Daily limits restrict the number of cars that can enter, so in summer it's best to either reserve ahead or to leave your car in Alberese and use the regular bus service. Contact the park's information office for bookings and to secure English-language guides. ✉ *Park Office, Via Bersagliere 7/9, Alberese* ☎ *0564/393211* ⊕ *parco-maremma.it* 🎟 *Free.*

Monte Argentario

Porto Santo Stefano: 60 km (37 miles) southwest of Saturnia, 118 km (74 miles) southwest of Siena, 186 km (116 miles) southwest of Florence.

Connected to the mainland only by two thin strips of land and a causeway, Monte Argentario feels like an island. The north and south isthmuses, La Giannella and La Feniglia, have long sandy beaches popular with families, but otherwise the terrain is rugged, dotted with luxurious vacation houses.

There are beautiful views from the panoramic mountain road encircling the promontory, and a drive here is a romantic sunset excursion. The mountain itself rises 2,096 feet above the sea, and it's ringed with rocky beaches and sheer cliffs that afford breathtaking views of the coast.

GETTING HERE

The Monte Argentario Peninsula lies just off the SS1 (Via Aurelia), which connects Rome and Pisa. It's a two-hour drive from either city. Intercity buses are not a viable option. The closest train station is in Orbetello Scalo, with local bus service available to both Porto Ercole and Porto Santo Stefano.

VISITOR INFORMATION

CONTACTS Monte Argentario Tourism Office. ✉ *Piazza delle Valle, Porto Santo Stefano* ☎ *0564/814208* 🌐 *www.monteargentario.info.*

Sights

Porto Ercole

TOWN | On the southeastern side of Monte Argentario, this small port town is the haunt of the rich and famous, with top-notch hotels and restaurants perched on the cliffs. ✉ *Monte Argentario.*

Porto Santo Stefano

TOWN | On the north side, busy and colorful Porto Santo Stefano is Monte Argentario's main center, with markets, hotels, restaurants, and ferry service to Giglio and Giannutri, two of the Tuscan islands. ✉ *Monte Argentario.*

Hotels

Il Pellicano

$$$$ | **RESORT** | Worldly cares are softly washed away by the comforts of the rooms (some damask linens, tapestry-like canopies, marble highboys), the superlative attentiveness of the staff, and the hotel's magnificent garden setting. **Pros:** spectacular setting and gardens; superlative service; excellent dining options. **Cons:** on a long dirt road; beach is rocky; isolated location. [$] *Rooms from: €923* ✉ *Località Lo Sbarcatello, Monte Argentario* ✥ *5 km (3 miles) west of Porto Ercole* ☎ *0564/858111* 🌐 *www.hotelilpellicano.com/en* 🕑 *Closed Nov.–Mar.* 🛏 *47 rooms* 🍴 *Free Breakfast.*

Massa Marittima

111 km (69 miles) southeast of Livorno, 48 km (30 miles) east of Piombino, 66 km (42 miles) southwest of Siena, 132 km (82 miles) southwest of Florence.

Massa Marittima is a charming medieval hill town with a rich mining and industrial heritage—pyrite, iron, and copper were found in these parts. After a centuries-long slump (most of the minerals having been depleted), the town is now popular simply for its old streets.

GETTING HERE

From Siena, the easiest way to reach Massa Marittima is to take the SP73bis, then the SP441. Bus service from Siena, provided by Tra-In, is not timed to make day trips feasible. Massa Marittima cannot be reached by train.

VISITOR INFORMATION

CONTACTS Massa Marittima Tourism Office. ✉ *Via Todini 3, Massa Marittima* ☎ *0566/902756* 🌐 *www.turismomassamarittima.it.*

Sights

Duomo

CHURCH | The central Piazza Garibaldi, dating from the 13th to the early 14th century, contains this Romanesque cathedral, with sculptures of the life of patron saint Cerbone above the door. ✉ *Via della Libertà 1, Massa Marittima.*

Museo Archeologico

HISTORIC SIGHT | The 13th-century Palazzo Pretorio, on Piazza Garibaldi, is home to this fascinating museum with plenty of Etruscan artifacts. A number of displays reconstruct the nature of daily life for the Etruscans who once inhabited the hills in this area. ✉ *Piazza Garibaldi 1, Massa Marittima* ☎ *0566/902289* 🌐 *www.museidimaremma.it* 🎫 *€4* 🕑 *Closed Mon.–Thurs., Jan.–Mar.; Mon. in Sept. and Oct.; and Mon.–Wed., Nov.–Dec. 20.*

Museo di Arte Sacra
ART MUSEUM | In the converted convent church of San Pietro all'Orto, this museum houses a large number of medieval paintings and sculptures gathered from churches in and around Massa Marittima. Perhaps the most important piece, Ambrogio Lorenzetti's early-14th-century *Maestà*, was discovered in the storage room of the church in 1866. ✉ *Corso Diaz 36, Massa Marittima* ☎ *0566/901954* 🎟 *€5* 🕑 *Closed Mon.–Thurs., Jan.–Mar.; Mon., Apr.–June and Sept.–Nov.; and Mon.–Wed., Nov.–Dec.*

Torre del Candeliere (*Tower of the Candlemaker*)
MILITARY SIGHT | **FAMILY** | Built to both defend and control their new possession after the Sienese conquered Massa Marittima in 1335, the Fortezza dei Senesi crowns the upper part of town. Just inside the imposing Sienese gate is the so-called Tower of the Candle Holder, a massive bastion that is connected to the outer walls by the Arco Senese, a high-arched bridge. A visit to the tower gives access to the arch and to the upper city walls, where commanding views open before you. ✉ *Piazza Matteotti, Massa Marittima* ☎ *0566/902289* 🌐 *www.museidimaremma.it* 🎟 *€4* 🕑 *Closed Mon., Apr.–June and Sept. and Oct.; closed Mon.–Wed., Nov. and Dec.*

Hotels

Rifugio Prategiano
$ | **B&B/INN** | **FAMILY** | Horseback trail rides through Tuscany's cowboy country are an integral part of the experience at this family-run country inn, where your hosts can arrange picnics, suggest itineraries, and organize weeklong tours. **Pros:** great for families with children; plenty of outdoor activities; peaceful setting with a swimming pool. **Cons:** no air-conditioning in some rooms; need a car to get around; very simple furnishings. [$] *Rooms from: €120* ✉ *Via dei Platani 3b, Località Prategiano, Montieri* ✥ *17 km (11 miles) west of Abbazia San Galgano* ☎ *0566/997700* 🌐 *www.hotelprategiano.it* 🕑 *Closed Nov.–mid-Mar.* 🛏 *24 rooms* 🍴 *Free Breakfast.*

Performing Arts

Balestro del Girifalco (*Falcon Crossbow Contest*)
FESTIVALS | **FAMILY** | On the fourth Sunday of May and again on the second Sunday in August, Massa Marittima's three traditional neighborhood groups dress in medieval costumes and parade through the town with much fanfare and flag throwing. The pinnacle of the event is a crossbow shooting competition between the town's districts. ✉ *Massa Marittima* 🌐 *www.comune.massamarittima.gr.it.*

Abbazia di San Galgano

32 km (20 miles) northeast of Massa Marittima, 33 km (20 miles) southwest of Siena, 87 km (54 miles) south of Florence.

Although time has had its way with this Gothic cathedral, it's still a hauntingly beautiful sight that's well worth a detour.

GETTING HERE

You'll need a car to get here, as bus and train service is not available. From Siena, follow the SP73bis, then take the SP441 south.

Sights

Abbazia di San Galgano
CHURCH | The church was built in the 13th century by Cistercian monks, who designed it after churches built by their order in France. But, starting in the 15th century, it fell into ruin, declining gradually over centuries. Grass has grown through the floor, and the roof and windows are gone. What's left of its facade and walls makes a grandiose and desolate picture. In July and August the

scene is enlivened by evening concerts arranged by the Accademia Musicale Chigiana in Siena. Contact the tourist information office at the abbey for details. ✉ *Strada Comunale di S. Galgano, Massa Marittima* ☎ *0577/049312.*

Eremo di Montesiepi

CHURCH | Behind the church of San Galgano, a short climb brings you to this charming little chapel with frescoes, by painter Ambrogio Lorenzetti (documented 1319–48), and a sword in a stone. Legend has it that Galgano, a medieval warrior and bon vivant, was struck by a revelation on this spot in which an angel told him to give up his fighting and frivolous ways forever. As a token of his conversion, he plunged his sword into the rock, where it remains today. ✉ *Strada Comunale di S. Galgano, Above Abbazia di San Galgano, Massa Marittima* ☎ *0577/750313* 🌐 *www.prolocochiusdino.it.*

Giglio

60 km (36 miles) south of Massa Marittima, 90 km (55 miles) south of Siena, 145 km (87 miles) south of Florence.

GETTING HERE

To get to Giglio, take one of the Toremar car ferries that run between Porto Santo Stefano on the Monte Argentario Peninsula and Giglio Porto. The trip, which costs €6.30 for passengers and €30 for cars, takes about an hour.

VISITOR INFORMATION

CONTACTS Giglio Tourism Office. ✉ *Via Provinciale 9, Giglio Porto* ☎ *0564/809400* 🌐 *www.isoladelgiglio.it.*

Sights

Isola del Giglio

ISLAND | This rocky, romantic isle, whose name translates to Island of the Lily, is an hour by ferry from Porto Santo Stefano but a world away from the mainland's hustle and bustle. The island's three towns—Giglio Porto, the charming harbor where the ferry arrives; Giglio Castello, a walled village at Giglio's highest point; and Giglio Campese, a modern town on the west side of the island—are connected by one long, meandering road. But to really explore Giglio you need a good pair of hiking boots. A network of rugged trails climbs up the steep hills through clusters of wild rosemary and tiny daffodils, and once you leave town, chances are your only company will be the goats who thrive on Giglio's sun-baked hills.

The island's main attraction, however, is at sea level—a sparkling array of lush coves and tiny beaches, most accessible only on foot or by boat. With the exception of Giglio Campese, where the sandy beach is as popular in summer as any mainland resort, most of the little island's coastline is untouched, leaving plenty of room for peaceful sunning for those willing to go off the beaten path.

Hotels

Pardini's Hermitage

$$$$ | **B&B/INN** | This ultraprivate hotel is free from noise except for the lapping of waves on the rocks; terraces and flowering gardens spill down a rocky cliff to private beaches below, and on the hill above, the owners raise purebred donkeys that you can ride over the mountain and goats that produce fresh yogurt and cheese for breakfast. **Pros:** hydromassages and mud baths are available at the hotel's spa; spectacular views; highly comfortable accommodations. **Cons:** isolation makes the hotel a poor base from which to tour the island; no air-conditioning; three-night minimum stay. [$] *Rooms from: €370* ✉ *Località Cala degli Alberi, Giglio Porto* ☎ *0564/809034* 🌐 *www.hermit.it* 🕒 *Closed Oct.–Mar.* 🛏 *12 rooms* 🍴 *All-Inclusive.*

🏃 Activities

HIKING

For day-trippers, the best hike is the 1,350-foot ascent from Giglio Porto to Giglio Castello. It's a 4-km (2½-mile) trek that takes about an hour and affords marvelous views of the island's east coast. Frequent bus service to and from Castello allows the option of walking just one way. The rest of the island's trails are reasonably well marked. Pick up maps at the tourist office in Giglio Porto.

WATER SPORTS

Boatmen

BOATING | Rent motorboats (usually with a skipper) for exploring the island's innumerable coves at this kiosk on the waterfront. Look for signs reading *noleggio barche* (boat rentals) near the ferry dock. ⊠ *On port, Via Umberto I, Giglio Porto* ☎ *349/350–8493.*

Elba

40 km (24 miles) southwest of Massa Marittima, 80 km (48 miles) southwest of Siena, 120 km (72 miles) southwest of Florence.

Elba is the Tuscan archipelago's largest island, but it resembles nearby verdant Corsica more than it does its rocky Italian sisters, thanks to a network of underground springs that keep it lush and green. It's this combination of semitropical vegetation and dramatic mountain scenery—unusual in the Mediterranean—that has made Elba so prized for so long, and the island's uniqueness continues to draw boatloads of visitors throughout the warmer months. A car is very useful for getting around the island, but public buses stop at most towns several times a day. The tourist office has timetables.

GETTING HERE AND AROUND

Toremar car ferries make the one-hour trip between Portoferraio and Piombino on the mainland. The cost is €14 for passengers and €34 for cars. From Piombino, Moby Lines also provides one-hour passenger ferry service to Portoferraio (no cars) for €17.87 per person.

Portoferraio is also a popular cruise-ship stop on Elba.

CAR AND SCOOTER

There are numerous places to rent transport on Elba, but may choose scooters or bicycles. Chiappi rents Honda and Yamaha scooters as well as campers, cars, and boats. Rent Modo rent bikes, scooters, motorcycles, or cars.

CONTACTS Chiappi. ⊠ *Calata Italia 38, Elba, Portoferraio* ☎ *0565/914366* ⊕ *rentchiappi.it.* **Toremar.** ⊠ *Piazzale Premuda 13, Nuova Stazione Marittima, Piombino* ☎ *199/117733 toll-free in Italy* ⊕ *www.toremar.it.*

FERRY

CONTACTS Moby Lines. ⊠ *Via Ninci 1, Portoferraio* ☎ *02/7602–7132, 199/303040 toll-free in Italy* ⊕ *www.moby.it.* **Rent Modo.** ⊠ *Via Renato Fucini 6, Portoferraio* ☎ *338/718–5735.*

VISITOR INFORMATION

For information about the flora and fauna to be found on Elba, as well as throughout the Tuscan archipelago, contact the Parco Nazionale dell'Arcipelago Toscano. The tourism office also has detailed walking and hiking maps.

CONTACTS Elba Tourism Office. ⊠ *Viale Elba 4, Portoferraio* ☎ *0565/914671* ⊕ *www.infoelba.com.*

👁 Sights

Marina di Campo

TOWN | On the south side of Elba, this small town with a long sandy beach and protected cove is a classic summer vacationer's spot. The laid-back marina is

A harbor on Elba

full of bars, boutiques, and restaurants. ⊠ *Marina di Campo.*

Monte Capanne

MOUNTAIN | The highest point on Elba, Monte Capanna is crossed by a twisting road that provides magnificent vistas at every turn; the tiny towns of Poggio and Marciana have enchanting little piazzas full of flowers and trees. You can hike to the top of the mountain, or take an unusual open-basket cable car from just above Poggio. ⊠ *Marciana.*

Montecristo

ISLAND | The most famous visitor to this island, about 50 km (30 miles) south of Elba, was fictional: Alexandre Dumas's legendary count. Today, the island is a well-protected nature preserve with wild Montecristo goats and vipers, peregrine falcons, and rare Corsican seagulls who make their home amid rosemary bushes and stunted pine trees. Scientific-research teams are given priority for permission to land on the island, and an annual quota of 1,000 visitors strictly limits even their number. ⊠ *Isola di Montecristo, Portoferraio.*

Museo Archeologico

OTHER MUSEUM | Exhibits at this museum reconstruct the island's ancient history through a display of Etruscan and Roman artifacts recovered from shipwrecks. The museum has experienced temporary closures, so check ahead on its status. ⊠ *Località Linguella, Calata Buccari, Portoferraio* ☎ *0565/944024* ⊕ *www. infoelba.it* ✉ *€7.*

Palazzina dei Mulini

HISTORIC HOME | During Napoléon's famous exile on Elba in 1814–15, he built this residence out of two windmills. It still contains furniture from the period and Napoléon's impressive library, with the more than 2,000 volumes that he brought here from France. ⊠ *Piazzale Napoleone 1, Portoferraio* ☎ *0565/915846* ⊕ *www. infoelba.it* ✉ *From €5* ☉ *Closed Tues.*

Porto Azzurro

TOWN | The waters of the port at Elba's eastern end are noticeably *azzurro* (sky-blue). It's worth a stop for a walk and gelato along the rows of yachts harbored here. ⊠ *Porto Azzurro.*

Portoferraio

TOWN | The lively port town where Victor Hugo (1802–85) spent his boyhood makes a good base for visiting Elba. Head right when you get off the ferry to get to the centro storico, fortified in the 16th century by the Medici grand duke Cosimo I (1519–74). Most of the pretty, multicolor buildings that line the old harbor date from the 18th and 19th centuries when the boats in the port were full of mineral exports rather than tourists. ⊠ *Portoferraio.*

Rio Marina

TOWN | Elba's quietest town is an old-fashioned port on the northeastern edge of the island. Here you'll find a pebble beach, an old mine, a leafy public park, and ferry service to Piombino. ⊠ *Rio Marina.*

Villa San Martino

HISTORIC HOME | A couple of miles outside Portoferraio, this splendid villa was Napoléon's summer home during his 10-month exile on Elba. Temporary exhibitions are held in a gallery attached to the main building. The Egyptian Room, decorated with idealized scenes of the Egyptian campaign, may have provided Napoléon the consolation of glories past. The villa's classical facade was added by a Russian prince, Anatolio Demidoff, after he bought the house in 1852. ⊠ *Località San Martino, Portoferraio* ☎ *0565/914688* ⊕ *www.infoelba.it* ⊠ *From €5.*

 Restaurants

Ristorante Pizzeria Il Mare

$$ | **ITALIAN** | Homemade pastas and fresh seafood are served here with a dash of style. The chef puts a creative spin on the classics, coming up with such delights as homemade vegetable gnocchi with scampi in a butter and saffron sauce. **Known for:** delicious pizzas; genial service; well-prepared octopus. $ *Average main: €15* ⊠ *Via del Pozzo 16, Rio Marina* ☎ *0565/962117* ⊘ *Closed Nov.–Mar.*

Trattoria da Lido

$$ | **SEAFOOD** | This well-established restaurant serves commendable primi and stellar *elbana* (whitefish baked with vegetables and potatoes). The bustling, casual trattoria is in the old center of Portoferraio, at the beginning of the road to the old Medici walls. **Known for:** pesce all'elbana (fish of the day baked with potatoes and vegetables); great waitstaff; gnocchetti di pesce (bite-size potato dumplings with a hearty fish sauce). $ *Average main: €16* ⊠ *Salita del Falcone 2, Portoferraio* ☎ *0565/914650* ⊕ *www.ristorantelido.org* ⊘ *Closed Sun. and mid-Dec.–mid-Feb.*

Hotels

Hermitage

$$$$ | **HOTEL** | This hotel on a private bay provides access to a sandy white beach from the bar and restaurant. **Pros:** wide range of sports equipment; several good restaurants; on a private beach and bay. **Cons:** can get very crowded; books up quickly; a car is necessary. $ *Rooms from: €600* ⊠ *Strada della Biodola 1, Portoferraio* ✛ *8 km (5 miles) west of Portoferraio* ☎ *0565/9740* ⊕ *www.hotel-hermitage.it* ⊘ *Closed Oct.–Mar.* ⊐ *130 rooms* ⦿ *Free Breakfast.*

Park Hotel Napoleone

$ | **HOTEL** | At this late-19th-century villa—in a park next to Napoléon's Villa San Martino—hand-painted medallions form the centerpieces of scrolled ironwork beds and chairs that are painted in colors coordinating with the draperies. **Pros:** in a gorgeous park; excellent restaurant; a great base for exploring the island. **Cons:** somewhat isolated; some furnishings show their age; hour-long walk to the beach and nearest town. $ *Rooms from: €103* ⊠ *Località San Martino, Portoferraio*

✥ *5 km (3 miles) west of Portoferraio's center* ☎ *0565/918502* 🌐 *www.elbaparkhotelnapoleone.it* ⏲ *Closed Nov.–Easter* 🛏 *64 rooms* 🍴 *Free Breakfast.*

Rio sul Mare

$ | **B&B/INN** | **FAMILY** | Convenient to Rio Marina's charming town center and gravel beach, this comfortable hotel has pretty sea views, especially from one of the five rooms that have terraces facing the sea. **Pros:** close to town center; very attractive sea views from all rooms; great value for money. **Cons:** the nearby beach is rocky; books up quickly; not all rooms have air-conditioning. [$] *Rooms from: €85* ✉ *Via Palestro 31, Rio Marina* ☎ *0565/924225* 🌐 *www.hotelriomarina.com* ⏲ *Closed Nov.–Mar.* 🛏 *35 rooms* 🍴 *Free Breakfast.*

Activities

BEACHES

Elba's most celebrated beaches are the sandy stretches at Biodola, Procchio, and Marina di Campo, but the entire island—and particularly the westernmost section, encircling Monte Capanne—is ringed with beautiful coastline. Indeed, it seems every sleepy town has its own perfect tiny beach. There are also some stretches accessible only by boat, such as the black-sand beach of Punta Nera. Try Cavoli and Fetovaia anytime but July and August, when the car-accessible beaches on the island are packed.

WATER SPORTS

Il Viottolo

BIKING | Adventurous types can rent sea kayaks and mountain bikes from this tour operator, which also offers three-day guided excursions on land or by sea. ✉ *Via Puccini 55, Marina di Campo* ☎ *329/736–7100* 🌐 *www.ilviottolo.com.*

Spaziomare

BOATING | Head here to rent a motorboat for a half or full day. Sailboats to rent by the week are also available. ✉ *Via Vittorio Veneto 13, Porto Azzurro* ☎ *0565/95112* 🌐 *www.spaziomare.it.*

Subnow

SCUBA DIVING | Contact this group of experienced divers for information on diving excursions in the waters of Elba's National Marine Park. ✉ *Via della Foce 32, Località La Foce, Marina di Campo* ☎ *348/158–0495* 🌐 *www.subnow.it.*

Capraia

60 km (35 miles) west of Massa Marittima, 90 km (55 miles) west of Siena, 110 km (66 miles) southwest of Florence.

GETTING HERE

Car ferry service from Livorno is provided by Toremar. The trip takes 2½ hours.

VISITOR INFORMATION

CONTACTS Capraia Tourism Office. ✉ *Via Assunzione 72* ☎ *0586/905071* 🌐 *www.prolococapraiaisola.it.*

Sights

Capraia

ISLAND | Only a handful of people actually live on the island of Capraia, which is frequented mainly by sailors. It's a rocky and hilly unspoiled national park, with only one sandy beach, Cala della Mortola, on the northern end of the island. the rest of the coast is a succession of cliffs and deep green coves with pretty rock formations. The 2½-hour ferry trip departs from Livorno and docks at the town of Capraia Isola, dominated by the Fortezza di San Giorgio up above. Nearby, an archway leads to an area that was once a prison.

Activities

Capraia Diving Club

SCUBA DIVING | Capraia's clear waters and undersea life draw raves from scuba divers. Equipment, boats for rent, and the guidance of qualified instructors are available through this diving service. ✉ *Via Assunzione 100/B, Capraia Isola* ☎ *333/317–2333* 🌐 *www.capraiadiving.it.*

Chapter 8

UMBRIA AND THE MARCHES

8

Updated by
Liz Humphreys

⊙ Sights	⑪ Restaurants	🛏 Hotels	⊕ Shopping	☕ Nightlife
★★★★☆	★★★★☆	★★★★☆	★★★☆☆	★★☆☆☆

WELCOME TO UMBRIA AND THE MARCHES

TOP REASONS TO GO

★ **Palazzo Ducale, Urbino:** A visit here reveals more about the ideals of the Renaissance than a shelf of history books could.

★ **Assisi, shrine to St. Francis:** Recharge your soul in this rose-color hill town with a visit to the gentle saint's majestic basilica, adorned with great frescoes.

★ **Spoleto, Umbria's musical Mecca:** Crowds descend and prices ascend here during summer's Festival dei Due Mondi, but Spoleto's hushed charm enchants year-round.

★ **Tantalizing truffles:** Are Umbria's celebrated "black diamonds" coveted for their pungent flavor, their rarity, or their power in the realm of romance?

★ **Orvieto's Duomo:** Arresting visions of heaven and hell on the facade and brilliant frescoes within make this Gothic cathedral a dazzler.

1 Perugia. Umbria's largest town, filled with university students.

2 Assisi. The fascinating city of St. Francis.

3 Gubbio. A medieval mountainous town in North Umbria.

4 Deruta. A 14th-century town famous for its ceramics.

5 Spello. A pretty hilltop town known for its cuisine.

6 Montefalco. A wine town nicknamed "balcony over Umbria."

7 Spoleto. Come to see the Piazza del Duomo.

8 The Valnerina. Valley of the River Nera.

9 Todi. Considered Umbria's prettiest hill town.

10 Orvieto. Carved out of volcanic rock and known for its cathedral.

11 Urbino. See the Palazzo Ducale here.

12 Loreto. Home to the House of the Virgin Mary.

13 Ascoli Piceno. A major producer of fruit and olives in the region.

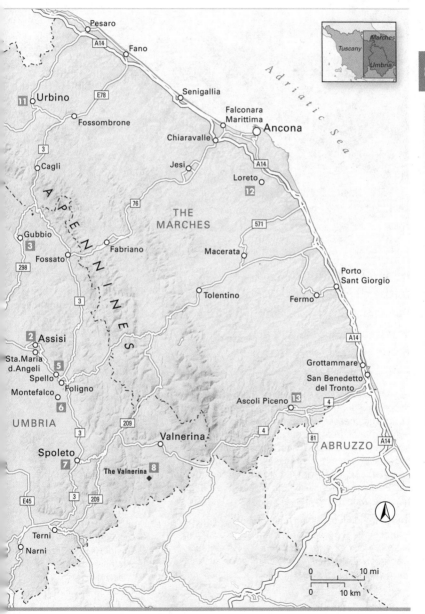

EATING AND DRINKING WELL IN UMBRIA AND THE MARCHES

Central Italy is mountainous, and its food is hearty and straightforward, with a stick-to-the-ribs quality that sees hardworking farmers and artisans through a long day's work and helps them make the steep climb home at night.

In restaurants here, as in much of Italy, you're rewarded for seeking out the local cuisines, and you'll often find better and cheaper food if you're willing to stray a few hundred yards from the main sights. Spoleto is noted for its good food and service, probably a result of high expectations from the international arts crowd. For gourmet food, however, it's hard to beat Montefalco and Bevagna, which have both excellent restaurants and first-rate wine merchants.

A rule of thumb for eating well throughout Umbria is to order what's in season; stroll through local markets to see what's for sale. Also, a number of restaurants in the region offer *degustazione* (tasting) menus that give you a chance to try different local specialties without breaking the bank.

TASTY TRUFFLES

More truffles are found in Umbria than anywhere else in Italy. Spoleto and Norcia are prime territory for the *tartufo nero* (reddish-black interior and fine white veins), prized for its extravagant flavor and intense aroma.

The mild summer truffle, *scorzone estivo* (black outside and beige inside), is in season from May through December. The *scorzone autunnale* (burnt brown color and visible veins inside) is found from October through December.

OLIVE OIL

Nearly everywhere you look in Umbria, olive trees grace the hillsides. The soil of the Apennines allows the olives to ripen slowly, guaranteeing low acidity, a cardinal virtue of fine oil. Look for restaurants that proudly display their own oil, often a sign that they care about their food.

Umbria's finest oil is found in Trevi, where the local product is intensely green and fruity. You can sample it in the town's wine bars, which often offer olive-oil tastings.

PORK PRODUCTS

Much of traditional Umbrian cuisine revolves around pork. It can be cooked in wood-fired stoves, sometimes basted with a rich sauce made from innards and red wine. The roasted pork known as *porchetta* is grilled on a spit and flavored with fennel and herbs, leaving a crisp outer sheen.

In Norcia, the art of pork processing has been handed down through generations, so much so that charcuterie producers throughout Italy are often known as *norcini*. Don't miss *prosciutto di Norcia*, which is aged for two years.

LENTILS AND SOUPS

Throughout Umbria, look for *imbrecciata*, a soup of beans and grains,

delicately flavored with local herbs. The town of Castelluccio di Norcia is particularly known for its lentils and its farro (a grain used by the Romans, similar to wheat), as well as for the variety of beans used in its soups. Other ingredients that find their way into thick Umbrian soups are wild beet; sorrel; mushrooms; spelt; chickpeas; and the elusive, fragrant saffron, grown in nearby Cascia.

WINE

Sagrantino grapes are the star in Umbria's most notable red wines. For centuries they've been used in Sagrantino *passito*, a semisweet wine made by leaving the grapes to dry for a period after picking to intensify their sugar content. In recent decades, Montefalco Sagrantino *secco* (dry) has occupied the front stage. Both passito and secco have a deep, red-ruby color, with a full body and rich flavor.

The abundance of *enotecas* (wineshops and wine bars) has made it easier to arrange tastings. Many establishments also let you sample different olive oils on toasted bread, known as bruschetta. Some wine information centers, such as La Strada del Sagrantino in the town of Montefalco, will help set up appointments for tastings.

Birthplace of saints and home to some of the country's greatest artistic treasures, central Italy is a collection of misty green valleys and picture-perfect hill towns laden with centuries of history.

Umbria and the Marches are the Italian countryside as you've imagined it: verdant farmland, steep hillsides topped with medieval fortresses, and winding country roads. No single town here has the extravagant wealth of art and architecture of Florence, Rome, or Venice, but this works in your favor.

Small jewels of towns feel knowable, not overwhelming, and the cultural cupboard is far from bare. Orvieto's cathedral and Assisi's basilica are two of the most important sights in Italy, while Perugia, Todi, Gubbio, and Spoleto are rich in art and architecture.

East of Umbria, the Marches (Le Marche to Italians) stretch between the Apennines and the Adriatic Sea. It's a region of great turreted castles on high peaks defending passes and roads—a testament to the centuries of battle that have taken place here. Rising majestically in Urbino is a splendid palace, built by Federico da Montefeltro, where the humanistic ideals of the Renaissance came to their fullest flower, while the town of Ascoli Piceno can lay claim to one of the most beautiful squares in Italy.

Virtually every small town in the region has a castle, church, or museum worth a visit—but even without them, you'd still be compelled to stop for the interesting streets, panoramic views, and natural beauty.

MAJOR REGIONS

Umbria's largest town, **Perugia,** is home to some of Perugino's great frescoes. **Assisi,** the city of St. Francis, is a major pilgrimage site that retains its medieval hill-town character. The quiet towns lying around Perugia include **Deruta,** which produces exceptional ceramics. A massive castle towers over **Spoleto,** which is home to the Piazza del Duomo and Filippo Lippi frescoes in its cathedral.

Of central Italy's many hill towns, none has a more impressive setting than **Orvieto,** perched on a plateau 1,000 feet above the surrounding valley. East of Umbria, the steep, twisting roads of this region lead to well-preserved medieval towns before settling down to the sandy beaches of the Adriatic.

Planning

Getting Here and Around

BUS

Perugia's bus station is in Piazza Partigiani, which you can reach by taking the escalators from the town center.

Local bus services between all the major and minor towns of Umbria are good. Some of the routes in rural areas are designed to serve as many places as possible and are, therefore, quite roundabout and slow. Schedules change often, so consult with local tourist offices before setting out.

BUS CONTACTS Flixbus. ⊕ *www.flixbus. com.* **Sulga.** ☎ *075/500–9641* ⊕ *www. sulga.it.*

CAR

The steep hills and deep valleys that make Umbria and the Marches so idyllic also make for challenging driving. Fortunately, the area has an excellent, modern road network, but be prepared for tortuous roads if your explorations take you off the beaten track.

On the western edge of the region is the Umbrian section of the Autostrada del Sole (A1), Italy's principal north–south highway. It links Florence and Rome with Orvieto and passes near Todi and Terni. The S3 intersects with the A1 and leads on to Assisi and Urbino. The Adriatica superhighway (A14) runs north–south along the coast, linking the Marches to Bologna and Venice.

Central Umbria is served by a major highway, the RA6, which passes along the shore of Lake Trasimeno and ends in Perugia. Assisi is served by the modern highway S75; the S75 connects to the S3 and S3bis, which cover the heart of the region. Major inland routes connect coastal A14 to large towns in the Marches, but inland secondary roads in mountain areas can be winding and narrow.

TRAIN

Several direct daily trains run by the Italian state railway, Trenitalia, link Florence and Rome with Perugia and Assisi, and local service to the same area is available from Terontola (on the Rome–Florence line) and from Foligno (on the Rome–Ancona line).

Intercity trains between Rome and Florence make stops in Orvieto. The main Rome–Ancona line passes through Narni, Terni, Spoleto, and Foligno.

Making the Most of Your Time

Umbria is a nicely compact collection of character-rich hill towns; you can settle in one, then explore the others, as well as the countryside and forest in between, on day trips.

Perugia, Umbria's largest and liveliest city, is a logical choice for your base, particularly if you're arriving from the north. If you want something a little quieter, virtually any other town in the region will suit your purposes; even Assisi, which overflows with bus tours during the day, is delightfully quiet in the evening and early morning. Spoleto and Orvieto are the most developed towns to the south, but they're still of modest proportions. Charming Montefalco is a required stop for wine lovers.

If you have the time to venture farther afield, consider trips to Gubbio, northeast of Perugia, and Urbino, in the Marches. Both are worth the time it takes to reach them, and both make for pleasant overnight stays. In southern Umbria, Valnerina and the Piano Grande are out-of-the-way spots with the region's best hiking.

Festivals

If you want to attend an event, make arrangements in advance. During festival time, hotel rooms and restaurant tables are at a premium. A similar caveat applies for Assisi during religious festivals at Christmas, Easter, the feast of Saint Francis (October 4), and Calendimaggio (May 1), when pilgrims arrive en masse.

★ Eurochocolate Festival

FESTIVALS | FAMILY | If you've got a sweet tooth and are visiting in fall, book early and head to Perugia for Europe's largest chocolate festival, held for 10 days in mid-October. ⊠ *Ruggero d'Andreotto*

19/E, ☎ 075/500–3838 ⊕ www.euro-chocolate.com.

★ **Festival dei Due Mondi**

FESTIVALS | The annual event, held in late June and early July, is one of the most important cultural happenings in Europe, attracting big names in all branches of the arts, particularly music, opera, and theater. ⊠ Piazza del Commune 1 ☎ 0743/776444 ⊕ www.festivaldispoleto.com.

★ **Umbria Jazz Festival**

FESTIVALS | One of the world's biggest jazz festivals attracts big names and big crowds to Perugia for 10 days in July and to Orvieto for five days in December or January. ⊠ Piazza Danti 28 ☎ 075/573–2432 ⊕ www.umbriajazz.it.

Hotels

Virtually every older town, no matter how small, has some kind of hotel. A trend, particularly around Gubbio, Orvieto, and Todi, is to convert old villas, farms, and monasteries into first-class hotels. The natural splendor of the countryside more than compensates for the distance from town—provided you have a car. Hotels in town tend to be simpler than their country cousins, with a few notable exceptions in Spoleto, Gubbio, and Perugia.

Restaurants

As befits a landlocked territory, the cuisine of Umbria is firmly based on local produce. Consequently, most restaurants in the region offer menus that are strictly seasonal, though locals have ensured that the food most associated with Umbria—tartufi, or truffles—is available year-round thanks to their mastery of freezing, drying, and preserving techniques.

Truffles are added to a variety of dishes, especially local pastas stringozzi (also written strengozzi or strangozzi) and

ombrichelli. Lamb, pork, and boar are the most common meats consumed in Umbria, and lentils grown around Castelluccio are highly prized.

Seafood from the Adriatic predominates in the coastal Marches region, often made into brodetto, a savory fish soup. Inland, Ascoli Piceno is renowned for its stuffed green olives.

Restaurant and hotel reviews have been shortened. For full information, visit Fodors.com. Restaurant prices are the average cost of a main course at dinner or, if dinner is not served, at lunch. Hotel prices are the lowest cost of a standard double room in high season.

WHAT IT COSTS in Euros			
$	$$	$$$	$$$$
RESTAURANTS			
under €15	€15–€24	€25–€35	over €35
HOTELS			
under €125	€125–€200	€201–€300	over €300

Visitor Information

Umbria Regional Tourism Office. ⊠ Piazza Matteotti 18 ☎ 075/573–6458 ⊕ www.umbriatourism.it.

Perugia

157 km (98 miles) southeast of Florence, 65 km (40 miles) east of Montepulciano.

Perugia is a majestic, handsome, wealthy city, and with its trendy boutiques, refined cafés, and grandiose architecture, it doesn't try to hide its affluence. A student population of around 30,000 means that the city, with a permanent population of about 165,000, is abuzz with activity throughout the year. Umbria Jazz, one of the region's most important music festivals, attracts music lovers

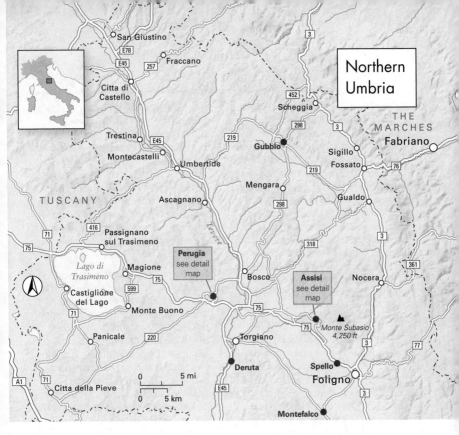

from around the world every July, and Eurochocolate, the international chocolate festival, is an irresistible draw each October for anyone with a sweet tooth.

GETTING HERE AND AROUND

The best approach to the city is by train. The area around the station doesn't attest to the rest of Perugia's elegance, but buses running from the station to Piazza d'Italia, the heart of the old town, are frequent. If you're in a hurry, take the *minimetro*, a one-line subway, to Stazione della Cupa.

If you're driving to Perugia and your hotel doesn't have parking facilities, leave your car in one of the lots close to the center. Electronic displays indicate the location of lots and the number of available spaces. If you park in the Piazza Partigiani, take the escalators that pass through the fascinating subterranean excavations

of the city's Roman foundations and lead to the town center.

Sights

Collegio del Cambio (*Bankers' Guild Hall*)
HISTORIC SIGHT | These elaborate rooms, on the ground floor of the Palazzo dei Priori, served as the meeting hall and chapel of the guild of bankers and money changers. Most of the frescoes were completed by the most important Perugian painter of the Renaissance, Pietro Vannucci, better known as Perugino. He included a remarkably honest self-portrait on one of the pilasters. The iconography includes common religious themes, such as the Nativity and the Transfiguration seen on the end walls. On the left wall are female figures representing the virtues, and beneath them are the heroes and sages of antiquity. On the

Umbria through the Ages

The earliest inhabitants of Umbria, the Umbri, were thought by the Romans to be the most ancient inhabitants of Italy. Little is known about them: with the coming of Etruscan culture, the tribe fled into the mountains in the eastern portion of the region. The Etruscans, who founded some of the great cities of Umbria, were in turn supplanted by the Romans. Unlike Tuscany and other regions of central Italy, Umbria had few powerful medieval families to exert control over the cities in the Middle Ages—its proximity to Rome ensured that it would always be more or less under papal domination.

In the center of the country, Umbria has, for much of its history, been a battlefield where armies from north and south clashed. Hannibal destroyed a Roman army on the shores of Lake Trasimeno, and the bloody course of the interminable Guelph–Ghibelline conflict of the Middle Ages was played out here. Dante considered Umbria the most violent place in Italy. Trophies of war still decorate the Palazzo dei Priori in Perugia, and the little town of Gubbio continues a warlike rivalry begun in the Middle Ages—every year it challenges the Tuscan town of Sansepolcro to a crossbow tournament. Today the bowmen shoot at targets, but neither side has forgotten that 500 years ago they were shooting at each other.

In spite of—or perhaps because of—this bloodshed, Umbria has produced more than its share of Christian saints. The most famous is St. Francis, the decidedly pacifist saint whose life shaped the Church of his time. His great shrine at Assisi is visited by hundreds of thousands of pilgrims each year. St. Clare, his devoted follower, was Umbria-born, as were St. Benedict, St. Rita of Cascia, and the patron saint of lovers, St. Valentine.

right wall are figures presumed to have been painted in part by Perugino's most famous pupil, Raphael. (His hand, experts say, is most apparent in the figure of Fortitude.) The *cappella* (chapel) of San Giovanni Battista has frescoes painted by Giannicola di Paolo, another student of Perugino's. ⊠ *Corso Vannucci 25, Perugia* ☎ *075/572–8599* ⊕ *www.collegiodelcambio.it* 🎫 *€5* ⊗ *Closed Sun. afternoon, also Mon. afternoon Nov.–Mar.*

Corso Vannucci

STREET | A string of elegantly connected palazzi expresses the artistic nature of this city center, the heart of which is concentrated along Corso Vannucci. Stately and broad, this pedestrian-only street runs from Piazza Italia to Piazza IV Novembre. Along the way, the entrances to many of Perugia's side streets might tempt you to wander off and explore. But don't stray too far as evening falls, when Corso Vannucci fills with Perugians out for their evening *passeggiata*, a pleasant predinner stroll that may include a pause for an aperitif at one of the many bars that line the street. ⊠ *Perugia*.

Duomo

CHURCH | Severe yet mystical, the Cathedral of San Lorenzo is most famous for being the home of the wedding ring of the Virgin Mary, stolen by the Perugians in 1488 from the nearby town of Chiusi. The ring, kept high up in a red-curtained vault in the chapel immediately to the left of the entrance, is stored under lock and key—15 locks, to be precise—most of the year. It's shown to the public on July

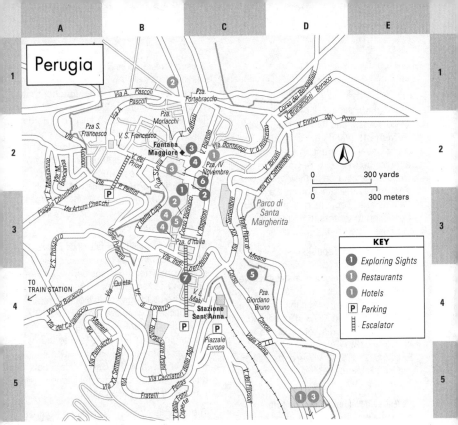

Perugia

KEY

- Exploring Sights
- Restaurants
- Hotels
- P Parking
- Escalator

Sights ▼	Restaurants ▼	Hotels ▼
1 Collegio del Cambio **B2**	1 Antica Trattoria San Lorenzo Simone Ciccotti **C2**	1 Le Tre Vaselle Resort & Spa **D5**
2 Corso Vannucci **C2**		2 Locanda della Posta.... **B3**
3 Duomo **C2**	2 Dal Mi' Cocco **B1**	3 Posta Donini 1579— UNA Esperienze **D5**
4 Galleria Nazionale dell'Umbria **C2**	3 Osteria a Priori **B2**	
5 Museo Archeologico Nazionale................. **C4**	4 Ristorante La Rosetta .. **B3**	4 Sina Brufani **B3**
6 Palazzo dei Priori **C2**	5 Ristorante La Taverna.. **B3**	
7 Rocca Paolina........... **B4**		

30 (the day it was brought to Perugia) and the second-to-last Sunday in January (Mary's wedding anniversary).

The cathedral itself dates from the Middle Ages, and has many additions from the 15th and 16th centuries. The most visually interesting element is the altar to the Madonna of Grace; an elegant fresco on a column at the right of the entrance of the altar depicts La Madonna delle Grazie. Sections of the church may be closed to visitors during religious services.

The Museo del Capitolo displays a large array of precious objects associated with the cathedral, including vestments, vessels, and manuscripts. Outside the Duomo is the elaborate Fontana Maggiore, which dates from 1278. It's adorned with zodiac figures and symbols of the seven arts. ⊠ *Piazza IV Novembre, Perugia* ☎ *075/572–3832* ⊕ *www.cattedrale.perugia.it* ⊠ *Museum €6* ⊗ *Museum closed Mon. Nov.–Mar.*

★ Galleria Nazionale dell'Umbria

ART MUSEUM | The region's most comprehensive art gallery is housed on the fourth floor of the Palazzo dei Priori. Enhanced by skillfully lit displays and computers that allow you to focus on the works' details and background information, the collection includes work by native artists—most notably Pintoricchio (1454–1513) and Perugino (circa 1450–1523)—and others of the Umbrian and Tuscan schools, among them Gentile da Fabriano (1370–1427), Duccio (circa 1255–1318), Fra Angelico (1387–1455), Fiorenzo di Lorenzo (1445–1525), and Piero della Francesca (1420–92). In addition to paintings, the gallery has frescoes, sculptures, and some superb examples of crucifixes from the 13th and 14th centuries. Some rooms are dedicated to Perugia itself, showing how the medieval city evolved. ⊠ *Corso Vannucci 19, Piazza IV Novembre, Perugia* ☎ *075/5866–8415* ⊕ *gallerianazionaledellumbria.it* ⊠ *€8* ⊗ *Closed Mon.*

Museo Archeologico Nazionale

HISTORY MUSEUM | An excellent collection of Etruscan artifacts from throughout the region sheds light on Perugia as a flourishing city long before it fell under Roman domination in 310 BC. Little else remains of Perugia's mysterious ancestors, although the Arco di Augusto, in Piazza Fortebraccio, the northern entrance to the city, is of Etruscan origin. ⊠ *Piazza G. Bruno 10, Perugia* ☎ *075/572–7141* ⊕ *www.musei.umbria.beniculturali.it* ⊠ *€5* ⊗ *Closed Mon.*

Palazzo dei Priori (*Palace of the Priors*)

GOVERNMENT BUILDING | A series of elegant, connected buildings serves as Perugia's city hall and houses three museums. The buildings string along Corso Vannucci and wrap around the Piazza IV Novembre, where the original entrance is located. The steps here lead to the Sala dei Notari (Notaries' Hall). Other entrances lead to the Galleria Nazionale dell'Umbria, the Collegio del Cambio, and the Collegio della Mercanzia.

The Sala dei Notari, which dates from the 13th century and was the original meeting place of the town merchants, had become the seat of the notaries by the second half of the 15th century. Wooden beams and an array of interesting frescoes attributed to Maestro di Farneto embellish the room. Coats of arms and crests line the back and right lateral walls; you can spot some famous figures from Aesop's *Fables* on the left wall. The palazzo facade is adorned with symbols of Perugia's pride and past power: the griffin is the city symbol, and the lion denotes Perugia's allegiance to the Guelph (or papal) cause. ⊠ *Piazza IV Novembre 25, Perugia* ⊠ *Free.*

Rocca Paolina

HISTORIC SIGHT | A labyrinth of little streets, alleys, and arches, this underground city was originally part of a fortress built at the behest of Pope Paul III between 1540 and 1543 to confirm papal dominion over the city. Parts of it were destroyed after the end of papal rule, but much still remains. Begin your visit by taking the escalators that descend through the subterranean ruins from Piazza Italia down to Via Masi. In summer, this is the coolest place in the city. ✉ *Piazza Italia, Perugia* 🎟 *Free.*

🍴 Restaurants

Antica Trattoria San Lorenzo Simone Ciccotti

$$ | **UMBRIAN** | Both the food and the service are outstanding at this popular small, brick-vaulted eatery next to the Duomo. Particular attention is paid to adapting traditional Umbrian cuisine to the modern palate, and there's also a nice variety of seafood dishes on the menu, both à la carte and in good-value tasting menus—the *pacchero* (pasta with smoked eggplant, cod, and scampi) is a real treat. **Known for:** fish and truffle tasting menus; modernized versions of local recipes; impeccable service. [$] *Average main: €24* ✉ *Piazza Danti 19/a, Perugia* ☎ *075/572–1956* 🌐 *anticatrattoriasanlorenzo.business.site* 🕒 *No lunch Sat.*

Dal Mi' Cocco

$$ | **UMBRIAN** | Favored by Perugia's university students, this casual spot with vaulted ceilings is fun, crowded, and inexpensive. Fixed-price meals change with the season and include starters, pasta, a main meat course, and dessert; each day of the week brings some new creation *dal cocco* (from the "coconut," or head) of the chef. **Known for:** abundant portions; honest prices; authentically casual feel. [$] *Average main: €15* ✉ *Corso Garibaldi 12, Perugia* ☎ *075/573–2511* 🌐 *www.facebook.com/ristorantedalmicocco* 🕒 *Closed Mon. and late July–mid-Aug.*

★ Osteria a Priori

$ | **MODERN ITALIAN** | This charming wine-and-olive-oil shop with a restaurant (featuring vaulted ceilings and exposed brick) tucked into the back offers up small plates using ingredients with a "zero-kilometer" philosophy: everything comes from local and artisanal Umbrian producers. Regional cheeses, homemade pastas, and slow-cooked meats steal the show, and, as might be expected, the selection of wine is top-notch. **Known for:** local, nontouristy atmosphere; knowledgeable servers; all Umbrian products. [$] *Average main: €13* ✉ *Via dei Priori 39, Perugia* ☎ *075/572–7098* 🌐 *www.osteriaapriori.it* 🕒 *Closed Sun.*

Ristorante La Rosetta

$$ | **ITALIAN** | The dining room of the hotel of the same name is a peaceful, elegant spot to get away from the bustle of central Perugia; in winter you dine inside under medieval vaults, and in summer, in the cool courtyard. The food is simple but reliable, and flawlessly served. **Known for:** professional service; refined versions of local meat dishes; elegant, old-fashioned setting. [$] *Average main: €18* ✉ *Piazza Italia 19, Perugia* ☎ *075/374–7858* 🌐 *www.ristorantelarosettaperugia.com.*

Ristorante La Taverna

$$$ | **UMBRIAN** | Medieval steps lead to a rustic two-story space where wine bottles and artful clutter decorate the walls. The regional menu features lots of delicious house-made pastas and grilled meats prepared by chef Claudio and served up in substantial portions, plus generous shavings of truffle in season. **Known for:** welcoming ambience; swift and efficient service; Umbrian specialties. [$] *Average main: €25* ✉ *Via delle Streghe 8, off Corso Vannucci, Perugia* ☎ *075/573–2536* 🌐 *www.ristorantelataverna.com* 🕒 *Closed Sun. and Mon.*

🛏 Hotels

Le Tre Vaselle Resort & Spa

$$ | **HOTEL** | **FAMILY** | Rooms spread throughout four stone buildings are spacious and graced with floors of typical, red-clay, Tuscan tiles; olive groves surround the outdoor pool, and the indoor

spa specializes in wine treatments. **Pros:** perfect for visiting the Torgiano wine area and Deruta; nice pool; friendly staff. **Cons:** service occasionally falters; amid an uninspiring village; somewhat far from Perugia. [$] *Rooms from: €149* ✉ *Via Garibaldi 48, Torgiano* ☎ *075/988–0447* 🌐 *www.3vaselle.it* 🛏 *52 rooms* 🍴 *Free Breakfast.*

★ **Locanda della Posta**

$$ | **HOTEL** | This friendly, centrally located, converted 18th-century palazzo off the bustling pedestrian-only Corso Vannucci features spacious rooms soothingly decorated in muted colors; some include original frescoes and beamed ceilings. **Pros:** some fine views; exudes good taste and refinement; central location. **Cons:** no gym or spa; no real lobby; some street noise. [$] *Rooms from: €139* ✉ *Corso Vannucci 97, Perugia* ☎ *075/572–8925* 🌐 *www.locandadellapostahotel.it* 🛏 *17 rooms* 🍴 *Free Breakfast.*

★ **Posta Donini 1579 — UNA Esperienze**

$$ | **HOTEL** | **FAMILY** | Beguilingly comfortable guest rooms set on lovely grounds—where gardeners go quietly about their business—along with a small but charming spa and a well-regarded restaurant make this historical hotel south of Perugia worth a stay. **Pros:** plush atmosphere; great restaurant; a quiet and private getaway. **Cons:** parking area can get full; uninteresting village; outside Perugia. [$] *Rooms from: €134* ✉ *Via Deruta 43, San Martino in Campo* ☎ *075/609132* 🌐 *www.postadonini.it* 🛏 *48 rooms* 🍴 *Free Breakfast.*

Sina Brufani

$$$ | **HOTEL** | Though a tad old-fashioned, this elegant, centrally located hotel dating from 1884 with a magnificent spa is the most upscale accommodation in town. **Pros:** wonderful location; excellent views from many rooms; unique spa area. **Cons:** service can be hit-or-miss; in-house restaurant not up to par; could use a refresh. [$] *Rooms from: €284* ✉ *Piazza Italia 12, Perugia* ☎ *075/573–2541* 🌐 *www.sinahotels.com* 🛏 *94 rooms* 🍴 *Free Breakfast.*

Nightlife

With its large student population, the city has plenty to offer in the way of bars and clubs. The best ones are around the city center, off Corso Vannucci.

Bottega del Vino

WINE BARS | This cozy wine bar offers a large selection of *vino* from around Italy as well as light meals; you can't go wrong with the *antipasti* (appetizers), cheese platter, or bruschetta. A live jazz band plays on Wednesday night. ✉ *Via del Sole 1, Perugia* ☎ *075/571–6181* 🌐 *www.labottegadelvino.net.*

★ **Living Café**

CAFÉS | Get the best views in town from the large terrace of this café-bar, attached to Ristorante del Sole. It's the most scenic spot in town for aperitivo; happy hour starts daily at 7 pm. ✉ *Via della Rupe 1, Perugia* ☎ *075/573–5031* 🌐 *www.ristorantesole.com.*

Zenoteca

WINE BARS | This informal hangout, with a living room atmosphere, serves up both Italian and international wines as well as craft beers. Regular live music nights draw an artsy crowd. ✉ *Via Prospero Podiani 14, Perugia* ☎ *0324/697–3490* 🌐 *zenoteca.business.site.*

Shopping

Stroll down any of Perugia's main streets, including Corso Vannucci, Via dei Priori, Via Oberdan, and Via Sant'Ercolano, and you'll see many well-known designer boutiques and specialty shops.

The most typical thing to buy is chocolate, which you can find almost anywhere. The best-known confections made by Perugina (now owned by Nestlé) are the chocolate-and-hazelnut-filled nibbles called Baci (literally, "kisses"). They're wrapped in silver foil that includes a sliver of paper, like the fortune in a fortune cookie, with multilingual romantic sentiments or sayings.

★ Chocostore by Eurochocolate

CHOCOLATE | The official store of the Eurochocolate festival sells bars, truffles, dipped fruits, and more chocolate goodies year-round. ⊠ *Piazza IV Novembre 7, Perugia* ☎ *075/573–2885* ⊕ *www. eurochocolate.com/store.*

Perugina

CHOCOLATE | At Baci Perugina's original home, you'll find these iconic chocolates in all shapes and sizes, along with chocolate bars and candies. ⊠ *Corso Vannucci 101, Perugia* ☎ *075/573–6677* ⊕ *www. sweetcityperugia.it.*

Assisi

28 km (17 miles) southeast of Perugia.

The small town of Assisi is one of the Christian world's most important pilgrimage sites and home of the Basilica di San Francesco—built to honor St. Francis (1182–1226) and erected swiftly after his death. The peace and serenity of the town are a welcome respite from the hustle and bustle of some of Italy's major cities.

Like many towns in the region, Assisi began as an Umbri settlement in the 7th century BC and was conquered by the Romans 400 years later. The town was Christianized by St. Rufino, its patron saint, in the 3rd century, but it's the spirit of St. Francis, a patron saint of Italy and founder of the Franciscan monastic order, that's felt throughout its narrow medieval streets. The famous 13th-century basilica was decorated by the greatest artists of the period.

GETTING HERE AND AROUND

Assisi lies on the Terontola–Foligno rail line, with almost hourly connections to Perugia and direct trains to Rome and Florence several times a day. The Stazione Centrale is 4 km (2½ miles) from town, with a bus service about every half hour.

Assisi is easily reached from the A1/E35 autostrada (Rome–Florence) and the SS75 highway. The walled town is closed to traffic, so cars must be left in the parking lots at Porta San Pietro, near Porta Nuova, or beneath Piazza Matteotti. Pay your parking fee at the *cassa* (ticket booth) before you return to your car to get a ticket to insert in the machine that will allow you to exit. It's a short but sometimes steep walk into the center of town; frequent minibuses (buy tickets from a newsstand or tobacco shop near where you park your car) make the rounds for weary pilgrims.

◉ Sights

Assisi is pristinely medieval in architecture and appearance, owing in large part to relative neglect from the 16th century until 1926, when the celebration of the 700th anniversary of St. Francis's death brought more than 2 million visitors. Since then, pilgrims have flocked here in droves, and today several million arrive each year to pay homage. But not even the constant flood of visitors to this town of 28,000 residents can spoil the singular beauty of this significant religious center, the home of some of the Western tradition's most important works of art. The hill on which Assisi sits rises dramatically from the flat plain, and the town is dominated by a medieval castle at the very top.

Even though Assisi is sometimes besieged by busloads of sightseers who clamor to visit the famous basilica, it's difficult not to be charmed by the tranquility of the town and its medieval architecture. Once you've seen the basilica, stroll through the town's narrow winding streets to see beautiful vistas of the nearby hills and valleys peeking through openings between the buildings.

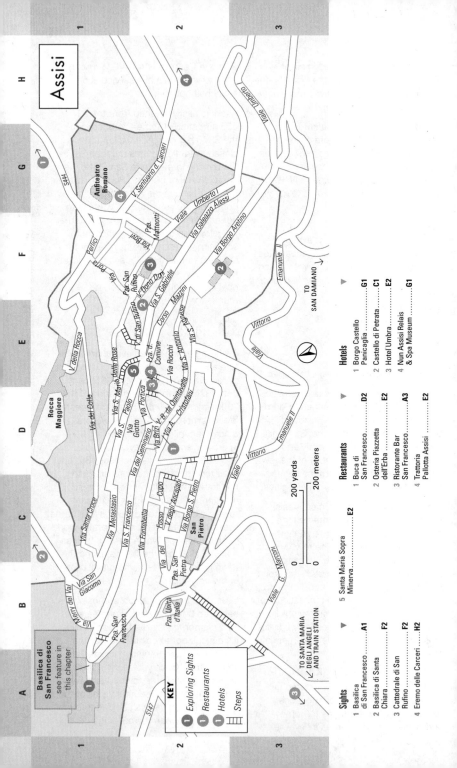

Assisi

Basilica di San Francesco
see feature in this chapter

Rocca Maggiore

Anfiteatro Romano

San Pietro

KEY

①	Exploring Sights
①	Restaurants
①	Hotels
⊞	Steps

Sights ▶

1 Basilica
  di San Francesco........**A1**
2 Basilica di Santa
  Chiara....................**F2**
3 Cattedrale di San
  Rufino....................**F2**
4 Eremo delle Carceri......**H2**

5 Santa Maria Sopra
  Minerva...................**E2**

Restaurants ▶

1 Buca di
  San Francesco............**D2**
2 Osteria Piazzetta
  dell'Erba.................**E2**
3 Ristorante Bar
  San Francesco............**A3**
4 Trattoria
  Pallotta Assisi..........**E2**

Hotels ▶

1 Borgo Castello
  Panicaglia...............**G1**
2 Castello di Petrata......**C1**
3 Hotel Umbra..............**E2**
4 Nun Assisi Relais
  & Spa Museum.............**G1**

0 ———— 200 yards
0 ———— 200 meters

TO SANTA MARIA
DEGLI ANGELI
AND TRAIN STATION

TO
SAN DAMIANO

★ **Basilica di San Francesco**

CHURCH | The basilica isn't one church but two: the Gothic church on the upper level, and the Romanesque church on the lower level. Work on this two-tiered monolith was begun in 1228. Both churches are magnificently decorated artistic treasure-houses, covered floor to ceiling with some of Europe's finest frescoes: the Lower Basilica is dim and full of candlelight shadows, while the Upper Basilica is bright and airy.

In the Upper Church, the magnificent frescoes from 13th-century Italian painter Giotto, painted when he was only in his twenties, show that he was a pivotal artist in the development of Western painting. He broke away from the stiff, unnatural styles of earlier generations to move toward realism and three-dimensionality. The Lower Church features frescoes by celebrated Sienese painters Simone Martini and Pietro Lorenzetti, as well as by Giotto (or his assistants). The basilica's dress code is strictly enforced—no bare shoulders or bare knees are permitted. ⊠ *Piazza di San Francesco, Assisi* ☎ *075/819–0084* ⊕ *www.sanfrancescoassisi.org* ☜ *Free.*

Basilica di Santa Chiara

CHURCH | The lovely, wide piazza in front of this church is reason enough to visit. The red-and-white-striped facade frames the piazza's panoramic view over the Umbrian plains. Santa Chiara is dedicated to St. Clare, one of the earliest and most fervent of St. Francis's followers and the founder of the order of the Poor Ladies—or Poor Clares—which was based on the Franciscan monastic order. The church contains Clare's body, and in the Cappella del Crocifisso (on the right) is the cross that spoke to St. Francis. A heavily veiled nun of the Poor Clares order is usually stationed before the cross in adoration of the image. ⊠ *Piazza Santa Chiara, Assisi* ☎ *075/812216* ⊕ *www.assisisantachiara. it* ☜ *Free.*

Cattedrale di San Rufino

CHURCH | St. Francis and St. Clare were among those baptized in Assisi's Cattedrale, which was the principal church in town until the 12th century. The baptismal font has since been redecorated, but it's possible to see the crypt of St. Rufino, the bishop who brought Christianity to Assisi and was martyred on August 11, 238 (or 236 by some accounts), as well as climb to the bell tower. Admission to the crypt includes the small Museo della Cattedrale, with its detached frescoes and artifacts. Visits to the crypt on weekends must be reserved at least one day in advance; see the website for details. ⊠ *Piazza San Rufino, Assisi* ☎ *075/812712* ⊕ *www. assisimuseodiocesano.it* ☜ *Church free, Crypt and Museum €4, Bell Tower and Museum €4, Bell Tower €2* ⊙ *Bell tower and museum closed Wed.*

Eremo delle Carceri

RELIGIOUS BUILDING | About 4 km (2½ miles) east of Assisi is a monastery set in a dense wood against Monte Subasio: the Hermitage of Prisons. This was the place where St. Francis and his followers went to "imprison" themselves in prayer. The only site in Assisi that remains essentially unchanged since St. Francis's time, the church and monastery are the kinds of tranquil places that St. Francis would have appreciated. The walk out from town is very pleasant, and many trails lead from here across the wooded hillside of Monte Subasio (now a protected forest), with beautiful vistas across the Umbrian countryside. True to their Franciscan heritage, the friars here are entirely dependent on alms from visitors. ⊠ *Via Eremo delle Carceri 38, 4 km (2½ miles) east of Assisi, Assisi* ☎ *075/812301* ⊕ *www.santuarioeremod-ellecarceri.org* ☜ *Donations accepted.*

Santa Maria Sopra Minerva

CHURCH | Dating from the time of the Emperor Augustus (27 BC–AD 14), this structure was originally dedicated to the Roman goddess of wisdom, and in later times it was used as a monastery and prison before being converted into a church in the 16th century. The expectations raised by the perfect classical facade are not met by the interior, which was subjected to a thorough baroque transformation in the 17th century. ✉ *Piazza del Comune 14, Assisi* ☎ *075/812361* 💲 *Free.*

 Restaurants

Buca di San Francesco

$ | UMBRIAN | In summer, dine in a cool green garden; in winter, under the low brick arches of the cozy cellars. The unique settings and the first-rate (though straightforward) fare make this central restaurant one of Assisi's busiest; try the namesake homemade spaghetti *alla buca,* served with a roasted mushroom sauce. **Known for:** warm and welcoming service; historical surroundings; cozy atmosphere. 💲 *Average main: €12* ✉ *Via Eugenio Brizi 1, Assisi* ☎ *075/812204* ⊕ *buca-di-san-francesco.business.site* ⊙ *Closed Mon. and 10 days in late July.*

★ Osteria Piazzetta dell'Erba

$$ | UMBRIAN | Hip service and sophisticated presentations attract locals, who enjoy Italian cuisine with unusual twists (think porcini mushroom risotto with blue cheese and blueberries), a nice selection of salads—unusual for an Umbrian restaurant—plus sushi options and intriguing desserts. The enthusiastic young team keep things running smoothly and the energy high. **Known for:** intimate ambience; inventive dishes; friendly staff. 💲 *Average main: €18* ✉ *Via San Gabriele dell'Addolorata 15/b, Assisi* ☎ *075/815352* ⊕ *www.osteriapiazzetta-dellerba.it* ⊙ *Closed Mon. and a few wks in Jan. or Feb.*

Ristorante Bar San Francesco

$$ | UMBRIAN | An excellent view of the Basilica di San Francesco from the covered terrace is just one reason to patronize this traditional restaurant, where Umbrian dishes are made with aromatic locally grown herbs. Menus change seasonally and include a fine selection of pastas and mains; appetizers and desserts are also especially good. **Known for:** pleasant staff; tasty seasonal dishes; prime Assisi location. 💲 *Average main: €20* ✉ *Via di San Francesco 52, Assisi* ☎ *075/813302* ⊕ *www.ristorante-sanfrancesco.com.*

Trattoria Pallotta Assisi

$$ | UMBRIAN | At this homey, family-run trattoria with a crackling fireplace and stone walls, the women do the cooking, and the men serve the food; try the *strangozzi alla pallotta* (thick spaghetti with a pesto of olives and mushrooms). Connected to the restaurant is an inn whose eight rooms have firm beds and some views across the rooftops of town. **Known for:** fast and courteous service; delicious meat plates, including pigeon and rabbit; traditional local dishes. 💲 *Average main: €18* ✉ *Vicolo della Volta Pinta 3, Assisi* ☎ *075/815–5273* ⊕ *www.trattoriapallotta.it* ⊙ *Closed Tues.*

Hotels

Advance reservations are essential at Assisi's hotels between Easter and October and over Christmas. Latecomers are often forced to stay in the modern town of Santa Maria degli Angeli, 8 km (5 miles) away. As a last-minute option, you can always inquire at restaurants to see if they're renting out rooms.

Until the early 1980s, pilgrim hostels outnumbered ordinary hotels in Assisi, and they present an intriguing and economical alternative to conventional lodgings. They're usually called *conventi* or *ostelli* ("convents" or "hostels") because they're run by convents, churches, or other Catholic organizations. Rooms are spartan but peaceful. Check with the tourist office for a list.

Continued on page 322

ASSISI'S BASILICA DI SAN FRANCESCO

The legacy of St. Francis, founder of the Franciscan monastic order, pervades Assisi. Each year the town hosts several million pilgrims, but the steady flow of visitors does nothing to diminish the singular beauty of one of Italy's most important religious centers. The pilgrims' ultimate destination is the massive Basilica di San Francesco, which sits halfway up Assisi's hill, supported by graceful arches.

The basilica is not one church but two. The Romanesque Lower Church came first; construction began in 1228, just two years after St. Francis's death, and was completed within a few years. The low ceilings and candlelit interior make an appropriately solemn setting for St. Francis's tomb, found in the crypt below the main altar. The Gothic Upper Church, built only half a century later, sits on top of the lower one, and is strikingly different, with soaring arches and tall stained-glass windows (the first in Italy). Inside, both churches are covered floor to ceiling with some of Europe's finest frescoes: the Lower Church is dim and full of candlelit shadows, and the Upper Church is bright and airy.

VISITING THE BASILICA

THE LOWER CHURCH

The most evocative way to experience the basilica is to begin with the dark Lower Church. As you enter, give your eyes a moment to adjust. Keep in mind that the artists at work here were conscious of the shadowy environment—they knew this was how their frescoes would be seen.

In the first chapel to the left, a superb fresco cycle by Simone Martini depicts scenes from the life of St. Martin. As you approach the main altar, the vaulting above you is decorated with the Three Virtues of St. Francis (poverty, chastity, and obedience) and St. Francis's Triumph, frescoes attributed to Giotto's followers. In the transept to your left, Pietro Lorenzetti's Madonna and Child with St. Francis and St. John sparkles when the sun hits it. Notice Mary's thumb; legend has it Jesus is asking which saint to bless, and Mary is pointing to Francis. Across the way in the right transept, Cimabue's Madonna Enthroned Among Angels and St. Francis is a famous portrait of the saint. Surrounding the portrait are painted scenes from the childhood of Christ, done by the assistants of Giotto. Nearby is a painting of the crucifixion attributed to Giotto himself.

You reach the crypt via stairs midway along the nave—on the crypt's altar, a stone coffin holds the saint's body. Steps up from the transepts lead to the cloister, where there's a gift shop, and the treasury, which contains holy objects.

THE UPPER CHURCH

The St. Francis fresco cycle is the highlight of the Upper Church. (See facing page.) Also worth special note is the 16th-century choir, with its remarkably delicate inlaid wood. When a 1997 earthquake rocked the basilica, the St. Francis cycle sustained little damage, but portions of the ceiling above the entrance and altar collapsed, reducing their frescoes (attributed to Cimabue and Giotto) to rubble. The painstaking restoration is ongoing. ⚠ The dress code is strictly enforced—no bare shoulders or bare knees.

FRANCIS, ITALY'S PATRON SAINT

St. Francis was born in Assisi in 1181, the son of a noblewoman and a well-to-do merchant. His troubled youth included a year in prison. He planned a military career, but after a long illness Francis heard the voice of God, renounced his father's wealth, and began a life of austerity. His mystical embrace of poverty, asceticism, and the beauty of man and nature struck a responsive chord in the medieval mind; he quickly attracted a vast number of followers. Francis was the first saint to receive the stigmata (wounds in his hands, feet, and side corresponding to those of Christ on the cross). He died on October 4, 1226, in the Porziuncola, the secluded chapel in the woods where he had first preached the virtue of poverty to his disciples. St. Francis was declared patron saint of Italy in 1939, and today the Franciscans make up the largest of the Catholic orders.

THE UPPER CHURCH'S ST. FRANCIS FRESCO CYCLE

The 28 frescoes in the Upper Church depicting the life of St. Francis are the most admired works in the entire basilica. They're also the subject of one of art history's biggest controversies. For centuries they thought to be by Giotto (1267-1337), the great early Renaissance innovator, but inconsistencies in style, both within this series and in comparison to later Giotto works, have thrown their origin into question. Some scholars now say Giotto was the brains behind the cycle, but that assistants helped with the execution; others claim he couldn't have been involved at all.

Two things are certain. First, the style is revolutionary—which argues for Giotto's involvement. The tangible weight of the figures, the emotion they show, and the use of perspective all look familiar to modern eyes, but in the art of the time there was nothing like it. Second, these images have played a major part in shaping how the world sees St. Francis. In that respect, who painted them hardly matters.

Starting in the transept, the frescoes circle the church, showing events in the saint's life (and afterlife). Some of the best are grouped near the church's entrance—look for the nativity at Greccio, the miracle of the spring, the death of the knight at Celano, and, most famously, the sermon to the birds.

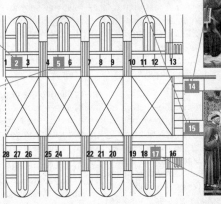

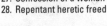

The St. Francis fresco cycle

1. Homage of a simple man
2. Giving cloak to a poor man
3. Dream of the palace
4. Hearing the voice of God
5. Rejection of worldly goods
6. Dream of Innocent III
7. Confirmation of the rules
8. Vision of flaming chariot
9. Vision of celestial thrones
10. Chasing devils from Arezzo
11. Before the sultan
12. Ecstasy of St. Francis
13. Nativity at Greccio
14. Miracle of the spring
15. Sermon to the birds
16. Death of knight at Celano
17. Preaching to Honorius III
18. Apparition at Arles
19. Receiving the stigmata
20. Death of St. Francis
21. Apparition before Bishop Guido and Fra Agostino
22. Verification of the stigmata
23. Mourning of St. Clare
24. Canonization
25. Apparition before Gregory IX
26. Healing of a devotee
27. Confession of a woman
28. Repentant heretic freed

★ Borgo Castello Panicaglia

$$$ | HOTEL | FAMILY | This rustic-chic, 17-room hotel between Assisi and Gubbio, dating from 1266 but thoroughly modernized inside, is a relaxing base for exploring the pretty Umbrian countryside. **Pros:** extremely family-friendly atmosphere; tasty and inventive meals; modern amenities in a historical building. **Cons:** location is quite rural; no spa; need a car to get around the area. $ *Rooms from: €208 ⊠ Località Panicaglia, Nocera ✛ 24 km (15 miles) northeast of Assisi ☎ 0742/81663 ⊕ www.borgocastello-panicaglia.com ⇨ 17 rooms* ⦿| *Free Breakfast.*

★ Castello di Petrata

$$. | HOTEL | Wood beams and sections of exposed medieval stonework add a lot of character to this 14th-century fortress, while creature comforts make each individually decorated room a delightful retreat. **Pros:** great views of town and country; peaceful pool; medieval character. **Cons:** limited choices in restaurant; far from Assisi town center; slightly isolated. $ *Rooms from: €142 ⊠ Via Petrata 25, Assisi ☎ 075/815451 ⊕ www.castello-petrata.it* ⦿ *Closed Sun.–Thurs. Jan. and Feb. ⇨ 20 rooms* ⦿| *Free Breakfast.*

Hotel Umbra

$ | HOTEL | Rooms on the upper floors of this charming 16th-century town house near Piazza del Comune look out over the Assisi rooftops to the valley below, as does the sunny, vine-covered terrace. **Pros:** very central; excellent valley views from some rooms; pleasant small garden. **Cons:** uninspiring breakfasts; some small rooms; difficult parking. $ *Rooms from: €110 ⊠ Via degli Archi 6, Assisi ☎ 075/812240 ⊕ www.hotelumbra.it* ⦿ *Closed Nov.–late Mar. ⇨ 24 rooms* ⦿| *Free Breakfast.*

★ Nun Assisi Relais & Spa Museum

$$$$ | HOTEL | Within walking distance of Assisi's restaurants and shops, this monastery built in 1275 has been converted into a thoroughly contemporary, high-end place to stay with a fabulous spa carved out of 2,000-year-old Roman baths. **Pros:** fantastic blend of the historical and modern; wonderful place to relax; excellent restaurant. **Cons:** split-level rooms with stairs difficult for those with mobility issues; on-site parking costs extra; on the expensive side. $ *Rooms from: €385 ⊠ Via Eremo delle Carceri 1A, Assisi ☎ 075/815–5150 ⊕ www.nunassisi.com ⇨ 18 rooms* ⦿| *Free Breakfast.*

Gubbio

39 km (24 miles) northeast of Perugia, 92 km (57 miles) east of Arezzo.

There's something otherworldly about this jewel of a medieval town, tucked away on the slopes of Monte Ingino. Even in the height of summer, the so-called Città del Silenzio (City of Silence) stays comparatively cool, and its dramatically steep streets remain relatively serene. At Christmas, kitsch is king. From December 7 to January 10, colored lights are strung down the mountainside in a shape resembling an evergreen, creating the world's largest Christmas tree.

Parking in the central Piazza dei Quaranta Martiri—named for 40 hostages murdered by the Nazis in 1944—is easy and secure. It's wise to leave your car there and explore the narrow streets on foot.

GETTING HERE AND AROUND

If you're driving from Perugia, take the SS318, which rises steeply up toward the Gubbio hills. The trip will take you 40 to 50 minutes. The closest train station is Fossato di Vico, about 20 km (12 miles) from Gubbio. Daily buses connect the train station with the city, a 30-minute trip. There are also many buses a day that leave from Perugia's Piazza Partigiani, the main Perugia bus terminal.

VISITOR INFORMATION

CONTACT Gubbio Tourism Office. ✉ *Via Repubblica 15,* ☎ *075/922–0693* 🌐 *www.ilikegubbio.com.*

Sights

Basilica di Sant'Ubaldo

CHURCH | Gubbio's famous *ceri*—three 16-foot-tall pillars crowned with statues of Saints Ubaldo, George, and Anthony—are housed in this basilica atop Monte Ingino. The pillars are transported to the Palazzo dei Consoli on the first Sunday of May, in preparation for the Festa dei Ceri, one of central Italy's most spectacular festivals. ✉ *Via Monte Ingino 5, Gubbio* ☎ *075/927–3872* 🌐 *diocesigubbio.it* 🎫 *Free.*

Duomo di Gubbio

CHURCH | Set on a narrow street on the highest tier of the town, the Duomo dates from the 13th century, with some baroque additions—in particular, a lavishly decorated bishop's chapel. ✉ *Via Ducale, Gubbio* ☎ *075/922138* 🌐 *diocesigubbio.it* 🎫 *Free.*

Funivia Colle Eletto

TRANSPORTATION | **FAMILY** | For a bracing ride to the top of Monte Ingino (where you can see the Basilica di Sant'Ubaldo), hop on the funicular that climbs the hillside just outside the city walls at the eastern end of town. It's more like an oversize metal birdcage than a cable car, and it's definitely not for those who suffer from vertigo. Operating hours vary considerably from month to month; check the funicular's website. ✉ *Via San Girolamo, Gubbio* ☎ *075/927–3881* 🌐 *www.funiviagubbio.it* 🎫 *€6 round-trip.*

Palazzo dei Consoli

HISTORY MUSEUM | Gubbio's striking Piazza Grande is dominated by this medieval palazzo, attributed to a local architect known as Gattapone, who is still much admired by today's residents (though some scholars have suggested that the palazzo was in fact the work of another architect, Angelo da Orvieto). In the Middle Ages, the Parliament of Gubbio assembled in the palace, which has become a symbol of the town and now houses a museum with a collection famous chiefly for the Tavole Eugubine—seven bronze tablets that are written in the ancient Umbrian language, employing Etruscan and Latin characters, and that provide the best key to understanding this obscure tongue.

Also in the museum is a fascinating miscellany of rare coins and earthenware pots. A lofty loggia provides exhilarating views over Gubbio's roofscape and beyond. For a few days at the beginning of May, the palace also displays the famous ceri, the ceremonial wooden pillars at the center of Gubbio's annual festivities. ✉ *Piazza Grande, Gubbio* ☎ *075/927–4298* 🌐 *www.palazzodeiconsoli.it* 🎫 *€7.*

Palazzo Ducale

CASTLE/PALACE | This scaled-down copy of the Palazzo Ducale in Urbino (Gubbio was once the possession of that city's ruling family, the Montefeltro) contains a small museum and a courtyard. Some of the public rooms offer magnificent views. ✉ *Via Federico da Montefeltro 2, Gubbio* ☎ *075/927–5872* 🌐 *www.musei.umbria.beniculturali.it* 🎫 *€5* 🕒 *Closed Mon.*

Restaurants

Ristorante Grotta dell'Angelo

$$ | **UMBRIAN** | In summer, the handful of outdoor tables are in high demand at this rustic trattoria, which is situated in a hotel of the same name at the lower part of the old town near the main square. The menu features simple local specialties, including *capocollo* (a type of salami), *stringozzi* (Umbrian wheat pasta), and lasagna *tartufata* (with truffles). **Known for:** homey atmosphere; good antipasti and grilled meats; reasonable prices. [$] *Average main: €15* ✉ *Via Gioia 47, Gubbio* ☎ *075/927–1747* 🌐 *www.grottadellangelo.it* 🕒 *Closed Tues. and Jan. 7–Feb. 7.*

★ Taverna del Lupo

$$ | **UMBRIAN** | One of the city's most famous taverns has a menu that includes such indulgences as lasagna made in the Gubbian fashion, with ham and truffles, and the *suprema di faraono* (guinea fowl in a delicately spiced sauce); save room for the excellent desserts. The restaurant also has two fine wine cellars and an extensive wine list. **Known for:** good wine list; alluring presentation; wide menu choice. $ *Average main: €20* ⊠ *Via Ansidei 21, Gubbio* ☎ *075/927–4368* ⊕ *www.tavernadellupo.it.*

Hotels

★ Castello di Petroia

$ | **HOTEL** | This atmospheric, 12th-century castle 15 km (9 miles) from Gubbio has spacious, antiques-filled, individually decorated rooms—some with decorated or beamed ceilings and stained glass, many with whirlpool tubs—as well as excellent in-house breakfasts and dinners. **Pros:** charming atmosphere; seasonal outdoor swimming pool; lovely breakfast buffet with handmade cakes and jams. **Cons:** temperature can be difficult to regulate in guest rooms; beds could be comfier; decor is on the simple side. $ *Rooms from: €120* ⊠ *Località Petroia, Gubbio* ☎ *075/920287* ⊕ *www.petroia.it* ۩ *Closed early Jan.–late Mar.* ➪ *13 rooms* ⦿ *Free Breakfast.*

Hotel Bosone Palace

$ | **HOTEL** | A former palace is now home to an elegant, if faded, hotel, where elaborate frescoes grace the ceilings of the two enormous suites and delightful breakfast room. **Pros:** friendly welcome; low rates; excellent location. **Cons:** can hear church bells ringing during the night; rooms and bathrooms on the small side; needs a refresh. $ *Rooms from: €62* ⊠ *Via XX Settembre 22, Gubbio* ☎ *075/922–0688* ⊕ *www.hotelbosone.com* ۩ *Closed early Jan. and Feb.* ➪ *30 rooms* ⦿ *No Meals.*

Deruta

19 km (11 miles) southeast of Perugia, 60 km (37 miles) southwest of Gubbio.

This 14th-century hill town is most famous for its ceramics. A drive through the countryside to visit the workshops is a good way to spend a morning, but be sure to stop in the medieval town itself.

GETTING HERE AND AROUND

From Perugia, follow the directions for Rome and the E45 highway; Deruta has its own exits. There are also buses from Perugia that take about 30 minutes to reach Deruta.

VISITOR INFORMATION

CONTACT Deruta Tourism Office. ⊠ *Via Biordo Michelotti 27* ☎ *075/972–8612* ⊕ *visitderuta.com.*

Sights

Museo Regionale della Ceramica

(*Regional Ceramics Museum*)

HISTORY MUSEUM | It's only fitting that Deruta is home to an impressive ceramics museum, which is housed in the 14th-century former convent of San Francesco. Panels in Italian and English explain artistic techniques and production processes, and the more than 6,000 items on display constitute the country's largest collection of Italian ceramics. The most notable are Renaissance vessels made using the *lustro* technique, which originated in Arab and Middle Eastern cultures some 500 years before coming into use in Italy in the late 1400s and which incorporates crushed precious materials such as gold or silver to create a rich, lustrous finish. ⊠ *Largo San Francesco, Piazza del Consoli 12, Deruta* ☎ *075/971–1000* ⊕ *www.museoceramicadideruta.it* ▦ *€7, includes Pinacoteca Comunale* ۩ *Closed Tues. and Wed.*

Pinacoteca Comunale

ART MUSEUM | The 14th-century Palazzo dei Consoli houses Deruta's Municipal Picture Gallery, open only on Sunday. The rich collection displayed over two floors includes frescoes and paintings by the Renaissance artists Perugino and L'Alunno, among other works from local churches. Upstairs, the Pascoli Collection features 17th- and 18th-century canvases, donated by a descendant of the prominent art collector and writer Lione Pascoli. Artists represented include Giovanni Battista Gaulli, Sebastiano Conca, and Francesco Trevisani. ⊠ *Piazza dei Consoli 12, Deruta* ☎ *075/971–1000* ⊕ *www.museoceramicadideruta.it* ⊠ *€7, includes Museo Regionale Della Ceramica* ⊘ *Closed Mon.–Sat.*

Shopping

Deruta is home to dozens of ceramics shops that offer a range of items, including extra pieces commissioned by well-known British and North American tableware manufacturers. A drive along Via Tiberina Nord takes you past one shop after another. If you ask, most owners will take you to see where they actually throw, bake, and paint their wares.

Spello

30 km (19 miles) southeast of Perugia, 12 km (7 miles) southeast of Assisi, 33 km (21 miles) north of Spoleto.

With well-appointed hotels, this hilltop town at the edge of Monte Subasio, just a short drive or train ride from Perugia or Assisi, makes an excellent base for exploring the region. Spello's art scene includes first-rate frescoes by Pinturicchio and Perugino, and contemporary artists can be observed at work in studios around town. If antiquity is your passion, the town also has some intriguing Roman ruins. And the warm, rosy-beige tones of the local *pietra rossa* stone on the buildings brighten even cloudy days.

GETTING HERE AND AROUND

Spello is an easy half-hour drive from Perugia. From the E45 highway, take the exit toward Assisi and Foligno. Merge onto the SS75 and take the Spello exit. There are also regular trains on the Perugia–Assisi line. Spello is 1 km (½ mile) from the train station, and it's a short, steep walk up to Porta Consolare.

From Porta Consolare, continue up the steep main street, which begins as Via Consolare and changes names several times as it crosses the little town. It also follows the original Roman road, so, as it curves around, you'll see winding medieval alleyways to the right and more uniform, Roman-era blocks to the left.

◉ Sights

Santa Maria Maggiore

CHURCH | The two great Umbrian artists hold sway in this 16th-century basilica. Pinturicchio's vivid frescoes in the Cappella Baglioni (1501) are striking for their rich colors, finely dressed figures, and complex symbolism. Among his finest works are the *Nativity, Christ Among the Doctors* (on the far left side is a portrait of Troilo Baglioni, the prior who commissioned the work), and the *Annunciation* (look for Pinturicchio's self-portrait in the Virgin's room). The artist painted them after he had already won great acclaim for his work in the Palazzi Vaticani in Rome for Borgia Pope Alexander VI. Two pillars on either side of the apse are decorated with frescoes by Perugino (circa 1450–1523). Hours to visit the cappella may be limited and vary by season; see the website for details. ⊠ *Piazza Matteotti 18, Spello* ☎ *0742/301792* ⊕ *www.smariamaggiore.com* ⊠ *€3 for Cappella Baglioni.*

326

 Hotels

Hotel Palazzo Bocci

$ | HOTEL | Lovely sitting areas, a reading room, bucolic ceiling and wall frescoes, and a garden terrace all add quiet, elegant charm to this slightly faded 14th-century property, where you could settle in for a week and take a cooking course or have the staff book you a bicycle or a horseback excursion. **Pros:** central location; abundant breakfasts; splendid views of the valley from public areas and some rooms. **Cons:** needs a spruce-up; not all rooms have views; noisy in summer months. $ *Rooms from: €103* ⊠ *Via Cavour 17, Spello* ☎ *0742/301021* ⊕ *www.palazzobocci.com* ⇥ *23 rooms* ⊙ *Free Breakfast.*

La Bastiglia

$ | HOTEL | Polished wood planks and handwoven rugs have replaced the rustic flooring of a former grain mill, and comfortable sitting rooms and cozy bedrooms are filled with a mix of antique and modern pieces. **Pros:** lovely terrace restaurant; fine views from top-floor rooms, some with terraces; leisure and wellness facilities. **Cons:** can use an overall refresh; no elevator and plenty of steps, so pack light; some shared balconies. $ *Rooms from: €110* ⊠ *Via Salnitraria 15, Spello* ☎ *0742/651277* ⊕ *labastiglia.com* ☉ *Closed 3 wks in Jan.* ⇥ *34 rooms* ⊙ *Free Breakfast.*

Montefalco

18 km (11 miles) south of Spello, 34 km (21 miles) south of Assisi, 48 km (30 miles) southeast of Perugia.

Nicknamed the "balcony over Umbria" for its high vantage point over the valley that runs from Perugia to Spoleto, Montefalco began as an important Roman settlement along the Via Flaminia. The town owes its current name ("Falcon's Mount") to Emperor Frederick II

(1194–1250). Obviously a greater fan of falconry than Roman architecture, he destroyed the ancient town, which was known as Coccorone, in 1249, and built in its place what would later become Montefalco. Aside from a few fragments incorporated in a private house just off Borgo Garibaldi, no traces remain of the old Roman center.

However, Montefalco has more than its fair share of interesting art and architecture and is well worth the drive up the hill. It's also a good place to stop for a meal, as is nearby Bevagna. You need go no farther than the main squares to find a restaurant or bar with a hot meal, and most establishments—both simple and sophisticated—offer a splendid combination of history and small-town hospitality.

GETTING HERE AND AROUND

If you're driving from Perugia, take the E45 toward Rome. Take the Foligno exit, then merge onto the SP445 and follow it into Montefalco. The drive takes around 50 minutes. The nearest train station is in Foligno, about 7 km (4½ miles) away. From there you can take a taxi or a bus into Montefalco.

VISITOR INFORMATION

CONTACT La Strada del Sagrantino. ⊠ *Piazza del Comune 17* ☎ *0742/378490* ⊕ *www.stradadelsagrantino.it.*

 Restaurants

★ Enoteca L'Alchimista

$$ | UMBRIAN | "The Alchemist" is an apt name, as the chef's transformations are magical, and everything can be paired with wines from the restaurant's extensive selection. Though pasta, veggie, and meat dishes change seasonally, the homemade gnocchi in Sagrantino sauce, always on offer, wins raves from guests, plus all the delicious desserts are made on the premises. **Known for:** refined but relaxed dining; congenial setting and atmosphere; extensive wine list. $ *Average main: €18* ⊠ *Piazza del Comune*

14, Montefalco ☎ *0742/378558* 🌐 *www.ristorantealchimista.it* 🕒 *Closed Tues.*

★ Redibis

$$ | **MODERN ITALIAN** | Housed in a Roman theater—built in the 1st century AD but brought up-to-date with mid-century modern furniture and sleek chandeliers—this restaurant has an atmosphere that's as unique as the food. The seasonally changing menu, featuring mainly zero kilometer products, aims to adapt ancient ingredients like Roveja wild peas of Colfiorito to sophisticated modern tastes, while offering a fine selection of Umbrian wines. **Known for:** beautifully presented dishes; focus on local producers; fascinating cavelike atmosphere. [$] *Average main: €23* ✉ *Via dell'Anfiteatro 3, Bevagna* ✥ *8 km (5 miles) northwest of Montefalco* ☎ *0742/362120* 🌐 *www.foodie.bio* 🕒 *Closed Tues.*

🛏 Hotels

★ Palazzo Bontadosi Hotel & Spa

$$ | **HOTEL** | This charming boutique hotel, set in an 18th-century palace overlooking the main square, has spacious, individually decorated rooms, where original frescoes and beamed ceilings contrast with modern furnishings and some bathrooms have deep soaking tubs. **Pros:** sophisticated, design-focused vibe; friendly service; spa in medieval cellars has a private Turkish bath and soaking pool. **Cons:** small breakfast selection; no gym; rooms facing the square can be noisy. [$] *Rooms from: €161* ✉ *Piazza del Comune 19, Montefalco* ☎ *0742/379357* 🌐 *hotelbontadosi.it* 🛏 *12 rooms* 🍴 *Free Breakfast.*

Villa Pambuffetti

$$ | **HOTEL** | If you want to be pampered in the refined atmosphere of a private villa, this is the spot, with the warmth of a fireplace in the winter, a pool to cool you down in summer, and cozy reading nooks and guest rooms year-round. **Pros:** peaceful gardens; excellent dining room; cooking courses offered. **Cons:** dated feel; grounds could be better kept; outside the town center. [$] *Rooms from: €140* ✉ *Viale della Vittoria 20, Montefalco* ☎ *0742/379417* 🌐 *www.villapambuffetti.it* 🛏 *15 rooms* 🍴 *Free Breakfast.*

Spoleto

24 km (15 miles) southeast of Montefalco, 46 km (29 miles) south of Assisi, 63 km (39 miles) southeast of Perugia, 80 km (50 miles) east of Orvieto.

For most of the year, Spoleto is one more in a pleasant succession of sleepy hill towns, resting regally atop a mountain. But for more than two weeks every summer the town shifts into high gear for a turn in the international spotlight during the Festival dei Due Mondi (Festival of Two Worlds), an extravaganza of theater, opera, music, painting, and sculpture.

As the world's top artists vie for honors, throngs of art aficionados vie for hotel rooms. If you plan to spend the night in Spoleto during the festival, make sure you have confirmed reservations, or you may find yourself scrambling at sunset.

Spoleto has plenty to lure you during the rest of the year as well: the final frescoes of Filippo Lippi, beautiful piazzas and streets with Roman and medieval attractions, and superb natural surroundings with rolling hills and a dramatic gorge. Spoleto makes a good base for exploring all of southern Umbria, as Assisi, Orvieto, and the towns in between are all within easy reach.

GETTING HERE AND AROUND

Spoleto is an hour's drive from Perugia. From the E45 highway, take the exit toward Assisi and Foligno, then merge onto the SS75 until you reach the Foligno Est exit. Merge onto the SS3, which leads to Spoleto. There are regular trains on the Perugia–Foligno line. From the train station it's a 15-minute uphill walk

The Sagrantino Story

Sagrantino grapes have been used to produce red wine for centuries. The wine began centuries ago as Sagrantino *passito*, a semisweet version in which the grapes are left to dry for a period after picking to intensify the sugar content. One theory traces the origin of Sagrantino back to ancient Rome in the works of Pliny the Elder, the author of the *Natural History*, who referred to the Itriola grape that some researchers think may be Sagrantino. Others believe that, in medieval times, Franciscan friars returned from Asia Minor with the grape. ("Sagrantino" perhaps derives from *sacramenti*, the religious ceremony in which the wine was used.)

The passito is still produced today and is preferred by some. But the big change in Sagrantino wine production came in the past decades, when Montefalco Sagrantino *secco* (dry) came onto the market. Both passito and secco have a deep ruby-red color that tends toward garnet highlights, with a full body and rich flavor.

For the dry wines, producers not to be missed are Paolo Bea, Terre di Capitani, Antonelli, Perticaia, and Arnaldo Caprai. Try those labels for the passito as well, in addition to Ruggeri and Scacciadiavoli. Paolo Bea's biodynamic wines are robust and long-lasting. Terre di Capitani is complex and has vegetable and mineral tones that join tastes of wild berries, cherries, and chocolate—this winemaker pampers his grapes and it shows. Antonelli is elegant, refined, and rich. Perticaia has a full, rounded taste. Caprai is bold and rich in taste. The Ruggeri passito is one of the best, so don't be put off by its homespun label.

At La Strada del Sagrantino in Montefalco's main square, you can pick up a map of the wine route, set up appointments, and book accommodations. Some wineries are small and not equipped to receive visitors. Visit the local enoteche, and ask the sommeliers to guide you to the smaller producers.

to the center, so you may want to take a local bus or a taxi.

VISITOR INFORMATION

CONTACT Spoleto Tourism Office. ✉ *Largo Ferrer 6* ☎ *0743/218620* ⊕ *www. comune.spoleto.pg.it.*

 Sights

The walled city is set on a slanting hillside, with the most interesting sections clustered toward the upper portion. Parking options inside the walls include Piazza Campello (just below the Rocca) on the southeast end, Via del Trivio to the north, and Piazza San Domenico on the west end. You can also park at

Piazza della Vittoria farther north, just outside the walls, or at one of several well-marked lots near the train station. If you arrive by train, you can walk 1 km (½ mile) from the station to the entrance to the lower town. Regular bus connections are every 15–30 minutes.

Like most other towns with narrow, winding streets, Spoleto is best explored on foot. Bear in mind that much of the city is on a steep slope, so there are lots of stairs and steep inclines. The well-worn stones can be slippery even when dry; wear rubber-sole shoes for good traction.

Several pedestrian walkways cut across Corso Mazzini, which zigzags up the hill, and three escalators connect the main

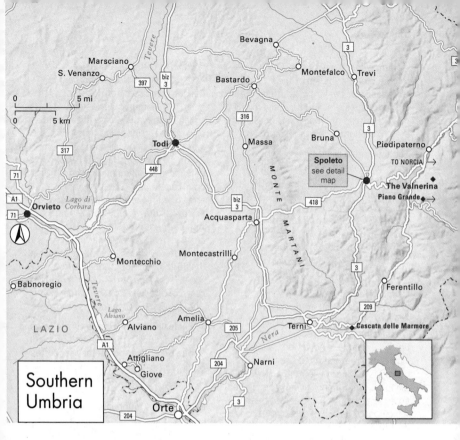

car parks with the upper town. A €9.50 Spoleto Card, sold at any of the town's museums, allows you entry to all the main museums and galleries over seven days.

Casa Romana (*Roman House*)

RUINS | Spoleto became a Roman colony in the 3rd century BC, but the best excavated remains date from the 1st century AD. Best preserved among them is the Casa Romana. According to an inscription, it belonged to Vespasia Polla, the mother of Emperor Vespasian (one of the builders of the Colosseum and perhaps better known by the Romans for taxing them to install public toilets, later called "Vespasians"). The rooms, arranged around a large central atrium built over an *impluvium* (rain cistern), are decorated with black-and-white geometric mosaics. ⊠ *Palazzo del Municipio, Via di Visiale 9, Spoleto* ☎ *0743/40255* ⊕ *www.*

spoletocard.it ✉ *€3; included with Spoleto Card* ⊘ *Closed Tues.*

★ Duomo di Spoleto (*Spoleto Cathedral*)

CHURCH | The 12th-century Romanesque facade received a Renaissance face-lift with the addition of a loggia in a rosy pink stone, creating a stunning contrast in styles. One of the finest cathedrals in the region is lit by eight rose windows that are especially dazzling in the late afternoon sun. The original floor tiles remain from an earlier church destroyed by Frederick I (circa 1123–90). Above the church's entrance is Bernini's bust of Pope Urban VIII (1568–1644), who had the church redecorated in 17th-century baroque; fortunately he didn't touch the 15th-century frescoes painted in the apse by Fra Filippo Lippi (circa 1406–69) between 1466 and 1469. These immaculately restored masterpieces—the

Annunciation, Nativity, and *Dormition*—tell the story of the life of the Virgin. The *Coronation of the Virgin,* adorning the half dome, is the literal and figurative high point. Portraits of Lippi and his assistants are on the right side of the central panel.

The Florentine artist-priest, "whose colors expressed God's voice" (the words inscribed on his tomb), died shortly after completing the work. His tomb, which you can see in the right transept (note the artist's brushes and tools), was designed by his son, Filippino Lippi (circa 1457–1504). ⊠ *Piazza del Duomo 2, Spoleto* ☎ *0577/286300* ⊕ *www.duomo-spoleto.it* ▣ *Free; €5 for audio guide.*

La Rocca Albornoz

CASTLE/PALACE | Built in the mid-14th century for Cardinal Egidio Albornoz, this massive fortress served as a seat for the local pontifical governors, a tangible sign of the restoration of the Church's power in the area when the pope was ruling from Avignon. Several popes spent time here, and, in 1499, one of them, Alexander VI, sent his capable teenage daughter, Lucrezia Borgia (1480–1519), to serve as governor for three months. The Gubbio-born architect Gattapone (14th century) used the ruins of a Roman acropolis as a foundation and took materials from many Roman-era sites, including the Teatro Romano.

La Rocca's plan is long and rectangular, with six towers and two grand courtyards, an upper loggia, and grand interior reception rooms. In the largest tower, Torre Maestà, you can visit an apartment with some interesting frescoes. The fortress also contains the Museo Nazionale del Ducato, 15 rooms dedicated to the art of the duchy of Spoleto during the Middle Ages. If you phone in advance, you may be able to secure an English-speaking guide. ⊠ *Piazza Campello, Spoleto* ☎ *0743/224952* ▣ *€8, including the Museo Nazionale del Ducato; included with Spoleto Card.*

★ Palazzo Collicola Arti Visive

ART MUSEUM | Spoleto's compact but delightful modern art museum, housed in an 18th-century palace, features a fine collection of works from Italian contemporary artists, including renowned Spoleto sculptor Leoncillo and Umbria-based American sculptor Barbara Pepper. International artists such as Alexander Calder and Richard Serra, are also represented, and an entire room is devoted to a large-scale wall drawing by Sol Lewitt. The Appartamento Nobile is a reproduction of an 18th-century nobleman's house, and the Pictures Gallery has paintings from the 16th to 19th centuries. ⊠ *Piazza Collicola 1, Spoleto* ☎ *0743/46434* ⊕ *www.palazzocollicola.it* ▣ *€9; included with Spoleto Card* ⊘ *Closed Tues. and Wed.*

★ Ponte delle Torri (*Bridge of the Towers*)

BRIDGE | Standing massive and graceful through the deep gorge that separates Spoleto from Monteluco, this 14th-century bridge is one of Umbria's most photographed monuments, and justifiably so. Built over the foundations of a Roman-era aqueduct, it soars 262 feet above the forested gorge—higher than the dome of St. Peter's in Rome. Though you can't walk across the bridge as it's being repaired due to earthquake damage, it's still a must-see, particularly on a starry night. ⊠ *Via del Ponte, Spoleto* ▣ *Free.*

Teatro Romano

RUINS | **FAMILY** | The Romans who colonized the city in 241 BC constructed this small theater in the 1st century AD; for centuries afterward it was used as a quarry for building materials. The most intact portion is the hallway that passes under the *cavea* (stands). The rest was heavily restored in the early 1950s and serves as a venue for Spoleto's Festival dei Due Mondi. The theater was the site of a gruesome episode in Spoleto's history: during the medieval struggle between Guelph (papal) and Ghibelline (imperial) forces, Spoleto took the side of the Holy Roman Emperor. Afterward, 400 Guelph supporters were massacred in the theater, their bodies burned in an enormous pyre. In the end, the Guelphs were triumphant, and Spoleto was incorporated into the states of the Church in 1354. Through a door in the west portico of the adjoining building is the Museo Archeologico, with assorted artifacts found in excavations primarily around Spoleto and Norcia. The collection contains Bronze Age and Iron Age artifacts from Umbrian and pre-Roman eras. The highlight is the stone tablet inscribed on both sides with the Lex Spoletina (Spoleto Law). Dating from 315 BC, this legal document prohibited the desecration of the woods on the slopes of nearby Monteluco. ✉ *Piazza della Libertà, Spoleto* ☎ *0743/223277* 🌐 *www.spoletocard.it* 🎟 *€4, included with Spoleto Card* 🕓 *Closed Mon. and Tues.*

🍴 Restaurants

Il Tartufo

$$ | **UMBRIAN** | As the name indicates, dishes prepared with truffles are the specialty here—don't miss the risotto al tartufo. Incorporating the ruins of a Roman villa, the surroundings are rustic on the ground floor and more modern upstairs; in summer, tables appear outdoors, and the traditional fare is spiced up to appeal to the cosmopolitan crowd attending (or performing in) the Festival dei Due Mondi. **Known for:** abundant portions, well presented; charming staff; recipes incorporating truffles. [$] *Average main: €18* ✉ *Piazza Garibaldi 24, Spoleto* ☎ *0743/40236* 🌐 *www.ristoranteiltartufo.it* 🕓 *Closed Mon. and early Jan.–early Feb. No dinner Sun.*

Il Tempio del Gusto

$$ | **UMBRIAN** | In charming shabby-chic environs, this welcoming eatery near the Arco di Druso (ancient Roman arch) serves up Italian with a subtle twist. Along with an extensive selection of thoughtfully chosen Umbrian wines, you'll find lots of veggie options, mounds of truffles in season, and, to finish things off, a superlative version of Spoleto sponge cake. **Known for:** quaint setting; friendly atmosphere; flavorful Umbrian cuisine. [$] *Average main: €16* ✉ *Via Arco di Druso 11, Spoleto* ☎ *0743/47121* 🌐 *www.iltempiodelgusto.com* 🕓 *Closed Thurs.*

★ **Ristorante Apollinare**

$$ | **UMBRIAN** | Low wooden ceilings and flickering candlelight make this monastery from the 10th and 11th centuries Spoleto's most romantic spot; in warm weather, you can dine under a canopy on the piazza. The kitchen serves sophisticated, innovative variations on local dishes, including long, slender strengozzi pasta with such toppings as cherry tomatoes, mint, and a touch of red pepper or (in season) porcini mushrooms or truffles. **Known for:** impeccable service; intimate and elegant setting; modern versions of traditional Umbrian dishes. [$] *Average main: €22* ✉ *Via Sant'Agata 14, Spoleto* ☎ *0743/223256* 🌐 *www.ristoranteapollinare.it* 🕓 *Closed Tues.*

Ristorante Il Panciolle

$ | **UMBRIAN** | A small garden filled with lemon trees in the heart of Spoleto's medieval quarter provides one of the most appealing settings you could wish for. Dishes, which change throughout the year, might include pastas served with asparagus or mushrooms, as well as grilled meats; more expensive dishes prepared with fresh truffles are also available in season. **Known for:** panoramic terrace; affable staff; authentic local cuisine. [$] *Average main: €14* ✉ *Via del Duomo 3/5, Spoleto* ☎ *0743/45677* 🌐 *www.ilpanciolle.it* 🕓 *Closed Wed. Sept.–Mar.*

Sights ▼

Restaurants ▼

Hotels ▼

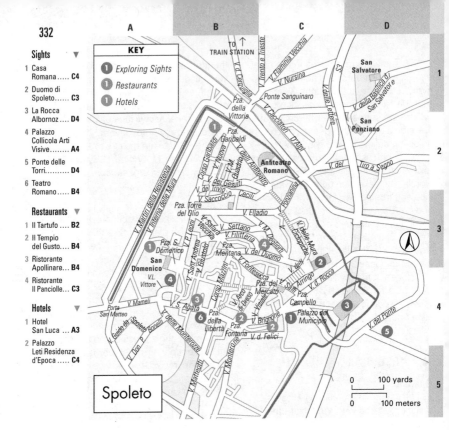

Spoleto

 Hotels

★ Hotel San Luca

$ | HOTEL | Hand-painted friezes decorate the walls of the spacious guest rooms, and elegant comfort is the grace note throughout—you can sip afternoon tea in oversize armchairs by the fireplace or take a walk in the sweet-smelling rose garden. **Pros:** very helpful staff; close to escalators for exploring city; spacious rooms. **Cons:** can feel soulless in winter; restaurant only open for groups; outside the town center. ⓢ *Rooms from: €104* ✉ *Via Interna delle Mura 21, Spoleto* ☎ *0743/223399* ⊕ *www.hotelsanluca. com* ⇄ *35 rooms* ⦿ *Free Breakfast.*

★ Palazzo Leti Residenza d'Epoca

$ | HOTEL | Fabulously landscaped gardens, complete with fountains and sculptures, along with panoramic views provide a grand entrance to this late 13th-century residence turned charming hotel high up in Spoleto's old town. **Pros:** feels like a private hideaway; friendly owners happy to help; unbeatable views. **Cons:** few amenities (no restaurant, gym, or spa); often booked far in advance; reaching on-site parking can be tricky. ⓢ *Rooms from: €120* ✉ *Via degli Eremiti 10, Spoleto* ☎ *0743/224930* ⊕ *www. palazzoleti.com* ⇄ *12 rooms* ⦿ *Free Breakfast.*

The Valnerina

The Valnerina is 27 km (17 miles) southeast of Spoleto.

The Valnerina (the valley of the River Nera, to the southeast of Spoleto) is the most beautiful of central Italy's many well-kept secrets. The twisting roads that serve the rugged landscape are poor, but the drive is well worth the effort for its forgotten medieval villages and dramatic mountain scenery.

GETTING HERE AND AROUND

You can head into the area from Terni on the S209, or on the SP395 bis north of Spoleto, which links the Via Flaminia (SS3) with the middle reaches of the Nera Valley through a tunnel.

Sights

Cascata delle Marmore

WATERFALL | FAMILY | The road east of Terni (SS3 Valnerina) leads 10 km (6 miles) to the Cascata delle Marmore (Waterfalls of Marmore), which, at 541 feet, are the highest in Europe. A canal was dug by the Romans in the 3rd century BC to prevent flooding in the nearby agricultural plains. Nowadays, the waters are often diverted to provide hydroelectric power for Terni, reducing the roaring falls to an unimpressive trickle, so check with the information office at the falls (there's a timetable on its website) or with Terni's tourist office before heading here.

On summer evenings, when the falls are in full spate, the cascading water is floodlit to striking effect. The falls are usually at their most energetic at midday and at around 4 pm. This is a good place for hiking, except in December and January, when most trails may be closed. ✉ *SP79, Terni* ✈ *10 km (6 miles) east of Terni* ☎ *0744/67561* 🌐 *www.cascatadellemarmore.info* 🎟 *€10.*

Norcia

TOWN | The birthplace of St. Benedict, Norcia is best known for its Umbrian pork and truffles, which you can sample at shops throughout town. Norcia exports truffles to France and hosts a truffle festival, Nero Norcia, every February. Though the town itself is still under reconstruction following a devastating 2016 earthquake, the surrounding mountains provide spectacular hiking. ✈ *42 km (25 miles) east of Spoleto, 67 km (42 miles) northeast of Terni.*

★ **Piano Grande.**

VIEWPOINT | A spectacular mountain plain 25 km (15 miles) to the northeast of the valley, Piano Grande is a hang glider's paradise and a wonderful place for a picnic or to fly a kite. It's also nationally famous for the quality of the lentils grown here, which are a traditional part of every Italian New Year's feast. ✉ *Teramo, The Valnerina* 🎟 *Free.*

Hotels

★ **Palazzo Seneca**

$$ | HOTEL | The Bianconi family oversees this elegant hotel, which is housed in a 16th-century palace—just around the corner from Norcia's main square—and features stone floors, vaulted ceilings, and a Michelin-star restaurant. **Pros:** lots of style and charm; central location; fabulous restaurant (book well in advance). **Cons:** no parking at the hotel; breakfast not up to par; no gym. $ *Rooms from: €178* ✉ *Via Cesare Battisti 12, Norcia* ☎ *0743/817434* 🌐 *www.palazzoseneca.com* 🛏 *24 rooms* 🍴 *Free Breakfast.*

Hiking the Umbrian Hills

Magnificent scenery makes the heart of Italy excellent walking, hiking, and mountaineering country. In Umbria, the area around Spoleto is particularly good; several pleasant, easy, and well-signed trails begin at the far end of the Ponte alle Torri bridge over Monteluco. From Cannara, an easy half-hour walk leads to the fields of Pian d'Arca, the site of St. Francis's sermon to the birds.

For slightly more arduous walks, follow the saint's path uphill from Assisi to the Eremo delle Carceri, and then continue along the trails that crisscross Monte Subasio. At 4,250 feet, the treeless summit affords views of Assisi, Perugia, far-off Gubbio, and the distant mountain ranges of Abruzzo. For even more challenging hiking, the northern reaches of the Valnerina are exceptional; the mountains around Norcia should not be missed.

Throughout Umbria and the Marches, most recognized trails are marked with the distinctive red-and-white blazes of the Club Alpino Italiano. Tourist offices are a good source for walking and climbing itineraries to suit all ages and levels of ability, and bookstores, *tabacchi* (tobacconists), and *edicole* (newsstands) often have maps and guides that detail the best area routes. Wear comfortable walking shoes or hiking boots, depending on your route, and bring plenty of water.

Todi

34 km (22 miles) south of Perugia, 34 km (22 miles) northeast of Orvieto, 46 km (29 miles) northwest of Spoleto.

As you stand on Piazza del Popolo, looking out onto the Tiber Valley below, it's easy to see why Todi is often described as Umbria's prettiest hill town. Legend has it that the town was founded by the Umbri, who followed an eagle who had stolen a tablecloth. They liked this lofty perch so much that they settled here for good. The eagle is now perched on the insignia of the medieval palaces in the main piazza.

GETTING HERE AND AROUND

Todi is best reached by car, as the town's two train stations are way down the hill and connected to the center by infrequent bus service. From Perugia, follow the E45 toward Rome. Take the Todi/Orvieto exit, then follow the SS79 bis into Todi. The drive takes around 40 minutes.

VISITOR INFORMATION

CONTACT Todi Tourism Office. ✉ *Piazza del Popolo 29–30* ☎ *0758/895–6227* ⊕ *www.visitodi.eu.*

Sights

Duomo di Todi (*Todi Cathedral*)
CHURCH | One end of the Piazza del Popolo is dominated by this 12th-century Romanesque-Gothic masterpiece, built over the site of a Roman temple. The simple facade is enlivened by a finely carved rose window. Look up at that window as you step inside and you'll notice its peculiarity: each "petal" of the rose has a cherub's face in the stained glass. Also take a close look at the capitals of the double columns with pilasters: perched between the acanthus leaves are charming medieval sculptures of saints—Peter with his keys, George and the dragon, and so on. You can see the rich brown tones of the wooden choir near the altar, but unless you have binoculars or request special permission

in advance, you can't get close enough to see all the exquisite detail in this Renaissance masterpiece of woodworking (1521–30). The severe, solid mass of the Duomo is mirrored by the Palazzo dei Priori (1595–97) across the way. ✉ *Piazza del Popolo 1, Todi* ☎ *0335/542–0520* 🌐 *www.chiesaditodi.it* 🎫 *Free.*

Piazza del Popolo

PLAZA/SQUARE | Built above the Roman Forum, Piazza del Popolo is Todi's high point, a model of spatial harmony with stunning views onto the surrounding countryside. In the best medieval tradition, the square was conceived to house both the temporal and the spiritual centers of power. ✉ *Todi* 🎫 *Free.*

🍴 Restaurants

★ Pane & Vino

$$ | **ITALIAN** | This charmingly rustic restaurant in Todi's historic center specializes in "dishes of the past" made from local ingredients. Choose from a fine selection of meat and cheese antipasti, house-made pastas and soups, and hearty meat dishes—accompanied by truffles in season—along with tempting daily specials, served with well-priced wines from a comprehensive list. **Known for:** focus on organic products from small producers; friendly, knowledgeable service; fabulous selection of wines from across Italy. [$] *Average main: €16* ✉ *Via Augusto Ciuffelli 33, Todi* ☎ *075/894–5448* 🌐 *panevinotodi.com* 🕒 *Closed Wed.*

Ristorante Umbria

$$ | **UMBRIAN** | Todi's most popular restaurant for more than four decades is reliable for its sturdy country food and the wonderful view from its terrace; because it has only 16 tables outside, make sure you reserve ahead. In winter, try lentil soup, risotto with saffron and porcini mushrooms, or wild boar with polenta; steaks, accompanied by a rich dark-brown wine sauce, are good any time of year. **Known for:** friendly atmosphere; terrific vista from terrace; traditional Umbrian dishes. [$] *Average main: €15* ✉ *Via San Bonaventura 13, Todi* ☎ *075/894–2737* 🌐 *www.ristoranteumbria.it* 🕒 *Closed Tues. and 3–4 wks in Jan. and Feb.*

🛏 Hotels

★ Relais Todini

$$$ | **HOTEL** | Inside a 14th-century manor house 9 km (6 miles) southeast of Todi, this elegant hotel sits adjacent to working vineyards (don't forget to sample the Todini wines) and features such welcome amenities as a spa, outdoor pool, and gym. **Pros:** quiet location; walking paths around the grounds; lots of relaxing public spaces, including a spa. **Cons:** reception not staffed 24/7; priced on the high side; decor feels a bit worn. [$] *Rooms from: €210* ✉ *Frazione Collevalenza, Todi* ☎ *075/887521* 🌐 *www.relaistodini.com* 🕒 *Closed weekdays Nov.–Mar.* 🔑 *12 rooms* 🍽 *Free Breakfast.*

Residenza D'Epoca San Lorenzo Tre

$ | **HOTEL** | Magnificent valley views are paired with 19th-century charm at this property filled with paintings, antique furnishings, and period knickknacks. **Pros:** old-world atmosphere; spectacular views; excellent central location. **Cons:** small, basic bathrooms; long flight of steps to enter; few modern amenities. [$] *Rooms from: €105* ✉ *Via San Lorenzo 3, Todi* ☎ *075/894–4555* 🌐 *www.sanlorenzo3.it* 🕒 *Closed Nov.–mid-Apr.* 🔑 *6 rooms* 🍽 *Free Breakfast.*

Orvieto

30 km (19 miles) southwest of Todi, 78 km (48 miles) southwest of Perugia, 81 km (51 miles) west of Spoleto.

Carved from an enormous plateau of volcanic rock high above a green valley, Orvieto has natural defenses that made the high walls seen in many Umbrian towns unnecessary. The Etruscans were the first to settle here, digging a honeycombed network of more than 1,200 wells and storage caves out of the soft stone.

The Romans attacked, sacked, and destroyed the city in 283 BC. Since then, it has grown up out of the rock into an enchanting maze of alleys and squares. Orvieto was solidly Guelph in the Middle Ages, and, for several hundred years, popes sought refuge in the city, at times needing protection from their enemies, at times seeking respite from the summer heat in Rome.

When painting his frescoes inside the Duomo, Luca Signorelli asked that part of his contract be paid in Orvietan wine, and he was neither the first nor the last to appreciate the region's popular white. In past times, the caves carved underneath the town were used to ferment the Trebbiano grapes used in making Orvieto Classico. Although local wine production has moved out to more traditional vineyards, you can still while away the afternoon with tastings at any number of shops in town.

GETTING HERE AND AROUND

Orvieto is well connected by train to Rome, Florence, and Perugia. It's also adjacent to the A1 autostrada that runs between Florence and Rome. Parking areas in the upper town tend to be crowded. A better idea is to follow the signs for the Campo Della Fiera parking lot, then take the escalators or elevator that carry people up the hill.

The Carta Orvieto Unica (single ticket) is expensive but a great deal if you want to visit everything. For €20 you get admission to nine museums and monuments, including the three major sights in town—Cappella di San Brizio (at the Duomo), Museo Etrusco Claudio Faina, and Orvieto Underground—along with entry to the Torre del Moro, with views of Orvieto, plus a bus and funicular pass. You can buy the card online or at any of the included museums.

CONTACT Orvieto Tourism Office. ✉ *Piazza del Duomo 24* ☎ *0763/341772* ⊕ *www. liveorvieto.com.*

Sights

★ **Duomo di Orvieto** (*Orvieto Cathedral*)
CHURCH | Orvieto's stunning cathedral was built to commemorate the Miracle at Bolsena. In 1263, a young priest who questioned the miracle of transubstantiation (in which the Communion bread and wine become the flesh and blood of Christ) was saying Mass at nearby Lago di Bolsena. A wafer he had just blessed suddenly started to drip blood, staining the linen covering the altar. Thirty years later, construction began on a duomo in Orvieto to celebrate the miracle and house the stained altar cloth.

The cathedral's interior is rather vast and empty; the major works are in the transepts. To the left is the Cappella del Corporale, where the square linen cloth (*corporale*) is kept in a golden reliquary that's modeled on the cathedral and inlaid with enamel scenes of the miracle. In the right transept is the Cappella di San Brizio, which holds one of Italy's greatest fresco cycles, notable for its influence on Michelangelo's *Last Judgment*, as well as for the extraordinary beauty of the figuration. In these works, a few by Fra Angelico and most by Luca Signorelli, the damned fall to hell, demons breathe fire and blood, and Christians are martyred.

The Museo dell'Opera dell Duomo next to the cathedral is worth a short visit to see its small collection of historical paintings and sculptures. ✉ *Piazza del Duomo, Orvieto* ☎ *0763/342477* 🌐 *www.opsm.it* 🎫 *€5, including Cappella di San Brizio and Museo dell'Opera dell Duomo; included with Carta Unica.*

Museo Etrusco Claudio Faina

HISTORY MUSEUM | This superb private collection, beautifully arranged and presented, goes far beyond the usual smattering of local remains displayed at many museums. The collection is particularly rich in Greek- and Etruscan-era pottery, from large Attic amphorae (6th–4th century BC) to Attic black- and red-figure pieces to Etruscan *bucchero* (dark-reddish clay) vases. Other interesting items include a 6th-century sarcophagus and a substantial display of Roman-era coins. ✉ *Piazza del Duomo 29, Orvieto* ☎ *0763/341216* 🌐 *museofaina.it* 🎫 *€6* 🕒 *Closed Tues.*

Orvieto Underground

RUINS | **FAMILY** | More than just about any other town, Orvieto has grown from its own foundations. The Etruscans, the Romans, and those who followed dug into the tufa (the same soft volcanic rock from which catacombs were made) to create more than 1,000 separate cisterns, caves, passages, storage areas, and production areas for wine and olive oil. Much of the tufa removed was used as building blocks for the city that exists today, and some was partly ground into pozzolana, which was made into mortar. You can see the labyrinth of dugout chambers beneath the city on the Orvieto Underground tour, which runs daily at 11, 12:15, 4, and 5:15 (more frequently in busy periods), departing from Piazza del Duomo 23. ✉ *Piazza del Duomo 23, Orvieto* ☎ *0763/340688* 🌐 *www.orvietounderground.it* 🎫 *Tours €7; included with Carta Unica.*

Pozzo della Cava

RUINS | If you're short on time but want a quick look at the cisterns and caves beneath the city, head for the Pozzo della Cava, an Etruscan well for spring water. On a walk through nine excavated caves you can see the fascinating ruins of medieval houses and unearthed archaeological artifacts. ✉ *Via della Cava 28, Orvieto* ☎ *0763/342373* 🌐 *www.pozzodellacava.it* 🎫 *€4; included with Carta Unica.*

🍴 Restaurants

Le Grotte del Funaro

$$ | **UMBRIAN** | Dine inside tufa caves under central Orvieto, where the two windows afford splendid views of the hilly countryside. The traditional Umbrian food is reliably good, with simple grilled meats and vegetables and pizzas—oddly, though, the food is outclassed by an extensive wine list, with top local and Italian labels and quite a few rare vintages. **Known for:** good choice of wines; crusty pizzas; unusual setting. [$] *Average main: €16* ✉ *Via Ripa Serancia 41, Orvieto* ☎ *0763/343276* 🌐 *www.grottedelfunaro.com* 🕒 *Closed Mon. and 10 days in July.*

Ristorante Maurizio

$$ | **UMBRIAN** | Off a busy pedestrian street near the Duomo, this welcoming, family-owned restaurant has an ultra-contemporary look but is actually housed in a 14th-century medieval building with arched ceilings. The Martinelli family's own products, including balsamic vinegar, olive oil, and pasta, are used in their robustly flavored dishes, and you can also sample their well-regarded Montefalco wines. **Known for:** local wines; traditional Umbrian dishes; complimentary balsamic vinegar tasting to start. [$] *Average main: €16* ✉ *Via del Duomo 78, Orvieto* ☎ *0763/341114* 🌐 *www.ristorante-maurizio.com.*

Trattoria La Grotta

$ | UMBRIAN | The vaulted, plant-filled dining area—where white walls are adorned with paintings, antique vases, and other knickknacks—makes a congenial setting for this small, rustic-style trattoria, which is lauded for its homemade pasta, perhaps with an artichoke, duck, or wild-boar sauce. Roast lamb, veal, and pork are all also good, and the desserts are supplied by Orvieto's most eminent pasticceria.
Known for: warm and welcoming service; fresh, local ingredients; tasty homemade pastas. Ⓢ *Average main: €14* ⊠ *Via Luca Signorelli 5, Orvieto* ☏ *0763/341348* ⊕ *www.trattorialagrottaorvieto.com* ⊙ *Closed Tues.*

 ## Hotels

Eremito

$$$$ | ALL-INCLUSIVE | For a more spiritual slant to your vacation, spend a night or two at this "modern monastery," where you'll sleep in a cell, eat vegetarian food by candlelight, practice yoga, and relax in a whirlpool tub. **Pros:** chance to meet other travelers; lovely scenery; truly getting away from it all. **Cons:** very simple accommodations (and no Wi-Fi); need a car to get there; on the pricey side. Ⓢ *Rooms from: €370* ⊠ *Località Tarina 2, Parrano* ✛ *28 km (17 miles) north of Orvieto* ☏ *0763/891010* ⊕ *www.eremito. com* ⤳ *14 rooms* ❙◯❙ *All-Inclusive.*

Hotel Palazzo Piccolomini

$ | HOTEL | This 16th-century family palazzo has been beautifully restored, with inviting public spaces and handsome guest quarters where contemporary surroundings are accented with old beams, vaulted ceilings, and other distinctive touches. **Pros:** private parking; good location; efficient staff. **Cons:** some rooms and bathrooms are small; four-star category not completely justified; underwhelming breakfasts. Ⓢ *Rooms from: €120* ⊠ *Piazza Ranieri 36, Orvieto* ☏ *0763/341743* ⊕ *www.palazzopiccolomini.it* ⊙ *Closed Jan. and Feb.* ⤳ *33 rooms* ❙◯❙ *Free Breakfast.*

★ Locanda Palazzone

$$$ | HOTEL | Spending the night in this 13th-century building just 5 km (3 miles) northwest of Orvieto is like staying in a sophisticated country home, albeit one with vineyard views, a private chef, and two-level rooms with modern furnishings. **Pros:** tranquil surroundings; tasty meals served nightly; extremely friendly owners and staff. **Cons:** split-level rooms can be difficult for those with mobility issues or young children; limited public spaces to lounge in; no à la carte menus. Ⓢ *Rooms from: €239* ⊠ *Località Rocca Ripesena 68, Orvieto* ☏ *0763/393614* ⊕ *www.locandapalazzone.it* ⤳ *7 rooms* ❙◯❙ *Free Breakfast.*

Urbino

230 km (143 miles) east of Florence, 116 km (72 miles) northeast of Perugia, 75 km (47 miles) north of Gubbio.

Majestic Urbino, atop a steep hill with a skyline of towers and domes, is something of a surprise to come upon. Though quite remote, it was once a center of learning and culture almost without rival in western Europe. The town looks much as it did in the glory days of the 15th century: a cluster of warm brick and pale stone buildings, all topped with russet-color tile roofs. The focal point is the immense and beautiful Palazzo Ducale.

The city is also home to the small but prestigious Università di Urbino—one of the oldest in the world—so its streets are usually filled with students, and it has the usual college town array of bookshops, bars, and coffeehouses. In summer, the Italian student population is replaced by foreigners who come to study Italian language and arts at several prestigious, private, fine-arts academies.

Urbino's fame rests on the reputation of three of its native sons: Duke Federico da Montefeltro (1422–82), the enlightened warrior-patron who built the Palazzo

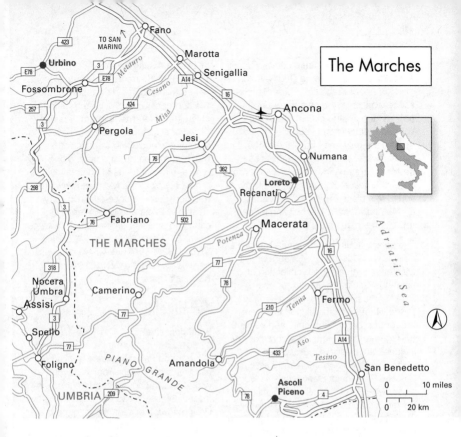

Ducale; Raffaello Sanzio (1483–1520), or Raphael, one of the most influential painters in history and an embodiment of the spirit of the Renaissance; and the architect Donato Bramante (1444–1514), who translated the philosophy of the Renaissance into buildings of grace and beauty. Unfortunately there's little work by either Bramante or Raphael in the city, but the duke's influence can still be felt strongly.

GETTING HERE AND AROUND
Take the SS3 bis from Perugia, and follow the directions for Gubbio and Cesena. Exit at Umbertide and take the SS219, then the SS452, and at Calmazzo, the SS73 bis to Urbino.

VISITOR INFORMATION
CONTACT Urbino Tourism Office. ✉ *Via Puccinotti 35* ☎ *0722/2613* ⊕ *www.turismo. marche.it.*

 ## Sights

Casa Natale di Raffaello
(*House of Raphael*)
HISTORIC HOME | This is the house in which the painter was born and where he took his first steps in painting, under the direction of his artist father. There's some debate about the fresco of the Madonna here; some say it's by Raphael, whereas others attribute it to the father—with Raphael's mother and the young painter himself standing in as models for the Madonna and Child. ✉ *Via Raffaello 57, Urbino* ☎ *0722/320105* ⊕ *www.casaraffaello.com* ✉ *€4.*

★ **Palazzo Ducale di Urbino** (*Ducal Palace*)
ART MUSEUM | The Palazzo Ducale holds a place of honor in the city. If the Renaissance was, ideally, a celebration of the nobility of man and his works, of the light and purity of the soul, then there's no place in Italy, the birthplace of the Renaissance, where these tenets are better illustrated. From the moment you enter the peaceful courtyard, you know you're in a place of grace and beauty, and the harmony of the building indeed reflects the high ideals of the time.

The palace houses the Galleria Nazionale delle Marche (National Museum of the Marches), with a superb collection of paintings, sculpture, and other objets d'art. Some pieces originally belonged to the Montefeltro family; others were brought here from churches and palaces throughout the region. Masterworks include Paolo Uccello's *Profanation of the Host,* Titian's *Resurrection* and *Last Supper,* and Piero della Francesca's *Madonna of Senigallia.* But the gallery's highlight is Piero's enigmatic work long known as *The Flagellation of Christ.* Much has been written about this painting, and although few experts agree on its meaning, most agree that this is one of the painter's masterpieces. ✉ *Piazza Rinascimento 13, Urbino* ☎ *0722/2760* 🌐 *www.gallerianazionalemarche.it* 🎟 *€8* 🕒 *Closed Mon.*

🍴 Restaurants

La Fornarina
$$ | **ITALIAN** | Locals often crowd this small, two-room trattoria near the Piazza della Repubblica. The specialty is meaty country fare, such as *coniglio* (rabbit) and *vitello alle noci* (veal cooked with walnuts) or *ai porcini* (with mushrooms); there's also a good selection of pasta dishes. **Known for:** hospitable staff; welcoming atmosphere; excellent starters. [$] *Average main: €18* ✉ *Via Mazzini 14, Urbino* ☎ *0722/320007.*

★ **Osteria Angolo Divino**
$$ | **ITALIAN** | Starred chef Tiziano Rossetti helms this long-standing restaurant in the center of Urbino, where tradition still reigns supreme. Elegant versions of regional dishes feature lots of local ingredients, including truffles, forest mushrooms, game, and pork, along with a wine list focused on small producers from the Marche. **Known for:** traditional osteria-style decor; quality cuisine with experimental elements; calm and pleasant ambience. [$] *Average main: €23* ✉ *Via S. Andrea 14, Urbino* ☎ *0722/327559* 🌐 *www.tizianorossetti.com/osterialangolodivino* 🕒 *Closed Wed. No lunch Thurs.*

🛏 Hotels

Hotel Bonconte
$ | **HOTEL** | Just inside the city walls and close to the Palazzo Ducale, this hotel has pleasant, if worn, rooms decorated with a smattering of antiques; those in front also have views of the valley below Urbino. **Pros:** pleasant views; good breakfast; central but away from the bustle. **Cons:** rooms and public spaces getting a bit shabby; some rooms are cramped; an uphill walk to town center. [$] *Rooms from: €110* ✉ *Via delle Mura 28, Urbino* ☎ *0722/2463* 🌐 *www.viphotels.it* 🛏 *23 rooms* 🍽 *No Meals.*

Loreto

150 km (93 miles) northeast of Perugia, 121 km (75 miles) southeast of Urbino.

There's a strong Renaissance feel to this hilltop town, which is home to one of the most important religious sites in Europe, the Santuario della Santa Casa (House of the Virgin Mary). Bramante and Sansovino gave the church its Renaissance look, although many other artists helped create its special atmosphere.

Today, the town revolves around the religious calendar. If you can be here on December 10, you will witness the Feast of the Translation of the Holy House, when huge bonfires are lighted to celebrate the miraculous arrival of the house in 1295.

GETTING HERE AND AROUND

If you're driving from Perugia, take the SS318 and then the SS76 highway to Fabriano and then on to Chiaravalle, where it merges with the A14 autostrada. The drive takes around two hours. Trains also go to Loreto, but the station is about a mile outside the town center. Regular buses leave from the station to the center.

VISITOR INFORMATION

CONTACT Loreto Tourism Office. ✉ *Via Solari 3* ☎ *071/970276* ⊕ *www.turismo. marche.it.*

 Sights

★ Basilica della Santa Casa

CHURCH | Loreto is famous for one of the best-loved shrines in the world: the Santuario della Santa Casa (House of the Virgin Mary), within the Basilica della Santa Casa. Legend has it that angels moved the house from Nazareth, where the Virgin Mary was living at the time of the Annunciation, to this hilltop in 1295. The reason for this sudden and divinely inspired move was that Nazareth had fallen into the hands of Muslim invaders, who the angelic hosts viewed as unsuitable keepers of this important shrine.

The house itself consists of three rough stone walls contained within an elaborate marble tabernacle. Built around this centerpiece is the giant Basilica of the Holy House, which dominates the town. Millions of pilgrims come to the site every year (particularly at Easter and on the December 10 Feast of the Holy House), and the little town of Loreto can become uncomfortably crowded.

Many great Italian architects—including Bramante, Antonio da Sangallo the Younger (1483–1546), Giuliano da Sangallo (circa 1445–1516), and Sansovino (1467–1529)—contributed to the design of the basilica. It was begun in the Gothic style in 1468 and continued in Renaissance style through the late Renaissance. ✉ *Piazza della Madonna 1, Loreto* ☎ *071/9747155* ⊕ *www.santuarioloreto.it* ✉ *Free.*

Ascoli Piceno

156 km (97 miles) southeast of Perugia, 88 km (55 miles) south of Loreto.

Ascoli Piceno sits in a valley ringed by steep hills and cut by the Tronto River. In Roman times, it was one of central Italy's best-known market towns. Today, with almost 52,000 residents, it's a major fruit and olive producer, making it one of the most important towns in the region.

Despite growth during the Middle Ages and at other times, the streets in the town center continue to reflect the grid pattern of the ancient Roman city. You'll even find the word *rua,* from the Latin *ruga,* used for "street" instead of the Italian *via.* Now largely closed to traffic, the city center is great to explore on foot.

GETTING HERE AND AROUND

From Perugia, take the SS75 to Foligno, then merge onto the SS3 to Norcia. From here, take the SS4 to Ascoli Piceno. There are also trains, but the journey would be quite long, taking you from Perugia to Ancona, 105 km (65 miles) to the north, before changing for Ascoli Piceno.

VISITOR INFORMATION

CONTACT Ascoli Piceno Tourism Office. ✉ *Piazza Aringo 7* ☎ *0736/298916* ⊕ *www.visitascoli.it.*

Sights

Piazza del Popolo

PLAZA/SQUARE | The heart of the town is the majestic Piazza del Popolo, dominated by the Gothic church of San Francesco and the Palazzo del Popolo, a 13th-century town hall that contains a graceful Renaissance courtyard. The square functions as the living room of the entire city and at dusk each evening is packed with people strolling and exchanging news and gossip—the sweetly antiquated ritual called a *passeggiata*—performed all over the country. ⊠ *Ascoli Piceno* 🖼 *Free.*

 Hotels

Hotel Pennile

$ | **HOTEL** | This modern, affordable, family-run hotel in a quiet residential area outside the old city center is pleasantly set amid a grove of olive trees. **Pros:** peaceful environment; easy parking; a good budget option. **Cons:** can hear some noise from other rooms; no restaurant; distance from town center. 💲 *Rooms from: €75* ⊠ *Via G. Spalvieri 13/A, Ascoli Piceno* ☎ *0736/41645* ⊕ *www.hotelpennile.it* 🛏 *33 rooms* ❙○❙ *Free Breakfast.*

Index

Photo Credits

Front Cover: Nataliya Nazarova/Alamy Stock Photo [Description: City panorama with houses and Ponte Vecchio across the river Arno, Florence, Italy]. **Back cover, from left to right:** Shutterstock / WDG Photo, Shutterstock/Igor Plotnikov, Shutterstock/Angelo Ferraris **Spine:** Shutterstock / Nickolay Vinokurov **Interior, from left to right:** BEST-BACKGROUNDS/Shutterstock (1) ronnybas frimages/shutterstock.com (2) Obscurenotion/Shutterstock (5) **Chapter 1: Experience Florence and Tuscany:** JaroslawPawlak/shutterstock.com (6) Stefano Termanini/Shutterstock (8) StevanZZ/Shutterstock (9) canadastock/Shutterstock (9) Sergii Koval/Dreamstime (10) Elena Odareeva/Shutterstock (10) Alexirina27000/Dreamstime (10) SJ Travel Photo and Video/Shutterstock (10) Jodi Nasser (11) Shaiith/Shutterstock (11) Tombor Szabina/Shutterstock (12) Thanida Siritan/Shutterstock (12) Freesurf69/Dreamstime (12) Adwo/Dreamstime (12) Veronika Galkina/Shutterstock (13) f11photo/Shutterstock (13) pixel creator/Shutterstock (14) DFLC Prints/Shutterstock (14) Stefano_Valeri/Shutterstock (15) Xbrchx/Dreamstime (16) Fabiobalbi/Dreamstime (16) StevanZZ/Shutterstock (16) Paolo Gallo/Shutterstock (16) karamysh/shutterstock.com (17) Scampari/Shutterstock (17) Canadastock/Shutterstock (20) StevanZZ/Shutterstock (21) Kiev.Victor/Shutterstock (22) Jasper Suijten/Shutterstock (22) Kip Garner/Dreamstime (22) Imagentle/Shutterstock (23) Nataliya Nazarova/Shutterstock (23) IriGri/Shutterstock (24) Gioncla/Dreamstime (24) HQuality/Shutterstock (24) Lisa Holmen Photography/Shutterstock (24) Emiko Davis (25) Leonid Andronov/Dreamstime (26) Luciano Mortula/Dreamstime (27) Everett Collection/Shutterstock (33) Everett Collection/Shutterstock (33) Marzolino/Shutterstock (33) Romas_Photo/Shutterstock (34) Steve Allen/Shutterstock (34) Giannit | Dreamstime.com (35) MisterStock/Shutterstock (35) Karl Allen Lugmayer/Shutterstock (35) Yuri Turkov/Shutterstock (35) Public Domain (36) Flickr/virtusincertus (36) CYSUN/Shutterstock (36) Flickr/jean louis mazieres (37) Bill Perry/Shutterstock (37) Flickr/Deb Nystrom (37) Planet Art (38 All Images) **Chapter 3: Florence:** Matej Hakl/Shutterstock (65) Coutesy Salcheto (68) George M. Groutas/Flickr (69) Lesya Dolyuk/shutterstock.com (69) Tt/Dreamstime (81) George Diamonds/Shutterstock (85) skovalsky/Shutterstock (87) Alfio Giannotti/viestiphoto.com (87) Rough Guides / Alamy (87) kritskaya/Shutterstock (88) Lornet/Dreamstime (92) Lornet/Dreamstime (93) Nicolesilvestri6/Dreamstime (103) Cubolmages srl / Alamy (123) Cubolmages srl / Alamy (123) Tibor Bognar / Alamy (123) Cubolmages srl / Alamy (123) Public Domain (All: 124) Ken Welsh / Alamy Zakrevsky Andrey/Shutterstock (125) Zakrevsky Andrey/Shutterstock (135) **Chapter 4: Pisa, Lucca, and Northwest Tuscany:** f11photo/Shutterstock (145) Marco Sallese/Shutterstock (155) Karl Allen Lugmayer/Shutterstock (156) Natalie Adamov/Shutterstock (156) leonori/Shutterstock (156) Alexandre Rotenberg/Shutterstock (157) Kristi Blokhin/Shutterstock (157) Dietmarrauscher | Dreamstime.com (157) Photology1971/Shutterstock (158) leonori/Shutterstock (158) Cubolmages srl / Alamy Marco (159) Crupi/Shutterstock (159) EQRoy/Shutterstock (160) New Africa/Shutterstock (160) davide bonaldo/Shutterstock (160) neil langan/Shutterstock (160) Photodisc (Own) (165) Alberto Masnovo/Shutterstock (172) Dutton Colin/simephoto (180) Dutton Colin/simephoto (181) Leonori/Shutterstock (191) **Chapter 5: Chianti, Siena, and Central Tuscany:** Lukasz Szwaj/shutterstock.com (195) clodio/iStockphoto (199) Black Rooster Consortium (211) Jarek Pawlak/Shutterstock (211) Boumen Japet/Shutterstock (211) Cephas Picture Library / Alamy (211) Elena.Katkova/Shutterstock (212) iacomino FRiMAGES/Shutterstock (213) HQuality/Shutterstock (213) Obscurenotion/Shutterstock (214) StevanZZ/Shutterstock (214) pmmart/Shutterstock (214) StevanZZ/Shutterstock (217) Wirestock Creators/Shutterstock (226) Public Domain (226) M. Rohana / Shutterstock.com (228) Fab38/Shutterstock (228) M. Rohana / Shutterstock.com (228) leonori/shutterstock.com (233) M. Rohana/Shutterstock (234) Photodisc (241) Perseo Media/Shutterstock (247) **Chapter 6: Arezzo, Cortona, and Eastern Tuscany:** StevanZZ/Shutterstock (249) Danita Delimont/Shutterstock (256) Danita Delimont/Shutterstock (257) **Chapter 7: Southern Tuscany:** Bertl123/Shutterstock (267) Walter Bibikow (277) Marco Rubino/Shutterstock (280) Julia Lopatina/Shutterstock (293) Balate Dorin/Shutterstock (298) **Chapter 8: Umbria and the Marches:** Sergey Dzyuba/Shutterstock (301) Vividaphoto/Dreamstime (304) 5 second Studio / Shutterstock (305) Bonchan/Shutterstock (305) StevanZZ/Shutterstock (319) Threerivers11 | Dreamstime.com (320) **About Our Writers:** All photos are courtesy of the writers except for the following: Liz_Shemaria by Ian Tuttle (352).

Every effort has been made to trace the copyright holders, and we apologize in advance for any accidental errors. We would be happy to apply the corrections in the following edition of this publication.

Notes

Fodor's FLORENCE & TUSCANY

Publisher: Stephen Horowitz, *General Manager*

Editorial: Douglas Stallings, *Editorial Director;* Jill Fergus, Amanda Sadlowski, *Senior Editors;* Kayla Becker, Brian Eschrich, Alexis Kelly, *Editors;* Angelique Kennedy-Chavannes, *Assistant Editor*

Design: Tina Malaney, *Director of Design and Production;* Jessica Gonzalez, *Graphic Designer;* Erin Caceres, *Graphic Design Associate*

Production: Jennifer DePrima, *Editorial Production Manager;* Elyse Rozelle, *Senior Production Editor;* Monica White, *Production Editor*

Maps: Rebecca Baer, *Senior Map Editor;* David Lindroth, Mark Stroud (Moon Street Cartography), *Cartographers*

Photography: Viviane Teles, *Senior Photo Editor;* Namrata Aggarwal, Neha Gupta, Payal Gupta, Ashok Kumar, *Photo Editors;* Eddie Aldrete, *Photo Production Intern;* Kadeem McPherson, *Photo Production Associate Intern*

Business and Operations: Chuck Hoover, *Chief Marketing Officer;* Robert Ames, *Group General Manager;* Devin Duckworth, *Director of Print Publishing*

Public Relations and Marketing: Joe Ewaskiw, *Senior Director of Communications and Public Relations*

Fodors.com: Jeremy Tarr, *Editorial Director;* Rachael Levitt, *Managing Editor*

Technology: Jon Atkinson, *Director of Technology;* Rudresh Teotia, *Lead Developer*

Writers: Liz Humphreys, Patricia Rucidlo, Liz Shemaria

Editor: Laura M. Kidder

Production Editor: Monica White

15th edition

ISBN 978-1-64097-537-8

ISSN 1533-1628

All details in this book are based on information supplied to us at press time. Always confirm information when it matters, especially if you're making a detour to visit a specific place. Fodor's expressly disclaims any liability, loss, or risk, personal or otherwise, that is incurred as a consequence of the use of any of the contents of this book.

SPECIAL SALES
This book is available at special discounts for bulk purchases for sales promotions or premiums. For more information, e-mail SpecialMarkets@fodors.com.

PRINTED IN CANADA

10 9 8 7 6 5 4 3 2 1

About Our Writers

Liz Humphreys is a transplant to Europe from New York City, where she edited for media companies including Condé Nast and Time Inc. Since then she's written for publications including *Condé Nast Traveler*, Michelin Green Guides, and Forbes Travel Guide. Liz has an advanced certificate in wine studies from WSET (Wine & Spirit Education Trust), which comes in handy when exploring her beloved Italian wine regions. Liz updated the Umbria and the Marches chapter for this edition. Follow her @winederlust_wanderings.

Patricia Rucidlo is a licensed tour guide in Florence and lives in the Tuscan countryside. She has masters degrees in Italian Renaissance history and art history. When she's not extolling the virtues of a Raphael masterpiece or angrily defending the Medici, she's at home puttering in her always-overgrown garden. She updated the following chapters: Florence; Pisa, Lucca, and Northwest Tuscany; Chianti, Siena, and Central Italy; Arezzo, Cortona, and Eastern Tuscany; and Southern Tuscany.

Liz Shemaria is an Italy-based journalist and third-generation Northern Californian who has trekked solo in Himalaya, interviewed artists in military-ruled Burma, and once rode an overnight train across Egypt on her birthday. She has contributed to more than a dozen travel and news publications including Fodor's guidebooks, *AFAR*, BBC Travel, and Roads & Kingdoms. Spontaneous dance parties are essential to her creative process. For this edition, she updated the Experience and Travel Smart chapters.